The Second Synod of Ephesus: Together with Certain Extracts Relating to It, from Syriac Mss. Preserved in the British Museum

Samuel Gideon Frederic Perry

ܟܘܢܫܐ ܬܪܝܢܐ ܕܐܦܣܘܣ ܐܘܟܝܬ
ܣܘܢܗܕܘܣ :

THE
SECOND SYNOD OF EPHESUS,
TOGETHER WITH CERTAIN EXTRACTS
RELATING TO IT,

From Syriac MSS. preserved in the British Museum,
and now first edited by

THE REV. S. G. F. PERRY, M.A.,
Vicar of Tottington, in the Diocese of Manchester.

ENGLISH VERSION.

"For, where two or three are gathered together in My Name,
there am I in their midst."—Matt. xviii. 20.

"The Mothers of the Catholic Faith."
Encyc. to Bishops, p. 374.

PRINTED AT THE ORIENT PRESS, DARTFORD, IN THE COUNTY OF KENT.
1881.

TO THE

ENGLISH SPEAKING PEOPLE

OF

"The Holy Church throughout the World,"

THIS WORK IS DEDICATED

BY

S. G. F. P.

The following has just (Dec. 1879,) arrived in England from Italy.

ACTORUM CONCILII CALCEDONENSIS VERSIO INEDITA.

Præcedunt tres epistolæ Imperatorum juxta versionem Codicis Vaticani, 1322.

Sequitur Ordo gestorum habitorum Calcedona, &c., juxta lectionem Coleti cum variantibus.

Deinde (   ) Synodi Constantinopolitani, sub P. P. Leone.

(a) Exemptum libelli Eusebii Dorylitani (versio medita).

(b) Gesta contra Eutychen Presbuterum (item).

(c) Relatio Flaviani Ep. CP. ad Papam Leonem (item).

(d) Alia Epistola Flaviani Ep ad Papam Leonem (id).

(e) Epistola Papae Leonis ad Flavium (cum nonnullis variantibus.

(f) Libellus Appellationis Eutychetis ad Papam Leonem (   ), adjectis SS. P.P. testimoniis ineditis nempe Juliis Athanasii, Gregorii Majoris Gregorii Naz. Petri Alex. celestini Romani. Felicis Romani et Synodi Romani et Synodi Ephesinæ, item contestatio ad Papylum Constantinopolitanium inedita.

(g) Acta Latrocinii Ephesini (versio inedita)

(h) Libellus Apellationis Flaviani Ep. CP. ad Papam Leonem.

(i) Libellus Apellationis ad Papam Leonem Eusebii. Daryleorum

THE SECOND

SYNOD

OF

EPHESUS,

(SECOND SESSION).

INTRODUCTION.

To be the means of presenting to the Church of the 19th Century an Oriental Document purporting to be the authorised Acts of an Œcumenical Council of the 5th Century, in its original quaint costume as well as in a modern dress, by which a new page of the Church's chequered life might be unrolled and deciphered, and in which, too, as in a picture would be represented, in its deadliest aspect, one ghastly struggle between The TRUTH Herself and the Dragon of Heresy, when He vomited forth upon Her Mystical Body his most poisonous venom, was the original, and not very unimportant, object of producing these two almost unique Volumes.

How far that object has been attained, and how useful the realisation of it, may be best judged perhaps by those who scrutinise their pages.

A brief sketch may not be uninteresting or unacceptable, though perhaps not absolutely necessary.

In the summer of 1867, whilst conning over

my transcript of the first part of the MS., numbered 14,530 Additional, which had been put into my hands in the British Museum, it occurred to me that that part could be finished and dedicated to the Pan-Anglican Synod, or Conference of Bishops of the Anglican Communion, to be assembled in the autumn at Lambeth under the auspices of the then Archbishop of Canterbury. A terse description of the MS., addressed to Archbishop Longley, soon brought his opinion that it must be a MS. "interesting to the Church at large," and a permission, most kindly expressed, to dedicate Part I. to the forthcoming Conference and its President.

By the ready help of the Oxford Clarendon Press, so many copies of Part I. were finished and presented to as many Metropolitans among the Bishops while in session, by the good Offices of the presiding Archbishop. Subsequently, a revised and corrected impression of Part I., with a type that an Oriental scholar designated as "sumptuous," was forwarded to all the Bishops who had attended the Conference, that to the President being accompanied by a second photograph, representing a page of the MS., which indicated, by internal evidence, the Œcumenicity of the Council which the Acts recorded. All the English and Irish Prelates, sometimes with a frank avowal of unacquaintance with the language in which our Lord spoke, made a polite acknowledgment of its receipt, but to the eighteen special copies which the American Bishops received at the hands of the late Bishop of Illinois— who, after writing the Presentee's and the Presentor's names and addresses in each copy, kindly offered them at the Convention held next after his return to America—no answer has ever been vouchsafed, except from three, of whom the Chief Bishop was one, viz., the late learned divine and scholar, Dr. J. H. Hopkins, of Vermont.

I feel bound, therefore, in justice to myself, to give others the opportunity of judging of the only part (for, the reproduction of the MS. itself, or the Latin translation given in Mansi of its documents, or the English of one by myself, could not possibly give offence) which must have had that effect I suppose, and which accounts for so unusual a phenomenon, viz.,—the "Prefatory Remarks," which are produced here verbatim, with the Dedication page, and to which the Metropolitan of Chios alludes in the translated letter of acknowledgment to me* subjoined, with approving emphasis.

---

* Most Reverend Father,

I owe many thanks to our common friend, most highly esteemed by me, the Reverend George Williams, because, even from afar, he does not cease to remember my Humility; and also from his good and kind disposition to make me known to his friends there.   It is certainly to the friendly commendation of this worthy man that I am now indebted, both for the honour of your letter, and the valuable work sent together with it, the Title of which is, 'An Ancient Syriac Document, &c."—a work having a special bearing on the Christians of the East.

Glory and honour to all those who occupy themselves in earnest works of this character, from which the dark parts of Ecclesiastical History will derive light,—amongst which men, without dispute, your Reverence—greatly desired by me—is also to be numbered, on account of your learned address prefixed, in memory of the Synod of the Venerable Anglican Bishops at Lambeth, in 1867.

And now, while acknowledging with gratitude your love in this valuable present, I pray from my soul (both for you and for all who contend for the truth, and for the union in one fold of all who call upon the all-holy name of Christ, "which is above every name") help from above, and illumination to walk without swerving in the direct and saving path of the one truth that is in Christ; which the Spirit-bearing Apostles of our Saviour, having received from Him, proclaimed; and their successors, the Divine Fathers, following them, by holy tradition, set forth both severally and in General Councils.

Your Reverence's (greatly desired by me) humble bedesman in Christ, and ready servant to your friendly commands,

The Metropolitan of Chios,

✛   GREGORY.

In Chios,
  8th September, 1869.

DEDICATION.

"To the Holy Synod of Bishops of Christ's Holy Catholic
"Church, Most Reverend and Right Reverend Fathers in God,
"in Communion with the See of Canterbury; convoked at
"the Instance of the Metropolitan and Bishops of Canada
"and of others, and holden at Lambeth Palace on 24, 25, 26, and
"27th days of September, in the year 1867, under the Presidency
"of his Grace the Lord Archbishop of Canterbury, in the spirit
"which animated "that gentle Father of his People," who says
"of "the Bishops assembled in Council"—"The Divine favour
"will bring it to pass, that we with the rest, our Colleagues,
"may stably and firmly administer our office, and uphold the peace
"of the Catholic Church in the Unity of Concord;" this attempt
"at an entire reproduction in fac-simile Estrangela characters, and
"at a translation of

"AN ANCIENT SYRIAC DOCUMENT

"(for centuries lost, and now generally unknown, to the Church),
"purporting to be an historical relation, in its chief features, of a
"certain Synod at Ephesus, summoned by Imperial Authority to be
"held in August, 449, A.D., as, and distinctly and authoritatively
"designated by itself when held to be an Œcumenical Synod of the
"Catholic Church, but, by reason of the outrage committed by its
"President and the violent perversion of its ends, for ever pro-
"nounced by SAINT LEO THE GREAT to be the

"'LATROCINIUM OF EPHESUS,'

"is, with Profound Veneration, as well as by Express Permission,
"Dedicated by a Priest of the Catholic Church in Communion
"with the See of Canterbury.

PREFATORY REMARKS.

"The original ancient Document, which the following pages
"indicate an attempt to reproduce in fac-simile type and to trans-
"late, forms one of those rich and magnificent Syriac treasures
"which the present Archdeacon of Bedford, Dr. Tattam, brought
"from the Syrian Monastery of St. Mary Deipara, in the Desert
"of Nitria or Scete, (ܪܘܚܐ ܟܢܝܫܬܐ ܕܝܠܕܬ ܐܠܗܐ
"ܐܡܐ ܕܐܝܠܝܢ ܐܣܟܡܐ ܘܗܝ ܕܒܡܕܒܪܐ), on the Western
"side of the Nile, between twenty and thirty years ago. The
"most important and most ancient of all those treasures have
"already been made known to the world by distinguished Oriental
"scholars, viz. :—

"(1) Clementis Romani Recognitiones, by Dr. P. de Lagarde of
         "Berlin.

"(2) Titi Bostreni contra Manichæos libri quatuor, by Dr. P. de
         "Lagarde.

"(3) Eusebius Bishop of Cæsarea on the Theophania or Divine
         "Manifestation of our Lord and Saviour Jesus Christ, with a
         "translation and notes, by Dr. Samuel Lee, late Professor of
         "Hebrew at Cambridge.

"(4) Ancient Syriac Documents relative to the earliest establishment
         "of Christianity in Edessa and the neighbouring countries,
         "from the year after our Lord's Ascension to the beginning
         "of the fourth century, with a translation, by Dr. Cureton,
         "and with a Preface by Dr. William Wright of the British
         "Museum.

"(5) Spicilegium Syriacum: containing remains of Bardesan, Meliton,
         "Ambrose, and Mar Bar Serapion, with a translation and
         "notes, by Dr. Cureton.

"(6) History of the Martyrs of Palestine by Eusebius, Bishop of
         "Cæsarea, with a translation into English, and Notes, by Dr.
         "Cureton.

"(7) An Ancient Syrian Martyrology, edited and translated by Dr.
         "William Wright of the British Museum, in the Journal of
         "Sacred Literature. 'The MS. of which it forms a part was
         "transcribed in the year of the Greeks 723, i.e. 412 A.D.'

"(8) Analecta Syriaca, with Appendix, by Dr. P. de Lagarde.

"(9) The Fragments of John of Asia, soon to be published by Dr.
" J. P. N. Land.

"(10) The Festal Letters of St. Athanasius, by Dr. Cureton.

"In this last work Dr. Cureton gives a full and very interesting
"history of the way in which these ancient Syriac monuments
"were discovered in the Syrian Convent, in the valley of the
"Nitrian Lakes, and brought by Dr. Tattam in 1842 to England,
"and afterwards deposited in the British Museum as the property
"of the nation in 1847, where they now form one of the most
"remarkable and important collections of the writings of antiquity
"which have ever been transported from East to West. Dr.
"Cureton mentions the share M. Pacho had in the purchasing
"these Manuscripts of the Cloistered Brethren of the Nitrian
"Valley. It turns out that M. Pacho himself, after having sold,
"according to agreement, the whole to the trustees of the British
"Museum, must have withheld part of them in some way or another,
"of which part the Imperial Public Library of St. Petersburg
"appears to be in present possession, certainly as far as the Syriac
"copy of the Ecclesiastical History of Eusebius, which Dr. Wright
"showed me, is concerned.

"Next after these very recherché specimens of Syriac literature
"above mentioned, ranks in importance and character, as I think,
"our Manuscript, which describes itself as

ܘܩܝܡ̈ܐ ܕܟܬܒ̈ܐ ܦܬܓ̈ܡܝ ܘܩܣܡܘܩ
܀ ܟܢܘܫܐ ܘܩܝܣܘܩ̈ܝܣ ܟܬܒܐ ܕܩܕܘ̈

"It is most probably a Syriac version, made about a century after
"the events it records, of a Greek original long since lost to the
"Church. It is numbered 14,530 among the Additional MSS. in
"the British Museum. It is very legibly and boldly indited on
"vellum in the Estrangělā character, and presents, as now bound
"up, only two blank leaves, indicating as few lacunæ* in the
"document. The generally excellent condition of the parchment

---

* There are in all five Lacunæ in the Original MS.

"leaves is no doubt due to the continuously dry and warm climate
"of the Desert, which has preserved it for our benefit during a
"period considerably exceeding one thousand years, according to
"the date so fortunately undefaced in this MS., as in many of its
"fellows, and placed at the end on the last page but one.

"The last page, however, presents difficulties of no ordinary
"kind; but its photographic representative, given in corresponding
"type at the end of our printed text, magnifying as it does the
"letters and the parts of letters that are discernible, as well as the
"marks of disfigurement, may induce some Syriac scholar to
"venture on an endeavour to decipher the sadly marred features of
"its dimly sombre visage, and so to offer some solution of those
"difficulties that have hitherto baffled some few not unskilful
"handlers of ancient Oriental MSS.

"The whole MS. consists of 216 pages, each page averaging
"about 28 lines. Sometimes towards the middle the lines number
"33 and 34. The portion of the Syriac text printed in this Part I
"is the beginning of the attempt at a reproduction of the docu-
"ment in its entirety, so that, page in our text nearly correspond-
"ing to page in the original, and line exactly to line, word for
"word, red type for red, and black type for black, we shall be
"enabled in the course of time, if encouraged, to accomplish the
"task of reproducing the whole document in fac-simile Estrangĕlä
"characters as contemplated.

"The translation strikes off with the Latin rendering of one of
"the documents already given in Mansi's L'Abbé. The English
"translation here given points to those very important matters
"connected with the characteristics of this MS.; for it relates to
"what occurred after August 8, and to the case of Ibas and to
"the unfolding of the unlawful acts of Dioscorus and partisans at
"the Synod, by which its President perverted it into a Concili-
"abulum and that Conciliabulum into the Latrocinium of Ephesus.
"The Emperor had summoned the Synod for August 1. Its first
"session, three extant fragments concerning which are given in
"Latin and Greek in L'Abbé's 'Conciliorum Collectio,' took place

" on August 8. It is the Session on Saturday, August 20, of
" which mention is made, and that on Monday, August 22, pro-
" ceedings of which are recorded, in these Acts alone.

" As the preceding remarks relative to the Syriac MSS. cannot
" be otherwise than apposite and pertinent to the matter in hand,
" so the subjoined reflections will not, I think, be considered
" inapposite or inopportune, which deal with the subject of
" Synods generally, although *at present* it appears to be not unwise
" to say little of that particular one, of which *much* is to be said
" and can be better said when all connected with it is complete.

" Now it is evident to all men (ܐܬ ܝ܇ܘ܀ܪܐ ܪܝܠܗܠ to use the
" first words of our document) reading the signs of the times, that
" the grand idea of the distinctive oneness of the ' one Body ' of
" Christ—so fully taught by the Holy Ghost, as well in the
" glorious Creeds of the Church Catholic as through the direct
" and immediate inspiration of Holy Writ—is receiving and
" growing into a vivid realization in this latter half of the nine-
" teenth century, which may witness, before its close, through that
" ' one Body ' being continually quickened and informed by the
" ' one Spirit,' a no inappreciable approximation to the Church's
" oneness of character in primitive times.   And there is also much
" reason to aver that the synodical system of the Church, by and
" in the highest form in which her articulate voice was in the ages
" of faith so faithfully uttered and obediently heard, and of which,
" I will add, our MS., coming up as it does through the long vista
" of those past ages from the unchanging East, is so singularly
" expressive, promises, by God's mercy to us, to receive such posi-
" tive and helpful encouragements as will afford to many, yearning
" for its joyful fulness, a warranty of hope and belief that that
" visible Oneness or Unity must be attended with an immediate
" and manifest accession.

" Now the Synodical Institutions of the Church Catholic are of
" Divine origin. The germ from which they are all evolved and
" the source to which they can be referred and traced back, as well
" in their first emergent and scarcely discernible development as in

"the grandest and most glorious, when the largest General Council
"could exultingly appropriate Christ's promise to itself, may be
"found in the Divine words containing that promise of our Lord's
"gracious presence : οὗ γάρ εἰσι δύο ἢ τρεῖς συνηγμένοι εἰς τὸ ἐμὸν
"ὄνομα, ἐκεῖ εἰμι ἐν μέσῳ αὐτῶν. The secondary meaning of these
"words, reality of belief in which has been abundantly and
"unprecedently evidenced of late years—may it still increase !—
"in the awakened consciousness of Churchmen to privileges and
"duties in connection with assemblies for Worship, needs certainly
"no elaborate elucidation ; whilst the primary, significative of
"order, discipline, and work, has surely been insufficiently regarded
"in the realization of blessings inherent of necessity in a guaran-
"teed promise to what is done, εἰς τὸ ὄνομα, by many or by few in
"authorised union and action.

"This year of grace, however, and this month of September,
"bear witness to a special and unprecedented instance of actual
"realization of the promise, in the Synod of Bishops, held at
"Lambeth, of Christ's Holy Catholic Church in Communion with
"the See of Canterbury :— special, whether there are regarded
"evidences of the special Presence attached, and the special office
"of teaching the truth of God assigned, to such Synods ; or it be
"looked on only as a συνόδος ἡ ἐνδημαύσα, like that at Constantinople
"in November A.D. 448, when the Hæresiarch was formally accused
"of a denial of the truth of the distinction of the two natures of
"Jesus Christ ;—unprecedented, as the annals of our whole Com-
"munion furnish no such instance of the ʻ Demonstrative Unity ' of
"its Chief Pastors. May this apostolic return by our Right
"Reverend Fathers in God to the earliest and normal rule and law
"of the Church, by which the primary signification of Christ's own
ʻ Words is manifestly attested and realized, exercise over the future
"of our one-third division of Christendom such a beneficial influ-
"ence as will encourage every member of that Division gladly to
"recognise his position in it, and to realise his ʻ vocation and
"ministry '—his calling from on high (ἡ ἄνω κλῆσις) and his office
"and function in the ʻ one Body '—as it regards that primary sig-

"nification, and such as may bear comparison with that of the great "Fathers of Nice over the whole history of Christendom, in the "actual past and present, as well as in its probable future.

"The received histories of the Catholic Church from the Day of "Pentecost, after the Apostolic Synod at Jerusalem in A.D. 51, held "to determine points of Ritual and to enact Canons, and another "under the presidency of the Bishop of that city, held to receive "a persecuted Apostle and his company, present us with at least "six recognised Œcumenical Councils or Synods—besides smaller "ones—which, viewed at a mere glance, may be perhaps epitomised "thus :—

	A.D.	
(1) At NICE—318 Bishops present—it attested to "the Deposit" and defined "the Faith once, and once for all, delivered"—Arianism condemned—Synodical Epistle—20 Canons	325	Convoked by *Constantine the Great.*
(2) At CONSTANTINOPLE—150 Bishops, it re-affirmed the faith and completed the Nicene Definition—condemned the Macedonian Heresy—before it Arianism fell—7 Canons	381	Convoked by *Theodosius the Great.*
(3) At EPHESUS—200 Bishops present—the great exposition of the faith by S. Cyril—the Nestorian Heresy condemned—8 Canons	431	Convoked by *Theodosius the younger.*
At Ephesus—130 Bishops present—Dioscorus President..........	449	*Convoked by Theodosius the younger.*
(4) At CHALCEDON—630 Bishops—the Creed (without filioque) now set forth as perfection, τὸ τέλειον—Eutychian Heresy anathematized—Leo's Tome, rejected at Ephesus, is accepted, and Dioscorus deposed and sentenced—30 Canons	451	Convoked by *Marcian,* great lover of the Faith.
(5) At CONSTANTINOPLE—165 Bishops—the three Chapters; miserable results, but this Synod has always been received and respected by the Church as condemning error	556	Convoked by *Justinian* against the Church's wish and desire.
(6) At CONSTANTINOPLE—170 Bishops—Agatho's Synodical letters—Definition of there being two natural Wills or Operations of Christ in One Person—Monothelite Error—Honorius, &c., anathematized	681	Convoked by *Constantine IV.*

The Quinisext Council is supplementary
  to the fifth and sixth, because they
  enacted no canons of discipline—and
  this made 102, confirming the doc-
  trine of the six General Councils,   692   Convoked by *Justinian*
  "the 85 Canons of the Apostles,"   *II.*
  &c.—The Code of the Universal
  Church complete ....

"At these Councils, all summoned by Imperial authority, the
"Holy Gospels were exalted on a Throne put in a prominent posi-
"tion, definitions and transactions were regularly recorded in the
"Acts, and Canons enacted. The Actio was the Session. A
"Patriarch had several Notaries attendant on him, and a Bishop
"always one or more. The primicerius was the Bishop's registrar.
"Bishops alone attested to the faith, alone determined, defined or
"settled points of doctrine, declaring together by virtue of their
"office, 'Thus believes the Catholic Church,' and separately
"endorsing with 'definiens subscripsi,' whilst any other wrote
"'consentiens subscripsi.' The Notaries had to write down or copy
"the Acts for the Bishops, who took to their provinces the defini-
"tions of the Faith and the Canons enacted. There were also
"apocrisiaries, or a sort of proctors, syncelli, and promoters,
"and committees, formed for special business, defenders
"and defendants, letters of citation, information demanded and
"declared before the Holy Gospels present so conspicuously, libels,
"or bills of indictment preferred against the accused, memorials,
"petitions. gravamina, &c., besides 'acclamations,' which formed a
"characteristic feature of the working of the ancient Synods, very
"similar, for instance, to the following :—'Such is the Faith of the
"Fathers. Such is the Faith of the Apostles. Peter has spoken
"by Leo. So the Apostles taught. Leo hath taught piously and
"truly. Cyril taught so. Eternal be the memory of Cyril.' These
"instances of freedom include a remarkable illustration in our
"document.

"Of these six Œcumenical Synods, the first, in the highest sense
"and in another, the greatest and most important undoubtedly was
"that at Nicæa. Besides enacting twenty Canons, and settling for
"ever the questions as to the time for the Church to keep Easter

" and the re-admission of certain schismatics into her communion,
" the Fathers of the first Synod said on behalf of God's truth, and
" said for all Christians for all time, 'Thus believes the Catholic
" Church.' That General Council is the foundation on which all
" the others were built and grounded. The second knit itself on
" to it. The third affirmed 'the faith of the cccxviii. and of the
" cl.' 'Those holy and venerable Fathers,' says S. Leo, 'who, at
" Nice having condemned Arius with his sacrilegious impiety,
" enacted laws of Ecclesiastical Canons to abide to the end of the
" world, live in their Constitutions among us and throughout the
" world.' 'All the Fathers reverenced the Nicene Council, as an
" oracle given from heaven.' That Council also regulated the
" holding of Synods of Bishops. Many such Synods had taken
" place frequently before; and Bishop Beveridge proves, at great
" pains, that many were held in the second and third centuries.
" They were the normal rule of the Church; and 'the *half-yearly*
" Synod of Bishops was then, by virtue of an authority acknowledged
" as supreme, appointed for the whole Church.'

" During the period intervening between the first and second
" Œcumenical Synods, when Arianism under various phases and
" forms vigorously and constantly assaulted, with a view to destroy,
" the Faith in God the Son, but finally fell before the Faith's
" victory at the latter Council, we have afforded to us notices of no
" less than eighty Synods; and though they were mostly unsatis-
" factory, being attempts to undo the work of God the Holy Ghost
" in the Church—waves dashing against the rocks of the true Faith,
" which 'foamed out their own shame,' as a Regius Professor so
" beautifully puts it (for I am here using his thoughts),—yet they
" testify to the practice of Synods of Bishops, to the regular custom
" that then obtained. All the then misbelievers seem to have been
" such misbelievers through failing to perceive, as some do now (for
" Arianism under another appellative is still moribund), that 'there
" is no middle point between the entire Oneness of the Nature of
" God the Son with the Father and His being a mere creature,' since
" what is not God of necessity is a creature of God,

"'Taken together, the first four general Synods rank above all
"others in importance and value to the Catholic Church. They
"chiefly concerned themselves about 'the whole state of our Lord
"Jesus Christ;' to make which 'complete,' Hooker (Book V.) says,
"'There are but four things that concur: His Deity, His manhood,
"the conjunction of both, and the distinction of the one from the
"other being joined in one. Four principal heresies there are
"which have in those things withstood the truth: Arians by bending
"themselves against the Deity of Christ, Apollinarians by maiming
"and misinterpreting that which belongeth to His human nature,
"Nestorians by rending Christ asunder and dividing Him into two
"persons, the followers of Eutyches by confounding in His person
"those natures which they should distinguish. Against these there
"have been four most famous ancient General Councils: the Council
"of Nice to define against Arians, against Apollinarians the Council
"of Constantinople, the Council of Ephesus against Nestorians,
"against Eutychians the Chalcedon Council. In four words,
"ἀληθῶς, τελέως, ἀδιαιρέτως, ἀσυγχύτως, *truly, perfectly, indivisibly,*
"*distinctly;* the first applied to His being God, and the second to
"His being Man, the third to His being of both One, and the fourth
"to His still continuing in that one Both: we may fully, by way
"of abridgment comprise whatsoever antiquity hath at large
"handled, either in declaration of Christian belief, or in refutation
"of the aforesaid heresies. Within the compass of which four
"heads, I may truly affirm, that all heresies which touch but the
"person of Jesus Christ, whether they have arisen in these latter
"days, or in any age heretofore, may be with great facility brought
"to confine themselves.'

"Now if there be one period in the whole history of the Church
"militant here on earth, which does or will demand of the readers
"of that history thoughts and reflections such as those so pithily
"and nervously indited in the Oxford translation of M. L'Abbé
"Fleury, it is that which comprises the period of heresy and the
"councils so succinctly reviewed and concisely summarized by
"Hooker. Our allusion is to the following: 'Most men who have

" considered the course which Church-history takes, have in some
" stage of their progress felt pain, if not misgiving, at the rapidity
" with which one heresy seems to follow upon another.   To minds
" in this state we may suggest, *first*, that as wars occupy a wide
" space on the page of civil history, though often affording scarcely
" any criterion of the aggregated happiness of a nation, so ecclesi-
" astical history is often compelled to dwell on the life of a single
" heretic, while thousands and tens of thousands are passing to
" their heavenly inheritance unnoticed and unknown.   *Secondly*,
" that from the disproportionate time spent in examining heresies
" we are apt to think too slightly of the periods of rest, those
" " intervals of sunshine between storm and storm " in which it " is
" God's will to gather in His elect little by little."   *Lastly*, that
" heresy is overruled to several of the best ends—to promote
" humility—to try our faith (I. Cor. ii. 19)—to rouse the careless
" to an attentive study, and the religious to a more earnest realiza-
" tion of the Christian verities, and to subserve the evolution of
" those verities in a dogmatic form.'

" And if there be one page of ecclesiastical history which more
" than another deserves and claims attention to the strikingly
" beautiful and thoughtful remark tersely embodying the sentiments
" expressed above, and placed by Dr. Burton in the forefront of his
" historical work, it is that which recounts the doings, especially
" when viewed by the additional light furnished by this ancient
" Syriac Document, of that Patriarch of the ancient and once
" glorious Church of Alexandria, who marred the splendour of the
" Throne of SS. Athanasius and Cyril, reduced one of the grandest
" institutions of Christ, designed for the benefit of His Church, to
" ' the Latrocinium of Ephesus,' and so brought a withering curse
" upon the whole of ' the Evangelical See ' of S. Mark, it may be
" for ever.

" It is hoped that, in this individual effort to do some honour to
" and to commemorate, the Synod of Bishops of Christ's Holy
" Catholic Church, holden at Lambeth in September 1867, may be
" considered, as included, a humble desire as well to promote the

" study of the oldest Church language and literature generally, as
" to draw their attention to, if not actually to bring to bear on
" those many fellow Churchmen of our common ' Civitas Dei ' in
" India, the Colonies, and other parts of the world, the rich literary
" Church treasures, and the accompanying advantages within easy
" reach, which we of the home Church possess in such great but
" not selfish abundance ; and last, but not least, to add a little link
" in that chain of fraternal love that is uniting together in closer
" brotherhood the members of the ' One Body ' living in the East
" and in the West, in the New World and in the Old.

" S. G. F. PERRY.

" TOTTINGTON PARSONAGE,
" IN THE DIOCESE OF MANCHESTER AND PROVINCE OF YORK,
" *September*, 1867."

Thus have I transposed, in their entirety, my
" Prefatory Remarks" of Part I., by which to enable
my readers to judge of them for themselves.   One
more paragraph at Page 19 I might adduce as
unfavourable to myself perhaps, but, as the matter
therein stated is purely historical, I forbear to do so.
The fellow copy of that presented to Archbishop
Longley was shewn among other articles of literary
curiosity at the Missionary Exhibition at Manchester,
undertaken a few years since by the enterprise of
the senior Member for that city—viz., Hugh Birley,
Esq. A notification of Part I. is made by Dr. W.
Wright in the three-volumed catalogue of the Syriac
MSS. in the British Museum.   Subsequently, on
finding the costliness of printing the whole Codex in
the " sumputous" type would be very considerable,

I followed the example of a Syriac scholar whose work had cost Oxford University £1,000, and made application, but in vain, to the Delegacy for assistance, and, although the Right Honorable W. E. Gladstone, during his first Premiership, offered me a sum of money from the Treasury, I ultimately resolved to adopt a smaller type, and to prosecute my object at my leisure and independent of all pecuniary assistance. Accordingly, when I had completed the transcript of the whole of it with my own hand, I dedicated my first printed edition of the Codex to the memory of S.W.P. and of M.E.P., in the personal "tribulation" connected with which I have never yet been able to be "joyful," and in the midst of the joy in the bitterness of the heart no stranger could possibly intermeddle. At the suggestion of a foreign scholar, who, though of an alien communion, sympathised with me both in my labours and my sorrows, I appended several appropriate extracts from various Syriac documents in the British Museum, and at the late Quarternian Centenary Commemoration of the University of Tübingen—QUINTUM SÆCULUM SUPERIORIBUS CLARIUS SURGIT (See Vol. ii. p. 305)—where thirty universities had representatives, and where such distinguished courtesy and kindness were manifested towards me as can never be effaced from my memory.   I was able to have the pleasure of presenting to the University and Royalty there my Tubingen Edition, including an English Version of the Codex, together with the first part of my Tetraglott Psalter, and the Rector Magnificus, at my request, proposed formally to those in Statu Pupellan a Prize Essay for the encouragement of Syriac Ltterature—a fact duly recorded in the beautiful Documents drawn up for the Commemoration.   In a new Edition of a Theological Encyclopœdia Professor Semischt afterwards called attention to the Syriac Volumes, and especially to the extracts that more or less refer to the Codex.   It will greatly add to my pleasure to offer these now completed Volumes, i. and ii., with some accompaniments, for the acceptance of Modern Victoria University, by which opportunity to the rising generation for encouragement to study may be afforded.   A Language and a Literature that are hallowed by associations affecting greatly our Blessed Lord and His Mission on Earth, and call to the whole Christian World in the unedited Paschetto for devout attention, and that appeal to this Nation especially in the unravelled MSS. of unrivalled Syriac Treasures in the British Museum.

CONTENTS OF THE BOOK.

ANALYSIS OF THE CODEX

The Great Syriac Codex, numbered 14,530 among the Additional MSS. in the British Museum, is by us designated A, which contains :—

Action taken against Ibas at Edessa.

Imperial letters to the Council urging it, since all classes witness against his Impiety, to appoint another Bishop in the stead of Ibas. [This is the Document (γ) not (δ) (38). Monks enter the Council, bearing Imperial Letters addressed to James and eleven other Archimandrites of Edessa, which letters are read, (39—41). At the instance of Dioscorus, the Commissioners, Photius, Eustatius, and Uranius, declare what took place before them on matters of The Faith as to Ibas, and as regards Daniel, he tendered his resignation (41—43).

[A.] Records of Transactions at Edessa in April last past before the Præses, Chæreas, including the vociferations of the Citizens on his entry on the borders and into the Church of Zachœus (44—54).

[B. First Formal Enquiry.] The Second Report. Document addressed to Roman Authorities by Chereas respecting the excited condition of the City (55—57). Copy of Records drawn up at Edessa in the Consulate of Zeno and Posthumian. Micallus brings a Petition of the Inhabitants of the City, which he and other Ecclesiastics had signed, and it is received and read (57—59). The Petition (59—66). "Every person subscribed to these Transactions and to the Presentation of the Petition" Then the Acclamations of the whole population (67—73). The Count notes the instancy on the Authorities, and Micallus offers the apology (73 and 74). Micallus assures the Count that it is with the good will of all present that the *Petition* and the *Oath* are proffered (75). Fifty attest to this (75—82).

[C. Second Formal Enquiry]. The Third Report. Document, despatched to Martialius by Chæreas, relative to the recurrence of the commotion excited in the City by the discovery of the false faith of its Bishop (84—87). A civic Dignitary, Theodosius, speaks of his efforts on a Sunday to repress disturbance, and, in the name of the community at large, presents a Petition for allaying it. He urges Ibas's accusers present to say what charges are preferred against him, in what counts convicted, and appeals to those present as to whether his statements are correct (87—90). Twenty-six witnesses attest to this (91—94). Samuel, Maras, and Cyrus took part in the presentment and indictment at Berytus (95). Samuel's account of his full Deposition made there, and of Ibas's Heresy—"I do not envy Christ's becoming God, &c.," (95—100). The testimony of six witnesses to this Heresy (100—103). That of sixteen others as to kindred Heresy (103—108). Theodosius urges the conveyance of these Instruments to the Authorities, and asks for a copy of Ibas's Letter to Maris be read before the Synod (108—109).   The Judge replies (110).   THE LETTER ITSELF (111—119).   Discussion as to the copy of the Letter (120—123).   Count Chæreas promises that all shall be notified to the Authorities (123).   Then ensue EXCLAMATIONS from the Synod (124—125). What Eulogius repeats as known, the Synod cries out should be put into writing (126).   More Exclamations of the Synod (127).   The President calls for silence (128).   A highly important Deposition made by Eulogius (128—133).   Sentence of Deposition pronounced upon the Bishop of Edessa judicially and severally by twenty chief Bishops of the Synod and unanimously by the Synod itself (134—145). [A note on their judgment (145—147).]

iii.   DEPOSITION OF DANIEL THE BISHOP OF CHARRÆ (HARAN).

[Introductory Note, containing part of the tenth "Actio" of the Chalcedon Synod referring to the "Crimina" with which Daniel was charged, and the relationship between Edessa and Charrae, and their Bishops (151—154).] Eulogius opens the case with charges made against Daniel, and requests the Commissioners to speak on the subject into which investigation had been made in their presence (155). One of them says he had forgotten the case (156).   Eustathius states Daniel was convicted to his face in open Court, but, during a delay, sent in letters of his Resignation to his Metropolitan.   In the end, the case was remitted for the settlement of the affair to this Œcumenical Synod (156—158).   Bishop Euranius speaks by an interpreter (159). Relying on the excellent name of the Commissioners, twelve Bishops or more pronounce sentence upon Daniel's Deposition from the Throne of the Priesthood (159—165).

iv.   DEPOSITION OF IRENÆUS THE BISHOP OF TYRE.

[Introductory Note, shewing that Irenaeus was a Count of the Empire, but subsequently consecrated to the Episcopate by Archbishop Domnus and not by Theodoret (168—170).] The Proto-Notary, after speaking of the Nestorian Doctrine which Daniel upheld, and of his having two wives, &c., urges the justice of a Synodical and Legal sentence (170—173).   The chief Bishops state that he ought to be deprived of the episcopal Dignity which he should not have had in the first instance, and, some add, of Communion in the Pure Mysteries.   The Synod assented (173—177).

xxviii.   CONTENTS.

APPENDICES.

EXTRACTS

Translated from Syriac MSS of different dates, in the British
Museum, relating directly or indirectly, sometimes quoting, the
Second Synod, or to the Great Nestorian Controversy.

THE SECOND SYNOD

WHICH ASSEMBLED

AT EPHESUS

IN THE DAYS OF THE

HOLY BISHOP DIOSCORUS.

A

ENGLISH VERSION.

I.

(a) THE AUTOCRATIC CÆSARS, THEO-
DOSIUS AND VALENTINIAN,
VICTORS AND ILLUSTRIOUS BY
VICTORIES, THE EVER-WORSHIP-
FUL, THE AUGUSTI, TO DIOS-
CORUS* :

It is evident unto all men that the Status of our
Government and (the condition of) all our human
affairs are strengthened and consolidated by (The
True) Religion, and that, when God is propitious,

---

* This Imperial Document of Theodosius ii. and Valentinian iii.,
convoking what was intended to be and was at first the 4th Œcumenical
Synod or Council of Christ's Catholic Church, and addressed to the
Successor of S. Mark in its 2nd See, was originally issued in Greek
and will be found in Labbe's "Sacro-Sancta Concilia" at Tom. IV.
99-102, and in Mansi's "Conciliorum nova et amplissima collectio" at Vol.
VI., 588-590. It has two Syriac Translations among the Add. MSS.
in the Brit. Museum, of one of which (the chief, and numbered 14,530)
my Vol. i. contains the Oxford Clarendon Press impression at the commencement. The other (in Add. MS. numbered 12,156) will be found
under the designation D among the Appendices of the same Vol. and

matters are readily administered and proceed according to our wish.   Called,* then, to reign by Divine Providence we of necessity exercise great solicitude for the peace and quiet of our subjects in order that Our Rightful Majesty may be upheld and Our Government carried on and flourish by (The True) Religion.†

---

its translation in this Vol. ii. under Appendix D. The Ecclesiastical Annals of Baronius contain only a Latin Version of it at Tom. VIII. p. 10 (Lucæ 1741). I have given another Latin version of it from Mansi's Labbe at p. 15, of my "Ancient Syriac Document, &c.," presented in 1868 to the late Archbishop of Canterbury, and since deposited by the present one in the Lambeth Library.

* Or, it may perhaps be rendered, but not so well,—"Called, then, to "reign by Divine Providence and supremely desirous of promoting the "peace and happiness of our subjects we shall take care that our Majesty "and our Government be distinguished by a true Piety."

† "By (The True) Religion." The Roman Empire found support, as to the matter of Government, in the true Principles embodied in a false Religion.   How much more would it in those of the True Religion, although at this period that Empire was on the decline and destined to fall ere long under the weight of its own vices, of which the historical fact of this Ephesine Assembly is a not inappropriate prelude, when viewed in the light of a great Council of the Church being turned into the nefarious purposes of the Chiefs of the Eutychean party, Chrysaphius, Eutyches, and Dioscorus, whom I designate the Ecclesiastical Triumvirate of the period.   In Dr. R. Payne Smith's Thesaurus Syriacus column 864, he distinguishes between (1) ܐ ܐ, Θεοσέβεια, and (2) ܐ ܐ, εὐσέβεια, religio, pietas and (3) ܐ ܐ ?, religiositas tua, which terms constantly occur throughout the original MS., as may be seen from my version in Vol. i. The last (3) I have uniformly translated *Your Piety* or *Your Reverence*, as *Your Religiosity* or *Religiousness* would hardly be an admissible appellative in accosting anyone.   At p. 3, l. 7, in my text ܐ ܐ ? seems to partake of both significations (1) and (2) which idea is confirmed by the corresponding term in Appendix D where it is ܐ ܐ ?, so that it might be translated also "*by a true Piety*." In correspondence with Dr. R. P. Smith, he was good enough to

Now, seeing that a certain controversy* has all on a sudden sprung up just lately touching Apostolic Doctrine and affecting the conservancy of our Orthodox Faith, which (controversy), by drawing men off into diverse opinions, agitates and disturbs their minds and affections, it has appeared to us that it would not be well to neglect a matter of this kind, disgraceful though it be, lest haply our disregard of it tend to the dishonour of God Himself; and for that reason we have given command that, when there have assembled together Pious and God-loving personages enjoying great reputation for Piety and

point out to me that the cognate word ‏ܠܐ‎ means (1) *adoratio*, *veneratio*, and (2) probably *res adoranda*, *idolum* as well as (3) the *respect* and *veneration*, claimed by the Roman Emperors and implied, I think, in the words Augustus, divus, divinus, &c. In Mansi's Labbe's " Conciliorum Collectio" it is rendered θρησκεία and *Religio*.

The term ‏ܠܐ‎ at the very beginning of this Imperial Document and ‏ܠܐ‎ in Appendix D mean *dignitas*, as well as *ordo*, *status* ; the Thesaurus Syriacus of Dr. P. S., at c. 1125 affording us an example in the expression ‏ܠܐ‎, *Splendores regiæ dignitatis.*

* " A controversy has all on a sudden sprung up just lately." In his letter to Proclus, the Proconsul of Asia, as given by Binius (Concilia iii. p. 56) in Latin and Greek, the Emperor says :—" Nunc et altera " iterum contra Divinam Fidem excitata est dubitatio (*a*), secundam hanc " in Epheso fieri Synodum Sanximus, mali radicem omnino excidere " cupientes. . . . . Elpidium (*b*) verum Spectabilem Comitem " nostri Consistorii et Eulogium verum Spectabilem, Tribunum et " Notarium, ad hanc causam degimus."

(*a*) In a beautiful little letter of S. Leo, addressed to this Second Ephesine Council, as given by Binius (Concilia iii. p. 14), he has explained in a few words the " fons et origo" of the great Controversy :—" Tu es, inquit, Christus Filius Dei : " hoc est, Tu, Qui es vere Filius hominis, idem vere es Filius Dei vivi : Tu, " inquam, verus in Deitate, verus in carne, et sub ea geminæ proprietate na- " turæ utrinque unus. Quod si Eutyches intelligenter ac vivaciter crederet " nequaquam ab hujus fidei tramite deviaret." The controversy itself concerned the true nature of Jesus Christ. See Introduction.
(*b*) See Vol. i. page 273, and Appendix D of this Vol., " Commonitory or Commission of Elpidius."

for being of The Orthodox and True Faith, such an accurate enquiry be instituted that the groundless controversy be composed, and The True and Orthodox Faith, so precious to God, become consolidated.

Your Piety, then, taking with you ten of the Holy Metropolitan Bishops of the Province, besides ten other Venerable Bishops adorned with (the qualifications of) eloquence and an upright manner of life, and, more than other men, distinguished for the knowledge and for the teaching of The True and Inerrant Faith, will, on the Calends of August next ensuing, take care to repair without delay to Ephesus the Metropolis of Asia—no other person, however, except those mentioned, must be allowed to trouble the Holy Synod—in order that, when all those Pious and God-loving Bishops, whom we have given command by Royal Letters to assemble together, shall have gone with promptitude to the City named above, and have instituted accurate investigation and enquiry, the whole Error may be uprooted and made to cease, whilst the Doctrine of The Orthodox and True Faith, so dear to Christ our Saviour, shall flourish as usual, and be consolidated ; which (Faith) it will be the duty of all men now living to preserve unshaken and (to transmit) inviolate to times hereafter, having God propitious. If any one, however, be bent on contemning this God-loving Synod — a Synod which necessity has demanded—and demur to proceed with all his ability at the time appointed, and to the place selected, not a single excuse will be found (available) for him before God or with our Clemency. But he who excuses himself insincerely* from attending this assembly of the Priesthood (though his excuse be accepted, yet) will, necessarily, feel punishment (injured) in himself.

Theodoret,† Bishop of the City of Cyrus, however, whom we have already commanded to confine himself to his own Church, we forbid to proceed to the Holy Synod, unless first it should seem fit to the whole assembled Synod for him also to go and take part in that Synod. But, if any division (of opinion) arise on his account, we determine that the Holy Synod shall meet and settle the business, as ordered, without him.

THIS ORDINANCE WAS ISSUED ON THE 30TH OF MARCH, THE THIRD BEFORE THE CALENDS OF APRIL, IN THE CITY OF CONSTANTINOPLE, AFTER THE CONSULATE OF THE ILLUSTRIOUS ZENO AND POSTHUMIAN.

---

* " Insincerely." Literally translated the Syriac phrase is " with no good conscience." The whole sentence's meaning is tersely expressed in Mansi's Latin :—" Sacerdotalem enim conventum non nisi quis malâ propriâ conscientiâ sauciatus evitat." The Œcumenical Synod of Nicæa in 325 A.D. was designated an assembly of the Priesthood. So this.

† These Acts will be found to furnish no unimportant materials for writing the history of this great and prominent character of the 5th Century, to which Dr. Newman has already contributed much.

Theodosius the Younger and Valentinian III. were "the Masters of the world." The former succeeded to the Imperial Purple in his 8th year and died in his 49th year, 450 A.D., leaving only one daughter, who married Valentinian III. The latter, the last of the family of Theodosius the Great, was publicly acknowledged Emperor of Rome Oct. 3rd, 423 A.D., although only in the 6th year of his age, and was murdered there in the 31st year of his reign, 454 A.D.

RECORDS OF PROCEDURE DIRECTED AGAINST IBAS,
THE BISHOP OF THE CITY OF EDESSA.*

(β) The Autocratic Cæsars, Theodosius and Valentinian, Victors and Illustrious by Victory, the
ever-Worshipful, the Augusti, to Dioscorus† :

On a former occasion‡ we ordered that Theodoret,
the Bishop of City of Cyrus, should not go to the

---

* The above heading of the legal action or of the " memorial of pro-
"ceedings," adopted both by this Assembly and by others, in relation to this
very celebrated and greatly canvassed character—so much so as to have
occupied the attention of no less than half-a-dozen Councils of the
Church—would perhaps have been far more appropriately placed by the
Scribe lower down in the original Acts or MS., since only one of the
following Documents relates specially to Ibas. The Report of his, the
first, cause tried by the Council occupies in these Acts the first 92 pages.
I have always rendered the word ‎ܐܝܗܒ‎ *Ibas*, although it is evident that
orthographically it should be *Hiba* and etymologically *Ihiba*.

† This Imperial Letter assigns the Presidency of the then immediately assembling Council to Dioscorus the Archbishop of Alexandria as
Successor to the Great Cyril in the second Church in rank in the then
Christendom, but through interested partizans at Court chiefly it was no
doubt that he obtained the appointment. The term " Alexan-
"dria the Great" which runs through these Acts would apparently
seem to indicate that the Greatness of the great Conqueror, its
Founder, was still retained in the minds of men in Vth Century
after Christ. This Letter views Theodoret, though his pastoral and
literary labours for the Catholic Church had been so great and successful
and his Services to the Empire not unimportant, yet because he was not
perfectly Orthodox, as a dangerous Heretic and a Teacher to be repressed
and silenced. His faithful adherence to his old and and cherished friend
Nestorius won for him chiefly the unenviable notoriety of being a
wilful participator in the great Error of that Heresiarch, whereas his
recantation before the Fathers of Chalcedon of all that might have been
heretical on his part would seem to modify, if not exonerate him from,
the charge. The letter is to be found in Labbe (Sacro-Sancta Concilia
IV., 110-112) and in Mansi (Concil. omnium amplis. collectio VI.,
599-600), reprinted in my " Ancient Syriac Document, &c." at page
16. A Second Syriac Version may be seen in Appendix D to Vol. i.
A Latin version of it occurs in Baronius's Annals.

‡ " On a former occasion," i.e., in the Imperial Letter (α) dated

Holy Synod until that Holy Synod had settled what
it willed concerning him. For, we have discounten-
anced his proceedings, seeing that he has ventured to
compose treatises* antagonistic to those which Cyril,
of Blessed Memory, who was Bishop of Alexandria
the Great, wrote concerning The Faith. Since,
however, it is possible that some of the partizans of
Nestorius will exhibit a degree of solicitude about
him so as by all means to enable him to go to the
Holy Synod, for that reason we have of necessity
concluded on addressing these Royal Letters to your
Piety ; and by them we notify to your Charity and to
the entire Holy Synod that, acting in conformity
with the Canons of the Holy Fathers, we have
assigned the Presidency and (Chief) Authority not
only over Theodoret, but also over all other Bishops
admitted to that Holy Synod now assembled, to
your Piety ; being assured, as we verily are, that
also the God-loving Archbishop of Jerusalem, Juvenal, and the God-loving Archbishop Thalassius,
and all who have a similar zeal and love for The

March 30, which, hereafter it will be convenient to remember, was the
Wednesday of the Easter Week in 449 A.D. The prohibition is
renewed in the above letter (β) dated the day before the opening of this
Synod.

* In Migne's Patrologia Græca, letter 112 of Theodoret, in which he
says his "sad soul sighs and laments" as he witnesses the preparations
made for the approaching Council, goes so far as to speak of
"the venom contained in the 12 Chapters," and of the Successor of
Cyril as daring "to pronounce an anathema on those who refuse to accept
"the 12 Chapters," which, as they are so frequently alluded to and so
remarkable and able, we have given below, for the benefit of the English
reader, from the Oxford Fleury.

B

Orthodox Faith, are of the same opinion with your Holiness, who are, by the grace of God, distinguished for gravity of life and integrity of Faith.

As for those who have ventured to affirm (any thing) in addition to, or in subtraction from, what has been determined on in matters relating to The Faith (the Symbol delivered) by the Holy Fathers at Nicæa and afterwards at Ephesus, we by no means allow them any liberty of speech at all that would accrue to them in Holy Synod, whilst we will (at the same time) that they submit to your judgment. For this reason, too, it is that we have decreed that the assembling of the Holy Synod should now take place.

This Ordinance was issued (granted) on the 6th of the month of Ab (August) on the 8th before the Ides of August, at Constantinople

———

The Autocratic Cæsars Theodosius and Valentinian, Victors and Illustrious by Victory, the ever Worshipful, the Augusti, to the Holy Synod assembled at Ephesus the Metropolis

Numerous Anaphoræ (Reports) from people at

———

Edessa, a City in the Province of Osrhoene, with Acts drawn up there, have been despatched hither, which contain the Depositions of many Venerable Clergy and God-fearing Archimandrites and Civic

---

the celebrated Commission which those (in one sense famous, but not so in another) Bishops Photius, Eustathius, and Uranius received at the bidding of the Masters of the world, when the Bishop Ibas's trial took place at Tyre-Berytus-Tyre. The difficulties connected with the history of that trial, which for so long a period were discussed by Tillemont and other historians, have received a complete solution by certain historical facts made known to us now for the first time by A. The Add. MS. numbered 14,602 in the British Museum contains passages—see Appendix E for their translation—referring not only to Dioscorus and to his Synod, by whose authority the Bishops of Edessa and Cyrus were expelled from their Episcopal Sees without even being cited to appear before that Tribunal, but specially relating also to the Commissioners Photius and Eustathius appointed to adjudicate in the case of Ibas, first at Tyre, by whose Bishop a reconciliation between the contending parties was initiated, and then at Berytus, where a decision was arrived at, and then back again at Tyre as being the Bishopric that claimed priority in point of Dignity and Rank.

As this case will afford a most evident instance of the important manner in which Extracts from MSS. in the Appendices named B, C, D, &c., bear upon the great Document A, like some minor attendant Satellites (if I may indulge in a simile) subserving one great Luminary, I will subjoin some *ipsissima verba* of MS. 14,602 for the purpose of instituting comparison respectively between MS., 14,530 or my Version A at pages 20 and 59, from lines 5 and 2, and 14,602 or E where occur the words ܡܢ ܡܚܕܐ ܩܘܡܝܘܢ ܗܘ ܕܣܝܡܐ ܕܟܠܗ܀

ܡܠܟܐ܂ ܥܡ ܠܣܘܦܐ ܘܝܣܝ ܠܣܘܩܬܐ ܩܘܡܝܘܢ : ܘܩܘܣܛܢܛܝܢܘܣ ܘܗܘܢܘܪܝܘܣ : ܡܠܟܘܢ ܘܐܡܕܝܢܝ ܂ ܘܒܬܪܝܗܘܢ ܘܒܥܠܕܒܒܝܟ

ܗܘܐ ܩܘܝܡ ܗܘ ܚܣܕܐ ܂

and between A at page 21 from line 10, and E, where the Bishops state—

ܡܕܝܢ ܕܝܢ ܡܬܘܕܝܢ ܣܠܝ ܠܣܘܦܣܛܝܣܝܘܢ : ܘܥܠ ܕܠܐ ܡܬܬܣܝܡܐ ܘܣܠܝ ܂ ܠܐ ܐܬܥܨܝܢ ܣܠܝ ܘܒܣܝܣܘܬܐ : ܕܡܪ ܚܣܕܐ ܗܘ ܕܐܬܐܡܪ܀

We would recommend a comparison also between the respec-

Dignitaries, and, so to speak, of the whole population of the same City, who witness against Ibas, Bishop of the City of Edessa, to a great deal of Impiety and Blasphemy.

Since, then, it appertains to (the office of) your Holiness to correct such Profanity--for, that the evidence of all these persons, Clerics and Monks and Civic Magistrates and Laics, should be false, your Holiness cannot fairly admit on reading the (formal) account of these matters with the (accompanying) affidavits—you will free that City from such Blasphemy (scandal) and appoint over it a man honoured for integrity of life, and renowned in The True Faith — one who is master of himself.* And, if anything else occur in those parts of a similar (scandalous) character, let it be suppressed ; for, if those who preside over Metropolitan

---

tive translations of these passages in this Vol.   My friend, Mons. Martin, has given me, before his own work is published, a clear instance, in the subjoined paragraph, of the value of our MS. named A in *re* the trial at Tyre and Berytus.   He says, " Il est evident aujourd'hui que la " conférence de Tyr et de Béryte avait eu lieu, quand se tint le " brigandage d'Ephèse.   Par conséquent la date des conférences de " Béryte (Mansi, VII., 211) est *fausse.*—Il n'y a eu qu'un seul arbitrage, " lequel commencé à Tyr, s'est continué à Béryte et est revenu se ter- " miner a Tyr vers le 25 février 448.   Voir Pagi daus Mansi, *Concil. omn.*, " VI , 499.—Tillemont, *Mémoires pour servir à l'histoire ecclesiastique* " XV., 474, et note 13ᵉ sur S. Léon, p. 897.   Cfr. Héfélé: *Histoire* " *des Conciles*, II."   About Archimandrites, &c., see below.

* This little sentence has always presented a difficulty to me.   Perhaps it will be best to take Martin's fluent rendering :—" In appointing " to preside over it (the City of Edessa) a man of irreproachable " character and of unassailable faith, you will succeed in imposing silence " upon those who, in the same country, may probably have been successful " in exalting themselves against Orthodox Believers."

Cities are Orthodox, the others (Bishops Suffragan) will as a matter of necessity follow their teaching. In reference to this same cause we have enjoined already that the Adjudicators of it should be the God-fearing Photius, Bishop of the Holy Church of Tyre, the Metropolis, and Eustathius, Bishop of Berytus, and Uranius, Bishop of the City of Himeria, whom also we now command to proceed to your Holy Synod in order to convey, in person, all these Instructions to your Holiness.

> This Ordinance was issued on the 5th before the Calends of July, which is the 27th day (of June, 449, A.D.), at Constantinople.

(δ) After (the year of) the Consulate* of the Illustrious Zeno and Posthumian, in the Month called by the Egyptians Mesori, on the 29th day of it, during (the continuance of) Indiction the third†, the Holy

---

* It will be remembered that Zeno was Consul for the East in 448 A.D., and Posthumian for the West. See Mansi's " Sac. Conciliorum Collectio," Tom VI., p. 441-451 (Florentiæ, 1761).

† " Third Indiction." It is well known that the Third Indiction did not begin till Sept. 1st, 449 A.D. So there must be here a mistake made. Yet, from Appendix D, it will be seen that the Addl. MS. marked 12,156 has *Indiction the third*, also. It, however, should be : *during the second Indiction.*　　　Baronius begins a Volume thus :

JX[1] Annus 449	Leonis Pap. Annus 10	Theodosii . 42 Valentiniani . 25 } Imp.

Pagins's Note {	SÆC. V. Olymp. 307	Anno Periodi Græco-Romanæ, 5942 ○ 10.　B.) 13.　P. 27 Mart.　**Indict. 2.** JX 449. .... Coss. Fl. Asturius et Fl. Protogenes.

Synod assembled at Ephesus in compliance with the command of the Christ-loving Emperors, when there sat in the Church called Mary the Pious and God-loving Bishops (following):—*

1 Dioscorus of Alexandria,†
2 Juvenal of Jerusalem,
3 Thalassius of Cæsarea of the First Cappadocia,

---

* The list of Bishops present at this Council, as ascertained from these Acts, differs from that in our Historians in several respects. First, the names omitted are—Domnus and Flavian, Archbishops of Antioch and Constantinople; Quintillus of Heraclea, who represented also Bishop Anastasius of Thessalonica; Cyriacus, Bishop of Trocmadæ, representing Theoctistus of Pisinontia in the Second Galatia; Theodorus of Tarsus and Romanus of Myra in Lycia; John of Nicopolis in the First Armenia; Eutychius of Adrianopolis in Asia; John of Messena of Achaia; Theodorus of Claudiopolis in Isauria; Etericus of Smyrna; Flavian of Adramytha; Meliphtongua of Juliopolis; Onesiphorus of Iconium; Longinus of Chersonesus; Eudoxius of Bosphorus; Timothy of Primopolis in Pamphilia; Isaac of Elearcha; Julian of Mostena (?).   At the end the Greek adds:—

The Priest Longinus replacing Dorotheus of Neocesarea;
     „   Anthymius   „   Patricius of Tyana in the Second
                                     Cappadocia;
     „   Aristonius   „   Eunomius in Nicomedia;
     „   Olympius   „   Calogera of Claudiopolis in Pontus;

Hilarius Roman Deacon and Dulcitius Roman Notary (Labbe, Sacrosancta Concilia, t. IV., col. 115-119).   The Greek omits and the Syriac adds—Maximian of Gaza; Paul of Andaha; Peter of Chronesos (Chersonesus?); Olympius of Sozopolis; Paulinus of Theodosiopolis; Gennadius of Gnosse Quaïoussa; Mortorius of Gortyna in Crete; Mara of Dyonisyada; Ananius of Quapatoulida.   In all 27 omissions and 9 additions in the Syriac.   Our Acts containing 111 names, that of Barsumas included, the number of Fathers at Ephesus 449 A.D. would then be 137 or 138.   We may perhaps explain these differences by saying that the Greek list contains only the names of the Fathers who figured in the first Session, while the Syriac list contains only the names of those who assisted at the second.   It is probable, in fact, that many Bishops left, when they saw into what an ambush they had been drawn under pretence of a Council.   See Martin's Etude in "Revue des Questions Historiques."

† Space forbids even the attempt of giving a shortened account of the

4 Stephen of Ephesus,

5 Eusebius of Ancyra of the First Galatia,

6 Cyrus of Aphrodisias of Caria,

7 Erasistratus of Corinth in Hellas,

8 Miletius of Larissa, who also filled the place of the Venerable Domnus, Bishop of Apamea,

9 Diogenes of Cyzicus,

10 John of Sebastia in the First Armenia,

11 Basil of Seleucia of Isauria,

12 John of Rhodes,

13 Photius of Tyre,

14 Theodore of Damascus,

15 Florentius of (Sardis in) Lydia,

16 Marinianus of Synnada,

17 Constantius of Bostra,

---

several Sees which the below-named Bishops occupied, but as a specimen of the history of the Patriarchates of Christendom we subjoin, as summarised by Dr. Neale, that of the Rise and Decline of the Church of Alexandria. We have traced it, he says, from the time when its Apostolic Founder laid down his life for his Lord: we have penetrated, as far as we might, the obscure annals of its earlier Patriarchs: we have seen it struggling with the persecutions of Valerian and Diocletian, and, by the blood of its martyrs, spreading the Faith into the wildest regions of Africa: we have seen it crushing the Sabellian heresy in the person of S. Dionysius, standing alone against an Arian world in that of Athanasius, overthrowing Nestorius, and wielding an Œcumenical Council in that of S. Cyril. We have seen it drawn into error by the vices and heresy of Dioscorus; thenceforward beset by a long and fearful schism, from which neither the Martyrdom of Proterius, nor the alms of S. John, nor the learning of S. Eulogius, could deliver it; and, finally, overwhelmed by the victorious arms of the Impostor of Mecca. We have struggled through the dark annals of its mediæval history: we have found heresy triumphant, the Church almost dropping the name of Catholic, persecution rife, apostasy frequent; scarcely one valiant action for the faith recorded; scarcely one noble athlete for his God chronicled. We have seen the dismal gulf yawn between the Eastern

18 Acacius of Ariarathia of the Second Armenia, who filled the place of the Venerable Constantius of Melitene,

19 Stephen of Mabug (Hierapolis),

20 Atticus of Nicopolis of Ancient Epirus,

21 Eustathius of Berytus,

22 Nunechius of Laodicea of the Trimitarian Phrygia,

23 Olympius of Constantia of Cyprus,

24 Candidian of Antioch in Pisidia,

25 Stephen of Anazarbus,

26 Gerontius of Seleucia of Syria,

27 Rufinus of Samosata,

28 Indamus of Irenopolis,

29 Timothy of Balanea,

30 Theodosius of Canotha,

31 Claudius of Anchismus of Ancient Epirus,

---

and Western Christendom; and we have noted the attempts made by Rome, and by Protestant Germany, to pass it. We have watched the progress of the Portuguese in Ethiopia, from their first hopes of success, through the absolute victory, to the entire fall of Rome. We have remarked the gradual rise of error in the mind of Cyril Lucar, and his fruitless, though conscientious, attempt to lead the Eastern Church into heresy. And now we behold the Church of S. Athanasius and S. Cyril, a shadow of its former self, without a Bishop, except the Patriarch, "persecuted, but not forsaken; cast down, but not destroyed." What remains but that we long and pray for those happier times when Alexandria and her sister Churches "shall shake themselves from the "dust," shall "loose the bands of their neck," shall no more be "forsaken "and hated," shall become "an eternal excellency, a joy of "many genera-"tions;" shall be freed from the Ottoman yoke, purged from ignorance, shall unite and be united with the Western Church, shall become
One Fold under One Shepherd, Jesus Christ our Lord,
to Whom, with the Father and the Holy Ghost
be all honour and glory,
world without end,
Amen.

32 Simeon of Amida of Mesopotamia,
33 Seleucus of Amasia,
34 Peter of Gangra,
35 Luke of Dyrrhacium,
36 Antony of Lychnidus,
37 Mark of Eubæa,
38 Vigilantius of Larissa,
39 Basil of Trajanopolis of the Province of Rhodopæa,
40 Docimasius of Maronea of the Province of Rhodopæa,
41 Constantine of Demetrias,
42 Alexander of Sebaste of Tarsus,
43 Sozon of Philippi,
44 Eusebius of Doberus in the First (Macedonia),
45 Maximianus of Serrai in the First Macedonia,
46 Luke of Beræa in the First Macedonia,
47 John of Messena,
48 Uranius of Himeria in the Province of Osrhoene,
49 Athanasius of Opas (Opuntus) in Achaia,
50 Leontius of Ascalon,
51 Marinianus of Gaza,
52 Photius of Lydda,
53 Anastasius of Arenopolis,
54 Paul of (Anthadacia) Antdaha,
55 Theodosius of Amathus (Amathontius),
56 Paul of Majuma,
57 Zotimus of Minois,

c

58 Epiphanius of Perga,

59 Baruch of Sozuza of Palestine,

60 Heraclius of Azotus,

61 John of Tiberias,

62 Musonius of Zoara,

63 Dionysius of Sycamazon (Sycomason),

64 Cajumas of Phaneæ (Faina),

65 Constantius of Sebastia,

66 Zebennus (Zebinus) of Pella,

67 Olympius of Bostra,

68 Polychronius of Antipatris,

69 Pancratius of Libyas,

70 Auxilaus (Bishop) of the Subjected Saracens,

71 Domninus of Platææ of Hellas,

72 Theodosius of Mastaura,

73 Cyriacus of Ægæa,

74 Cyriacus of Lebedos,

75 Leontius of Magnesia of the Mæandra (Menandra),

76 Eutropius of Pergamos in Asia,

77 Gennadius of Teos,

78 Olympius of Evasa,

79 Maximinus of Trallis,

80 Julian of Hypæpa,

81 Chrysanthius of Baga,

82 Polycarp of Gabala,

83 Paul of Tripolis of Lydia,

84 Peter of Chersonesus (Cherronesus),

85 Olympius of Sozopolis,

86 Paulinus of Theodosiopolis,
87 Gennadius of Cajusa,
88 Martyrius of Gortyna of Crete,
89 Maras of Dionysias (Dinosyda),
90 Anianus of Capitolias (Capitolida),
91 Theopempus of Cabassa,
92 Calosirius of Arsinoe (Arsinoetus),
93 John of Hiphæstus (Ephestus),
94 Heraclius of Heraclea,
95 Gemellinus of Erythrum,
96 Apollonius of Tanis,
97 Gennadius of Hermopolis the Great,
98 Cyrus of Babylon,
99 Athanasius of Busiris,
100 Photinus of Teuchira,
101 Theophilus of Cleopatris,
102 Pasmejus of Paralus,
103 Sozias of Sozusa,
104 Theodulus of Tisila,
105 Theodorus of Barca,
106 Rufus of Cyrene,
107 Zeno of Rhinocorura,
108 Lucius of Zygra,
109 Ausonius of Sebennytus,
110 Isaac of Tava,
111 Philocalus of Zagylis (Zagulon),
112 Isaiah of Hermopolis the Less,
113 Barzumas, Presbyter and Archimandrite.

[*RESUMPTION OF THE BUSINESS OF THE COUNCIL ON MONDAY, AUGUST THE 22ND, 449 A.D.,]

AT THE

[SECOND SESSION.]

---

* The reader will have observed that, from the preceding Documents, the Chief Bishops of the whole Church were directed to meet in Œcumenical Synod for the dispatch of business on 1st Aug., 449 A.D. The Synod's proper work, however, does not appear to have begun till 10th Aug., after Formalities on 8th, and then to have continued—no doubt with intervals and with necessary arrangements for minor, as well as major, matters—until Thursday, the 18th or Friday, 19th, of Aug., on one of which days the affair of Eutyches was brought to a conclusion. THAT, then, we may correctly designate the First Session, at and by which the President and his party considered the *first* part, actually accomplished, of the end and object for which the Council was convoked and which first part was declared by authority to be—" To terminate a " question of Faith that has arisen between Flavian and Eutyches." At this the Second Session, on the Business of which the Council now enters, the assembling on "the first day," i.e. Saturday, Aug. 20th, being preliminary to it, we shall see *how* they attained the *second* part of that end and object, avowed to be—" To eject from the Church all who " maintain and favour the Error of Nestorius."   In Appendix E there is laid down a principle and a rule, embodied in one of the "Canons of the Apostles" and usually adopted in all legal procedure, even when the vilest criminals are arraigned, of which principle, however, and rule what trace can be found, we ask, at this Court and Tribunal of the Church, when Bishops, some of them of no ordinary character, are summoned and tried at the bar of Justice, and on a charge so serious as that of a Depravation of THE FAITH and of Heresy.

(1) Jons, Presbyter of Alexandria and Proto-
Notary, said : -

On the first day of the assembling of your Holy
and Great Synod, those* who fill the place of the
Pious and God-loving Archbishop of Rome, Leo,
and the God-loving Domnus, the Bishop of the
Church of Antioch, stayed away and did not come
(to the Synod) ; upon which your Holiness, acting
in accordance with the Canons, gave order that certain of the God-fearing Bishops, with some other
Clerics attendant on them, should go to them and to
him, and should remind them that they ought to
come *to-day* and assemble with your Holiness.
Since, then, they are now here present, who were
selected for the purpose of reminding both these
parties, that is to say, those from Rome, and the
God-fearing Bishop Domnus, I notify this circumstance for your pleasure (to deal with it).

Juvenal, Bishop of Jerusalem, said :-

Let the Holy Bishops now report the reply they
received from those persons who occupy the place

---

* The names of the Envoys, at this Council, of S. Leo the Great have
occasioned much discussion, but Quesnel's and other conjectures now fall to
the ground.　We are certain of the name of Julius of Pozzolo as ascertained from Appendix D, where Timothy Ælurus, who was at this
Council and a successor of Dioscorus, plainly distinguishes between this
Julius from Julian of Cos and speaks of the former as " occupying the
" place, or being the representative, of the Holy Bishop of the Church
" of Rome," and he afterwards quotes the advice of "Julian Bishop of
" Cos."　　S. Leo himself surely deserves to be called " the Great."
For, as a man, who cannot admire his patriotic, yea his heroic, great-

of the God-loving and Holy Bishop of the Church
of Rome, Leo, and from the God-loving Bishop of
the Church of Antioch, Domnus.

The God-fearing Bishops, OLYMPIUS of Evaza,* and
JULIAN of Hypæpa and MONTANIUS, Deacon of
the Holy Church of Aphrodisias, and EUPHRONIUS,
Deacon of Laodicea, said :—

In pursuance of the Orders of this Holy and
Œcumenical Synod, we proceeded to the place where
those (representative) persons reside who had been
despatched from celebrated and Royal Rome, to wit,
the God-loving Bishop Julian and the Deacon
Hilarius. We did not, however, find them (there).

---

ness in approaching, in the way he did, the savage Huns, headed by their
Leader recognized as "the Scourge of God," whom he caused to
withdraw from Italy, as well as in dissuading Genseric to retire from
the very gates of Rome. As a Doctor of the Church, what better
instance can be desired of his intellectual and literary greatness than the
fact that his grand Epistle (XXVIII.) written to Flavian, Archbishop of
Constantinople—the celebrated Tome that was rejected by Dioscorus,
to whom these Delegates in vain produced it before the Synod, but
heartily accepted by the Fathers of Calcedon in 451 A.D. as consonant with
the Symbol of the CCCXVIII. and of Constantinople, as well as with
what was settled by Cyril of Alexandria at Ephesus 431 A.D.—should
become, like the three celebrated Epistles of S. Cyril, Œcumenical in the
Church, the common property and heritage of the Faithful and binding
for ever on the faith of the Church. Great was he, also, as an unsurpassed Administrator and Governor of the Church, notwithstanding his
ambition to unduly exalt his own See. (See Bright's "18 Sermons of Leo.")
And lastly Great was Leo in foreseeing and, as far as possible, in coun-
teracting the evils and miseries that would befall the Church, if the great
Eutrchian party should succeed in bringing about, and then in over
ruling, a second Ephesine Council.

* Evaza, called also Theodosiopolis, and but very little known it
seems, was an Episcopal City of Asia Minor with Ephesus for its me-

Then we had an interview with Dulcitius, the
Notary, who was unwell ; and we told him that the
Holy Synod was re-assembled but was retarded in
(deferred) the act of adjudication in the hope that
they would again come to the assembly after one
day, that is, on the following Monday.   And the

---

tropolis.   Its first Bishops, according to Richard and Giraud, were (1)
Eutropius who appeared at the Council of Ephesus (431 A.D.) as an
opponent of Nestorius.   (2) Bassian (ordonné nalgré lui par Memnon
d'Ephèse) was at Calcedon 451 A.D.   (3) N ——— succeeded
Bassian.   (4) Olympius who assisted at the Latrocinium of Ephesus,
where he was favourable to the cause of Eutyches, but retracted two
years afterwards at Calcedon 451 A.D.   (Bibliotheque Sacrée.   Tom,
9, 10.   Daaler Sanahæ.   Fehre Paris, 1822-23.)

Lucas Holstenius, in his "Annotationes in Geographiam Sac. Caroli à
S. Paulo" (Romæ, 1666) at p. 135, says:—Evaza.   Hieroclis Notit.
Olympius Evazorum Episcopus Concil. Chalced. Act. i. et Eutropius in
Epheso.   Eidem ordinatus fuerat Ecclesiæ Bassianus, ut Concil. Chalcedon. Act. ii.   Εὐαστηνοῖς scripsit Basilius Mag. ep. 12. quam
ad Evazam pertinere existimo, ut Εὐαζηνοῖς potius isthic legendum
sit.   Hierocles in his 'Synecdemus' only gives the name as one of the
forty Bishoprics of Asia Minor.   Martinière adds nothing to the above
except that he says Olympius was at a Council at Rome in 503 A D.
Baluze in his "Nova Collectio Conciliorum" mentions the See and its
Bishops Bassianus and Eutropius.   On Bassian he has a Note sub anno
440 in connection with the Council at Ephesus (foll. 949, 950) giving
some account of Bassian's course.   The name of Εὐάζα does
not occur in the list of cities given by Hierocles in his Synecdemus
where it follows Διὸς Ἱερόν (Jovis Fanum).   Not even the name
occurs in the Notitiæ Græcæ Episcopatuum, edited by G. Parthey (Ber-
olini, 1866) ; but, curiously enough, the name which follows Διὸς
Ἱερόν in almost everyone of the Episcopal Notitiæ is Αἰγάζα or,
rather ὁ Αἰγαζων,=Episcopus Augazorum.   Augaza is not mentioned
by Hierocles, but he has Algiza, which Parthey thinks may be the same:
it, however, is absent from all the other lists.   Knowing the extraordi-
nary transformations some of these names undergo in the hands of the
Scribes, he asks—Is not Evaza as likely to be Augaza as Algiza ? and
on the whole thinks I have the true form.   (Note from H. Cowper.)

Hypæpa, Aphrodisias in Caria, and Laodicea in Asia are tolerably
well-known places needing no special remarks.

Notary replied that the God-fearing Bishop was* out in the country, and the Venerable Deacon at the Church (Martyrium)† of the Glorious S. John, but he promised to send to them to say that they should go. However, we did not rest content here, after this conversation, but again in the morning of the (subsequent) Day, Sunday, we proceeded thither, and had another interview with the same Notary, who informed us it was quite impossible for them to

---

* Perhaps, "in the suburbs of Ephesus."

† Martyrium implies the hallowed spot or ground where a true Saint of God glorified Him by his sufferings and Martyrdom. On such spots the Primitive Christians frequently erected a Church. Hence the Martyrium came to be synonimous with the Church. The word occurs again lower down, Martyrium or Church of Zaccheas, where the Inhabitants of Edessa met the Roman Governor, Cheıeas, who was Præses of the Province of Osrhoene and Hegemon of its Capital.

After explaining the general names given to Churches such as *synodi, concilia, conciliabula,* Bingham speaks of some which had particular appellations assigned them for reasons which could not extend to all. "Such "as were built over the grave of any Martyr, or called by his name to "preserve the memory of him, had usually the distinguishing title of *mar-* "*tyrium,* or *confessio,* or *memoria* given them for that particular reason. "Thus Eusebius observes of Constantine, that he adorned his new city "of Constantinople with many oratories and martyries, and, as it were, "consecrated his city to the God of the Martyrs. And from this time "in all Christian writings of the following ages, a martyry is always put "to signify such a Church. Socrates speaks of the Martyry of S. "Thomas the Apostle at Edessa, and of SS. Peter and Paul at Rome, "and of the Martyry of Euphemia at Chalcedon, where the body of "that Martyr lay buried, which was the Church where the famous "Council of Chalcedon was held, whence, in the Acts of that Council, "it is so often styled Μαρτύριον Ευφημίας, the Martyry of Euphemia. "And, upon the same reason, because our Saviour Christ was the Chief "Sufferer and Great Martyr of his own religion, therefore the Church "which Constantine built at Mount Golgotha, in memory of His passion "and resurrection, is usually by Eusebius and others styled *Martyrium* "*Salvatoris,* the Martyry of our Saviour." "The Latins, in- "stead of *martyrium,* use the name *memoria martyrum* for such kind of "Churches." (Bk. VIII., Chap. I., Sect. 8.)

assemble with the Holy Synod, even if it should send ten times, in consequence of the letters, with which they were accredited from Leo, the Archbishop of Illustrious and Royal Rome, containing no other commission whatever than the order for them to proceed to the Assembly of the Holy Synod (only) until the affair should be settled about the God-fearing Presbyter and Abbat Eutyches ;* and so, those matters, of which we have had cognizance, we have (now) reported before your Holiness.

JOHN, Bishop of Sebastia of the First Armenia, and ONESIPHORUS, Bishop of Iconium, and NONNUS, a Deacon of Ephesus, and PHOCAS, a Deacon of Tyre, said :—

As your Piety commanded, on the first day which was last Saturday, we went to the Pious and God-fearing Bishop of the City of Antioch, Domnus, and we found him prostrate on a couch† and complaining, when he asseverated—"It is on account of "illness that I am wanting (in the Synod)." We, notwithstanding, were not wanting (in our duty) ; but we made known to him your instructions to us, sta-

---

* S. Leo's representatives had sought in vain to get a hearing at the first Session of the Council, and, as Eutyches was there acquitted, notwithstanding all remonstrance, by the imperious and overbearing Dioscorus, the commission they had received at the hands of the great Champion of Orthodoxy at Rome was at an end ; and so they left Ephesus, or at least withdrew officially from the Synod.

† The word ܟܣܐ *stomach*, in my text is indistinct in the MS., and on taking a magnifying lens into the Library of the British Museum, when the Sun shone, I discovered it to be ܥܪܣܐ, *couch, bed*.

ting to him that it was only right and proper for him to betake himself *this very day* to your Holy and Œcumenical Synod. He readily replied that he was intending to go, and that he felt (quite) inclined to assemble with your Blessedness, provided only he could have a little respite from the sickness that had seized him. Then, to-day, in the morning he sent (appealed) to us ; and, regarding it as (only) right and just on our part to give a (complete) definite Report to your Piety, we proceeded to the said God-fearing Bishop and found him in the same condition (as before), bitterly complaining, whilst he entreated that, by our means and mediation, it might be reported to your Holiness that he was, contrary to his wish, prevented from attending you (in Synod) in consequence of the (bodily) debility that had seized him, but that as to all those measures your Holiness had taken against the parties who, infected with the horrible Impieties of Nestorian opinion, have written or were writing (in their defence), he (Domnus) ratifies your Decision and is of the same opinion as yourselves.

(2) THALASSIUS, Bishop of Cæsarea of the First Cappadocia, said :—

Our being* detained (so long) in this City occa-

---

* They had been convoked for Aug. 1st, 449 A.D. Some had arrived on that day at Ephesus. It was now Monday, Aug. 22nd, when they re-commenced business and began the trial of those Bishops named in these Acts against whom bills of indictment had been preferred.

sions much inconvenience to all the God-fearing and Pious Bishops, as well as injury to (their) Holy Churches ; and not that only, but the Gracious and Christ-loving Emperor also wishes that there should be a rapid dispatch (of the rest of the business) of this Synod, in order that we may ascertain with exactitude what is determined on (to which we hold ourselves).

Since, then, Formality, befitting and proper to the Holy Synod, has been observed—for, the God-loving the Bishop Julian and the Venerable the Deacon Hilarius, who occupy the place of the Holy and God-loving Leo, Archbishop of Rome, have been reminded by those God-loving Bishops, who were sent (for that purpose, viz.) Olympius of Evaza, and Julian of Hypæpa, and Montanius Deacon of Aphrodisias, and Euphronius Deacon of Laodicea, and have declined assembling here with us—I give it as my opinion that there is no necessity for deferring the matter ; but if the Holy Synod command it, let this business proceed, lest the monks, too, who are here present should receive annoyance from (be troubled at) the delay.

Here intervenes really the first of the Lacunæ in the original MS. (14,530 Additional) in the British Museum, although this hiatus in the Vol. of that MS. is not indicated by the insertion of a blank vellum leaf, as are the other Lacunæ ; and I have not noted it in my Version by any blank leaf in Vol. i., occurring at the 14th line of page 17 in the part of the Syriac Text that the Clarendon Press printed for me six or seven years ago.

IBAS.

This Champion in the great Controversy concerning The True Person of Jesus Christ occupies a most prominent position in its history as well as, in some respects, a perfectly unique one in the history of the Church. He must be ranged among the upholders of Nestorius and his Doctrine. He had for his predecessor in the See of the great Capital of Osrhoene the noble Rabulas or Rabbūlas who, well-nigh unsurpassed by the Great Cyril, adhered to the true Doctrine as settled by the third Œcumenical Council of the Church, and who had been proclaimed "the Glory of the City of Edessa;" and for his successor Nonnus* who had occupied the Bishopric during the forced absence of himself.   In Vol. I. of his "Bibliotheca Orientalis" J. S. Asseman tells us that the Author of "The Chronicle of Edessa" describes all three Bishops thus:

Cap. LI. In 723 (i.e., 412 A.D.), *Rabulas* Edessenum Episcopatum accepit. Hic, Imperatoris jussu, ædificavit Templum S. Stephani, quod antea Domus Sabati, id est, Synagoga Judæorum fuerat.

Cap. LIX. In 746 (i.e., 435 A.D.), die 8 Aug. ex hoc sæculo Rabulas Edessæ Epis: cui magnus *Ibas* suffectus est. Hic

---

* In the series of Bishops of Edessa given by Asseman (in Vol. I., p. 424) from the year of the Greeks 624 to 1080 " Ex Chronico Edesseno et ex Dionysio," the names preceding the above three are recorded thus :

I. Cono to 624 ; II. Saades to 634 ; III. Aetallahas to 657 ; IV. Abraham to 672 ; V. S. Barses Charris, Edessam translatus anno 672, obiit in exilio mense Martis anno 689 ; with VI. S. Eulogius ; VII. Cyrus ; VIII. Silvanus ; IX. Pachidas ; X. Diogenes.

Le Qulen in his " Oriens Christianus," Tom. II., c. 955, precedes this list by (1) Thaddæus, (2) Maris, (3) Bartymæus Martyr, omits the name of the 4th and makes Cono the 5th Bishop.

In Asseman, also, from the " Compendiaria rerum gestarum Historia," we learn that Kings began to reign at Edessa " anno cen- " tesimo octogesimo," and ex Chronico Dionysii we may read a list from " Orrhoës Heviæ filius qui Primus Edesseni Regni institutor" fuit to " Abgarus Maani F. Edessenorum Regum postremus." The whole Chapter (IX.) in the Bibl. Orient. is prefaced with the three following particulars necessary to be remembered, viz.— (1) Chronici Edesseni Auctor Orthodox. floruisse videtur circa annum Christi 550 ; (2) Græcorum Epocha utitur quæ Christianam vulgarem annis trecentis undecem ex ejusdem mente antecedit ; (3) Initium Chronici ab anno Græcorum 180. Finis verò in anno 851.

novam ædificavit Ecclesiam quæ hodie Apostolorum appellatur.

Cap. LXIV. In 759 (i.e., 448 A.D.) Ibas Epis. Edessa excessit die Januarii: cui *Nonnus* substitutus fuit die 21 Julii, tenuit que Sedem annis duobus, et fecit Sacrarium* in Ecclesiâ.

Cap. LXVII. In 769 (i.e., 458 A.D.) die 28 Octobris requievit Ibas Edessæ Epis. et in locum suum reversus Nonnus ædificavit Templum S. Joannis Baptistæ, et Nosocomium pauperum invalidorum, extra Portam Bethsemes. Extruxit autem in eodem Nosocomio Templum S.S. Cosmæ et Damiani. Præterea Monasteria Turresque excitavit. Sed et pontes fecit et vias exæquavit.

Ecclesiastical History informs us distinctly that the first and great Œcumenical Council of Ephesus held in 431 A.D., notwithstanding its having determined The Faith, was very indifferently received in parts of the East, John the Archbishop of Antioch appearing almost to be the head of the disaffected, and that, although an agreement between him and the great Champion of the Orthodox Faith, at Alexandria, was to the latter's great joy happily effected, through the good offices of Paul of Emesa, in 433 A.D., yet two great divisions of religious thought on the great Doctrine characterized the Clerical body in too many Dioceses. This was the case with the Catholic Church at the capital which rivalled Antioch in splendour, influence, and power—the celebrated City of Edessa.† Mons. Martin, in his Etude referred to before, writes truly that at the period when

---

* On the word Sacrarium Asseman has this note respecting its use by the Author of the Chronicle of Edessa :—

"Auctor noster Græca voce ἱερατεῖον. . . . Est autem ἱερατεῖον locus sacer ac venerandus, tabulato inclusus, Clericis tantùm, viris sæcularibus rarò, mulieribus nunquam penetrabilis, ut ex Græcorum Euchologio observat Suicerus in Thesauro.

† Robertson (Vol. I., p. 457) says that Nestorianism, suppressed in the Roman Empire, found refuge beyond its bounds. At Edessa was a flourishing School of Clergy for the Persian Church. Its head, Ibas, was favourable to Nestorianism and translated some of the works of Theodore of Mopsuestia and Diodore of Tarsus into Syriac. Rabbulas broke up the Institution in 435 A.D., but Ibas re-established it, and it kept till the reign of Zeno, by whom it was suppressed in 485 A.D. From this Seminary Nestorianism was propagated in Persia and India, and the Doctrine continued to have a powerful influence on the Christianity of the East. From Asseman (Vol. I., Chapter XV.) we learn that Ibas, whilst yet a Presbyter of the Church of Edessa, along with the greater part of its Clergy, bitterly opposed the efforts of Rabbulas his Bishop in

the first Great Synod assembled at Ephesus, Rabbulas, its Bishop, a converted heathen, maintained warmly the part of S. Cyril. It was even he who first raised, against the memory of Theodorus of Mopsuestia and Diodorus of Tarsus, that long controversy which terminated, at length, in the middle of the following century by the condemnation of the THREE CHAPTERS. Ardent in strife, excessive in his attacks, precipitate in his measures, even the wisest of them, Rabbulas did not defend S. Cyril without finding near his person opponents as ardent as himself, and it is perhaps to the resistance attempted on their part that we must attribute some of his proceedings which have sometimes been taxed with exaggeration. Amongst these opponents, figured in the first line the Persian school of Edessa, a school whose celebrity goes back as far as the epoch when Nisibis fell again under the rule of the Sassanidæ, in the middle of the preceding century (364 or 365 A.D.).

Then, in fact, most of the Christians who inhabited that city emigrated to the capital of Osrhoene, and founded there, under the protection of the Empire, a sort of University, where every one belonging to the Persian Church, most distinguished by birth and fortune, came to be taught. How did this school partake of the opinions of Nestorius? It is not for us to say just now; it constituted however a focus of opposition, whose masters and pupils Rabbulas hoped he was right in forcibly dispersing (432 A.D.). Thus at least, it seems to us, we ought to interpret the words of the writers of the epoch. Once returned to Persia, these masters and pupils continued to follow, with passion, a strife in which they had participated, and on the issue of which they vaguely imagined their future to depend. Thence, no doubt, came an exchange of correspondence

---

condemning the writings of Theodore of Mopsuestia, as Andrew of Samosata shows in a letter to Alexander of Hierapolis (See Assem. Vol. I., p. 198). Hence, as soon as he obtained the Bishopric of Edessa, he incurred the envy and enmity of the friends of Rabbulas. He was therefore accused before the Emperor Theodsius and Proclus, the Patriarch of Constantinople, by Samuel, Cyrus, Maras, and Eulogius, Presbyters of the Church of Edessa, of being auctor and fautor perniciosissimus of the disturbances between the Egyptians and the Orientals, of having translated the Books of Theodore into the Syriac Language, and of having disseminated them over the East.

which has for the most part perished; but, one famous piece of which, however, remains to us—a piece which, since its appearance, has had an echo superior to that of the anathemas of S. Cyril and Nestorius, and which has perhaps caused the loss of the Persian Church. In this letter, written during the lifetime of Rabbulas (about 434 or 435 A.D.), the priest Ibas gave his correspondent the history of the Nestorian controversy (428-435 A.D.). He did not attribute the blame to S. Cyril, but he branded especially the conduct of his Bishop, whom he called a tyrant. What shows the power of the party opposed to Rabbulas is that, when once this Bishop was dead, it was precisely his most marked and inveterate antagonist who succeeded him in the direction of his Church. Ibas was nominated Bishop of Edessa. This happened about 435.*

Having attained to the Episcopate under such circumstances, the Bishop of Edessa could not long enjoy the repose, of which he had need, to govern his faithful in peace. Those who had supported the ideas of Rabbulas and Cyril, could not fail to get up a vigorous opposition to him, the more so as the East was very much divided, and war brooded in men's hearts everywhere. Did Ibas give occasion to his adversaries to attack him by the manner in which he administered his Diocese, and in particular by his management of the ecclesiastical property? The reiterated complaints of his enemies lead us to believe it; and in the judgments, of which his life has been the object, are found the means both of charging and of defending his memory.† It was but a short time after he obtained the Episcopate, that his enemies accused him, probably at Alexandria, but

---

* Ibas was, in fact, already Bishop of Edessa during the life-time of John of Antioch, see Labbe, Sacro-Sancta Concilia, t. V., col. 412-414, 500-511. Cf. Asseman's Biblioth. Orient., t. I., p. 424. Moreover, we read in our Acts that "Ibas ruined religion in the City of "Edessa, for 13 or 14 years." (See Vol. I., p. 99, l. 8, and p. 38, l. 6, and the corresponding passages in this Vol.) One vociferator even wishes that "the bones of John of Antioch should be disinterred" because he had ordained him (Ibid). If, in 449 A.D., Ibas had been Bishop of Edessa for 13 or 14 years, it must have been in 435 or 436 A.D. that he was consecrated.—Tillemont, Memoires pour servir à l'Histoire Ecclesiastique, t. XIV., p. 823; t. XV., p. 966.

† We have only to compare the Council of Chalcedon (451 A.D.) with the Second Œcumenical Council of Constantinople (551 A.D.) to see that the ecclesiastical opinion has wavered a little before fixing upon the judgment which Ibas merited.

certainly at Constantinople. Proclus, Patriarch of this latter
city, wrote about it to John of Antioch, who does not appear to
have instituted any proceedings, and to Domnus, successor to
John, who delivered, in a Council held at Antioch, a little after
Easter (448), a first judgment in favour of Ibas; but the complainants did not consider themselves beaten: they effected so
much by their intrigues at Court, where they were supported
by a party already powerful, that they obtained the revision of
this first judgment. These events passed probably about the
middle of the year 448 A.D.: for, it would appear certain (the new
documents compel us to believe) that the events were not con-
secutive, as has been imagined until now. The signatures and
the dates, which figure at the head of the Sessions 9 and 10 of
the Council of Chalcedon, have led many ecclesiastical writers
into error.   The order of events would appear to be thus.

Having arrived at Constantinople, the enemies of Ibas, the
Clerks of Osrhoene, who had stranded near Domnus of Antioch, obtained, by their protectors, new judges—judges even in
part hostile to the accused. The Court of Constantinople had
not yet entered resolutely upon the path which was to lead
fatally to the BRIGANDAGE OF EPHESUS. It was wearied with the troubles of Asia, it wished to put an end to them,
but it would not employ *any* means. It was necessary that
new contradictions and new miscalculations should come to increase, with the credit of the heterodox factions, the anger of
the feeble Emperor Theodosius II. At the moment, of which
we now speak, he was displeased only with those who were
treated as Nestorians. On the 26th October, 448 A.D., he charged
the tribune and notary Damascius to have examined by Photius
of Tyre, Eustathius of Berytus, and Uranius of Himeria, the
cause of Ibas of Edessa, Daniel of Charrae, and John of Theo-
dosianople, against whom complaints had been submitted to
the Imperial Government. The accusers of Ibas set out again
in company with Damascius and the deacon Eulogius, whom
the Patriarch of Constantinople, Flavian, sent to follow the
proceedings, and probably also to keep him informed of all
that was done. Matters were in this position when the Council of Constantinople (8th Nov., 448), having condemned
Eutyches, changed the good designs which the Emperor

seemed to entertain. Eutyches, being condemned, had recourse to the eunuch Chrysaphius, and this latter, meditating the destruction of Flavian, took it into his head to get rid also of all those who supported him or could support him. Whilst he organized the plan of campaign with Dioscorus and Eutyches, the Oriental Bishops, led into error as to the dispositions of the Government by the condemnation of the Heresiarch, sent delegates to Constantinople to protest against all the calumnies, of which they were the object, on the part of certain interdicted Priests or of certain turbulent Monks of Osrhoene. Domnus and Theodoret took the initiative, and we have then the letters which the Bishop of Cyrus addressed to the most influential personages of the Court. Whilst this was going on, the judges named by Theodosius met first at Tyre, then transferred their sittings to Berytus, on account of the tumult made by the monks who accused Ibas, and returned at last to conclude the difference at Tyre by a friendly arrangement (25th Feb., 449). It has been supposed till now, generally at least, that the compromise of Tyre took place in February, 448, whilst the Synod of Berytus assembled on the 1st September in the same year; but that opinion cannot be maintained.

First, our Acts never distinguish these two assemblages; then the date of the Acts of Tyre and of Berytus places them in 449. Now, certainly, in that year there was no assembly at Berytus (Sept. 1st), whilst the Synod of Ephesus was already finished at that time. In short, the date of the 25th of February alone explains to us clearly the succession of events, and alone agrees exactly with what we read in a supplication of the Clergy of Edessa to the judges of Ibas. It is said that, the festival of Easter being near at hand, the judges of Tyre were entreated to send back the Bishop to Edessa that he might assist in the paschal ceremonies. It is evident that this language is comprehensible enough on the hypothesis that the Synods of Berytus and Tyre are placed in February, 449, whilst the festival of Easter fell in that year on the 27th of March; but this language would have no right to be used in the month of September of the preceding year, about seven months before paschal solemnities.

We may, lastly, set off, against the common opinion, a last

reason which has its weight : that is, the date of the Ordination
of Photius Bishop of Tyre, which took place on the 9th of
September, 448, seven months after the deposition of Irenæus
(17th Feb., 448).   Domnus of Antioch gives us this detail in a
letter to Flavian, preserved amongst the Syriac Acts.   Now, it
is indubitable that Photius was already Bishop of Tyre when
he was charged to judge Ibas; he could not then execute the
order of the Emperor in February, 448 A.D., since he was not
Bishop at that time.   It is to be seen, that everything compels
us to place the grave events which were passing in the East,
in the course of the year 449 A.D., from the month of February to
the month of September.

DATES AND FACTS WORTHY OF BEING REMEMBERED.

It was a little before Easter, April 11th, in the year 448 A.D., that
the Archbishop of the Province, Domnus, was beset with complaints and accusations against the Suffragan-Bishop of the
City of Edessa, Ibas.

It was in February, 448 A.D., that the Chiefs of the
great Eutychian party obtained, through their unboun-
ded influence with the Emperor and the Court, an
Imperial Edict directed against the Bishop of the Metropolitan City of Tyre, Irenæus; and Archbishop Domnus
pronounced a first judgment in the case of Ibas which did not
satisfy the monks of Osrhoene, not long after Easter.

Whilst several monks, headed by one Theodosius who
exercised great influence at Edessa, were excited at Alexandria
to calumniate the Archbishop Domnus and the Bishop of Cyrus,
Theodoret, the principal accusers of Ibas proceeded to intrigue
at Constantinople.

In the year 448 A.D.

During *May—June* the Imperial Order for Theodoret to confine
himself within his own Diocese was issued.

On *Sept. 9th* the Consecration of Photius to the Bishopric of
Tyre took place.

End of September the celebrated Letter of the Archbishop
Domnus to Flavian, the Archbishop of Constantinople, was
written.

On October 26th the Imperial Decree was issued ordering the
revision of the proceedings in the case of the Bishop of
Edessa,

During November 8th—22nd, at the Council held at Constantinople with Flavian as President the arraignment of the Archimandrite Eutyches by his friend Eusebius, Bishop of Doryleum, and his condemnation were effected.

In the year 449 A.D.

During February 1—25th, the Synod of Tyre-Berytus-Tyre was held under the direction of the Imperial Commissioners, Photius, Eustathius, and Uranius.

On March 30th, after the vexation and recrudescence of fury of the Eutychian party, the summoning of the Second Ephesine Council was brought about.

On April 8—13—27th the revision of the formal condemnation of Eutyches at the Constantinoplitan Synod was accomplished.

On April the 12th (Tuesday), *the* 14th (Thursday), and *the* 18th (Monday) the inquiry on the Judgment given at Tyre-Berytus was gone through at Edessa before Praeses Chaireas, as ordered by the Roman Government.

End of April, the despatch of the Reports, drawn up after the Enquiry at Edessa, by Chaireas, took place.

On May 13th and *June* 13th letters of convocation to the Second Ephesine Synod of the Oriental Monks were issued.   And

On August 8—23rd The First and Second Sessions of the Synod were held under the Presidency of Dioscorus, the Archbishop of Alexandria.

CRIMES LAID TO THE CHARGE OF IBAS, AS GIVEN BY ASSEMAN IN HIS "BIBLICTHECA ORIENTALIS."

Crimina.   Samuel, Cyrus, Mara, and Eulogius in libello, quem Photio Tyri et Eustathio Beryti Episcopis contra Ibam obtulerunt, duo-de-viginti Criminum capita eidem objiciunt.

1. Quod ex mille quingentis solidis, quos ad captivorum redemptionem civitas Edessena contulerat, quingentos ille sibi vindicasset.

2. Quod calicem gemmatum eidem Ecclesiae ante annos undecim a quodam pio viro oblatum, non reposuisset in Ecclesia.

3. Quod de Ordinationibus acciperet.

4. Quod Abrahamium, maleficum hominem, Batenorum Episcopum Ordinasset.

5. Quod Balleum seu Valentium adulterum Presbyterum

creasset, eosque, qui ordinationes contraxere, puniendos judici tradidisset.

6. Quod Danielem, suum ex fratre nepotem, juvenem adhuc eumque luxuriosissimum, Charrensem Episcopum fecisset. *Hellenopolis*, seu *Paganorum civitatis* Episcopum vertit Latinus Interpres: *Charras* enim seu *Haran* Syri appellare solent *Paganorum urbem*, quod ab ea idolorum cultus initium duxerit.

7. Quod omnes Ecclesiaticos redditus fratri suo, vel consobrinis conferret.

8. Quod hæreditates et munera et quæcunque Eccelsiæ offerebantur, in eorumdem usum converteret.

9. Quod ea, quæ in expensas detenterum in carcere eroganda fuerant, in domos suorum erogasset cognatorum.

10. Quod modicum et vitiosum vinum ad Sacrificium Altaris daret, ita ut vix Populo communicanti sufficeret; ipse verò multum et optimum vinum haberet.

11. Quod Nestorianus esset, et S. Cyrillum hæreticum appellasset.

12. Quod Daniel Episcopos quosdam suæ maximè intemperantiæ faventes Clericos ordinaret.

13. Quod Pirozum Presbyterum volentem relinquere sua propria Ecclesiis nullos redditus habentibus, prohibnisset, dicens, cautionem ejus se habere trium millium et ducentorum solidorum.

14. Quod Danielem Epis., testantem et relinquentem omnem facultatem suam Challoæ amicæ suæ ejusque nepotibus, minime redarguisset.

15. Quod Challoa, Danielis Epis. amica, quæ prius nihil habebat, multis rebus Ecclesiasticis abutens, quæ apud ipsam erant, ducentos et trecentos solidos fæneraretur: ut ex hoc manifestum fieret, unde esset harum rerum collectio.

16. Quod Abrahamius Diaconus, primitus pauper et nihil ferè habens, multas et innumeras res habuerit, quæ reverà Edessenæ erant Ecclesiæ. Volentem autem eas eidem Ecclesiæ ac pauperibus in testamento relinquere, hortatus est Daniel Epis., ut sub scripto testamento suam in ipsum transmitteret hæreditatem, jurans ei, eam post ejus mortem se pauperibus erogaturum: Postquam autem hanc Daniel adeptus est, Challoæ amicæ suæ dedisset.

17. Quod a Paganis Haranitis in sacrificiorum impietatem lapsis accipiens Dan. Epis. sportulam, remitteret crimen, negotians et hinc sibimet lucrum.

18. Quod à prædio Lafargaritha Ecclesiæ Edessenæ silvas cædentes portassent ad prædia Challoæ amicæ Daniel Epis., et quæ voluerunt, ædificassent. Porrò Dan. iste Charrarum Episcopus, unà cum Iba avunculo suo, depositus fuit in Latrocinio Ephesino, eique Joannes substitutus, qui Concilio Chalcedonensi subscripsit. Idem Daniel in causa Ibæ sub Domno subscriptus legitur in Concilio Antiocheno, licet in Græco pro *Charris* malè *Beræa* ponatur.

Another grave charge, given in Mansi and Baronius, and abundantly witnessed to, as we shall see, in these Acts is this—that Ibas publicly gave utterance to this Blasphemy, viz., *Non invideo Christo facto Deo: in quantum enim ipse factus est, et ego factus sum.*

The above "Crimina" are stated more fully, and sometimes differently, in Labbe (1670) Tom. IV., p. 648, compared with the same in the Bibliotheca Orientalis. The 1st charge, *e.g.*, is put thus. Civitate conferente ad redemptionem captivorum usque ad mille et quingentos solidos, et positis apud custodem sacrorum* ministeriorum usque ad six millia solidorum, et paulo amplius, præter redditus, quos scripsit ipsius frater, habens in vasis argenti sacri usque ad libras ducentas, ea vendidit pro† mille solidis solum (sicut nos cognoscimus, non direxit) in semet-ipsum reliqua conferens.

Differently expressed is the 13th Charge. "Piroso Pres-"bytero bene testante et sua propria disponente, et res "quas habuit, relinquente ecclesiis redditus nullos habenti-"bus, accensus noster Epis. Ibas cautionem ejus se habere "dixit mille ducentorum solidorum: et significavit ei, "volens ejus infringere voluntatem, et eam per tristitiam "perimere."

---

* Vasorum.

† Et nonnisi mille solidos, ut cognovimus, misit, reliquos ad seipsum abstulit.

II.

[ACTION TAKEN AGAINST IBAS THE BISHOP OF EDESSA.]

(1) [JOHN, Presbyter and Prime Notary, reads]

The Autocratic Cæsars, THEODOSIUS and VALENTINIAN, Victors and Illustrious by Victories, the ever-Worshipful, the Augusti, to the Holy Synod at Ephesus.

Many Anaphoræ (Reports) from people at Edessa, a City of the Province of Osrhoene, with the (Documentary) Acts, etc., as written above.*

(2) JOHN, Presbyter and Prime Notary, said :—

Monks from the City of Edessa are standing outside and state that they are bearers of Royal Letters. What, therefore, does your Holiness enjoin respecting them ?

EUSEBIUS, the Bishop of Ancyra in the First Galatia, said :—

Let the God fearing Bishops Photius, Eustathius, and Uranius recount what seemed good to them to be done in the cause of Ibas and what was the decision they came to ; and, since the God-fearing

---

* This is the beginning of that Imperial Document (δ above), addressed to the Council in relation to the celebrated Bishop Ibas, which should be read, and ought no doubt to have been inserted, in this place.

Presbyter and Proto-Notary made mention of Royal Letters, let those God-fearing Monks enter the Holy Synod in order that the Letters of the Gracious Emperors, with which they are accredited, may be notified to the Holy Synod.

And, when those Monks had entered,

(2) John, Presbyter and Proto-Notary, read (the following) :*

The Autocratic Caesars, Theodosius and Valentinian, Victors, the ever-Worshipful, the Augusti, to James :—

It has not been concealed from Your Clemency in how great a contest God-fearing Presbyters and Archimandrites have been engaged in contending for The True Faith in the land of the East against certain Bishops of that land who, infected with the Impious tenets of Nestorius, have rendered them-

---

* This Circular Letter, addressed to one of the principal Archimandrites or Abbats of Edessa, was written at the time when the Consul of the West—Asterius—had not become known yet in the East, as we see from the place of date of the Letter. (Zeno and Posthumian were the Consuls of the year 448 A.D. ; and Protogenes and Asterius (Asturius), according to Clinton's Fasti, those of the year 449 A.D.) It is similar to the Royal Rescript to Barzumas in May, 449 A.D., given in Labbe, Tom. IV., p. 106 (Paris 1671), and reprinted at p. 22 of my "Ancient Syriac Document, &c." The Monks, judging from a similarity of names of those mentioned in Mansi were possibly, if not probably, the very same who wrote to the Synod of Berytus in favour of Ibas. We see now, what was unknown before, the reason why so many Monks were present at Ephesus. They came to it deeply interested in the great case of the Bishop of Edessa, as witnesses or partizans. The first Session, wherein Flavian was condemned and Eutyches acquitted, being completed, the Monks now pressed on the Council,

selves retrograde (infamous), while the God-loving
Archimandrites have been sustained by the Faithful
Laity.

Since, then, we will that in every way the Orthodox Faith should shine forth, it has for this reason
seemed to us just and right that your Piety, distinguished for purity of life and integrity of faith,
should repair to Ephesus, a City of Asia, on the
Calends of August and take a seat in the Holy
Synod which is appointed to meet there, and, in
concert with the rest of the Holy Fathers, the
Bishops, accomplish that which is well-pleasing to
God.

This Ordinance was issued on the 13th of Hazi-
ran, on the day of the Ides of June, at Constantinople, during the Consulate of the
Illustrious PROTOGENES and of him who is (yet)
to be notified.

JOHN, Presbyter and Proto-Notary, said :—

Copy of the Gracious Letters addressed—

To Abraham, Presbyter and Archimandrite.
To Elias, Presbyter and Archimandrite.
To Pacidas, Presbyter and Archimandrite.
To Isaac, Presbyter and Archimandrite.
To Eulogius, Presbyter and Archimandrite.
To Habib, Deacon and Archimandrite.
To Abraham, Deacon and Archimandrite.
To Ephraim, Presbyter and Archimandrite.

To Polychronius, Archimandrite.
To Benjamin, Archimandrite.
To Andrew, Archimandrite.*

DIOSCORUS, Bishop of Alexandria, said :—

These distinguished, God-loving, Archimandrites are here present at what is being done, in pursuance of the command of the Gracious Emperor.

Now, let the God-fearing Bishops, Photius, and Eustathius, and Uranius, declare, in compliance with the direction of the God-loving Bishop Eusebius, what

---

* Archimandrites, usually of the Order of Presbyters both for the performance of Divine Offices and the exercise of Discipline among those over whom they were superiors, were the Patres or heads of Monasteries in Eastern Christendom, corresponding to Abbats or Abbots in Western and possessing great absolute power.   In order that the members, who were often very numerous, of these confederate communities might the better perform their several and respective duties, Bingham says that " the monasteries were commonly " divided into several parts, and proper officers appointed over them. " Every ten monks were subject to one who was called the *decanus*, or " dean, from his presiding over ten : and every hundred had another " officer, called *centenarius*, from presiding over a hundred. Above these " were the *patres*, or the fathers of the monasteries, as S. Jerom and S. " Austin generally term them ; which in other writers are called *Abbates*, " abbots, from the Greek 'Aββάs, a father : and *hegumeni*, presidents ; " and archimandrites, from *mandra*, a sheepfold ; they being as it were " the keepers or rulers of these sacred folds in the Church."   " The " Abbots or Fathers were also of great repute in the Church. " For many times they were called to Councils, and allowed to sit and " vote there in the quality of Presbyters. As Benedict in the Council " of Rome under Boniface II., anno 531 ; which I relate on the au- " thority of Dr. Cave who has it from Antonius Scipio in his Eulogium " Abbatum Cassinensium. The like privilege we find allowed in the " Council of Constantinople under Flavian, anno 448, where 23 Archi- " mandrites subscribe with 30 Bishops to the condemnation of Eutyches, " as appears from the fragments of the Council related in the Council of " Chalcedon." (Bk. VII., Chap. III., Sect. 11 and 13.)   Had he known of these Acts, Bingham might have instanced this Council of 449 A.D. at Ephesus.

F

transactions took place in their (official) presence relative to Ibas.

(3) The God-loving Bishops, Photius of Tyre, and Eustathius of Berytus, and Uranius of Himeria, said :—

In reference to Ibas, matters concerning The Faith were mooted in our presence ; and because witnesses for this case were requisite, and a long space of time would have intervened, we commanded that those who belonged to the clerical body (κληρος) of the City of Edessa, should affirm on Oath upon the Gospels, whatever they were cognizant of in reference to the accusation advanced against him (Ibas) touching The Faith.   Now, on this matter a great commotion was made, and a considerable amount of talk took place, at Edessa, which circumstance also was notified to our Gracious and Humanitarian Emperor: and it is because we have thus been apprised of the Victorious Emperor having notification of this matter and of his having received the Affidavits of all those whose names are notified in the Records,*

---

* These Records were the Documentary Acts drawn up at Edessa. Like many other words in our MS., this one ‫ܗܘܦܘܡܢܐܛܐ‬, which so frequently occurs in it, is only the Greek word ὑπομνήματα Syrianized, and, with them, shows clearly enough that this MS. or these Acts of the Second Synod of Ephesus were originally written in Greek.   In a note on p. 178 of Dr. Cureton's " Ancient Syriac Documents" he says that " Valesius, in his notes to Eusebius, *Hist. Eccl.*, B. I., c. g. n. b. writes, "' Acts were Books wherein the Scribes that belonged to the several " places of Judicature recorded the sentences pronounced by the Judges. " See Calvin's Lex. Jurid., the word Acta.'   And again, on B. VII., " c. XI., r. d., ' For the Greeks use Ὑπομνήματα in the same sense as " the Latins use their word *Acta*.   Those which wrote these, the

as your Holiness has just now heard, that we request these same Records to be read.

As regards Daniel, Bishop of Harran (Charræ), he was charged with an (immoral) course of life ; and, as we perceived that he would be evidently convicted, we wanted to effect his Deposition, so that we might not be put to shame (so as to avoid scandal). He, however, perceiving what was expedient for himself to do, chose to tender Letters of Resignation. To your Holiness, therefore, it appertains to exercise your authority and to decree what seems fit to you. We, however, signify to your Holiness that, after the trial *we* conducted, we have not consented (i.e., we refuse) to hold communication with the same Ibas.*

(4) CYRUS, Bishop of Aphrodisias, said :—

If your Piety command it, let the affair of Ibas be first investigated and brought to a conclusion : then, if it choose, let your Holy Synod give orders that the Records of the Action, taken in reference to him, be read.

"'Υπομνηματογραφοι, the Latins call *Ab actis.*' Bishop Pearson "writes thus : 'Ut enim actus Senatus et acta diurna Populi Romani "conficiebantur ; sic et in Provinciis Romanis idem a Presidibus et Cae-"sarum Procuratoribus factum est ; qui ad Imperatores saepissime de "rebus alicujus momenti Epistolas scripserunt, ut passim observare est in "historiis Romanis. *Lect. in Act. Apost.*, p. 50, &c."

. * It is quite evident from this that the conferences at Tyre and Bery-tus on the affair of Ibas had taken place before the Second Synod of Ephesus. Consequently the date given in Mansi VII., 211, is wrong, as M. Martin has shown. There was only one procedure of Arbitration, commencing at Tyre, continuing at Berytus, and ending at Tyre 25th Feb., 448 A.г.

[A]

ARRIVAL AT THE METROPOLIS OF THE
JUDGE* CHARGED WITH INSTRUCTIONS
FROM THE ROMAN GOVERNMENT RELATIVE
TO THE DIFFERENCES BETWEEN THE INHABI-
TANTS AND THE BISHOP OF EDESSA.

(1) JOHN, Presbyter and Proto-Notary, read thet
Acclamations of the citizens (of Edessa) :—

After the Consulate of the Illustrious Flavians,
Zeno and Posthumian, on the day before the Ides
of April (12th April, 449 A.D.) during (the continuance of) Indiction the Second, there assembled all
the inhabitants of the City of Edessa, the Metropo-

---

* This person, Cheræas or Chaireas, although apparently unknown
to the writers of this Epoch, is disclosed by the great MS.
named A to our historical view to be the Civil Governor and
Judge, under the Roman Power, of the vast Province, Osrhoene,
and by E in the Appendices of Vols. i. (p. 310, l. 16) and ii. is further
discovered to be the Hegemon of its great Capital.   He had
been ordered by the Imperial Court, probably through the intrigue of the
heads of the Eutychian party who resolved on using this Council as a
means of effecting their secret designs, to repair to Edessa for the purpose of examining the serious differences between the Bishop and Clergy
of that city.   The accusers of Ibas, who hastened to meet him and to
conduct him to the Martyrium, situated perhaps on the ܬܚܘܡܐ, *limes,*
march, or *boundary* of their town district, greeted him with Acclamations and Clamours raised against Ibas, that recur during the entire
proceedings.   The Acclamations, recorded with repeating and arranged minuteness, enable us both to get a correct insight into
the way in which those proceedings were directed to shape their
course, giving us an idea what kind of justice Ibas will receive, and
into the way, also, in which the Administration of an Oriental province of
the Roman Empire was managed in the fifth Century, before the close of
which human society belonging to it fell, on the decay of those principles
that alone weld it together compactly and render it stable and secure.

† Acclamations, both in the course of the business of a Synod and
of the worship in the Church or elsewhere given, were one distinct and
recognized mode of the people's expressing their approbation, or praise, or

lis, together with the Venerable Archimandrites and Monks and women and men of the same City, who proceeded to meet the Great and Glorious Chaireas, Count of the First Rank and Judge (Præses) of Osrhoene ; and when he came and stood at the boundary and (then) entered into the Church* (Martyrium) of the Holy Zachæus, they vociferated all these acclamations :—" (There is only) *One* God. " Victory to the Romans—the Lord be merciful " towards us. May our Sovereigns be ever vic- " torious. May the Victory of Theodosius increase ! " May the Victory of Theodosius the August be " perpetual ! The Victory of Valentinian the " August increase—the Victory of our Sovereigns " multiply ! The Victory of the God-fearing in- " crease !—to the Orthodox many years. One God ! " (Give) Theodosius Victory. One God ! (Give) " to Valentinian Victory. To the Eparchs many

---

assent, and give us Occidents a close insight into Oriental customs and manners by disclosing to us what influence public assemblies exercised. They are all included by the Greeks in the word κρότος. " The first " use of this custom," says Bingham (Bk. XIV., chap. IV., sect. 27), " was only in the Theatres. From thence it came into the Senate, and, " in process of time, into the Acts of the Councils, and the ordinary " assemblies of the Church." We have abundant instances of Synodi- cal acclamations, as well as distinct allusions to similar expressions of praise and delight with great Preachers in Church, in these Acts.

* " The Church (Martyrium) of the Holy Zachæus." Under the word Martyrium, which Du Cange defines as *Ædes sacra, Deo sub Martyrum invocatione dicata*, he quotes Isidorus lib. 15, cap. 9 :— " Martyrium, locus Martyrum, Græca derivatione, eo quod in Memoriam " Martyris sit constructus, vel quod sepulcra sanctorum ibi sint Martyrum. " Walafridus Strabo lib. de Reb. Eccl. cap. 6: Martyria vocabantur " Ecclesiæ, quæ in honore aliquorum Martyrum fiebant : quorum sepul- " cris et Ecclesiis honor congruus exhibendus in Canonibus decernitur." (Glossarium mediæ et infimæ latinitatis, Tom. IV., p. 307.)

"years—to Protogenes many years. To the Illus-
"trious ones (the Consuls) many years. A statue of
"gold for the Eparchs! May* the Augusti be
"preserved. May the Court be preserved. To
"Domnus many years. To the Christ-loving many
"years. To the Consul many years. To the Or-
"thodox many years. *One* is the God who guards you.
"To Zeno many years.   To the General many
"years. An Icon of gold for the General. You
"are the Glory of the General. You are the
"Angel of Peace. You are the trusted confidant
"of the Victors. May the Roman power be pre-
"served. May the Augusti be preserved. A
"Statue for the General. Icons of gold for the
"Victor. To Anatolius many years—to the Patri-
"cian many years—thou art the Father of the
"August—thou art the trusted confidant of our
"Sovereigns. In all, Anatolius (is) one (with us).
"The Trinity (is) with the Patrician. To Theodosius
"many years—to the Count many years—all the
"City offers its gratitude to Theodosius—all the

---

* Or " Prosperity to the Augusti" (or Roman Cæsars)—"prosperity
"to the Roman Court." The Sovereigns alluded to were, of course,
Theodosius II. and Valentinian III.   Protogenes was the Consul
for the East in 449 A.D.; Zeno, Master of Divine Offices, was the General of the Army; Anatolius, the Patrician, was a friend of Theodoret;
and probably Theodosius (to be mentioned hereafter) the important personage at Edessa; and Domnus the Archbishop of the Province, in which
Edessa was situated.   Ibas, a name so often shouted, was by the
Edessenes repudiated as holding Doctrines identified with the tenets of
the Archheretic Nestorius.   So constant and manifest are references to the
circumstances and "crimina" connected with Bishop Ibas made in these
Acclamations of the people that, in order to understand most of them, the
Reader need only be directed to the Introductory Note under Ibas, p. 25.

" City praises the Count. To Cheræas many years.
" To the Count many years. To the Christians many
" years—thou arrivest and all rejoice—the Augusti have
" justly honoured thee—thou art worthy of the Au-
" gusti. May the Palace (the Court) be preserved.
" Another Bishop for the Metropolis—no man accepts
" Ibas—no one accepts a Nestorian—perish the (whole)
" race of the Nestorians. Let what belongs to the
" Church be restored to the Church. Drive Ibas
" from the Church—the Church ought not to suffer
" violence. There is (but) *One** God—Christ the
" Victor. Our Lord! be merciful to us! All of
" us are of one mind—nobody, in one word, accepts
" Ibas—in short, no man wants a Nestorian Bishop.
" August Theodosius! have pity on Thy own City.
" Nobody wants a second Nestorius. Nobody
" wants a man who wars against Christ. No man
" wants the enemy of Christ. No man wants the
" hater of Christ. No man receives the destroyer
" of Orthodoxy. No man receives a Judas for a
" Bishop. An Orthodox Bishop for the Metropolis
" —let him (Ibas), who is departing, (at once) take
" his departure. We¶ beg of thee imme-

* "*One*" would be emphasized by the voice of the vociferator, by im-
plication, refuting the Nestorian dissolver of the unity of the Person of Christ.
¶ Or " Make these wishes known, (Count!) we beg, to our Mas-
" ters (Imperial) and to the General (Commandant)—To the fire with the
" partizans of Ibas—to the fire with the Votaries of Nestorius.
" We want Pirouz for Steward." Pirouz—a regular Persian word—
appears to have been a Priest of the Church of Edessa and a Λογοθέτης,
Œconomus, *Steward, officer of the accounts* in the Church there.
Pirouz's name occurs in the Acts of the Synod of Berytus (Mansi,
Conciliorum omnium amplissima collectio, t. VII., col. 226, No. 13.)

" diately manifest it. Let our Emperors know these
" things. Let the General be informed of them—
" let his race (partizans) be forthwith burnt —
" let the race of Nestorians forthwith be burnt.
" Pirouz be Logothet to the Church. Pirouz be
" Steward to the Church. Whoèver for Christ's
" sake would die, they are (really) living."

Likewise, on the day after the Ides,* which is the
14th of Ijar, during Indiction the Second, there
came to the Council Chamber (Cabinet) of the Lord,
the Noble and Illustrious Flavius Cheræas, Count
of the First Dignity and Governor of Osrhoene,
Venerable Clerics and God-loving Archimandrites and
Monks and Vowed† Persons, who made Depositions
notified in writing. There came, too, workmen and
inhabitants from the Metropolis of Edessa who
requested to enter the Council Chamber : and, having entered, they uttered these acclamations :—

" Our Lord be merciful towards us. May our
" Sovereigns be ever victorious—the triumph of
" Theodosius increase— our Sovereigns many years

---

* On April 14th, A.D. 449, then, took place the first sitting of the Judge.
Let the Reader note particularly, as he proceeds, the order of events
and the arrangements made in the Administration of Justice.

† There is a little difficulty here in the Original Syriac concerning, nor is it easy to find an exact English rendering of, the expression
ܒ̈ܢܝ ܩܝܡܐ every time it so frequently occurs. In his Thesaurus
Dr. R. P. Smith gives *monachi*, and ܒܪ ܩܝ̈ܡܐ *filius fœderis, qui fœdus
iniit*, presertim *coenobita, monachus* and ܒܪܬ ܩܝ̈ܡܐ *monialis, virgo sacra*.
Also "redditur ܒܢܝ ܩܝܡܐ *devoti, voto obstricti*." " Vowed persons"
will be the equivalent term, perhaps, comprehending the entire class.

" —the Orthodox many years—the victory of Valen-
" tinian increase—our Sovereigns many years—
" (Thou, the) *One* God! (give) to Theodosius victory
" There is *One* God—to Valentinian victory—(O Thou)
" *One* God! (give) to the Romans victory. To the
" Eparchs many years—to Protogenes many years.
" Icons of gold for the Eparchs—to Nomius* many
"years—to the Orthodox many. *One* is God who
" protects thee. To Zeno the General many years
" —to Chrysaphius† many years—Urbicius‡ many
" years—to Anatolius the Patrician many years.
" May Anatolius be preserved to the Roman Em-
" pire. To Senator‖ many years. To Count Theo-

---

* I believe this person was not the Count, as my Syriac text would seem to
indicate, but ܢܘܡܝܘܣ Nomius, sometimes written Nomus, as further on,
who was Consul in the year 445 A.D., Master of divine Offices in 439
and 443 A.D., a Patrician in 446 A.D., and a Partizan of Eutyches, as
well as present at the General Council of Chalcedon in 451 A.D. (Mansi,
Concil. omn. ampl. et nova Collectio, Vol. VI., c., 1023 B). It
was to Nomus, when Ex-Consul, that Theodoret wrote that famous letter
in which, in a brief compendium, he writes a short history of his whole
life, and describes what (numerous) results had been accomplished during
his Episcopate, as Baronius informs us in Tom. VII., p. 618 of his
Ecclesiastical Annals.

† This Chrysaphius was the wretched, intriguing, Eunuch who, so
powerful at the Imperial Court, and so deadly an enemy to Archbishop
Flavian, turned the Synod into an instrument for his own sinister ends
and for effecting the objects of the great Eutychian party. Though
once in such high power and influence, and now so greatly applauded, yet
in the end he was exiled and put to death. Tillemont writes of him
in his Memoires. XV, and in his Histoires des Empereurs. VI.

‡ Urbicius was Præfect of the Prætorium in 449 A.D.

‖ Senator was a great benefactor to Edessa, its Chronicle in Bibl.
Orient. I. speaking of him thus—LX. Anno Græcorum 749 (Christi
438) sub præstantissimo Ibâ obtulit Senator ingentem mensam argenteam
librarum septies centum et viginti, quæ in veteri Edessæ Ecclesia reposita
fuit.

G

" dosius many.   To Cheræas many—may he be
" preserved to the Augusti.   Ibas for bishop no
" man accepts—The Simonian no man accepts—The
" enemy of Christ no man wants—a man who is the
" envier of Christ no man wants—no man wants a
" depraver of Orthodoxy.   The confidant of Nestorius
" into exile—the man who has confessed in writing the
" doctrine of Nestorius nobody accepts—his fellow
" Counsellor nobody—the spoliator of the Temple (of
" God) to exile—the companion of Nestorius to exile—
" the man who agrees with Nestorius ought to dwell in
" exile—Ibas has desolated the Church—Ibas alone has
" robbed the Church—his relatives detain the goods
" of the Church—what belongs to the Church should
" be restored to it—what belongs to the poor should
" return to the poor—no man receives the corruptor
" of Orthodoxy—none receives the enemy of The
" Faith—none receives the Iscariot—a rope (the gib-
" bet) for the Iscariot.   Holy Rabbulas !* be instant
" together with us—Ibas has depraved thy Faith—
" Ibas has depraved the Holy Faith of The Synod—
" Ibas has corrupted The Faith of Ephesus—Ibas

---

* Rabbūlas was the immediate predecessor of, and much opposed by,
Ibas.   He still lived in the memory and hearts of the people whom they
had known as the faithful adherent of S. Cyril and upholder of the
Faith as established by the first Ephesine Synod.   He holds nearly as
prominent a position in the Nestorian Controversy as that great Champion
of The Truth himself.   His Sermon preached to the people in the great
Church at Constantinople is given by Overbeck in his " Selecta Opera"
(pp. 239-244), who also notes the fact that the translation into Syriac
by Rabbulas of Cyril's treatise " De Naturâ Humanâ Domini nostri"
still exists in the British Museum (Addl. MSS. No. 14557, foll.
94-123).

" has corrupted the True Faith of Cyril. Gracious
" Sovereigns! reject him. Orthodox Sovereigns! re-
" ject him—do you preserve your own metropolis—do
" (preserve) your faithful servant¶—another Bishop
" for the Metropolis.   To Dioscorus, the Arch-
" bishop, many years.   An Orthodox Bishop for the
" Metropolis.   May Alexandria be preserved a city
" of the Orthodox. Dagalaiphas* Bishop for the
" Metropolis—Holy Rabbulas! be instant with us.
" Ibas melted down the Service of (Plate be-
" longing to) the Church—Ibas has carried off pos-
" sessions that are the common property of all—
" August Theodosius! be merciful to thy City—
" the relation of Ibas has detained the goods
" of the Church.   Our Lord! be merciful to-
" wards us.   Unbeliever¶ and misbeliever! go

¶ Or, "Do you deliver your Believing Handmaid" (that is, Edessa),
is a rendering that brings out the force of ܐܠܕܣܐ. See Cureton's An-
cient Syriac Documents relative to the earliest establishment of Chris-
tianity in Edessa and the neighbouring countries from the year after our
Lord's Ascension to the beginning of the fourth century. *Blessed* and
Believing were the two Epithets specially applied to the City of Edessa.
In Dr. Payne Smith's Thesaurus, he says, at column 612, "Saepe etiam
urbes vocantur ܡܒܪܟܬܐ, sic Haran ab ethnicis vocabatur ܡܒܪܟܬܐ,
B H Chr. 176; ܡܒܪܟܬܐ ܡܕܝܢܬܐ ܗܝ ܕܠ urbs benedicta *Tel
Tura*, ib. 258; præsertim sic vocabatur a Christianis urbs Edessa, propter
Abgarum, B. O. i. 32; ܐܘܪܗܝ ܡܒܪܟܬܐ ܡܕܝܢܬܐ, ib. ii. 45;
ita ut ubi ponatur absolute pro Édessa, e.g., ܐܠܗܐ ܢܛܪܝܗ,
Doc. Syr. ܝܓ . 3."

* Daglaiphas or Dagalaïfa (ܕܓܠܐܝܦܐ) is one of the three men whose
names (Vol. I., p. 40, l. 6) the people cried out to be Bishop in the
place of Ibas, with Flavian and Eliades. It is a strange word.

¶ 'Or, perhaps, "The unbeliever shall have a difficulty in remaining with us."

"your way to Nestorius, your fellow. An Orthodox
"Bishop for the Church—the enemy of The True
"Faith none receives—the lover of Jews none re-
"ceives—the enemy of God none receives—take
"Ibas away and rid the world (of him)—the hater
"of Christ to the dogs—the race of the polluters to
"the Stadium—they have in their possession the
"goods of (the Church of) God—let our Sovereigns
"be acquainted with this—let the Eparchs be in-
"formed of this—let* the Master (of the Forces)
"learn this—let the Senate learn it. Another
"Bishop for the Metropolis—Ibas has ruined
"Osrhoene—Ibas has plundered many Churches:
"the goods of the Church he now sells. Notify, we
"beg, these things directly. In short, no man re-
"ceives Ibas. Let Eusebius, his brother, be
"delivered over to the Council (for trial). No man
"receives a liar for a Bishop—the (partisan) race of
"Ibas to the Stadium—let the race of Ibas be burnt
"alive—let him, who is about to depart, take his
"departure forthwith. By the life of our Sove-
"reigns (Count!) notify (this) immediately—let
"Eulogius,† the Presbyter, depart soon—let the hater
"depart forthwith. In Sarug Ibas left nothing.

---

* Or, "The Master of divine Offices." The Chancellor of the Imperial
Palace at Constantinople was in 449 A.D. Flavius Areovindas Martialius.
(Mansi VI., 832.) Under the head of "Magister Officiorum," Du
Cange (Tom IV., c. 324) defines the Office thus—Dignitas magna in
Palatio Imperatorum qui præerat Palatinis et Principis Ministris, scholis
in Palatio militantibus, fabriciis et limitaneis ducibus.

† This Eulogius was probably a friend and partisan of Ibas. Sarug
(Batnæ) was a city in Mesopotamia, of which the Illustrious Jacob or
James was Bishop, to whom as a Father the Illustrious Jacob of Edessa

" He is a curse* (warning) to the Authorities. (There
" is) *One* God, Christ, the Victor. Our Lord ! be mer-
" ciful to us.   Another Bishop for the Metropolis—
" no man receives Ibas. Oh ! the impudence of
" that Courtezan. August Theodosius ! come to the
" rescue of thy City—no man accepts an unbeliever
" for a Bishop.   In short, no man receives a
" Nestorian as Bishop. Great Zeno, remove him—
" take away him who brought violence upon the
" City. To the Eparchs many years—to the General
" many years.   A city of Christians will not
" brook violence. The possessions (of the Church)
" are ever such—Daniel and Challoa† have con-
" sumed them (in pleasure). The City is ruined
" because of Ibas. There is no Verity (proclaimed),
" Count ! and no man to expound (the Faith). As
" for Ibas, no man accepts him. There is none to
" expound and Ibas is the cause of it—because
" an Orthodox man has not come, there is none to
" expound. The writings of Nestorius have been
" found with Ibas. Who is the mendacious Bishop ?
" Who is the Bishop that sends in false Reports ?
" The commands of our Sovereigns Ibas has eluded.
" Let Ibas receive the sentence of Nestorius—let ¶

once or twice appeals.   See Wright's Catalogue.

* The word ܩܘܣ̈ܙ is παραγγελία *præceptum, mandatum* (2)
Ambitus, petitio, magistratus cum prebensatione.   Ph. *denunciatio, con-
dictio, interdictio.*   (Hederick.)

† Daniel was the Bishop of Harran and nephew of Ibas, and Challoa was the woman with whom he was accused of having criminal
intercourse.   See the " Crimina" on page 35.

¶ Or, better, " Let the confidence of the Orthodox be restored."

" the Orthodox have liberty of speech.   Ibas perse-
" cuted the Holy Saints.   Ibas received Nestorians·
" Take away him who is an oppressor of the Church.
" Another Bishop for the Metropolis—an Orthodox
" Bishop for the Metropolis—all the people desire
" this—all the people cry out for this.   For four-
" teen* years has Ibas been teaching error.   This is
" a City of Christians—Edessa is a City of Chris-
" tians, which is also blessed† of God.   There is one
" Ibas and there is but one Simon (Magus).   Mu-
" sarais‡ the magician has prevailed.   Ibas has pre-
" vailed—do you (Simon and Musarais) take your
" fellow.   Holy Rabbulas! intercede with us.   An
" orthodox Bishop for the Metropolis—no man
" receives Ibas—let his name be erased out of the
" Diptychs.   Holy Rabbulas! send Ibas into exile
" —let Ibas go to the Mines.   We are en-
" treating, we are not by any means commanding
" (viz., you, our Superiors).   All these things we do
" for Christ's sake."

---

* " For (full) thirteen years Ibas has been teaching us error."
See Vol. I., p. 38, l. 16.   He had been ruining Religion for 13 or
14 years.   So that Ibas must have been Bishop since 435 A.D.

† The meaning of this is brought out in the Petition (below) pre-
sented by Micallus, and perhaps an allusion is made here to the Corre-
spondence between the Saviour and the Toparch, Abgarus, of Edessa,
Toparch being a generic term applied to designate the Kings of that
City, as Pharaoh, Cæsar, &c., to those of Egypt, Rome, &c.   Dr.
Cureton believed in the genuineness of that Correspondence.   See p. 51.

‡ Possibly ܠܝܡܘܣܟ was written by the Scribe in the MS. for the
word ܠܝܫܘܡ, the *Samaritan* (magician), but it may be correctly
Anglicised into (Mous'r''ia) Musarais.

[B]

[THE FIRST FORMAL ENQUIRY.]
THE SECOND REPORT.*

1 To the Noble and Glorious Flavians, FULRIS ROMANUS PROTOGENES, (Consul) for the second time and Consul Ordinary, and ALBINUS and SAIIMON, Eparchs, the Flavian CHERÆAS (sends) Greeting.†

How the City of Edessa was affected toward its Bishop, the Venerable Ibas, and how much people were (perpetually) exclaiming and declaring him to be a follower of Nestorius and that they would (not continue to) accept him (as Bishop) in their City, and how much commotion and what seditions it (the city) suffered in consequence¶—not without danger did I consider that these circumstances could be concealed from your High Potencies; and this I have‡ already made known to your Ex-

---

* Literally—"Another, the Second of the Anaphoræ."

† This superscription seems to have somehow undergone alteration and presents difficulties, the solution of which we would defer to a future handling, remarking at present only that Hoffman considers the names of Fulris (Florus or Florentius), Romanus, Protogenes, indicate three different persons, and that Martin believes that, as regards Salomon, we have no information left us whatever in any Libraries. Albinus and Salimon are evidently referred to as the Great and Glorious Eparchs, as well as Flavius Areobindas Martialius as the Glorious and High Master (of Divine Offices), further on in the Petition (or Instruction) presented by Micallus and issuing from the Inhabitants, as well as signed by the Clergy, of the City of Edessa.

¶ Or, perhaps, but not so well—"I had consequently to put up with."

‡ What follows goes upon the supposition that Cheræas had already

alted Throne, Noble and, in every way, Glorious
Lords ; being then persuaded, as I am now also, that
it would not have been without danger (to the
public tranquillity), had we failed to apprize your
Highnesses of these same occurrences.

But under what circumstances, and on whose account these commotions and seditions took place—
these I pass over in silence. What, however, transpired after the letters of our Humbleness to your
Noble and Exalted Throne, I, with brevity, now
narrate.

The whole Body* of the Clerks of the Holy
Catholic Church at Edessa, the Metropolis, accompanied by the Heads and Principals, who undertake
the Government of the Monks, and the Wise-men,
assembled together and approached my Humbleness;
and they prayed me about a Petition, including
certain Resolutions, which proceeded from them and
from others entrusted with authority, but inferior to
them in rank, as well as from Artificers,† inasmuch as
some even whose life is spent in daily labour put
their seals to this (Petition) of theirs, as their signatures testify. Others, too, lower than Artificers
adopted this Petition. They prayed our Humbleness would receive it of them and convey it to the
knowledge of your Gloriousness—for, I shrank‡ from

---

written. The Scribe has here for ܐܘܪܗܝ written plainly another
word which, however, I have not altered in my Text.

  * See p. 59, note ‡.

  † The lines 26 and 27 in Text are exegetical of ܐܘܡܢ̈ܐ.

  ‡ " I tried (i.e.) to avoid making you hear them."

forcing unpleasant subjects upon the attention of your Gloriousness; but, because they had overpowered (constrained) me by an Oath from which I could not be released, I consider it would have been presumptuous (in me) to have spurned the Prayer of the whole City together and have violated the formidable Oath, especially as they invoked (therein) the name of our Victorious Sovereigns.

For this reason I have taken in hand (drawn up) these Documents which give information of the matter, having also appended to them their Petition with the Record of the Acts occasioning it, so that your Orders may be executed, Noble and, in every way, Glorious Lords.

May you ever continue in health and prosperity be accorded to you by God! We pray you may live many years, Noble and, in every way, Glorious Lords.

(b) Copy of the Acts which were drawn up at Edessa, in the year following the Consulate of the Flavians, Zeno and Posthumian, in the presence of Asterius and Patroinus* and of Micallus and other Presbyters; and of Sabbatius and Sabbas and other Deacons; and of Callistratus and Euporus and other Sub-Deacons, of the Holy Church of Edessa; and of Elias, Jamblicus and other Monks; of others

---

* The name of Patroinus occurs in the Acts of the Council at Chalcedon, as given in next page, and that of Sabbatius at p. 669 of Actio X. Also those of Edessene Clergy.

H

besides (viz.), certain Apparitors* (of the Court) and Attendants on its Officers, &c.

The Venerable MICALLUS,¶ Presbyter of the Holy Church of the City of Edessa, says:

We bring a petition which proceeds from the inhabitants of this City and is subscribed by us¶ Ecclesiastics; and we pray your Illustrious Highness,† with a view to quelling the commotions that have overtaken the City and the Holy Church, by reason of this affair (of Ibas), to order it to be received and read, and to be deposited among the Records (Acts), then to forward it to the Noble and Glorious Lords, the Eparchs, and to the High

---

* Ταξεῶται were *Apparitores* and παλατῖναι, *Ministri* or *Attendants* on the High Officials of the Court, or were, rather, *under-Officials* (1) of the Civil Governor of the Province and (2) for raising the State Taxes in the Province and for the Crown Demesne.

¶ Or, perhaps, Micalas.

¶ Literally: "in which there is the subscription of us (بمد) "ecclesiastical persons." Micallus speaks on behalf of the Clergy as well as for himself. Subjoined are a few specimens of subscriptions, made in Greek and Latin at the General Council of Chalcedon held in 451 A.D., extracted from the 4th (p. 661) of the splendid Folio Volumes of Labbe (1671).

Μίκαλλος πρεσβύτερος πεποίημαι τὴν διδασκαλίαν ταύτην ἅμα ἑτέροις.
        [Opposite to this is the same in Latin.]
Πατρωῖνος ποεσβύτερος πεποίημαι, &c.
        [Opposite to this is the same in Latin.]
Εὐφράσιος ὑποδίακονος πεποίημαι τὴν διδασκαλίαν ταύτην ἅμα ἑτέροις. καὶ ἡ ὑπογραφη Συριακή.
Euphrasius, subdiaconus, similiter.   Et subscriptio Syra.
Adelphius, Lector feci hanc petitionem cum sociis.
Leontius, Presbyter feci hanc instructionem cum sociis.
Bassus, Presbyter, similiter.

† The scribe writes |ﻠﻗ, as it is in my Text, but no doubt it should be |ﻠﻗ, εὐπρεπής, "We pray your Eminence to despatch it to......... "that they may take cognizance of its contents."

and Glorious Count, Master of divine Offices, and to the Great and Glorious General Zeno* Ex-Consul (for them to take cognizance) of its contents.

FLAVIUS THOMAS JULIANUS CHERÆAS, High and Glorious Count of the First Rank and Judge (Governor), replied :—

Let the Petition be received which is proffered by the Venerable and God-loving persons, and let it be read.

And he (the Proto-Notary) read (as follows) :—

(3) To Your EMINENCE, from Illustrious† Municipal Dignitaries and the Clerks‡ and Archi-

---

* The ܩܘܢܣܘܠܐ is only the Greek ατο ὑπατων Syrianized—vir Consularis—one who has served the Office of Consul, and ܐܘܦܩܐ is Officia. Tillemont (IV., 212, 287) gives the origin and development of these High Offices.

† For ܐܘܦܩܐ ܥܠܝ̈ܐ the Greek has προπαιουχοι and the Latin Triumphatores. Here the second word stands alone. Πολιτευόμενοι or *Decuriones* or, rather, *Curiales* were those who administered the public affairs of the City, as a kind of Alderman,—were members of the Municipal bodies of the Roman towns, called *Curiæ*. The predominence of the municipal form and spirit, which the Roman Empire bequeathed to Modern Europe, characterized the commencement and the integrity, the decline and the fall of that Empire, whilst there was not the same necessity for that form in its Eastern Domains where human society was constructed on a different basis from that in the West. Still we observe it here.

‡ The Clerks or *Clerici* (ܩܠܝܪܝܩܘ), from κλῆρος (ܩܠܪܝܩܘ or ܩܠܪܘ) and *Canonici*, from κανών the *Register* or *Roll* of any particular Church, were terms of its functionaries, at first exclusively applied to the Higher or Superior Orders of Clergy, viz., Bishops, Presbyters or Priests, and Deacons ; but, says Bingham (Bk. I., Chap. V., Sect. 7), in the 3rd Century when many inferior Orders were appointed, as subservient to the Deacon's Office, such as Sub-Deacons, Acolythists, Readers, &c., with (I may venture perhaps to add) ܒܢܝ̈ ܩܝܡܐ *Vowed Persons*, so often and prominently alluded to in our Acts, then those had the common name of *Clerici*, too. He instances S. Cyprian, Ep. 24, al, 22 ed, Ox., how he

Archimandrites and Monks and Artizans, and from the whole City of Edessa together (is salutation offered).

From of old, even from the beginning, by the grace of God, Illustrious in The Faith has been this our City*; first, indeed (made so), through the Blessedness with which He blessed it, Who is Creator of Heaven and Earth, when He willed in

---

calls the Ordination of a Sub-Deacon and a Reader *Ordinationes Clericæ.* Also Cyprian's contemporary, Lucian the Martyr, speaks the same of Exorcists and Readers. The Council of Nice itself (Can. 3) gives the appellation κλῆρος to others besides Bishops, Presbyters, and Deacons: and the 3rd Council of Carthage made the Canon—"*Clericorum* nomen "etiam lectores, et Psalmistæ, et ostiarii retineant." · Con. Antioch, c. 1, speaks of the Roll, in which the names of all the Ecclesiastics belonging to a Church were written, as "ἄγιος και ὦν," *the sacred roll;* and the Apostolical Canons, c. 13, 14, &c., κατάλογος ἱερατικὸς, *the catalogue of the Clergy.* And in Con. Nic., Can. 16 and 17 and in Con. Antioch, Can. 2 and 6 the term οἱ ἐν τῶ κανόνι is put to denote the Clergy of the Church. So the terms *Clerici* or *Canonici* would include all those whose names were in the Church's Books to receive maintenance, such as Monks, Virgins, Widows, &c., as well as the *Capiatæ* who interred the dead, and *Lecticarii* for carrying biers at funerals, and the *Decani*—of very different rank from the Decani of the Palace—who saw to the proper interment of the dead, the *Defensores* who righted the wronged, the poor, &c., and *Logothetæ* (λογοθέτης), *Œconomi, stewards,* who looked after the revenues, and, as Chancellors of Finance, had to pay the Ecclesiastics out of those Revenues (Du Cange, Glos. Græc. 823.)

Bingham takes special care to distinguish between the Higher and Lower Orders of the Clerici, the former being called ἱερωμενοι *holy* and *sacred,* and the latter *insacrati, unconsecrated,* the one ordained at the Altar, with solemn rite of imposition of hands, the other, commonly without it, being ἀχειροτόνητος ὑπηρεσια. The chief difference, however, was in the exercise of their office and function. The one were ordained to minister before God, as Priests to celebrate the Sacraments, expound his word publicly, &c., whilst the other attended only upon such Priests and performed lower offices in connection with the Church and the spiritual requirements of the Faithful.

* For information about Edessa's reception of "the Word of the "Kingdom," see Cureton's "Ancient Syriac Documents" at pp. 140, 142, &c.

His Own Mercy and determined for our Redemption
and for the (Eternal) Life of us, the sons of men, to
become INCARNATE; and next, because it (the
City) was deemed worthy of being the Depository* of
the Relics† of the Apostle Thomas, who was the

* In the original MS. the word is ܐܬܣܘܡܐ (or ܐܬܣܟܘܡܐ.)
What is particularly germane to the subject, opened up here, may
be gathered from Asseman, Vol. 1., whose ipsissima verba are
these:—De Edesseno S. Thomæ Apostoli Templo hæc leguntur in
Chronico Edesseno. . . . Anno Græco 705 (A.D. 394), die 22
Aug. advexerunt Arcam S. Thomæ Apostoli in Templum magnum eidem
dicatam diebus S. Cyri Epis. . . . Anno Græc. 753 (i.e., A.D. 442)
Anatolius militiæ Præfectus fecit argenteam arcam in honorem ossium S.
Thomæ Apostoli. Also in Asseman Vol. I., Caput IX., under
XXVII., we find to this—" In 750 (i.e., 439 A.D.) Mense Aug. die 22,
"advexerunt Arcam Mar Thomæ Apostoli in Templum magnum eidem
"dicatam diebus Mar Cyri Episcopi"—at foot of the page is
appended this note: ' Thomæ Apostoli. Sacrum ejus corpus Edessam
translatum fuisse, testatur etiam Rufinus Lib. 2, Cap. 5, cui Hieronymus,
aliique Martyrologi suffragantur: " Indeque Indiarum Nestoriani, qui
" Sancti hujus Apostoli Corpus usque ad sæculum elapsum sese conser-
"vasse effutiere, valide confutantur," ut bene notat Pagius ad annum
327. Ejus vero Templi mentionem, præter auctorem Vitæ S.
Ephraemi, pag. 49, faciunt etiam Socrates Lib. 4, Cap. 18 et Sozomenus
Lib. 6, Cap. 18.'

† "Relics." This term would seem to some to need apology or explanation. The Church of England, teaching us to hold to what may be gathered
out of the writings of the Fathers and Doctors of the Undivided
Church, attracts us to, and does not withdraw our view from, "the cus-
"toms of the Churches." One of those customs was a chastened veneration and honour for Martyrs and their remains. Now, at what
Doctor's feet of the Primitive Church could we English Churchmen
more worthily sit as humble and teachable disciples than John Chrysostom's? Schooled under the teaching of the most distinguished
Rhetorician of the age, as so many Fathers and Apologists were in Law
or Rhetoric—recommended by a discerning and powerful politician of
the Imperial Court to the Patriarchal See whose occupant would come in
close contact with it (the Eunuchs Eutropius and Chrysaphius acted the
very opposite parts in reference to Chrysostom and Flavian)—unparalleled
in efforts as an Administrator and a Teacher of The Truth to the people—
unbiassed and critically just in his great Commentaries of Holy Writ—
he seems to stand prominently forward as a Doctor and Father of the
Early Church, in whom we might repose implicit trust. The Golden-

first to confess* our Redeemer to be the Lord GOD.

Now, it has been customary hitherto for us to love and honour our own Orthodox Bishops and to venerate them as the Coadjutors (of God)¶; and this has been our practice up to the present time. And, as regards Bishop Ibas, although his reputation had become sadly sullied by reason of his (mal-)administration of the property (the treasure) belonging to the Holy Church, as well as on other accounts, yet even then we still continued in this way to pay him honour, until, grievous charges being urged against him, he was arraigned on matters, relating to the Orthodox Faith.¶

---

mouthed (as he will probably be designated for all time) Teacher's sentence on the Relics of Ignatius the Martyr should disarm in thoughtful minds all prejudice against their mention.   It will be remembered that, after the lion's devouring jaws had been satiated in the presence of 87,000 spectators at Rome, what remained (some of the larger bones) was forwarded as a precious treasure to the people of Antioch.   So Chrysostom says—
" Short was the time for which God took him from you, and with greater
" grace hath He restored him to you again.   And as they who borrow
" money return that which they have borrowed with usury, so God ta-
" king from you this precious treasure for a little while that He may dis-
" play it at Rome, returned it to you with the greater glory.   Ye sent
" him forth a Bishop, ye received him back a Martyr: ye sent him forth
" with prayers, ye welcomed him home with crowns; and not ye only,
" but all the cities in the intervening lands."   The date of this Martyrdom, according to Baronius or rather his Critic Pagius, is 116 A.D.   The abuse of Relics, of which all know there was abundance in after ages and, must we not add, is in our own time, ought to be distinguished from their devout use in the Primitive Church.

  * See S. John's Gospel, chap. xx., 21.

  ¶ Or, "as our great Benefactors."

  ¶ Or, " It was only when his Orthodoxy was questioned and when
" we had verified the justness and the truthfulness of the charges pre-
" ferred against him by means of his own Letters addressed to Persians,
" which he found it impossible to disown—it was only then and on that
" account that we refused to receive him (as Bishop); anxious (as we
" were) to preserve (inviolate) The Faith which we have held from the

And (then) when we established the just character of this accusation by those letters which were written by him to Persia and which he was unable to deny, we on that account no longer consent to accept him (as Bishop), being ourselves anxious to preserve (inviolate) The Faith which we have held from the beginning, and seeing that of no slight moment is the harm occasioned by his Letters already, even in Persia.

Now it is a fact, ascertainable from these circumstances, that he is a Heretic. Henceforth it was only right and just for him, in consequence, spontaneously to have abdicated the Bishopric, instead of attempting, by coercion, to thrust himself upon our City in order to teach us a Faith other than, and in excess of, THE TRUTH. We, therefore, pray your Highness to write to him not to presume to (re-)enter our City, ere commands (to that effect) have been despatched from our Gracious Sovereigns. We make further request that you would notify these same circumstances to the Noble and Glorious Eparchs, and to the Glorious and High Master (of the divine Offices), so that, when officially informed (of what has passed), the Serene and Christ-loving Sovereigns may give order that a Record of those proceedings which took place at Berytus may be conveyed to, and be read before, your Clemency ; by

---

" beginning, and great (as we knew) the prejudice (injury) to be among
" Persians, occasioned by what Ibas had written. From all which cir-
." cumstances it becomes an ascertained fact that he is a Heretic."

which you will be apprized how wretchedly unorthodox are the opinions of Bishop Ibas.¶

We, likewise, pray your Highness to send up and notify to the Great and Powerful General, and Ex-Consul, Zeno, not to be anticipated (circumvented) by Ibas, since he is quite disposed to avail himself of the Roman troops in order by force to enter our City.

We are, however, of opinion that, instructed by your Illumination, that high Authority will not be prevailed upon by Ibas, and that his Highness will not be induced to lend the help of the Roman forces against the Orthodox, who honour and observe The Faith of our Sovereigns, the Gracious Emperors. His Gloriousness, on the contrary, is anxious to establish and defend, and in everything to put into execution the Commands proceeding from our Gracious Sovereigns.   For, already, it has reached the ears (the hearing) of all of us, the Orthodox, that the new* Edict (Law) has been put into ure by their

---

¶ Perhaps this might be translated—" In how wretched, and in how " unorthodox, a manner Bishop Ibas has been conducting his Pastorate."

* "The new Edict."   Mansi gives it thus: Statuimus ut Irenæus qui hac de causa (Nestorianismi) nostram indignationem olim incurrit, et postea, nescio quomodo, post secundas nuptias, sicut accepimus, contra Apostolicos canones, Tyriorum urbis Episcopatus creatus est, a sanctâ quidem Tyriorum ecclesiâ expellatur, privatus autem in patrio tantum solo degat, habitu et nomine sacerdotis prorsus exutus.   See page 238, Vol. I., containing my Syriac Text.

We also have in Labbe, Tom. V., p. 419 (1671), " Edictum pro-
" positum a præfectis.   .   .   .   adversus Porphyrium et Nestorium et
" Irenaeum: Piissimus Imperator noster cum probe noverit orthodoxam
" religionem esse *qua Leges et respublica ipsa* consistunt suo edicto omne
" semen impietatis abstulit," &c.   Likewise
at p. 418, we have " Exemplum sacræ legis.   .   .   .   Theodosii.
.   .   .   adversus Nestorianos, et adversus Irenæum Tyriorum Episco-

Clemency—that one which removed from the Priesthood Irenæus,* formerly Bishop of Tyre.   These matters, too, we pray may be notified to the God-loving Archbishop (of the Province).   Further, because at the trial that took place at Berytus, when his Homilies were produced, he refused to avow them to be his, and when he withdrew therefrom the witnesses competent to testify to that fact, because he had been travelling in company with his prosecutors,† we beg of those who are here present and are well aware from his various Homilies, how he preached in contravention of the Orthodox Faith, each one to come forward separately and depose in writing what he heard from Ibas, when delivering those Homilies, that is contrariant to The Faith. For, we have been constrained, through having perceived so much Impiety (false faith) in Bishop

---

"pum : Regiam Nostram Majestatem decere arbitramur ut, &c.   .   ."

* "That (Law) which removed Irenæus from the Priesthood." In the MS. the Scribe writes Arius by mistake for Irenæus.   In Baronius, Tom. VII. (Lucæ 1741). Pagius (448 a.c.) II. Anno ii. ad xix.—Theodosius Imperator vetuit libros Porphyrii et contra Cyrilli scripta editos, decrevitque etiam, ut quicunque nefariam Nestorii doctrinam quovis motu sectarentur, ex Ecclesiis expellantur. Ac denique statuit, ut Irenæus qui Nestorio faverat, et contra canones Tyriorum Episcopus Ordinatus fuerat, Sacerdotio penitus exueretur. Legitur Edictum illud Tom. III., Concil. pag. 1216.   We may add that this Law against the Nestorians was published April 18th, 448 a.d., and is called "new" in contradistinction with the Law against them enacted in the year 435 a.d.

† Ibas, i.e., having travelled with his accusers, took a new line of defence, adopted in consequence of what he had learnt on the way, and threw overboard (as it were), and did not call, his witnesses, but challenged the opposite party to prove that the Homilies were his. If, however, the word ܗܘܐ refers to the witnesses, then he did not cite them to appear " on the pretext that they had travelled in company with his

I

Ibas, to manifest some zeal for our Faith, and to eulogize (render homage to) the Gracious Lords of the Earth, and to pray of you to make known all these circumstances to the Noble and Distinguished Authorities above mentioned, seeing that we honour Rank in every quarter and are especially solicitous in every possible way for the Orthodox Faith. Lastly, we pray your Highness, adjuring you most solemnly, in the name of Almighty God and of His Christ and of the Holy Spirit, and by the Victory of the Gracious Masters of the World, the Gracious Flavians, Theodosius and Valentinian, the Ever-August, to receive this Petition from us and to take and notify it to the Princely Authorities aforesaid.

(Here follow) the subscriptions of the whole City. I, Flavius Theodosius, was present at these Transactions.

Then subscribed the whole body of the Clerks,* and the Archimandrites,* and the Monks, and the Vowed Brethren,* and the (Civic) Dignitaries, and the Municipal Authorities, and the Roman Officials, and the Colleges† of the Armenians and of the Persians and

"accusers." This latter view I prefer on further consideration.

 * About these several classes of persons see previous notes, as being consonant with some of which we may here refer to the expression—" the "Priest and Clerks"—which more than once occurs in the Prayer Book of the Church of England.

 † Investigation into Asseman's Bibliotheca Orientalis, the " Acta Sanctorum," &c., would doubtless furnish us with material, interesting and abundant enough for a Dissertation on these Christian Schools or Colleges, constituting an University for the Christian youth of Persia, Armenia, and Syria, the fact of whose existence at the populous City of Edessa with the number of members of the Church there that we meet with in these Acts, speaks volumes for the progress The True Religion.

of the Syrians, and (then) the Artizans and all
the City.   Every person, with his own hand, subscribed and assented to these Transactions and to the
Presentation of the Petition.   And there was a
clamour for three or four days when the whole population of the City shouted (thus) — together with
the whole body of Clerics, including the Presbyters
and the Deacons, and the Sub-Deacons and the
Readers, and the Holy Monks, and all the Deaconesses,
and the Vowed Sisters, and the Soldiers, and the
women and children, with the rest of the entire City—
" Our Lord be merciful to us !—(there is) *One* God,
" Christ the Victor !—our Sovereigns be ever vic-
" torious —- the victory¶ of Theodosius increase.
" Victory of Valentinian increase—the victory of
" the Christ-loving increase—this City belongs to
" the Augusti—this City belongs to Christians—
" Edessa is a City of the Orthodox.   To the Ep-
" archs long life (or many years)—to Nomius* many
" years—-to the Patriciant many years--to Zeno many

¶ Or, " increased be victory to Theodosius," and so also similar acclamations.

* " To Nomius many years or a long life." At p. 37, lines 18, 19,
20, the word is clearly in the MS. ܠܘܡܝܐ and at p. 25, l. 2, it is ܢܘܡܝܐ.
As in p. 39, l. 10, it should be ܠܘܡܐ or ܢܘܡܐ.   At p. 37, l. 23
ܢܘܡܝܘܣ may perhaps have been meant for ܩܘܡܣ *comes*, as at p. 24,
l. 19, but if not, then no doubt it should be Nomius.   It is Nomius at p.
37 undoubtedly. (Nomius would seem to have been a partizan of Eutyches mentioned as present at the Council of Chalcedon in 451 A.D.)
At p. 25, l. 9, it is ܢܘܡܝܘܣ, the second letter of which word in the
MS. looks like ܒ but it is not that letter, I think, and at p. 37 I found
it to be ܢܘܡܝܘܣ on further scrutiny.

† The great teacher of the greater Vossius (G. J.) writes thus :

"years—to the General many years—to Urbicius
"the Præfect (of the Prætorium) many years—
"Chrysaphius many years—Anatolius many years.
"May the palace (Court) of the Orthodox (Empe-
"rors) be (preserved).   Our Sovereigns be ever
"victorious.   Ibas, the Nestorian, no man receives
"—what was for the service of the Church he* ap-
"propriated for himself,¶ and on the Holy Day

—Patricius est nomen viri constituti in certa dignitate et præfectura,
cujus origo est a Constantino Magno.   Patricii sedebant supra præfectum
prætorii, et in ecclesia episcopis præponebantur.   Patriarchis pares habe-
bantur quippe proximi ab imperatoribus.   Ut imperator ἐπιστημονάρχης
dicebatur et ecclesiæ prærat rebusque ecclesiasticis, velut supremum
caput: ita patricius aliquis ejus locum tenebat, et ὑπεκκλησίων hac
de re appellabatur.   Ita Occidentales *patricios Romanorum* dixerunt,
quos nunc reges appellare mos est.   Tamen patriciis non semper in
Oriente sua dignitas constitit; quippe cum aliquando ante eos fuerit
Magister officiorum.   Vide Gloss. Græco-L. Meursii.   Turneb. lib. 15,
16, "Patricius pater imperatoris vocabatur, πατὴρ βασιλέως.   Olim
"igitur Patricii ex eo appellabantur, quod patrem cierent, postea quos
"imperator patres ciebat, quod quidem et Franciæ reges imitati sunt,
"quosdamque satrapas *patricios* vocant, quos antiquitatis ignari *Pares*
"appellarunt."   (Matthiæ Martini Lexicon Philologicum, Tomus
Secundus, p. 191.)

* At p. 38, l. 6, it is ܩܕ and at p. 27, l. 2, it is ܩܕ.

¶ Or, "Ibas melted down the Service (of Plate, the Vessels) be-
"longing to the Church," &c.   These, and the like expressions, all refer
to the same series of "Crimina," given in Labbe's Concilia, Chal.
Act 10ᵃ, Libellus Samuelis, &c., and in Asseman's Bibl. Orient (as quoted
above in pp. 35-37).   "He plundered the Holy Church" is another
acclamation understood at the time no doubt to refer to what is contained
in the Crimina.   See the 2nd of the Crimina on p. 35 above.

We quote in full the Charge as stated by Mansi.   X. Quia dum memoria fieret sanctorum Martyrum, non est datum vinum(a) ad sacrificium
altaris ad sanctificationem et populi distributionem, nisi admodum(b) exig-
uum et vitiosum, ac lutosum, ac quasi eo tempore vindemiatum: ut ex
hoc cogerentur, qui deputati fuerant ministrare, de tabernis omnino viti-
osi comparare sex sextarios, qui nec suffecerent: ita ut his qui sanctum
corpus distribuebant, innueret ut ingrederentur, qui sanguis non inveniretur;

(a) Ut offerretur sancto altari, et sanctificaretur, et populo distribuaretur.
(b) Omnino paululum et hoc infectum.

" nobody communicated (with him). Let our Sov-
" ereigns know this—let the Orthodox Emperors
" know this—take away one man and (liberate) save
" our City—he has sold the Holy Thomas*—he has
" plundered the Holy Church—he gave the pos-
" sessions of the poor to his relatives.† All the
" people know this. Let Ibas be despatched to the
" Stadium—Ibas, the Nestorian, into exile—the
" whole City prays for this. Let the bones of John
" (of Antioch) who ordained him be taken up—for
" 13 years he has been deceiving us—Ibas into exile
" —this City belongs to the Augusti—Ibas has pre-
" vailed—Simon has prevailed—Musarias the Ma-
" gician has prevailed. Ibas has prevailed—do you
" (Magicians) take your fellow. This man oppressed
" the poor. This man pillaged (made a spoil of) the
" Church—he secreted† (or appropriated to himself)
" the Holy Vessels—he made use of the Holy Ves-
" sels for his own purposes—Christ-loving Kings!
" eject him—man-loving Kings! let him go into
" exile—all the people desire this. Philanthropic
" Kings! show clemency to our City—this City is

---

illis bibentibus, et tunc ac semper habentibus(a) diversum et mirabile vinum.
Et hæc acta sunt conscio et admonito eo, qui potestatem ministeriorum
habebat : cui et dictum est, ut et ipse admoneret episcopum cum fiducia.
Et cum nihil fecisset, illo tempore coacti sumus nos et ipsum reverendissi-
mum episcopum suum admonere. Et cum didicisset, permotus non est,
sed contempsit, ita ut multi nostræ civitatis hinc scandalizarentur.

* " The Holy Thomas." Probably the Relics of which Asseman
speaks, as we have seen, and especially in the words—De iisdem Thomæ
Apostoli reliquiis in eodem Chronico (Edesseno) anno Christi 442, &c.

† This is a constant charge urged against Ibas. See the Crimina.

(a) Excellens.

" one of believers.   The writings of Cyril, the Or-
" thodox, he (Ibas) depraved—he depraved the
" Catholic Doctrine of the Holy Rabbulas —he
" has depraved the Orthodox Doctrine of the
" CCCXVIII.*   Take away (this) one man and
" deliver the City—this is a City of Christians.
" The victory¶ of Theodosius increase—the victory
" of Valentinian increase—the victory of the Ortho-
" dox increase—let the race of Christians increase—
" Clement Sovereigns ! be clement towards us—
" Ibas into exile—Ibas to the mines—Ibas, the Nes-
" torian, into exile.   Holy Thomas ! be instant to-
" gether with us—by thee, let us be remembered, Holy
" Rabbulas,—by thee, Holy Cyril, let us be remem-
" bered.   They,† it was, who established Orthodoxy.
" Ibas and Nestorius depraved it—they have de-
" praved (the Faith of) the Synod of Ephesus—the
" writings of Nestorius have been found with Ibas
" —the writings of Theodore‡ have been found with
" Ibas.   This man has violated your Edict, (O Empe
" rors).   All the City knows that—all the people suppli-
" cate this (viz.)—wipe this man out of the Diptychs.§

* The CCCXVIII—τὸ τῶν τριακοσίων δεκαστῶν σύμβολοι —mean
the 318 Fathers of the Great Council of Nicæa in 325 A.D.

¶ Or, " to Theodosius numerous or increasing victories."

† At the General Council of Ephesus 431 A.D. when The True
Faith was re-affirmed and re-established, and Nestorius and others like
him deposed.

‡ Ibas was a disciple of Theodore of Mopsuestia as well as of Diodore of
Tarsus, and translated their books.   The Edict of the Emperor forbade
the Faithful even the possession of the writings of Heretics.

§ The Diptychs were the Holy Books, from which the Deacon read
out the names of Bishops, Martyrs, &c., called so from being folded together.   To erase the names either of men or of Councils out of these

"Another Bishop for the Metropolis—we will not
"receive this man—nobody wants a Magician—no-
"body wants a (common) driver*—nobody receives
"a driver (for a Bishop).   He took for his own
"clothing the sacred vestments† (preserved) in (the
"Church of) S. Barlaha.‡   Abraham§ of Kirkis
"(Circesium) ordained him (Priest).   Holy Eliades be
"Bishop for (our) City—Flavian be Bishop for the

Diptychs was the same thing as to declare that they were Heretical, says Bingham, Book XV.   The above Theodore's name was
struck out after his death, about whom see more further on.   The
largest number of names ever inserted at once in the Church's Diptychs
were the 16,000 of that innumerable host of Martyrs who, in the great
persecution of Christians by Sapor the Persian King who may be ranked
with Pharaoh or Antiochus Epiphanes in hostility to the Church, laid
down their lives for Christ's sake.   Asseman writes—Imperatoris Justin-
iani Dei amantis cura providentiaque factum est ut Sanctæ quatuor Synodi
Ecclesiæ Diptychis adscriberantur : Nicæna, viz., Constantinopolitana,
Ephesina prima et Chalcedonensis (Vol. I., Chron. Edes. LXXXVIII.).

* The word ܗܢܝܘܟܐ ἡνίοχος, auriga probably represents any unfit,
unqualified, person.   This very word is used of Ibas in Appendix E.
Hoffman seems to make jockey of it.

† The word ܐܘܬܒܐ may be one or more of the ὀθόνια linteamenta,
coverings, or palls of fine Linen connected with the Sacrament of the
Altar.   Bingham (Bk. VIII., c. VI., s. 21) mentions another man
Proculus, as having done what is here attributed to Ibas.

‡ The Church of Barlaha (ܒܪܐܠܗܐ, Son of God) at Edessa is recorded, see Asseman (Vol. I., B. O, p. 416), in the Chronicle of
Edessa, thus :—Ex hoc sæculo migravit Mar Andreas Episcopus, et
conditus est in æde S. Barlahæ propè ossa Mar Nonni et Mar Asclepi ;
eique subrogatus Adæus, Edessam ingressus est die 28 Augusti Anni 844.

ܘܐܬܩܒܪ ܗܘܐ ܓܢܒ ܟܬܝܟܐ ܕܠܐ ܡܪܢܘܣܝܘܣ ܘܒܝܬ ܢܘܢܝ ܐܦܣ

ܘܥܠ ܐܣܟܡ . ܘܗܘܐ ܦܩܘܕܝܗ ܣܘܒܩܘ ܐܕܝ

§ The Bishop Abraham is mentioned more than once in the Acts of
Chalcedon Council, 451 A.P.   Here is the IVth Charge as given by
Labbe :—Abraamus quondam diaconus nostri cleri fuit.   Hic, Joanne
quodam malifico deprehenso, cujus amicus est et conscius coram reve-
rendis. Ep. nostro et omni clero convocato ad Audientiam Abra-

"City—Dagalaiphas be Bishop for the City.   Grant
"one of these three for the City — these are
"Orthodox men.   The whole City desiderates this.
"Ibas to the mines—Ibas into exile—no man re-
"ceives such an one as he for Bishop.   An Orthodox
"Bishop for the Metropolis.   Those who judge
"in favour of Ibas into exile.   Basil, the Arch-
"deacon, into exile — Abraham, the hospitaller,*
"(inspector of hospitals) into exile—Isaac and
"Cajumas, (the one belonging to) the Decani and
"(the other to) the sub-Decani,† depravers, into
"exile — Notarius, and Hypatius, and Theodo-
"sius, Sub-Decani, into exile.   Maronius,‡ the

ami diaconi, monstratum(a) est eodem confitente conscium esse, ut
pænam sustinuerit excommunicationis, et omnibus odio fuerit, et omnium
insectationi patuerit multo tempore.   Post hæc (neximus quomodo per-
suasus) satisfactione ab eo nullatenus proveniente, tentavit eum Batanorum
civitatis ordinare Episcopum et prohibitus ab eo, qui tunc Archidiaconus
erat, indignatus est.   Et hunc quidem, qui morti erat obnoxius, apud
semetipsum decrevit esse Episcopum.   Illum vero qui turbam(b) incitav-
erat civitatis, et dixit justum non esse hoc fieri, removit de proprio loco,
et excommunicavit, et expulit ab ecclesia.   Et quia de Episcopo ei non
processit, compulsus est eum facere xenodochum.   Et retinet chartam
magicarum incantationum reverendiss. Epis. noster, qui debuit ad judicem
provinciæ(c) hunc, qui ita execrabilis est, offerre secundum consuetudi-
nem(d) legum.

* Dr. R. Payne Smith, in his Thesaurus Syriacus, p. 185 defines the
Syriac word thus—" is cujus fidei commissum est quicquid ad ægrotos in
hospitio."

† These Decani and Sub-Decani were inferior officers of the Church
who took care of corpses (Oxford Fleury, Vol. I., p. 279), or Sacris-
tans.   The word is |ܡܝܠܐ, in the Original Document.

‡ Maronius, Deacon, is mentioned in the Petition for Ibas (Chal.
Act. X).   Here is his subscription at that Council :—Μαρώνης διάκονος πεποίημαι τὴν διδασκαλίαν ταύτην ἅμα ἑτέροις   In Latin it is—

(a) Convictus est ipso confitente conscius esse, adeo ut.
(b) Sermonem qui in civitate jactabatur, indicaverat, ac dixerat justum.
(c) Crimen deferre secundum.
(d) Consequentiam.

"Deacon, into exile—the writings of Nestorius were
"found in this man's possession—those (writings
"which) Bishop Ibas (well) knew.   Abbas,
"Presbyter, the Nestorian, into exile—this man is
"an abettor of the evil.   Babbai, and Barzumas,
"and Balasch,* Persians, into exile—these men have
"been the cause of miseries.   Let our Sovereigns
"be informed of that.   Holy Rabbulas! expel Ibas
"—Holy Rabbulas! intercede together with us.   Our
"Sovereigns be ever victorious.   Our Lord!
"ever have pity on us."

The COUNT said :—

It would be a rash act and one fraught with danger
for us persistently to trouble the Glorious and Most
Noble Authorities about these same affairs; for,
you yourselves must be well aware it was (only)

Maronius Diaconus similiter (i.e. feci hanc suggestionem) simul cum
ceteris.

* Balasch, if the same as Ballius, is mentioned in the Vth of the
Crimina (p. 35). He and Barzumas and Babbai seem to have held important positions in the Persian College at Edessa, and to have propagated
Nestorianism in Persia.   These and the after-named persons num-
bering 51, and consisting of 10 Presbyters, 20 Deacons, and
9 Sub-Deacons, and 12 Monks, forming an important though a
small part of the Catholic Church at Edessa, and the partizans of Ibas
who are not enumerated, and many of his enemies who are passed over in
silence, and the Schools or Colleges constituting the University of Edessa
for the education of Persian, Syrian, and Armenian youth are evidence of
the growth of The Truth and, in their degree, of the strong hold The Faith
had gained over men's minds in the extensive region of Osrhoene and its
neighbourhood and afford us an insight into the victories the Church had
obtained over some of the strong holds of Heathendom up to the middle of
the 5th Century, from Apostolic days when S. Thaddæus, the Brother
of the Apostle Thomas, first proclaimed That Truth to King Agbarus
and established that Church among his people of Edessa.

K

yesterday* that I assented to your request (Pe-
tion) and drew up the Anaphoræ (Reports,
two of them) — the one indeed for the High
and Exalted Throne and the other for the Glori-
·ous Master (of divine Offices).   I have not, therefore,
failed to make known to the Great and Powerful Authorities your wishes.¶   How is it, then, that,
as though you had forgotten what was done *yesterday, to-day* you come again, and you re-
quest¶ a (re-)presentation of them (to the
Authorities) ?

MICALLUS, Presbyter, replied :--

Beseeming and proper is that (pronounced) will of
the Tribunal, and we eulogize in every respect Your
Highness.   Still, seeing that but a few days have
elapsed—for the Anaphoræ (Reports) were despatched
(only) *yesterday*—we have (to-day) now brought this
Petition which has been read, praying and adjuring
you, by the dread Oath to the Almighty God and
His Christ and His Holy Spirit, and by the victory
of our Gracious Lords, the Flavians, Theodosius and
Valentinian, the ever-August, to notify this our
Petition to the Most Noble Authorities as the (only)
means of putting an end to the agitation that has
overtaken the City and the Holy Church and what-

---

* Yesterday would be April, the 10th.   The Count was evidently
fearful of importuning his Superiors too much.

¶ Or, those circumstances (in the Reports) proceeding from you.

¶ Or, " To present to me nearly the same Report."

ever comes upon us every day on account of this
same affair (about Ibas).

The COUNT continued :—

As regards the Oath (Adjuration) you now proffer, is it with the goodwill of the entire body of
the Venerable Persons who are now here present,
that you have proffered it ?

MICALLUS, Presbyter, rejoined :—

It is assuredly with the goodwill of all the Venerable Presbyters and Deacons and of all the Clerics
and of the Monks, that I have presented this Petition (Instruction), as well as the Oath which I
proffered ; and I beg that, while now standing, they
will say that it was for this purpose that we approached this Tribunal.

The COUNT said :—

Let each person say what he chooses as to that
which the Eloquent and Venerable Presbyter has
mentioned.

8 (*a*) ASTERIUS, Presbyter, said :—

It is with my consent that the Venerable Micallus,
Presbyter, presented this Petition ; and the selfsame
Oath (as he did) I proffer to your Highness.

(*b*) PATROINUS, Presbyter, said :—

The same Oath I also proffer to your Highness ;

and the Petition the Venerable Micallus, Presbyter, presented with my goodwill.

(c) EULOGIUS, Presbyter, said :—

With my goodwill the Venerable Micallus presented the Petition, and I proffer the same Oath.

(d) URSICINUS, Presbyter, said :—

With my goodwill the Venerable Micallus has presented the Instruction, and the Oath to your Highness ; and I also proffer the self same.

(e) ZOURA, Presbyter, said :—

I present this Oath to your Highness ; that Oath and Petition the Venerable Micallus, Presbyter, presented with my goodwill also.

(f) JAMES, Presbyter, said :—

It was with my goodwill that the Venerable Micallus, Presbyter, presented the Petition and the Oath ; and the same Oath I, likewise, proffer to your Highness.

(g) EULOGIUS, Presbyter, said :—

With the common goodwill the Venerable Micallus presented the Petition and the Oath.

(h) SAMUEL, Presbyter, said : —

And I present the Oath to your Highness ; for the Venerable Micallus, also with my good presented the Petition and the Oath, (*i*) BASSUS, Presbyter, said :—

With our goodwill the Venerable Micallus presented the Petition and the Oath; and the same Oath I myself, also, proffer to your Highness.

9 (*a*) SABBATIUS, Deacon, said :—

With our goodwill the Venerable Micallus presented the Petition and the Oath; I also proffer myself the same Oath to your Potency.

(*b*) MARAS, Deacon, said :—

With our goodwill the Venerable Micallus presented to your Highness the Petition and the Oath ; and I myself proffer the Oath, also.

(*c*) JOHN, Deacon, said :—

With the goodwill of us all was the Petition and the Oath presented to your Highness by the Venerable Micallus ; and the same Oath I present also.

(*d*) SABBAS, Deacon, said :—

I likewise present the same Oath to your Highness. The Petition and the Oath with our goodwill the Venerable Micallus presented.

(*e*) PATRICIUS, Deacon, said :—

With our common goodwill the Petition and the Oath were presented to your Highness by the Venerable Micallus ; and I present myself the same Oath.

(*f*) CYRUS, Deacon, said :—

With my goodwill the Venerable Micallus presented the Oath ; I also myself present the Oath.

(*g*) ABRAHAM, Deacon, said :—

And I present the Oath to your Highness ; and with our common goodwill likewise the Venerable Micallus presented the Petition and the Oath.

(*h*) HYPATHIUS, Deacon, said :—

With our common goodwill the Venerable Micallus presented the Petition and the Oath, and I myself present the Oath, also.

(*i*) EUSEBIUS, Deacon, said :—

With our goodwill the Petition and the Oath were presented by the Venerable Micallus ; and I also present the Oath.

(*j*) PAUL, Deacon, said :—

With the goodwill of us all the Venerable Micallus presented the Petition and the Oath, and I also present the Oath myself.

(*k*) ROMANUS, Deacon, said :—

Of the goodwill of us all the Document and the Oath were presented by the Venerable Micallus ; and the Oath I also myself present to your Highness.

(*l*) CYRUS, Deacon, said :—

And I present myself the Oath to your Highness ;

both the Document and the Oath with the goodwill of us all presented the Venerable Micallus.

(*m*) MARONIUS, Deacon, said :—

With the common goodwill the Venerable Micallus presented the Document ; both the Oath and the Document I also myself present.

(*n*) THOMAS, Deacon, said :—

And I proffer the Oath to your Highness ; for the Petition and the Oath Micallus also presented.

(*o*) LUCIAN, Deacon, said :—

This Oath I proffer to your Highness ; for with our goodwill the Document and the Oath the Venerable Micallus presented likewise.

(*p*) ABRAHAM, Deacon, said :—

With our goodwill the Petition and the Oath presented the Venerable Micallus ; and I also proffer the Oath to your Powerfulness.

(*q*) PAUL, Deacon said :—

It is with our goodwill that the Petition and the Oath were presented by the Venerable Micallus, and the Oath I also proffer to your Highness.

(*r*) MARAS, Deacon, said :—

It is with our common goodwill that the Venerable Micallus presented the Petition and the Oath to your Highness.

(s) EUPHRODANIUS, Deacon, said :—

And I proffer the Oath to your Highness; with our goodwill the Oath was also proffered to your Highness by the Venerable Micallus.

(t) SABBAS, Deacon, said :—

I also proffer the Oath to your Powerfulness; for, what Micallus said, he said with our goodwill.

10 (a) CALLISTRATUS, Sub-Deacon (said) :—

I, likewise, present the Petition to your Highness, as well as the Oath.

(b) EUPORUS, Sub Deacon :—

I present to your Highness the Petition and the Oath.

(c) ANTHONY, Sub Deacon :—

The Petition and the Oath I present to your Highness.

(d) MARAS, Sub-Deacon :—

I, too, give the same instructions and present the same Oath.

(e) ELIAS, Sub-Deacon :—

The Petition and the Oath I present to your Highness.

(f) MARAS, Sub-Deacon :—

The Petition and the Oath 1 present to your

Highness.

(*g*) EUSEBIUS, Sub-Deacon :—
I do the same ; and, whilst I offer the same Peti-tion, I present the Oath.

(*h*) THOMAS, Sub-Deacon :—
I, too, present the Petition and the Oath.

(*i*) PACIDAS, Sub-Deacon :—
I, likewise, present the Petition.

11 (*a*) ELIAS, Monk :—
It was with our goodwill (in our name) that the Venerable Micallus presented the Petition and the Oath to your Highness ; and that Petition and Oath we ourselves, likewise, now present.

(*b*) JAMBLICUS, Monk :—
We, too, (now) ourselves present the same Petition to your Highness ; and the Oath and the Petition were with our goodwill presented by the Venerable Micallus.

(*c*) HABIB, Monk :—
It was with my goodwill that the Oath and Peti-tion were presented by the Venerable Micallus, and I (now), also, myself proffer the Oath.

(*d*) DIANIUS, Monk :—
I, likewise, proffer the same Oath to your Highness, whilst I (at the same time hereby) certify that it was

L

with our goodwill that the Venerable Micallus presented the Petition and Oath.

(e) ABRAHAM, Monk :—
    With our goodwill it was that the Venerable Mi-
callus presented the Petition and Oath ; and I myself (now) proffer the Oath.

(f) EUPORUS, Monk :—
    This Petition I, likewise, tender to your High-
ness, and the Oath.

(g) SIMEON, Monk :—
    The same I say, too, profferring the Oath referred to.

(h) ELIAS, Monk : —
    This Petition I, likewise, myself present, as well
as the Oath, to your Highness.

(i) ASTERIUS, Monk :—
    The same from me also, whilst (at the same time)
I proffer the formidable Oath.

(j) ABRAHAM, Monk :—
    I, too, present myself the Document to your
Highness, as well as the Oath.

(k) ANDREW, Monk :—
    The same I likewise pray, proffering (at the same
time) the formidable Oath.

12 FLAVIUS THOMAS JULIANUS CHERÆAS, Count of
the First Rank, said :—

Although I felt indisposed to yield to your*
Petitions (Instances),—(Petitions) written and unwritten — I am compelled to it by the formidable Oath, which has been proffered by you, in
which invocation is made to the Consubstantial
(co-essential) Trinity and to the Mystery of Redemption and to the Victory of the Masters of the
World.   1 will, therefore, now proceed and notify to the Crowned and Glorious Auditory (of the
Emperors) your behests.

---

* "Instances." As a term of Law no doubt the Syriac expression
may be so rendered, but ordinarily *urgency, entreaty, prayer*. The words
ܠܩܘܡ ܠܡܥܕܐ of course refer to the Petitions, written and unwritten,
the latter of which may be designated Instructions. In p. 49 of my
Syriac Text, ܐ should be added to the end of the 1st line, though it is
omitted in the MS., and erased from that of the 5th, while it is correctly retained at the end of the 24th, in the word signifying Notification.
Of the two terms Consubstantial or Co-essential the latter is decidedly
to be preferred.
We may make a short pause here both to invite the Reader to remember that it is in the assembled Council that these various Documents are
read and to note here the several points in this great trial going on at this
tribunal of the Church. It was a business, not like that which took
place at the Synod assembled at Berytus, Tyre, and Antioch, in consequence of complaints emanating from private individuals. The complaints
here preferred have been dealt with by the Civil Governor of a Roman Province through the influence and at the solicitation, probably, of the great
Eutychian party and by order of the Roman Government. The complainants, Ecclesiastical and Lay, had formulated their Libels or Acts of
Accusation and presented them to that Governor (Cheræas) at Edessa, who
had forwarded these Documentary Acts, &c., preceding them by his Formal
Report. And now, in the Council assembled in August, 449 A.D., these
Documents are read, and discussed, and dealt with in the way we now
read of in this, hitherto unknown, because undiscovered, Syriac Manu-
script numbered 14,530 among the Additional Manuscripts in the British
Museum, which MS. we designate A in Vol. I,

[C]

[SECOND FORMAL ENQUIRY.]

THE THIRD REPORT.

(1) To The Great and Glorious FLAVIUS MARTIA-
LIUS,* Count and Master of divine Offices,
, FLAVIUS CHERÆAS (offers) Salutation.

¶The Power of our Emperors, Illustrious by Victory and Invincible, your Piety and the zeal of our
humble person have prevented the Metropolis of
Edessa from forfeiting (falling from) the rank of
City : but a bad Demon (evil Genius) has caused
there a (horrible) conflagration, as our humble self

---

* Flavius Areobindas Martialis (or Martialius).   In the text it
is Martilalius. In Mansi he is designated—magnificentissimus comes
et Magister (magistratus) sacrorum Officiorum.   As Chancellor of the
Imperial Palace at Constantinople he had the superintendence of all the
Offices of the Imperial Household and, by that very position, possessed
an immense influence at Court.   Under this Μαγιστρος τῶν Θείων
ὀφφικιών were the Μαγιστριανοι—some of them address the Council
soon—who ranked as the Officers and Agents of Martialius in the Roman Provinces.   See Du Cange's "Glossarium´ mediæ et infimæ
Latinitatis," 1V., p. 179.   We have now
arrived at the 3rd part of the whole Report, which part begins
with the letter addressed by the Roman Governor of Osrhoene to the
Chancellor of the Empire, in which the former brings afresh the troubles
at Edessa, recommencing and threatening the public peace, to the cognizance of the Military Commandant, because he believes the latter alone
competent to terminate the popular agitation. This letter precedes this
3rd Report in the same way, in which Cheræas's letter to Romanus
Protogenes and the Eparchs, its receivers, precedes the 2nd Report in
which are recorded the formal Libels or Acts of arraignment, against
Bishop Ibas, adopted by the Clerks and Inhabitants of Edessa.

¶ This whole passage may be rendered, perhaps, more literally thus :
—The Imperial Authority of our Sovereigns, Illustrious by Victory and
Invincible, the fear of you, and the solicitude of our Humbleness, have

apprized you of before, by the Notification which was despatched to your Highness. (All happened), then, as I informed you ; but now, in order to extinguish the new flames there is nothing less required than the authority of your (all)-powerful name ; for, everyone in the City proclaims loudly that this trouble will only end, when you yourself, on being informed of it, put a stop to what is going on. I felt reluctant, by writing, to annoy your Highness, but it has appeared to me that the

prevented the Metropolis of Edessa hitherto from forfeiting its rank among the number of Cities. For, an evil Demon excited in it a (terrific) conflagration, as I also at first made known to your Highness in a Notification* despatched from my Humbleness. Indeed, at that time and now, too, it was, as I said, nothing else whatever that could avail to extinguish it, save only your great and (all)-powerful name ; for, everybody of all classes of society perpetually exclaims that there is no means of appeasing the excitement stirred up, except that *you*, having been informed of it, should yourself give the matter its determination. And, although I was unwilling to write and trouble your Highness, yet it seemed to me that this was the sole healing and remedy for the calamities that have overtaken this City (viz.), that the occurrences should be brought to your knowledge. Accordingly, I have described with exactitude in what manner and from what causes these seditious movements took place, and I have despatched a Report which will afford you information of what you ought to be acquainted with. When the City, having for a moment recovered its order, was enjoying quiet and acting as usual, after some very few days had elapsed, again did the evil Demon set itself about (re-)kindling the extinguished conflagration : and it will devastate everything, unless you are found competent to (re-)extinguish the flame by those injunctions (naturally) expected from you and by (the help of) those most qualified. The mischief resulting from these clamours will not be restrained, unless, again, on your being apprized of them, you will apply the remedy to them.

Now, all those (present) occurrences, as well as the past which I have already notified to your Exalted Throne, arise from the hatred and great enmity entertained towards the Venerable Bishop Ibas whose Episcopate

---

* This Notification does not accompany the other Documents in these Acts, i.e. in MS. designated by A.

only means of healing and remedying the evils
which have overtaken this City, was to bring the
occurrences under your notice.   I have, therefore, stated carefully how, and by whom, all this
tumult has been excited, and I have sent you a
Report which will enlighten you (instruct you thoroughly).   After having for a moment regained
its habitual tranquillity, the City was, some days
afterwards, (brought anew into uproar) by a bad
Demon, who has done his best to revive the extinguished fire; and now this conflagration will destroy
everything, if you do not succeed in extinguishing a
second time the flames, by the orders which we
(naturally) expect from you and by the co-operation
of those most competent (to give it).   The evil resulting from all this clamour will not be extirpated
(removed), before you, on being apprized of it,
administer a remedy.   How has all this, and
all that which I have already brought under the
notice of your exalted Throne, been brought about ?
It is through the hatred and great enmity, by which
Ibas is prosecuted : no one will have him as Bishop

---

and Pastoral charge they repudiate, even though all the inhabitants of the
City should have to enter the fire (for doing so) ; since there is no evil
thing they decline to say or do, on only his name being mentioned.   But
no more of this ; for, I consider it would not be without peril for me to
(afflict) trouble your ever-wise ear with anything superfluous, (especially)
as the Report (Instruction) made at the time and appended below, will
enable you to become thoroughly acquainted with all that has transpired
in this matter, Noble and, in every way, Glorious Lords !

That my Illustrious and Glorious Lords (so) beneficial to the community, may ever enjoy good health is my frequent prayer to God,
Noble and Glorious Lords !

and Pastor : the inhabitants of the City (of Edessa) would prefer going through the fire (rather than receive him again as such). There is nothing so bad but they say it and do it, at the mere mentioning of his name. But enough of this, since it would not be without danger, if I wearied your ever-wise ear with anything superfluous. Moreover, from the annexed Reports you will be able to obtain an accurate knowledge of all that has transpired, Noble, and, in all respects, Glorious Lord!

May you always continue in good health, Masters and Benefactors of Society. I wish you many years of life, Noble and Glorious Lords.

(2) Copy of Records of procedure adopted at the City of Edessa (against Ibas) in the presence of the Civic Dignities, among whom is the Count Theodosius, and (in the presence of) the Clergy, named above, of the Church of the same Edessa, and of the Monks, &c.

The same Count Theodosius said :—

¶In order to put a stop to the recurrence of all commotion in the Metropolis, I have been obliged to have recourse to this Instruction (Petition). For, after

---

¶ Or, it may be translated thus—In order to stop the recurrence of all commotion in the Metropolis, I have been compelled to have recourse to this (Instruction) Petition. For, after all the City had assembled in the Holy Church* yesterday which is the Holy Day of the Week (Sunday),

---

* This Church would, no doubt, be the great one at Edessa, of which much mention is made in Asseman's Bibliotheca Orientalis. *Yesterday* would be April 17th, 449 A.D.

all the City had assembled in the Church yesterday
which is the Holy Day (Sunday) of the Week, and
when everybody had asked for the (formal) charges preferred against Ibas, who was the Bishop, to be made
publicly known ; the Service having terminated, your
Highness was obliged to proceed to the Holy Church,
in order to extinguish any spark of disturbance.   I
was, also, obliged to go there myself in order, by all

---

and when all had asked for the (formal) charges, preferred against Ibas
who had been Bishop, to be made publicly known, the Service having
ceased, your Highness was obliged to proceed to the Holy Church in
order to stifle all commotion.   I was likewise obliged to go, to the end
that, by every means, peace might accrue to the City.   All those persons, however, who were assembled together could, with difficulty, be induced to preserve silence, when your Highness promised that I should go
the very next day to enquire into the matter.   And I, too, promised
them in conjunction with your Highness the same, with the view of our
allaying the agitation.   Nevertheless, things are still in the City in a state
of confusion ; and your Highness will perceive that we can not be allowed to enjoy quiet and repose in our homes.   In sight of this spectacle
I am myself more especially regardful of what had been previously enjoined by him who is in every way the Great and Powerful General of
the East and the Ex-Consul who, solicitous for the peace of the City,
gave (peremptory) order for the whole disturbance to cease.   For this
reason I am obliged, in consequence of the commotions that have taken
place, to offer this Instruction (Petition) to your Supreme Highness, in
order to render it possible for you, as I believe it will, to allay the commotions that have been going on ; and I have proceeded to draw up this
Document with the common consent of the entire community of Clerks,
and Abbats, and Vowed Persons, as well as of the Civic Magistrates and
other Proprietors who now stand here, whereby I entreat your Highness
to repress the turbulence of the people, and to give order that the commotions that have been going on must terminate.   For, these occurrences
have arisen in consequence of the categorical charge preferred against
Bishop Ibas at the City of Berytus, whereby the people learnt that he is
inimical to the Orthodox Faith and has given utterance to a great deal of
Blasphemy.
    I pray, therefore, your Highness, in order to the termination of these
evils (unfortunate occurrences) to compel those his (Ibas's) accusers now
standing here to state what the deeds are that he has committed, and
what are the charges preferred against him, and under what counts he was

possible means, to restore peace in the City : it was
not, without difficulty, that we succeeded in silencing
the assembly ; your Highness (knows it, for you)
had to promise to investigate the matter the next
morning.   I myself, also, made the same promise, as
your Highness, for the purpose of putting an end to
the tumult, (and still) the City is all astir yet.
Your Highness is perfectly aware that it is impossible for us to enjoy quiet (peace) in our own homes,
whilst having this scene before our very eyes ; and
remembering the Orders, given before by the Ex-
Consul, the High and Powerful General of the East,
(and) desirous of putting a stop to this agitation in
the City—(seeing it, I say myself)—I have considered
it my bounden duty to present to your Highness
this Petition which seems to me to be calculated
to appease all.   I submit it to you in the name of the
community, (that is) of all the Clerics, the Abbats, and
the Vowed Persons, as well as of the Magistrates and

---

convicted.*   For, since I have been requested by the High Dignitaries
and by the Noblemen Curial, as well as by Venerable Clergy and Abbats
and by the Artizans here present (and I am myself equally anxious with
hem to repress the state of confusion† which breaks out (bursts forth)
daily about The Faith and threatens to become universal), I have therefore presented the Petition, and I request all those persons (mentioned
above) to say if the case is, as I state it.

---

* The word ܝܨܪܐ seems to be classed under the 2nd meaning of
ܝܨܪ *subegit*, if not *prosecutus est*, or ܝܨܪ Naser *deprehendit* (in Dr. R. P.
Smith's Thesaur. Syr.).

† In my text p. 54, l. 3 is exactly given a fac-simile of, as the Scribe
has written, the word with the stroke for correction. In line 4 ܡܚܒܠ
which generally signifies πονηρευειν, or *dolosè egit*, and can hardly mean *consentiens* as one would at first suppose, is fem. part. agreeing with ܟܢܘܫܬܐ.

M

of the rest of Proprietors,—in short, in the name
of all the inhabitants of Edessa—here present.

Thereby I pray your Highness to repress the
violence of the people and to put an end to the tumult which the Accusation made against Bishop Ibas,
in the City of Berytus, has occasioned, through which
the people have learnt that he is no longer Orthodox,
that he has uttered a host of Blasphemies, (and) that
he has committed many acts subversive of the Laws
and adverse to the Christian Faith.

For the termination, therefore, of these disas-
trous occurrences, I beseech your Highness to compel Ibas's accusers here present to tell us what
has occurred, what charges have been made against
the Bishop, and on what counts he has been convicted. So, requested by the High Dignitaries, the
Noble Magistrates, the God-fearing Clergy and Archimandrites, and the Artizans here present, and,
eager for the repressing of this commotion about
The Faith which breaks out (afresh) every day and
threatens to become universal, I now present to
you this Petition and request those present to say, if
things are such (as I have stated).

(3) Flavius Thomas Julianus Cheræas, the Count,
    said :—

Now that you have heard what the High and
Glorious Count Theodosius has said—those who are
standing here—(I mean) the Noble and Illustrious
personages, as likewise the Venerable and God-

loving Presbyters, and the Dignitaries (Curial) of this Metropolis, and the Venerable Monks—let them make known, if they wish, their opinion by means of their depositions.

(a) Count EULOGIUS replied :—

It is with the (particular) desire of all of us the Notables of the City, and the Clerics, and the Monks, as well as of the inhabitants of this City, as he has stated, that his Highness, the Glorious Count Theodosius, has presented this Petition.

(b) FAUSTINUS, a Magistrian, said :—

I also admit the same (viz.), that it is by my desire, and that of the whole City, that his Excellency, the Glorious Count Theodosius, has presented the Petition.

(c) THEODORE, a Magistrian, said :—

It is by my consent, and by that of all those who are now present, that the Petition has been presented by his Excellency, the Glorious Count Theodosius.

(d) The Venerable Micallus, the Presbyter, said :—

We all of us requested his Excellency, the Glorious Count Theodosius, to supplicate this of your Highness, and we regard it as a gracious act (on his part) that he consented to our request.

(e) RHODONIUS, and ZOARAS, and ISAAC, and ASTERIUS, and PATROINUS, and the other Venerable

Presbyters, said :—

We all requested of his Excellency, the Glorious Count Theodosius, to present, on our behoof, this Petition to your Highness.

(*f*) ABRAHAM, and MARTYRIUS, and LUCIANUS, and SABBATIUS, and the rest of the Venerable Deacons, said :—

We, all of us, too, prayed his Excellency, the Glorious Count Theodosius, to present, on our behoof, this Petition to your Highness.

(*g*) JOHN, and CALLISTRATUS, and MARAS, and THOMAS, and EULOGIUS, and the rest of the Sub-Deacons, said :—

By all of us was his Excellency, the Glorious Count Theodosius, supplicated to present this Petition to your Highness.

(*h*) JAMBLICUS, and ELIAS, and DIAS, and ABRAHAM, and EPHRAIM, and other Venerable Monks, said :—

By us, likewise, his Excellency, the Glorious Count Theodosius, was requested to present this Petition to your Clemency.

(*i*) CONSTANTINE, and JOHN, and SERGIUS, and the rest of the Vowed Persons, said :—

On his Excellency, the Glorious Count Theodosius, being supplicated by us, he presented the Petition to your Highness.

(*j*) Constantius said :—

I, likewise, attest that it is with the good pleasure of the entire City that his Excellency, Count Theodosius, presented the Petition to your Highness.

(*k*) Bias said :—

We prayed his Excellency, the Glorious Count, to present this Petition on our behalf.

(*l*) Gainas said :—

I, too, along with my compeers and the whole City, prayed his Excellency, the Glorious Count Theodosius, to present the Petition to your Highness.

(*m*) Asclepius said :—

Having been requested by all the City together and by its Principals, the Glorious Count Theodosius presented the Petition to your Clemency.

(*n*) Andrew said :—

On being requested by us and everybody, his Excellency, Count Theodosius, presented in place of us this Petition to your Potency.

(*o*) Eusebius said :—

Exactly as my compeers have stated it, so the case is. For, being entreated by everybody to do it, his Excellency, the Count Theodosius, presented the Petition to your Highness.

(*p*) Prince (Chief) Aurelian said :—

I, likewise, make the same affirmation.

(*q*) ABGARUS, Law-Advocate,* said :—

His Excellency, the Glorious Count Theodosius, received our expressed desire (for this purpose) ; and his Highness, acting in a manner worthy of himself, presented the Petition to your Highness.

(*r*) DEMOSTHENES said :—

The case is just as the Noble Civilians have informed (you). For, it was at the prayer of all together that his Excellency, the Glorious Count Theodosius, presented the Petition to your Highness.

(*s*) PALLAD(IUS) said :—

What has (just) been said by my compeers is the truth ; for, it is in compliance with the prayer made to his Excellency, the Glorious Count Theodosius, that he consented to present this Petition, in conformity with the Laws, to your Highness.

(4) The JUDGE said :—

An obligation, as it appears to me, manifestly attaches to your Highness, (viz.) that you, by your Deposition, should also make known the names of those Venerable Presbyters who (personally) participated in the presentment and indictment.

---

* "Law-Advocate"—σκολαστικος. In his Thesaurus Syriacus Dr. Payne Smith quotes J. Bar-Bahlulis Lexicon Syro-Arab,, under ܐܣܟܘܠܣܛܝܩܐ as giving two meanings, (1) *judex*, (2) *qui sapientiæ studet*, &c., adding, ܗܘ ܕܚܟܡ ܘܒܕܝܢܐ ܕܪܘܡܝܐ ܐܝܬ ܥܡ ܗ . ܘܩܦܣܝܘܙ: ܕܝܢܐ ܡܬܩܪܐ ܒܝܕ ܕܝܢܐ ܕܪܘܡܝܐ ܘܥܠ ܡܥܒܕܐ. dignitas fuit in imperio Romanorum, cujus munus fuit sententiam et pœnas statuere in malefactores.

The Count THEODOSIUS replied :—

They are the Venerable Presbyters, Samuel, Maras, and Cyrus.

The JUDGE said :—

Now that the Venerable Clergy have (just) heard what has been said by his Excellency, the Glorious Count Theodosius, (let them state), according to their own pleasure, what they wish.

(5) The Venerable SAMUEL, Presbyter, said :—

Far superior to our Deposition, and far more worthy of credit, would be testimony of the person who has adjudicated in the matter in pursuance of the commands of the Gracious and Christ-loving Emperors. Now, that person is the God-fearing Uranius. He is not, however, present here at this moment. But, perhaps, on account of this very cause he has been obliged to repair to the Emperors and inform them of the negotiations.   Besides, there is likewise absent one of us—the Venerable Eulogius ; so that about this same business there have come, then, hither three persons (complainants), of whom I am one.   Now, this much I state in a Deposition (viz.) that, after enduring all sorts of hardships everywhere and suffering from intrigues connected with the Bishop Ibas, and on account of his chicane and his habit of everywhere scattering gold abroad for the condemnation of The Truth,* it was

---

* (i.e., in order to get a verdict contrary to the Orthodox Faith).

with difficulty that we obtained what we desired, on our approaching the Clement Emperor, (with the view) that Judges should be granted us, whose names are the God-fearing Bishop Photius of Tyre, and Eustathius, Bishop of Berytus, and the Holy Uranius, Bishop of Himeria, whom I have just now mentioned ; and, while the matter was conducted before them by Documents, they decided certain points, as it seemed good to them, minutes of which relating to the business were laid up (preserved) with them : which (minutes) we have frequently asked leave to publish, and I do not know for what reason they have refused us leave to have them published. But if we are required now, also, here to plead the cause again before your Excellency, pointing out the origin of the trouble which has thrown confusion into the affairs of the City which suffered (so), and as to which everybody shares in sadness, (then) what we have to say is this—this is no light matter of which we were complainants, as all the Clergy are well aware, and who, I think, would likewise testify to the correctness of our statement. Acting in submission to what the Canons prescribe, we proceeded to the City of Antioch the Great and approached the Archbishop of that City, the Venerable Domnus, presenting to him certain precise counts (of complaint). When he had acquired accurate knowledge of them and perceived that everyone of them (the counts) would bring capital punishment on the offender, he sent us away at his pleasure (about our business).

Subsequently, as we could not get the better of his negligence, we were obliged to proceed to the Royal City and prefer our complaint to the Synod of the West --- I should say, to the Venerable Archbishop Flavian and, similarly, to our Gracious Emperor Theodosius,— bringing not only the same charges as we had preferred at Antioch and presented in authentic Documents, but also in the interest of The Faith (one of Heresy against Ibas). But as regards these heads (of accusation), if your Excellency command it, seeing that we are not able at the present moment to recount all of them before you, (yet) we do proceed to lay before you the order of them, (in which they are arranged in the Depositions).

He (Ibas) was, then, arraigned on a charge of Heresy, in the manner following.

In giving our account of the matter we affirm that in the Hall of the Episcopal Residence, at the time when the Heortastica (gifts on Feast Days) were distributed—for, it was the custom every year, when he presented the Heortastica to the Venerable Clergy, for him to deliver a Homily, and then to distribute his gifts—he (Ibas) said, in the presence of many persons : "I do not envy Christ becoming God : for, "in so far as He has become (God) I have become "so : for, He is of the same nature as myself."*

---

* This remarkable sentence is thus given by Baronius in his Ecclesiastical Annals :—"Non invideo Christo facto Deo : in quantum factus "est, et ipse factus sum ;" Vel ; " Si voluero, et ipse ut ille fieri."

N

Many of the Clergy know, if they fear God, that I immediately testified against him ; and, from that time up to the present, I have never received anything from the Church, nor have I had any communication with him, because I was cognizant of his Blasphemy.

Similarly (they know), too, that I attempted to rise and make a stir, at the very moment, but those, seated by me, would not allow me ; for, they said that there would be a row (scandal). But, after I had descended (from the Triclinium), they questioned me (about it), when I replied to them by calling to their remembrance the fact that he had said so (and so). This he (Ibas) denied in the presence of the Commissioners (Judges) granted (by the Emperor). He even anathematized himself in these terms :— " If I said so, I should have anathematized myself " and deposed myself from the Episcopate."

Although, then, he well knew this,* yet, aiming at justifying himself in this matter with the object of turning aside this accusation,* (in order that he might bring discredit on these men as witnesses), he maintained that they were under censure,† and therefore could not be received as Witnesses according to the Laws.

Whereupon we made reply—" If you excommuni- " cated them for any other reason, you have spoken

---

* (i.e., what my accusation was, and that he had actually uttered those words.)

† Under his ban, i.e., they might not come to the Holy Communion.

" sensibly : but, if it is only done in order that they
" might not be (qualified to) bear witness, just as you
" have excommunicated me because I was your accuser
" —(if your object is) that they may not (formally)
" accuse you, (in that case) they ought to be received
" as Witnesses.　But, if it is for any other cause—and
" an offence was charged against them previously to
" this affair (of your excommunicating them)—(then)
" they ought not to be admitted as Witnesses.
" (Only) say which."

He was unable to assign any other reason than this
sole averment.　He accused (limiting himself to
abusing) the Witnesses, by asserting that "they were
" with you at Constantinople :" and the Judges,
whether as being favourable to him (Ibas) or not, I
cannot say, would not consent so far as to receive
these as Witnesses alone, but refused, affirming that
it was befitting and proper for others also to appear.
It happened, however, by the will of God, that there
came the Venerable Eulogius, Presbyter, son of the
good Hypatius, of worthy memory, on that evening
with the Pious Presbyter James.　Seizing these persons, also, the very next day, we hurried them off to
go to appear and give evidence (before the Judges).
But these, too, the Judges refused to admit, stating
(every time) that it was befitting and proper for others
to be summoned.　To this we have replied at length,
as it is yet contained in the Documentary Acts, in
which is my own averment, that we are treated
wrongfully (in violation of Law), the Laws not

objecting to admit five. Accept, then, either the first ones, or these (the second), or all of us together; but, as that did not please them (the Judges), the matter remained thus in abeyance, as far as that head was concerned. Now, seeing that it is (only) in accordance with justice that those, who did not there make their Depositions, should at least now declare them here in writing, I again request of your Excellency (to demand) of those, also, who were found with us at Berytus, and all those who are cognizant of this count (in the indictment) to state what they know of the matter.

6 The JUDGE said:—

Whatever was said at Berytus by the God-fearing Samuel, the Presbyter, the (Documentary) Acts admit as evidence; but, what these other Venerable Presbyters also have to inform us of, let them declare if they will.

(a) The Venerable MARAS, Presbyter, said:—

That is the case; the chief count was discussed; and we request those, who have knowledge of it, to speak.

(b) The Venerable CYRUS, Presbyter, said:—

Yes: it is so. Let those, who have information on this head, state, with a view to enhance the value of the Acts, what they know.

(c) The JUDGE said:—

There is no bar to any of those who presented themselves at the City of Berytus, or Tyre, when the investigation (of the matter) took place there, (freely) stating whatever they know, if they will.

(d) The Venerable EULOGIUS, Presbyter, said:—

In my presence, together with (that of) my fellow-clergy, in the Bishop's House, Ibas said—"I do not "envy Christ's becoming God; for, I am become so "no less than He, since He is of the same nature as "myself." And I was prepared, on going to Berytus, if I were summoned, to testify to the same fact.

(e) The Venerable MARAS, Deacon, said:—

When I was with my venerable compeers, the Clergy, in the Episcopal Residence, Bishop Ibas said, in the course of a Homily, "I do not envy "Christ's becoming God: for, I am become so no "less than He, since He is of the same nature as "my own." And I bear witness before God and before men (to this fact). And when I was at Berytus, if I had been summoned, I was prepared to give the very same evidence. Moreover, I heard him, when delivering his Homily, (say), "That God the Word, "in His foreknowledge, knew that Christ would "justify Himself by His works, and therefore dwelt "in Him."

(*f*) DAVID, a Venerable Deacon, said:—

In my presence, whilst Bishop Ibas was delivering his Homily, he said, "I do not envy Christ's becom-"ing God; for, I am become so no less than He, "since He is of the same nature as myself." And if I had been summoned at Berytus, when I was there, to testify to that fact, I should not have declined.

(*g*) SAMUEL, Venerable Presbyter, said:—

Some of those who were at Berytus are now far off; for instance, Sabas and James.   There are, however, others among the Venerable Clergy, who equally with them (Sabas and James) have knowledge of this fact; and I request of them to depose in writing and on Oath whatever they know.

7 The JUDGE said:—

Let this be done by all who are cognizant of the circumstances having reference to this business, if agreeable.

(*a*) SAMUEL, Venerable Presbyter, said:—

I request, first of all, that the Venerable Leont(ius), Presbyter, would say, if I did not there and then, when we were sitting near each other, invoke him as Witness and, in the Episcopal House, adjust myself for immediately rising, but was not permitted by him (to do so); and if, after we came down (from the Bishop's House) when I was questioned, I did not tell him all that I have just said.

(b) LEONT(IUS), Venerable Presbyter, replied:—

What the Venerable Samuel, Presbyter, has (just) said, he has said with (perfect) truth. I was present when those words, which are deposed to by my compeers, were spoke by Ibas, (viz.)—"I do not "envy Christ's becoming God, for I am become so "no less than He, because He is of the same nature "as myself."

(c) The Venerable BASSUS said:—

I was present with my colleagues the Venerable Clergy, and heard Ibas say—"I do not envy Christ's "becoming God; for, 1 am become the same, as He "became; since He is of the same nature as my "own."*

(d) EULOGIUS, Deacon, said:—

I was present and heard Ibas say—" I do not envy "Christ's becoming God: for, I am become the same as He became, since He is of my own nature."

(e) URSACINUS, Presbyter, said·—

I heard Ibas say, in the course of a Homily, in the Church, that John the Evangelist has said:—"In the beginning was the Word,"† but Matthew, the Evangelist, has said:—" The Book of the Gene-

---

* Literally, questionless it might be with more correctness rendered, "because He is held in honour and I am held in honour."

† Chap. i, 1.

"ration of Jesus Christ, the Son of Abraham, the
"Son of David:"* and, commenting (on these two
passages), Ibas asked—"Is not the former one thing
"and the latter quite another?"   Again, on
an Easter Day†, he (Ibas) was giving his Exposition on the Bema.‡ when he affirmed—"It is
"to-day Christ became immortal."   And, at another time, in discoursing with Theodotus, a Senator
of very high Rank, on the subject of Hell (Gehenna), he (Ibas) affirmed that—"*that* was written
"(only) as a threat to terrify."¶   And I am certain
of it and heard it from him (himself).

(*f*) The Venerable SABAS, Deacon, said:—

I, likewise, heard Ibas say on the day of the Resurrection: "This day Christ became immortal."

(*g*) BARZUMAS, a Venerable Presbyter, said:—

I heard Ibas say on Easter Day—"This day
"Christ became immortal."   He, likewise, made

---

* Chap. i, 1, He is said to be "the Son of David, the Son of
"Abraham."

† These conferences took place at Edessa, on the 17th and 18th of
April, 448 A.Γ.

‡ *The Bema* (βῆμα from ἀναβαίνω, as also is *ambo*) was here probably the Ambo, or reading desk, whence he delivered his Targum or
Exposition.   The word, says Bingham, is of various significations, at
different times, meaning the Altar—the seats or thrones of the Bishop
and Presbyters—the whole space where those thrones and the Altar
stood (Bk. VIII., Chap. VI.), whence also the Clergy were termed οἱ
τοῦ βήματος and τάξις τοῦ βήματος, "the order of the Bema or the
"Sanctuary."

¶ Or, "that the word Gehenna (Hell) was only a simple trope or
"figure of speech for threatening."

this observation:—"We must discreetly make a dis-
"tinction between God and Man, and make a sepa-
"ration between Him Who was assumed by Grace
"and Him Who assumed Him by Grace."

(*h*) Lucian, Deacon, said:—

I heard Ibas say that "the word Gehenna (Hell)
"occupies only *the place of a threat* (a Metaphor)."
For, I am certain that he has in his possession the
blasphemous writings—blot out the name of Nestorius (for ever).¶

(*i*) Arsenius, Presbyter, said:—

I heard Ibas, when giving his Homily to the
people in the Church, (say)—"the Jews could not
"boast; for, they only crucified a mere man."

(*j*) Abraham, Deacon, said:—

And I heard Ibas say that "the Jews could not
"boast, since they did not crucify God, but a man,
"simply a man."

(*k*) John, a Vowed Person, said:—

I heard Ibas, when expounding in Church, say:—
"It was one Person who died, and another who was
"in Heaven, and that was one Person who was with-
"out beginning, and that was another who is subject
"to a beginning; and He was one Person Who is of

¶ Or, "For I knew that he was in possession of the Impious and
"publicly-proclaimed books of Nestorius," alluding to his name being
erased from the Diptychs. See note p. 70.

o

"the Father, and He was another Who is of the
"Virgin." And he added—"If God were dead,
"who is there to raise Him to life?"

(*l*) The Venerable MARAS, Presbyter, said to Constantine:—

By the God whom you worship, and by the Holy
Trinity, what did you hear (Ibas), in his Homily, say?

(*m*) CONSTANTINE replied:—

By reason of the necessity that is laid on me, in
consequence of the Adjuration (Oath) with which
the Venerable Samuel appealed to me, I will state
that of which I am fully persuaded. The Lord God
of truth knows it: and all those persons, who were
present and heard (him), can also bear me witness
that frequently have I heard him (Ibas), when discoursing, say:—"As the disgrace of the *purple*, as
"soon as it is disgraced, *passes over* to the King, so
"the suffering passes over to God." Often I left
him and went out, and I can have the evidence of
several from the City to (prove) this fact.

(*n*) THEODORUS said:—

Whilst Ibas was discoursing in his own Hall on
Doctrine and was handling the subject of the Resurrection of our Lord Christ, he said that His Body
was not the same before, as after, the Resurrection;
and when I urged as an objection against it—"How,
"then, could Holy Thomas, the Apostle, when

"seized by doubt, have drawn nigh to (touch) His
"(Christ's) side, according to His command, and
"have seen the places, in which the nails were fixed,
"and have heard from our Lord, 'be believing and
"'not unbelieving?'"*   Ibas to this replied that *that*
took place (only) in phantasy.   Astonished, therefore, at such a statement, I went to several Monks,
one by one, to tell them what Bishop Ibas had said.
They replied:—"Let the man, who says so, be ana-
"thema."

(*o*) SERGIUS, one under a Vow, said:—

Always has Ibas been in the habit of making a
division between the Divinity and the Humanity (of
Christ): and often I have, on the Bema, made complaint in reality about it.

(*p*) JAMES, a Monk, said:—

I heard Ibas say:—"The Jews had no reason to
"boast, as if they elevated (on the cross) One Who
"was God; they crucified a (mere) man."

(*q*) SERGIUS, a Vowed Person, said:—

On the Thursday, in the Great Week, at night,
Ibas said:—"The Jews could not boast that they
"crucified God: they did not crucify GOD."

(*r*) ABRAHAM said:—

I, too, heard Ibas say, "The Jews had no cause

---

* John, xx, 27, "Be not faithless, but believing."

"to boast of having crucified God ; for, they cruci-
"fied (only) a man."

(*s*) JOHN, a Vowed Person, said:—

I heard Ibas, as he was going out of the Baptis-
tery, in the evening (at vespers), declare:—"To-day
"Christ became immortal."

(*t*) CONSTANTINE, a Vowed Person, said:—

I, too, heard Ibas, on returning from the Baptis-
tery, at vespers, say:—"This day is Christ become
"immortal;" and, on another day, as he was giving
a Homily, he said:—"That is one Person Who is of
"the Father, and that is another Person Who is of
"the Virgin.   What the purple is to the King, that
"the Body is to Christ."

(*u*) The Venerable SAMUEL said:—

I heard Ibas say:—"As a King¶ is treated with
"insult through his purple, so did God The Word
"receive ignominy through His Body."

(*v*) The Count THEODOSIUS said:—

The matters deposed to, against Ibas, who was
Bishop of this Metropolis, your Excellency has (now)
taken cognizance of from these several Depositions
(just now) individually made.   It is in order to your

¶ "Just as the Purple is that which has insult shown it, when insult
"is offered to a King ; so also (the attributing) suffering to God is of-
"fering insult to Him."   Or, "When they despise the Purple, it is the
"King on whom the contempt falls, so the Passion is fallen on to God."

giving peace to this so-distracted City that I intreat your Highness—and I conjure you by the Holy Trinity and by the Clemency and Victory of the Masters of the world and by our own Master Theodosius, whom may the Son of God bless, to rejoice us !¶ — to convey these Instruments to his Excellency, the Master of divine Offices, so that, through the means of his Excellency, the Victorious and divine Crown may be informed of them, and to the Glorious and Illustrious Eparchs, and to the Powerful General of the two Armies, the Ex-consul. Will your Highness also instruct, by your Letters, the Holy Archbishops of Constantinople the Opulent, and of Alexandria (the Great), as well as the Venerable Domnus, the Archbishop of Antioch, and the Holy Bishop of Jerusalem, Juvenal, and Eustathius and Photius, the Holy Bishops of Tyre and Berytus, who have had to be Judges in this affair ? I desire, too, that a copy of the Syriac Letter spoken of, as that which Ibas wrote to Maris the Persian, may be read in the presence of the Venerable Clergy and all those in attendance here, and that it be deposited (afterwards) among the Documentary Acts. For, this is what I assented to do at the instance of the Venerable Clerics and Monks and of all the citizens, as their Depositions make evident.

(*h*) 8 The JUDGE said:—

The Declarations (Anaphoræ, Report) made at the

¶ Or it may be rendered "in whom the Son of God, to grant us "joy, may be pleased."

Court (Tribunal), so far as they have already gone, we have given information of to the Princely and Exalted Powers. That is in accord with the Instruction now delivered to the Tribunal, as well as with the formidable Oath, made in reference to the afore-mentioned subject.

We are, also, going now to write, as is obligatory upon us, to those God-loving Bishops just now alluded to by the Glorious Theodosius.

Now let the Letter,* which the Illustrious man made mention of, be received and read.

---

* That is, the Copy of the Syriac Letter which Ibas wrote to Bishop Maris, or Mares, the Persian. This very celebrated Epistle, which formed for a lengthened period the subject matter of a great Controversy in the Church that only terminated, in the following century, with the Condemnation of the Three out of the Fifteen κεφάλαια or Chapters, about Theodore of Mopsuestia, Theodoret of the City of Cyrus, and Ibas, will be found in Latin and Greek in parallel Columns 241 and 242 of the 7th Volume of Mansi's " Conciliorum omnium amplissima Collectio," accompanied by the valuable Notes of Baluze, the first of which informs us that " Tres " istius fragmenti editiones habemus, istam nimirum, aliam inter acta " Concilii Quinti, tertiam in libro sexto Facundi."

Details, also, both interesting and abundant, in relation to this Letter, may be met with in the history of the Controversy about the Three Chapters, as given by Fleury and other ecclesiastical historians, as well as much information about Ibas himself found in connection with the Vth Œcumenical Council. Taken in its entirety the Epistle may be justly regarded as being capable of interpretation of a double and opposite character, the Orthodox party seeing in it an exposition of their doctrinal views and the Heterodox a confirmation of theirs. This Council or Brigandage of Ephesus we shall soon see condemned it and its Author, although Ibas had been acquitted at the Synodical Assembly held at Tyre-Berytus-Tyre in the spring of the same year in which that Council took place, whilst some Bishops of the Great Œcumenical Council of Chalcedon held in 451 A.D. pronounced Ibas and his Epistle to be Orthodox.

(i) TRANSLATION* OF THE LETTER WHICH WAS WRITTEN BY THE VENERABLE IBAS TO MARIS, THE PERSIAN.

—Soon after the beginning (IBAS says):—

But we have taken pains to make known, in a brief manner, to that clear discernment of yours which recognizes great things through small ones, the events that have so lately taken place here. Besides, we know that, when we write to your Piety, what interests us is brought to the knowledge of those who dwell in your country, through your indefatigable efforts.

Now, those Scriptures which have been granted (to us) by God have not suffered the least alteration.

---

* The following is, of course, an English Version of the aforesaid Document. The actual letter which Ibas wrote to Maris was in Syriac. That was again, doubtless, translated into Greek and so formed part of the Original Acts, now lost, of this Ephesine Synod. That Greek one, with the rest of those Acts, was again rendered into Syriac by our Scribe, of whom see his own note at the end of A in Vol. I, and its translation at the end of A in this Vol.

In the Original MS. in the British Museum, copied in our A in Vol. I, the word Cyril is always written by the Scribe in vermillion, or some sort of red inditing, out of honour to the great name. As regards the Original Letter, Asseman, in Biblioth. Orient. III, pp. 203 and 204, writes:—" Scripsit famosam Epistolam ad Marin Per-" sam quum adhuc Orientales cum Egyptiis contenderent." Again, he says, in B. O. I, p. 350:—" Ab Iba accepit. Mares(a) quidam ex " urbe Hardiscir: atque exinde cœpit Persarum regio Nestorianismo " infici per Ibæ epistolas, et per versiones(b) Orationum et Commen-" tariorum magistrorum ejusdem."

(a) Mares. Celeberrima est Ibæ ad Marin Persam Epistola. . . . Cujus hic urbis in Perside Epis. fuerit nunc primùm ex Beth-Arsamensi cognoscimus.

(b) Expositiones. Theodori Mopsuesteni Libros è Græco in Syriacum sermonem transtulisse Ibam, eosque per omnem Orientem disseminasse, conqueruntur ejusdem Accusatores in Concil. Berytensi ac Tyrio, Act 9 et 10. Concil. Chalcedon. Alios Diodori, Nestorii, cæterorumque ejusdem farinæ hæreticorum Libros in Edessena Persarum Schola Syriacè conversos fuisse, testatur Auctor Catalogi Patriarcharum Chaldæorum ad calcem Epistolæ Simeonis nostri.

So, I make beginning of my account by those Words in which you are fully conversant, (those of Scripture).

A controversy has arisen, since your Piety was here, between those two men—Nestorius and Cyril —who have written against each other blasphemous statements, occasioning scandal to those who hear them. For, Nestorius stated, in his discourses, as also your Piety well knows, that "the Blessed Mary "is not the Mother of God." Accordingly, many have considered him as belonging to the Heresy of Paul of Samosata, who affirmed that Christ was a mere man. Cyril, however, while aiming to refute the affirmations of Nestorius, has been found to fall into the Dogma of Appollinarius, seeing that he himself has written in a similar way, (affirming) that "God, the Word, became Man," so that there could (in that case) be no distinction between The "Temple and Him Who dwells in it." For, he has written Twelve Chapters,* as also, I think, your

---

* THE TWELVE ARTICLES, CHAPTERS, OR ANATHEMAS DRAWN UP BY S. CYRIL, THE ARCHBISHOP OF ALEXANDRIA:—

I. If any man confess not that Emmanuel is truly God, and consequently the Holy Virgin, Mother of God (since by her, according to the flesh, was conceived the Word of God Who became flesh); let him be anathema.

II. If any man confess not that the Word which proceeds from God the Father is united to the flesh hypostatically, and that with His flesh He makes but One only Christ, Who is both God and Man; let him be anathema.

III. If any one, after confessing the reason, divide the hypostases of the only Christ, joining them indeed together, but only by a connection of dignity, authority, or power, and not by a real union; let him be anathema.

IV. If any attribute to two persons, or to two hypostases, the things which the Apostles and the Evangelists relate, as spoken concerning Christ by the Saints or by Himself, and apply some to a man conceived of sepa-

Piety knows, in which (he says) "there is One Na-
"ture constituting the Divinity and the Humanity
"of our Lord Jesus Christ," and that "we ought
"not, (so he says), to distinguish between expressions
"which our Lord made in reference to Himself and
"those which the Evangelists (made) in reference to
"Him." But, how impious such statements are,
your Piety will, even before we can declare it, have
been quite persuaded. For, how can this—"In the

---

rately, as external to the Divine Word (ὡς ἀνθρώπῳ παρὰ τὸν ἐκ Θεοῦ λόγον ἰδικῶς νοουμένῳ), and others (such as he deems worthy of God) solely to the Word proceeding from the Father; let him be anathema.

v. If any dare to say that Christ is a Man Who bears God within him (Θεοφόρον ἄνθρωπον) instead of saying that He is God indeed, as only Son, and Son by nature,—inasmuch as the Word was made flesh, and partook of flesh and blood, even as we; let him be anathema.

vi. If any dare to say that the Word proceeding from God the Father is the God or Lord of Jesus Christ, instead of confessing that the same is entirely both God and Man,—since, according to the Scriptures, the Word was made flesh;—let him be anathema.

vii. If any man say that Jesus as man was possessed by (ἐνηργῆσθαι) God the Word, and clothed with the glory of the Only Son, as if He were not identical with Him; let him be anathema.

viii. If any dare to say that the Man assumed (ἀναληφθέντα) by the Word ought, along with the Word, to be glorified and adored and called God, as if the one existed within the other (for this is the notion suggested by the perpetual repetition of the phrase *along with*), instead of honouring Emmanuel with one entire adoration, and rendering to Him one entire glorification,—forasmuch as the Word was made flesh;—let him be anathema.

ix. If any say that our Lord Jesus Christ was glorified by the Holy Ghost, as having received from Him a power of acting against unclean spirits and working miracles upon men, which was foreign to Himself, instead of saying that the Spirit by which He worked them belonged to Him essentially (ἴδιον αὐτοῦ); let him be anathema.

x. Holy Scripture says (Heb., iii, 1) that Jesus Christ was made the High Priest and Apostle of our Faith, and that He offered Himself for us to God the Father as a sweet-smelling sacrifice (Eph., v, 2); if any man, therefore, say that since the time when our High Priest and Apostle was made flesh and man like us, He is not the Word of God

P

" beginning was The Word"*—be taken to refer
to The Temple which was born of Mary? or, this—
" Thou hast made Him a little lower than the An-
" gels"†—be spoken of the Divinity of the Only
Begotten?   It is thus that the Church expresses herself, as your Piety, also, has from the beginning,
taught, and has allowed yourself to be confirmed by
the definition of the Blessed Fathers in Her Divine
teaching:—Two Natures,—One Power,—One Person,
—the Same Who is the Only Son, the Lord Jesus
Christ.

In consequence of this controversy, the Victorious
and Gracious Emperors gave order to the Archbishops to (proceed to, and) assemble (in Synod) at,
the City of Ephesus, and that, before them all, the
controversy of Nestorius and Cyril, should be adjudicated upon.   Before, however, all the Bishops,
who were summoned to assemble, could reach Ephesus, Cyril arrived first; and, having previously

---

but a man born of a woman, as if this man were a different person from
the Word ; or if any say that Christ offered the sacrifice for Himself,
instead of saying that it was solely for our sakes, (for He Who knew no
sin (2 Cor., v, 21) stood in no need of any sacrifice) ; let him be anathema.

xi. If any man confess not that the flesh of the Lord gives life, and
belongs essentially (ἰδίαν) to the Word Himself Who proceeds from the
Father, and attribute it to another who is only joined to Him in respect
of dignity, or by virtue of a divine indwelling, instead of saying that it
gives life because it belongs essentially to the Word, Who has the power
of quickening (ζωογονεῖν) all things ; let him be anathema.

xii. If any man confess not that the Word of God suffered according
to the flesh, was crucified according to the flesh, and was the first-born
among the dead,—forasmuch as He is Life, and giveth life, as God ;—
let him be anathema.

    * S. John's Gospel, c. i, v. 1.   † Psalms, viii, 5.

gained the ear of them all, he pre-occupied them with poison that is wont to blind the minds of (even) the wise. But he took occasion, from the hatred (entertained) by him towards Nestorius, to do so: and, before the God-loving Archhishop John could arrive at the Synod, they deposed Nestorius from the . Episcopate, without a trial and without an investigation. But, after two days from this Deposition, we arrived at Ephesus; and, as soon as we learnt that, in the act of Deposition,* which was decreed by them, they adopted, and confirmed, and assented to, the Twelve Chapters written by Cyril, just as if they were consonant with, while they are in reality adverse to, The True Faith, all the Bishops of the East deposed Cyril, and decreed Excommunication against those other Bishops who assented to the Chapters.† After this breach of (Canonical) order, each returned to his own City. Nestorius, however, by reason of the hatred entertained towards him by his own City and its Magnates, was unable to return thither; and the Synod of the East, remained, excommunicating the Bishops who communicated with Cyril. Consequently, there was much bitterness among both parties, and Bishops were in contention with Bishops, and people with people; and that which is written, in fact, received its fulfilment:—"A man's enemies

---

* That is, in the body of the sentence pronounced upon Nestorius at the General Council of Ephesus in 431 A.D.

† Enigmatic allusion is made to some other Synod held in the Patriarchate of Antioch.

"will be those of his own household."* Hence, too, arose many detracting remarks against us, among the unbelievers and the heretics; for, none ventured either to go from City to City, or from one country to another; but each pursued his neighbour as his enemy. Many persons, likewise, who had not God before their eyes, assuming, as a pretext, zeal on behalf of the Churches, eagerly took the opportunity to manifest by act that hatred they secretly entertained in their hearts. Such was, for instance, the TYRANT† of our Metropolis, a person not unknown to you, who, under pretext of the Faith, not only wreaked his revenge on the living, but on those likewise who had departed to the Lord, amongst whom is the Blessed Theodore,‡ that preacher of the

---

* S. Matthew's Gospel, Chap. x., v. 36.

† On these words, or rather the Latin ones (ex quibus unus existit nostræ Tyrannus civitatis), Baluze distinctly asserts : "Id est, Rabbulas "Episcopus Edessenus."

‡ This is the great Scholar of Diodorus of Tarsus, the bosom friend of the affectionate Chrysostom, and the learned but mistaken Divine, who was the real Father of Nestorianism. A clever and thoughtful Dissertation about him and modern thought—in which, however, I cannot hold with all the writer advances—appears in No. 1 of Vol. I of the *Church Quarterly Review.* Asseman says of him :—*Theodorus* patria *Antiochenus,* dignitate *Mopsuestiæ in Cilicia Episcopus,* apud Syros, maximè Nestorianos per excellentiam [ܠܡܦܫܩܢܐ], hoc est, *Commentator* seù Interpres dictus, quia multis in sacram Scripturam commentariis inclaruit, *qui licet ab eo homine profecti* (inquit Renaudotius Tom. 2, Liturg. Orient., pag. 622) *cujus fides corrupta erat opinionibus illis, quas Nestorius publicavit, ipsis Orthodoxis non contemnendi visi sunt adeò ut Catenis græcis multa illorum fragmenta occurrant.* Auditores habuit Nestorium et Theodoretum, qui Lib. v. Hist. Eccl., cap. vi, hoc Magistrum suum Theodorum encomio exornat, *totius Ecclesiæ doctor, et qui adversùs omnes hæreticorum catervas strenuè decertavit :* in plurimos tamen ipse errores delapsus, maximè Pelagianorum et Nestorianorum, quo-

Truth, that Doctor of the Church, who, not in his life-time only, stopped* the mouth of Heretics with The True Faith, but (has done so), also after his death, by leaving to the Sons of the Church spiritual armoury in his writings. (Now) he, who exceeds everybody in audacity, has openly in the Church dared to anathematize him (Theodore) who, out of zeal for God, not only led back his own City from Error to The Truth, but who has also instructed by his teaching Churches that are afar off: and, as

---

rum pater rectè appellatur : eamque ob causam, in Quinta Synodo, post mortem damnatus est. In Chronico Edesseno notatur Epocha temporis, quo Scripturam exponere aggressus est : *Anno Græcorum* (inquit Tom. 1 Biblioth. Orient., pag. 400) *septingentesimo Mopsuestiæ Episcopus sacram Scripturam commentari cæpit.* Is erat nonus Theodori Episcopatus annus, ut loc. cit. ostendi : obiit autem Theodorus anno Christi, 429, quum triginta sex annis Mopsuestenam Ecclesiam rexisset, ut Theodoretus notat. Ejus libros è Græca in Syriacam linguam olim convertos, testatur Liberatus in Breviario cap. x. Ibam Edessenum Episcopum eam versionem procurasse conqueruntur ejusdam accusatores Samuel, Cyrus, Maras, et Eulogius Presbyteri Edesseni in Concil. Berytensi ac Tyrio Act. 9 et 10, Concil. Chalced. ut Tom. 1 Biblioth. Orient., pag. 200 notavi. . .
. . . Abrulbarcatus in lib. de divin. Offic. cap. vii, hæc Theodori Commentariæ recenset. Theodorus, inquit, Commentator Syrorumque (puta Nestorianorum) doctor, habet expositionem quarundam epistolarum Pauli et Actuum Apostolicorum : magnamque obtinet apud gregales suos doctrinæ famam, etc. (B. O., Tom. 3, P. I, p. 30, cap. xix.) Ebed-Yeshua gives a list of his whole works (see Asseman Biblioth. Orient., Tom. 3, P. I, p. 30). Lagarde has published some fragments in his Analecta Syriaca, Leipzig, 1858, and Sachau more fragments, with a Latin translation, Lipsiæ, 1869, from the MSS. brought from the Monastery of S. Mary, Deipara, besides a Dissertation "on the Remains "of the Syriac Translations of Classical Greek Literature, exclusive of "Aristotelian, among the Nitrian MSS. in the Brit. Museum."
Diodorus Tarsensis composuit libros numero sexaginta, quos Ariani combusserunt—Magister Nestorii, cujus hæresi in libris suis nimium favere deprehensus est : quam ob causam à Nestorianis quidem summis laudibus tanquam ipsorum doctor et pater unàcum Theodoro Mopsuesteno et Nestorio Episcopo effertur. (B. O., Tom. 3, P. I, cap. xviii, p. 28.)
* The Syriac word means *to strike in the mouth, to silence, to beat down.*

regards his writings, there was everywhere a great search for them, not on account of their being alien and adverse to The True Faith, (for, certainly, whilst he (Theodore) was living, he constantly eulogized him, and used to read his writings), but because of the enmity he had secretly entertained towards him on his having reprehended him in Synod openly.   While all this mischief was going on between them, and each one "walking in his own way,"* as it is written, our adorable God, Who, in His mercy, is at all times solicitous for His Holy Churches, stirred up the heart of our faithful Emperor to send a great and distinguished man of his own Palace, in order to oblige the Holy and God-loving Bishop of the East,† Mar John, to be reconciled to Cyril, whom he had deposed from the Episcopate.   Then, after having received the letters of the Emperor, he (John) despatched the revered and God-loving Paul, Bishop of Emesa, with letters to Alexandria, sending by him, at the same time, (a Confession of) the True Faith, and commanding him to communicate with Cyril, if Cyril should assent to This Faith and anathematize those who affirm that the Divinity suffered, as well as those who affirm that there is (Only) One Nature of the Divinity and of the Humanity.   But the Lord, Who is ever concerned for His Holy Church which was redeemed (purchased) by His Blood,‡ had willed the subduing the heart of the Egyptian,‖ so that he

---

* Acts, xiv, 16.   † Or "The Lord John" of Antioch.
‡ Acts, xx, 28.   ‖ That is, Cyril of Alexandria.

might be able, without trouble or objection, to assent to and receive The Faith and anathematize all those whose belief is at variance with That Faith.

So, after they (John and Cyril) had communicated together, the controversy disappeared and peace arose upon the Church, and now the schism has ceased in it and peace reigns as heretofore.

Now, what the God-fearing Archbishop (John) wrote, and the reply which he received from Cyril— these letters 1 have attached to this one, which I dispatch to your Piety, so that, when you have read them, you can make known to all those our Brethren whom you consider lovers of peace, that the controversy is composed and the middle wall of enmity broken through, and those who so inordinately exalted themselves against the quick and dead, have become abashed, apologizing for their folly and teaching the very opposite to their former Doctrine. For, no man ventures (now) to affirm that there is One Nature (only) of the Divinity and the Humanity (of Christ), but men (openly) avow The Temple and Him Who dwells in it to be the One (Only) Son Jesus Christ.

Now this Letter I have written to your Piety out of the great affection I have for you, being well assured that your Holiness, by night and by day, occupies yourself in the Doctrine of God (Divine Learning), in order that you may be of service to the community.

(*j*) The JUDGE said:—

This writing, which has just been read, is, as also you have learnt, a copy of the Letter; for, *this* the Deposition of the Glorious Count makes evident. How, then, can it be received as authentic and deposited among the (Documentary) Acts, in order to its being notified to the God-loving Bishops already named?

(1) SAMUEL, Presbyter, said:—

¶This letter appears in the Accusation we have preferred against Ibas, and the accused himself recognized it as his own. The Acts of Berytus are witness of it. Those Acts were drawn up in the presence of the Judges who were given to us by the grace and order of the Emperor. Amongst these Judges was the Pious Bishop Uranius who has asserted, and does still assert, that Ibas has acknowledged himself the Author (of this Letter). There are other persons here who were present at Berytus when it was read—they know that it was (written) by Ibas; I beg them, therefore, to make their Depositions.

¶ Or it may be rendered thus:—There is distinct proof as regards Ibas, who was accused by us, that this is a copy of the Letter, and he (Ibas) acknowledged it to be his own : and this is on the credibility of the (Documentary) Acts, which there, at the City of Berytus, were drawn up in the presence of those persons, who, by the grant and order of the Emperor, were assigned to us as Judges, one of whom was the Venerable Bishop Uranius, who bore then, and still now bears, witness that it (the Letter) was acknowledged by him (Ibas) to be his own. There are, too, here (present) other persons ascertained at that time to be there (at Berytus), who are assured of the same fact (viz.), that it was shown and read as his own ; and I request of them to make their depositions.

(*k*) The JUDGE said:—

If, at the investigation (into the affair) instituted at the City of Berytus, in the presence of the God-loving Bishops who were granted as Judges by the divine Commands, the copy was shown of the Letter, which has just now been read, in the presence of these same Pious Bishops, and was acknowledged by the Venerable Ibas to be authentic, as coming from himself, (then), according to the instruction of the Venerable Samuel, let those parties who are acquainted (with this fact) certify us of it.

(*a*) MARAS, a Deacon, said:—

I was there (at Berytus) when Ibas owned, in my presence, that the letter was his, by saying—" I acknowledge it to be so;" and I have believed this to be the case up to the present day; and, if the Emperor were to decree and order me to be cut in pieces, I should still believe it to be so.

(*b*) EULOGIUS, Presbyter, said:—

At the City of Berytus I heard the Venerable Bishop Uranius affirm that Ibas owned it (the letter) to be his, and that of this his letter *that* is a copy which has been (just now) named; and so I believe.

(*c*) DAVID, Deacon, said:—

I also heard the Holy Bishop Uranius, at the City of Berytus, say that Ibas acknowledged the same letter to be his, and avow that he believed

Q

so. He said, too:—"If I were killed and if the "Emperor commanded me to die,"—I should still believe it was so, and not otherwise.

(*d*) ASTERIUS, Presbyter, said:—

I heard Ibas make this avowal—"From the "authentic letter of mine is that copy (taken)," which was produced and read before the Judges at Berytus.

(*e*) EUSEBIUS, Deacon, said:—

I heard Ibas say—"They exhibited a copy of my "letter; and, immediately on their beginning to read "it, I acknowledged it to be mine."

(*f*) EULOGIUS, Priest, said:—

I was not, indeed, inside (the Judgment Hall), but outside, when I heard Ibas say—"The copy of the "letter which has been read is certainly that of "mine"

(*g*) BAIVUS,* Priest, said:—

Ibas wrote a letter here, (in which he said)— "(My) enemies and accusers produced this letter I "wrote several years ago to Maris, the Persian; then "they began reading it, and, immediately on their "beginning to read it, I acknowledged it to be the "copy of a letter that had been written by me." And all the clergy know this.

---

* It may possibly be Banius or Bianæus. The word is very indistinct in the original MS. The word put thus, Baiv[u]s, is best, perhaps.

(*h*) EUSEBIUS, Deacon, said :—

Maronius, the Deacon, read to us the letter of Ibas, which asserts : "My enemies and accusers have "presented a copy of the Letter which was written by "me to Maris, the Persian :" as Ibas himself admitted also at Berytus that the Letter was *his*.*

(*i*) FLAVIUS THOMAS JULIAN CHERÆAS, Count of the First Rank and Judge, said :—

These circumstances that refer to the copy of the Letter have been sufficiently elucidated in their Depositions, by the Venerable Clergy, made this day according to the Instruction (Petition) which the Glorious Count Theodosius has, on behalf of the whole community, presented and exhibited.

All this will be notified to the Illustrious, Noble, and Exalted Authorities.

I will, likewise, write what is obligatory on my part to those persons whom the God-fearing Bishops mentioned ; for, we could not possibly contemn such formidable Adjuration, as we have just now heard.

---

* Ces diverses dépositions relatives à la lettre d'Ibas et à fon authenticité sont extrêmement importantes pour nous, non pas que cette lettre fut douteuse,—les Actes du iv et du v. Concile Œcuménique suffisent à démontrer son authenticité,—mais parcequélles nous permittent d'affirmer un fait qu'on avait simplement soupçonné jusqu' á ce jour. La partie des *Actes de Beryte et de Tyr*, qui fut relue au Concile de Calcédoine dans les sessions ix. et x., est évidemment tronquée dans les editions qui nous en restent. Il suffit de lire Mansi (Conciliorum Omnium, etc., VI. 242 B, et 230) pour voir qu'il y a une lacune. Maintenant la lacune devient certaine, car les Actes de Béryte que nous avons ne contiennent aucun des aveux quel'on préte ici à Ibas. (Martin.)

NOW, AFTER THESE DOCUMENTS HAD BEEN READ AT
EPHESUS, THE HOLY SYNOD SAID :—

"These things pollute our ears—to Cyril be eter-
"nal remembrance, because of the Archbishop Dios-
"corus—Cyril is immortal. May Alexandria (ever)
"abide the City of the Orthodox."

The HOLY SYNOD said :—*

"These proceedings are well accomplished. He
"(Dioscorus) is the crown of the whole Synod."

The HOLY SYNOD said :—*

"These things pollute our ears—they are fit (only)
"for Heathens! Spare our ears — these things
"ought not to be spoken. Spare our ears—spare
"our souls (pity us)—spare (peace to) the Orthodox.
"Let Ibas be burnt in the middle of the City—let
"Ibas be burnt in the middle of the City of Anti-
"och—let Ibas be burnt for the correction of others.
"These things not even have Demons spoken—these
"things not even Pharisees have said—these things
"not even the Jews have given expression to.
"Such language befits the Heathen—this is lan-
"guage worthy of Satan—thus (speak) those who
"do not believe in God. The Devils (proclaimed)
"owned Christ to be God—Ibas has not: Devils
"are much more modest (pious) than Ibas: the
"Devils owned Christ to be the Son of God—Satan
"is more modest than Ibas. The Tempter is more

---

* The same repeated superscriptions, as Hoffman remarks, indicate
that the Acts were interrupted with these words in several places.

"modest than Ibas—Ibas is the disgrace of the
"whole world. Let-Ibas be burnt together with
"those who are of his opinions—let Ibas be burnt
"with those who support him. Whoever does not
"hate Ibas is a Demon—whoever loves Ibas re-
"sembles Satan—whoever does not hate Ibas is not
"Orthodox—whoever loves Ibas is a Nestorian—
"whoever would not condemn Ibas to the fire is not
"Orthodox. Satan cares for the blasphemy of Ibas.
"We pray you, O Emperors! put to death Ibas.
"We pray you, O Emperors! let Ibas be burnt
"alone—let this be done for an example to Heretics.
"Let Ibas be burnt in Antioch. Rid us of one man
"and deliver the (whole) world—make one to burn,
"and deliver many. Nestorius and Ibas should be
"burnt together—let Nestorius and Ibas be burnt
"in the middle of Antioch. Exile is of no use—
"exile damages the City. Nestorius and Ibas
"should be burned together. Exile is nothing to
"them. Nestorius has gained by exile—exile for
"them is nothing. Nestorius and Ibas ought to be
"burnt together! Satan and his Son to the fire
"both together. Patriarch! help the Orthodox—
"do thou cast out all these. Let none remain of
"the whole Company of Pharaohs."

(n) DIOSCORUS, Bishop of Alexandria, said :—

Do you not perceive what this Demon (really)
said? He said—"I do not envy Christ becoming

"God; for, how could God be what he was not?"¶

The Holy Synod said :—

"To the Patriarchs¶ many years !—Dioscorus and
"Cyril have confirmed The Faith of the Fathers,—
"the Patriarchs many years !—the Orthodox many
"years !"

Dioscorus, Bishop of Alexandria said :—

"*That* you do not shout of yourselves alone.   But
"it is the Holy Ghost Who exclaims in you.   It is
"the Christ that Ibas persecutes."

The Holy Synod said :—

"All the world knows thy Faith— Dioscorus is a
"personage unique in the world."

And, when Eulogius, Presbyter of Edessa, entered
and repeated something well known, which had
taken place at Antioch, the Holy Synod cried out

"We request that *that* may be stated in writing—
"*that* relates to The Faith—let it be stated in wri-
"ting—it is directed against Christ—it ought to be
"put in writing."

(1) Dioscorus, Bishop of Alexandria, said :—

Is it your pleasure that that which has been
spoken should be put in writing or not ?

¶ Or, "(But) how could he become God, (except) by becoming
"what he was not ?"
   ¶ Or, " Long live the Patriarchs."

The HOLY SYNOD said :—

"We all request this—that it should be stated in
"writing. We ask this—that what he (Eulogius)
"stated, he should state in writing. It concerns the
"Faith. It should be stated in writing. It ought
"to be put down in writing. It ought to be made
"known to the Emperor. It ought to be made
"known to the Gracious Emperor. It ought to be
"made known to the Orthodox Emperor. The Faith
"is in peril—it should be stated in writing. We,
"the Orthodox, desire that it may be stated in wri-
"ting. The Christ is insulted—let it be stated
"in writing. Away with the Heretic—turn out the
"Heretic—eject those who are the adversaries of
"Christ. You have received the full authority—(so)
"turn out the Heretic."*

(3) DIOSCORUS, Bishop of Alexandria, said :—

Give silence to the Synod; for, it is written that
"the words of the wise should be listened to in si-

---

* After the reading to the Assembly of the Depositions, collected
by Cheræas, according to the formal instructions given him, and containing
nothing but the old Charges of Heresy, bad habits, &c., which had been
set aside in the trial at Tyre-Berytus, had been heard by it in silence,
that assembly, conscious as many of them, and privy as not many less,
must have been to the designs and objects of the Eutychian party, on the
one hand applauded Dioscorus as "the Crown of the Synod," as "the
Defender of the Faith," as "a person unique in the world," whilst on
the other, we see, they gave utterance to such maledictions, duly (i.e., by
Monophysite hands) preserved in these Acts, as the multitude belonging
to the City of Edessa did not venture to give vent to. If this be a correct
view, "O Tempora! O Mores!" might Mons. Martin, in his thoughtful Etude, well exclaim.

"lence."* Do not make a disturbance. Give not
occasion to the Heretics (to accuse us)—I know it is
your God-loving affection; for, rest assured that that
impels Bishops, and Clergy, and Laity to speak on
behalf The Faith, but still order must rule here.

EULOGIUS, Presbyter of Edessa, said :—

After the occurrence of much mischief and sad
troubles in the Church of Edessa, occasioned by the
Venerable Bishop Ibas, in consequence of matters
relating to The Faith and to other transactions in
the Church—as plundering of the Sanctuary and the
rest—we, all of us who lived in that City, became
profoundly distressed, not knowing to whom to resort
(for redress) about the matter; but, after having
deliberated on what it was obligatory upon us
to do, we proceeded and addressed ourselves to the
Holy Archbishop Domnus and submitted to him
specified counts (or heads of indictment). We
were, however, advised, by certain inhabitants
of the City of Antioch, well known for their
correct faith, not to raise any subject having relation
to The Faith before him who occupied the Throne of
Antioch. For, they said, in particular, you would,
if you did so, lose altogether the expenses (or resti-
tution relating to them) you will incur in sustain-
ing the Charge of the plundering the Sanctuary and
the rest. Now, when we thought over this, and felt
assured that those heads referring to the (complaint of)

---

* Eccles., chap. ix, part of verse 17, "The words of wise *men are*
"heard in quiet." Eng. Version.

of Sacrilege would suffice for the riddance of our City of Ibas, we concluded on urging no complaint relating to The Faith.

Subsequently, on the occasion of a Gracious and Orthodox Edict (σακρα) being published in the City of Antioch the Great, on the Sunday we went into the (worshipping) Assembly, feeling desirous, according to custom, of joining it which was held in the Church, where we found a vast number of people, among whom were mixed certain Readers belonging to the Clerks of Antioch and some of those who are termed Lecticarii.

The Holy Archbishop Domnus was presiding, and, seated near him, was the Venerable Bishop Theodoret. And we heard there such shoutings as these—"Cast "out the Edict: nobody believes in (by) a Decree." Taking cognizance of this, again we did not venture to speak of, or discourse upon, any matter touching The Faith, but we mooted only the five Counts (of Indictment), one of which was that of the pillaging the Sanctuary (Sacrilege).

Now, although we convicted Ibas before the God-fearing Archbishop Domnus of having melted down the Vessels of the Sanctuary amounting to 200lbs. of silver, and although he had proclaimed, in the Church of the Metropolis of Edessa, that, who-ever felt disposed, might contribute to the Redemp-tion (of the Captives) and, by taking part in the matter, would be doing a good work; although we proved that he had withdrawn, also, from this capital sum a Loan of nearly 500lbs., and that he had, too, received from the Treasurer two Chests and one Bag which amounted, according to what the Treasurer himself had stated, to 6,000 Denars—all which sums he (Ibas) declared he had sent away and (therewith) redeemed the Captives, whilst we proved that he sent only 1,000 (golden) Darici, which he owned to be the case, whereby he was found to have perjured himself (lied on Oath)—yet, when we urged that (for these criminal acts) he ought to receive punishment, we discovered that nobody replied a word to us on the matter, but, (on the contrary, we found) that in everything the Archbishop Domnus supported him, affirming that it was in his administrative power to act as he did.

And when we appealed to the Holy Canons, and for two days asked for them to be read, and prayed for a judgment in pursuance of what those Canons prescribe, we were not deemed worthy of a reply. So we there and then made a Statement to this effect.

May it please your Reverence : —

¶Whereas the Holy Vessels have been melted down, and (whereas) 1,500 Denars have been collected as the income for (or as offerings made by) Widows and Orphans and women, and in sums almost

---

¶ Another translation of this piece is here subjoined—
This is the Statement (request) we made at Antioch.

Please (to consider) :

That the sacred Vases have been melted down, that fifteen hundred Dinars have been collected by means of direct taxation ; about a hundred and fifty Loumé received from the hands of Widows, of Orphans, and (every time) amounting to 50 and 100 Lumin, and have been, too, received from the Treasurer, whilst there were sent, for the Redemption of the Captives only 1,000 Denars, those Captives to be redeemed being Monks and Nuns, who, the Monks, have been obliged to minister to Idols and to worship them with the barbarous Arabs, and the Nuns forced to become harlots and to stand in the squares (Halls) (for all that is the custom among the Barbarians),—whereas Ibas has received the payment (for their redemption), and deposited it at his Brother Eusebius's house—Do you judge what you consider right upon this question.

Now, when this Statement had been made by me, and we were not deemed worthy of any reply, except that two of us were deposed in their absence, who, becoming alarmed on seeing the dexterity in this business and the expenses brought to bear against us, repaired to the Gracious Emperor, but those (other) two of us, who remained to sustain the trial as complainants in those five heads, were excommunicated.

Women ; that six thousand Dinars have been taken from the Treasurer ; that they have only sent for the ransom of the Captives one thousand Dinars, although the Captives were Monks and Nuns ; and that, besides, these Monks found themselves constrained to serve the Idols adored by the Barbarian Arabs, while the Nuns were obliged to become Courtezans and to stand in the public place : these are, indeed, the customs of the barbarians ; that Ibas received all these sums and that his Brother Eusebius has kept them.

(Considering all that)

Please to judge according to what you know.

We have been released from this excommunication by your prayers, since the matter touching The Faith has been seen into by the Holy Bishops —Eustathius, Photius, and Uranius.

After having gone thence (from Antioch) we turned to the Synod at Constantinople, to which we submitted the very same complaints against Ibas. We addressed ourselves, also, to the Gracious Emperor who, regardful of our distress, asked us—"For " what reason did you not deal with this head touch- "ing The Faith before Domnus, the Archbishop of " Antioch ?"

After having remained silent, and refusing to go from one thing to another, (for, we set our face to- wards Ibas), we were obliged, in the presence of the whole Court in the Apostolic Church of the Holy John, to declare that "we have our suspicions of " him." He, therefore, asked—" Whence is this pre- " text of suspicion ?" And we were obliged to tell him—for, how was it possible to dissimulate before so great a Lord of the world, who upholds Ortho- doxy—that "Whilst in Church was seated Arch- " bishop Domnus, and after the Edict of your Clemency " against Nestorius, and against Irenæus, who was " Bishop of the City of Tyre, had been published " (there), we entered the Church and heard certain " men shouting out—'Throw out the Edict : 'nobody " 'believes in (by) a Decree'—without our observing " anybody to remonstrate with them, so that such ne- " gligence (silence) only encouraged them the more."

For this reason the Emperor, touched by our
misfortune, despatched us to those already spoken
of, (viz.,) the Holy Bishops, Photius and Eustathius
and Uranius: and it was before them that those
transactions were negotiated, the (record of) which
has been read before your Holy Synod.

---

* In an historical point of view, this Deposition of Eulogius is highly
important and valuable, and, including the particulars referred to therein,
deserves a separate Dissertation, which however would be too long to
insert in these notes. Not to mention words already explained, it may
suffice to remark upon the following ones. The word ﺍﺯﻓﻮ on p. 85,
l. 22, means *the necessary charges* or *expenses*, forming the *debitum*, and
ﺍﻛﻤﺪﻛﻠﻌﻣﺍ in p. 86, l. 20 would be *silver* libræ, but not ﺍﻛﻤﺪﻛﻔﺪﻣﺣﻤﺳ,
and the ﺍﺯﺯﻳ et ﺣﺸﻤ in p. 86, l. 27, or *Two Chests and One Bag*,
would indicate a money bag with a specified amount or weight of gold.
The ﺍﺭﻣﺪﻳ *Denars* on p. 87, l. 2 and 19 and 26, are the same as are
referred to in Mat., c. xx, v. 9 and 10. There is the nummus, aureus et
argenteus; and Dr. P. R. Smith, in Thes. Syr. after quoting Bernst.,
says, he adds, " denarius aureus pondus habet sesquidirhemi s. sesqui-
"drachmæ, pretiumque circa ducati, et valet xxv denarios argenteos s. susas,
" Ar. d'rhemus. On the ﺯﺪﻣﺣﺪﺗ and the ﻛﻘﺼﻛ, we may note that
about the *Daricus*, the name of a Persian coin and mentioned in Esdr., ii, 69,
viii, 27, Neh., vii, 70, 71, 72, Dr. P. R. Smith quotes Bernst.—" Ap.
" Theophanem νομίσματα χίλια, sed νόμισμα, i.e., Solidus=12 milliaren-
" sibus ;" and, concerning the latter word Lumin (equivalent to Pholles),
Matthew Martin in Tom. Primus, p. 462, describing their different
kinds, says—" Et, ut ait Hesychius illustris Philosophus, Phollis pondus
" est, alio nomine dicta balantium : trahit autem donos ducentos quinqua-
" ginta, hoc est, libras cccxii et uncias vi, singuli vero doni libram unam,
" uncias xii, comprehendebant. . . . Et est alius Phollis, a duabus
" auri libris incipiens, et usque ad octo procedens." And *Solidus* he
defines thus :—" *Solidus*, numus quidem aureus et argenteus. Solidus
" Romanorum aureus sextulæ pondus æquabat, et pendebat Attica grana
" 96. . . . Sic Isid., Lib. xvi, cap. xxiv. *Solidus nuncupatur, quia*
" *nihil illi deesse videtur. Solidum enim antiqui integrum dicebant et*
" *totum. Solidus apud Latinos alio nomine sextula dicitur, quod de iis*
" *sex uncia compleatur. Hunc vulgus aureum solidum vocat, cujus tertiam*
" *partem ideo dixerunt tremissem, eo quod solidum faciat ter missus.*"
(Lexicon Philologicum præcipue Etymologicum Tom. Secund., p. 657.
Amstellodami, M,DCCI.) Castell makes Nummi and Lumin convert-
ible terms, it seems. See Mansi's nova et amplis. Collectio, VII, 221
and 222, I°, &c. ; J. S. Asseman's Biblioth. Orient. I, 350 ; &c., &c.

THE SENTENCES OF JUDGMENT PRONOUNCED
BY THE BISHOPS OF THE SYNOD UPON THE
BISHOP OF EDESSA HERE FOLLOW.

(1) Dioscorus, Bishop of Alexandria, said :—

Ibas, who has estranged (deprived) himself from
the Honours of the Episcopate by those so great
Impieties on which he ventured and by those unmea-
sured statements¶ contrariant to (The Truth of the
Nature of) our Redeemer he advanced, as if he were
competent of himself to unravel The Mystery of the
Gospel,¶ has brought upon himself from on High, condemnation in this world and in that which is to come,
by showing himself undeserving of the Mercy of God.
We ourselves, likewise, conforming entirely to a desire to act in the fear of God, have decreed that he be
deprived of the Honours of the Episcopate and of
Communion with the Laity. For, it is not right for
him, who denies the Mysteries of Christ and tramples
under foot His Word, to communicate in, or be
deemed worthy of (receiving), the Blessed Mystery.
And this, too, I consider obligatory, (viz.,) that, together with the canonical sentence of Deposition
which he has received, he should be compelled to
restore all the Church's gold (he has taken) where-
with to prevent his acquiring increase to his Impiety.

(2) Juvenal, Bishop of Jerusalem, said :—

Ibas has been shown, by what has been read, to

¶ Or, " words unlawful against our Redeemer."
¶ Or, " solve the Mystery of the Incarnation."

. have been guilty of an immense deal of Impiety against our Lord Jesus Christ ; and, therefore, also, the Lord (Jesus) Christ removes him from His Priesthood and decrees him deprived of all Priestly Rank, as well as of Communion with the Laity.

We, then, for our part, desirous of proceeding in accordance with the Will of our Redeemer Jesus Christ, excommunicate him, and do decree that he be deprived, of all the Honour of the Priesthood, and, together with this, of Communion with the Laity.   Moreover, the Church's treasure he must restore in order that the Holy Church may sustain no damage, and that he who is so Impious might not enjoy treasure offered to God.

(3) THALASSIUS, Bishop of Cæsarea in the First Cappadocia, said :—

Those who have blasphemed the Son of God are unworthy of the Blessings promised by Him ; for, they alienate themselves from Mercy, through their Blasphemies against Him. In consequence, therefore, of Ibas having inflated himself against the opinion and feelings of the community of men, and of having dared to move the tongue of Blasphemy against our Redeemer Jesus Christ, as we know from what has been just read, he has deprived himself of the Priesthood, and of the Dignity of the Episcopate, and of Communion with the Laity.

(4) STEPHEN, Bishop of Ephesus, said :—

Surpassing all is the Blasphemy which has been

audaciously uttered against God and our Redeemer
Jesus Christ by Ibas, who is altogether Impious.   Let him, therefore, be excluded from the Episcopate, and from Communion in the Pure Mysteries,
and from all Ecclesiastical Rank, by the Sentence also
of my Humbleness, seeing that there is not even a
single excuse (for him), either now or in the world
to come, for having thus dared (to use so) loose (depraved) a tongue.   Moreover, let the goods of the
Church be demanded (and obtained) of him ; for, it
is not right and just that he, who has been proved
to be so thoroughly Impious, should be allowed to
enjoy what has been consecrated to God.¶

(5) Eusebius, Bishop of Ancyra of Galatia, said :—

Ibas, who was the originator of foul and damning
Blasphemies worthy of Satan, will receive indeed in
Hell (Gehenna) the judgment due to his audacity,
but, before the death of his body, the Christ, whom
he has blasphemed, declares him not only estranged
from the Priesthood, but likewise from the name of
Christian.   Those things, likewise, that of right

¶ This speech of this man may be thus freely rendered :—The
Blasphemies of the great Infidel against God and our Saviour, Jesus
Christ, surpass all (that can be imagined).   Let him be excluded from
the Episcopate, from participation in the Divine Mysteries, and from any
ecclesiastical Office, by the sentence of our Humbleness ; for, he has no
excuse to give, either now or in the world to come, for having dared to
employ language so depraved.   Let the property of the Church,
also, be resumed ; for, he who has been convicted of such Impieties
ought not to enjoy things consecrated to God.

At this Synod the treatment this man received at the hands of
Dioscorus is by himself described at the Œcumenical Council held in
451 A.D., at Chalcedon, as given by Mansi.

belong to the Holy Church, ought to be demanded of Ibas.   It is only fitting and proper that the enemy of (the True) Religion should not be allowed to revel in treasure belonging to the Poor.

(6) EUSTATHIUS, Bishop of Berytus, said :—

Ibas has given proof that he agreed with, if he did not precede, Nestorius, and has become a teacher of that Impious Heresy.   For, he had the audacity to surpass him (Nestorius) in Impiety.   It is due to him, therefore, according as it seems just also to your Blessedness, that he should be deposed from the Dignity of the High Priesthood, seeing that he has, by the use of his tongue, rendered himself alien to it, (unworthy of it).   He ought, also, to be inhibited Communion in the Pure Mysteries, because he has rejected the help of the Grace of God. According to your decision, too, all the treasure of the Church ought to be demanded of him.

(7) CYRUS, Bishop of Aphrodisias of Caria, said :—

A Deposition, on principles of Justice and in accordance with the Canons, has been conclusively arrived at by this great and Œcumenical Synod respecting Ibas who whetted his foul tongue against Orthodoxy.   Seeing he has scandalized many and caused them to err by his evil and polluted Doctrine, which appertains to Satan, he ought likewise to be inhibited intercourse with the Laity, by means of those parties, who should also make him restore

s

the treasure of the Church to the Holy Church.
(8) DIOGENES, Bishop of Cyzicus, said :—

From the Documents, which have just now been
read to this Great and Holy Synod, having reference
to Ibas, we ascertain this fact—that he has held
opinions, and written what is, alien to the Decisions of
the Fathers. For this reason I, also, for my part following the example of the Holy Fathers, do adjudge
him to be alien to (removed from) the Dignity of the
Episcopate and to Communion in the Pure Mysteries.
Moreover, (I decree) that he restore the treasure of
the Church to the Holy Church, which he has tyran-
nically extorted.

(9) JOHN, Bishop of (Sebastia in) the First Armenia, said :—

Those, who utter calumnious sentences against
Heaven, deserve to have to descend to the Abyss below
(Sheol). For, when a man exalts himself by Blasphemy, (obtruding) himself where he ought not, he
ends in a fall.¶ Ibas, then, who, while yet in the
grade of the Priesthood, was sadly infected with
Blasphemy, and who has, during the Realization of
the High Priesthood, carried it to such an extent
as not only to fill with Impiety the Church with
which he was entrusted, but has, also, like a (flame
of) fire, devoured with his tongue, inimical to God,
even the land of the Persians, must be re-

¶ Or, " to such a pitch is a man borne on in what is unbefitting that
" the pollution of Blasphemy sticks to him."

moved from the Priesthood and from the communion
of Christians. For, it is not just and right that he,
whose blasphemies are manifest from those Documents which have been read, as well as from his
own words, should fill again with his Heresy, like a
disease, the flocks entrusted to his charge. So, also,
must sentence be pronounced against him for the pillaging the Sanctuary : for, it is not becoming and
proper that those things, which have once been reli-
giously devoted (to God), should become means for
subserving Impiety, and, contrary to (all) justice, be
applied in pursuance of the will of the defrauder.

(10) BASIL, Bishop of Seleucia of Isauria, said :—
The words of the impious Ibas are foreign, and
antagonistic, to (those of) the Church, and are much
more (in harmony) with the vain religion of the
Pagans, with whom Mythologies have made Gods
out of men.¶   As for ourselves, we worship not a
temporal God, but we worship the Only Begotten
(Son*) Jesus Christ—(the God*) Whom, because of
His Mercy, we worship (as) the Only* Begotten Son,
Co-essential† (Consubstantial) with the Father, God
The Word,* our Lord Jesus Christ—(the God) Who,
by reason of His Mercy towards us, willed to become*

¶ Or, "for certain makers of parables (Myths) have, by a sort of
"perversity, formed God out of man."
    * 1 S. John, v, 20; John, i, 1.
    † The term "of One Essence," or Co-essential, is preferable to, as
being more correct or less inadequate than, the term "of One Substance"
or Consubstantial. So, also, in the Nicene Creed. See John, x, 30.
    * John, i, 14; John, iii, 16, 18.

MAN (INCARNATE). Ibas, therefore, has no need of being condemned by our tongue (sentence) ; for, he has cut off himself from the members of the Church, by means of all this his Blasphemy. We do entirely depose him by what justly proceeds from our mouth, and we stone him with stones, and expel him from all Function of the Priesthood and from Communion with the Laity. Further, we consider it befitting and proper that, in consequence of his robbery of the Church of her treasure and his wanting to rob our Lord Jesus Christ of (His) Glory, that he should not be allowed to rejoice in (the possession of) those goods as to which he audaciously pillaged the Sanctuary (committed sacrilege), but that he should restore to the Church the Church's treasure.

(11) JOHN, Bishop of Rhodes, said :—

By the Documents which have just now been read, Ibas is shown to be alienated from (unworthy of) the Priesthood. I, for my part, therefore, pronounce that he be void of the Honour of the Episcopate and of Communion in The Mysteries, whilst (at the same time) he is bound to restore the Church's treasure, in order to his having no fruit of his Impiety.

(12) PHOTIUS, Bishop of Tyre, said :—

For a long time since has the Falsity of the depraved Faith of Ibas, who was Bishop of Edessa, been objectionable to (reprobated by) myself; but especially from what has now been

read before your Blessedness, is he proved guilty,
and unworthy of (to be alienated from) the Ecclesiastical Throne; for, those who hold the Satanic opinions
and (so) become involved in the Heresy of Nestorius,
are destitute of all excuse, being antagonistic to Him
Who is the Redeemer. I, therefore, also for my
part, assent to what has been decided on by your
Piety, pronouncing him to be removed (alienated) from all the Honour of the Priesthood and
from Communion with the Laity. But, especially, ought he (to have preserved and) to render a
return of the Church's treasure, according to your
holy Decision.

(13) FLORENTIUS, Bishop of (Sardis in) Lydia, said :—

As regards Ibas who, abundant in criminal acts
and rich in Impiety, in conscience is poor towards
God, whilst, in robbery of the Holy Vessels and
in the perfection of infamy, he is a true Iscariot,
he ought to be dismissed from the Dignity of the
Priesthood. He, in whose mouth Impiety (has·
acted), as a bad servant, because of his cursed hate
of God, should be cut off from the body of the entire
Priesthood, forasmuch as he dared to rend the Church
of God with the Impiety of his tongue. He must,
likewise, render an account of the treasure of the
Church which he has robbed, because it appertains to
the nature of the law that any man who, under the
appearance of goodness, takes an oblation and is
induced therewith to work evil, should render up

the accounts of the Church without (any) damage.

(14) MARINIANUS, Bishop of Synnada, said :—

Ibas who, from what has been read, is proved to be full of Impiety, must, by the Grace of God, be separated from the Honour of the Priesthood and must cease from Communicating in the Holy Mysteries, receiving (at the same time) also punishment for pillaging the Sanctuary, and returning the treasure of the Church which was wrongfully pillaged.

(15) CONSTANTINE, Bishop of Bosra (Bostra), said :—

The Blasphemy and Impiety of him, who has hitherto been Bishop of the City of Edessa, being evident, from all that has been read, and your Holy and Great Synod having pronounced a correct sentence of punishment on him, depriving him of all the Function of the Priesthood and of the Dignity of the Episcopate, I likewise give my assent to what has been correctly determined on by your Holiness; and I pronounce him alien from (unworthy of) all the Function of the Priesthood, and the Dignity of the Episcopate, and the Communion of the Holy Mysteries. As regards the treasure, also, I for my part decide in reference to him the same as your Holiness also has determined.

(16) ACCACIUS, the Bishop of Ararat, who supplied also the place of the Venerable Bishop CONSTANTINE of Militine (Melitene), said :—

Against himself, Ibas should subscribe himself

rejected from the Priesthood and from Communion
in the Holy Mysteries, who, contrary to (all) Piety, so
whetted his polluted tongue against our Lord Christ.
Together with the punishment, then, which has come
upon him, let there be demanded of him, also, the
treasure belonging to the poor, inasmuch as it ought
to be given back to them for whom it was (originally) designed.

(17) ATTICUS, Bishop of Nicopolis of Ancient
    Epirus, said :—

By reason of those his Blasphemies with which he
was filled against our Lord, the Redeemer, Jesus
Christ, it was proper that Ibas should receive the
sentence of the punishment he deserved.   Furthermore, adhering to the righteous Judgment
of our Holy Fathers, we also, because he aspersed our Lord, the Redeemer Christ, with them
decree that he be excluded from all the Function of
the Priesthood and from Communion with the Laity,
whilst (at the same time) he be required to restore
the money of the poor, whom he robbed, in accordance with your Canonical Judgment.

(18) NUNECHIUS, Bishop of Laodicea (in Phrygia)
    Trimitaria, said :—

Human intelligence is incapable of discovering a
punishment adequate to the Impiety of Ibas. Because, however, it is obligatory on an Œcumenical
Synod to make the least matter, as well as many and

great ones, the subject of attention,—for, not through the means of the magnitude of a severe punishment is a power useful—I, likewise, for my part, decree him deserving the Deprivation of the Dignity of the Priesthood and of Holy Communion. He must, also, restore all that property of the Church to It, so that his Blasphemy may not be lucrative to him, and replace the Holy Vessels (he) impiously (took).

(19) CANDIDIAN, Bishop of Antioch in Pisidia, said:—

Ibas, who lent his tongue to his Father, the Calumniator, in violation of (all) Justice, is deservedly regarded by the Lord of all, Jesus Christ, as an enemy. And, he is now also cut off from the Priesthood and from Communion, by your Great and Holy Synod. I, for my part, share with you in the sentence of his condemnation, as well as in all those matters that have been determined on by your Synod in reference to him.¶

(20) SELEUCUS, Bishop of Amasia, said:—

Ibas, who, by means of his Blasphemies and his Impiety, has condemned himself, I, also, adjudge to be removed from the Dignity of Episcopate and from Communion with Christians, whilst (at the same time) what he ventured to pillage from the Sanctuary should be demanded of him.

(21) LEONTIUS, Bishop of Ascalon, said:—

Who can have pity for an Incantator (Juggler) whom

¶ Or, rather, "in what your Synod has decreed against him."

the Serpent bites? and what Christian could have pity for Ibas who, whilst carrying a spiritual Serpent in his soul, not only hurries himself into the depths of Hell (Sheol), but desires also to lead other souls into error by Impiety? I, therefore, remove him from the Office of the Priesthood and from Communion with the Laity. Also, he ought to restore to the poor of the Church the treasure he despoiled them of.

(22) DIOSCORUS, Bishop of Alexandria, said:—

Because (sufficient) time does not remain for all your Reverences to pronounce one by one his separate judgment, let there be given assent, by the (united) voices of the whole company, if you please, to what has been decreed.

(23) The HOLY SYNOD said:—

"The (same) things all of us say—this is the "decision of us all—all of us reject him who con-"tends (disputes) with God—as with one mouth all "of us condemn him."*

---

* Thus ends the trial, by his Compeers, of Bishop Ibas at this tribunal of the Church. They strip him of all the Honour, and the Dignity, and the Function belonging to the Office of a Bishop in the Church; they inhibit him from Communion in the Pure Mysteries, or Holy Eucharist: and they condemn him to what was more humiliating than "lay communion." Now, Lay Communion, says Bingham, "in a layman was no punishment, but a privilege, and one of the greatest privileges that belonged to him as a Christian: for it was entitling him to all the benefits and advantages of Christian Communion. But in a clergyman it was one of the greatest of punishments, reducing him from the highest dignity and station in the Church to the level and standard of every ordinary Christian. . . . . This supposes a power in the Church not only of conferring Clerical Orders at first to men, and promoting them from laymen to be Bishops, or Presbyters, or Deacons, but

T

also a power of re-calling their offices, and divesting them of all power and authority belonging to them, by degrading clergymen upon just reasons, and reducing them to the state and quality of laymen again."

This punishment was more severe than that called *peregrina communio*, or "the communion of strangers" and defined in the 33rd of "the Canons "of the Apostles" thus: "Let no strange Bishop, or Priest, or Dea-"con be received without letters commendatory: and when they are "brought, let them be examined carefully: and if they are messengers of "Piety, let them be received: but if not, after furnishing them with what "is necessary for their wants, do not receive them into fellowship: for "many are surreptitious." For, whereas the Order of the Church admitted those who had been reduced to "the Communion of strangers" to become capable of being restored to their office, according to the Canons of the Church, provided their prescribed penance was of a private, and not of a public, nature, the punishment of "lay communion" totally and perpetually degraded them from their Orders, excluding them ordinarily from their Office and compelling them ever after to abide in the state of Layman. Letters commendatory are based on 2 Cor., iii, 4.

Ibas, also, was accused of Sacrilege and of diverting what belonged to the Church to his private use. The Order of the Ancient Church was severely directed against this; for, the 73rd of "the Canons of the Apostles" says :—"Let no one convert to his own use any consecrated "vessel of gold, or silver, or linen: for it is against the law; and, if any "one be detected, let him be punished with excommunication." Besides the Holy Vessels, even in respect of the 'οθονοι, *linen*, Ibas lay under an imputation (see the Acclamations). Nor does the same Bishop appear to be clear of that serious crime which the Primitive Christians made so many severe laws to abolish and correct, viz., that of "murdering the poor," as it was called. The 2nd Council of Vaison, as quoted by Bingham, made this Canon :—"They who detain the oblations, and re-"fuse to give them to the Church, are to be cast out of the Church; "for such a provocation of God is a denying of the Faith; both the "faithful who are gone out of the body, are defrauded of the plenitude "of their vows, and the poor also of the comfort of their food and ne-"cessary subsistence. Such are to be esteemed murderers of the poor, "and infidels, with respect to the judgment of God." (Bingham, Bk. 17.)

Clergymen, when guilty of this and cognate crimes, were visited with such punishment as "communio peregrina." "Bishops, who were intrusted with the goods and revenues of the Church, were not allowed to alienate any part of them, except it were in great necessity, to relieve the poor, or redeem captives; in which case, St. Ambrose himself and many disposed of the plate of the Altar, and the vessels and utensils belonging to the Church, thinking it better that the inanimate temples of God should want their ornaments, than that the living temples should perish for want of relief." This, continues Bingham, "was not sacrilege in the eye of the law, either ecclesiastical or civil, but an act of mercy allowed by both; for the laws against sacrilege, next to the honour of God, have always a view to the necessities of the poor." But Ibas was charged with misappropriating the very revenues of the Church expressly devoted to the Redemption of the Captives. (See Crimina on p. 35.) So he was condemned accordingly. He was excluded from external communion with the visible Church in all offices. His Excommunication—ἀφορισμὸς—was complete. In S. Paul's words Ibas " was delivered over to " Satan" (1 Cor., v., 5).

In Schenkl's " Institutiones Juris Ecclesiastici," the 11th Edition, Tom. 2, p. 604, after dilating upon the three " Pœnæ Ecclesiasticæ," he subjoins this note :—Huic pœnæ affine, imo quoad rem ab ea haud diversum quidam arbitrantur illud animadversionis genus, quo Clerici ad communionem laicam (a) quondam detrusi sunt : a qua communio peregrina (b), suspensionis species quædam, distinguenda est. (c)   A friend, who sends me the quotations at the foot of the page, informs me that Maurus Schenkl, born in 1749 A.D. and of the Benedictine Order, brought out the first Edition of this work in 1790 A.D., that the 9th and 10th were prepared by Joseph Scheill and the 11th " a quodam juris " ecclesiastici Professore Publico," but that it is not one of the best Handbooks of Ecclesiastical Law in Germany, though much used in Bavaria.

It will be easily perceived by the Reader that this Sentence of Excommunication upon Bishop Ibas was effected—such was the flagrant perversion of Justice—without the accused having the opportunity of answering for himself at the Tribunal, or even having a summons to appear at it. It was the result of the intrigues and powerful influence of the great Eutychian party, headed by the Ecclesiastical Triumvirate named at first.

At the end of the 10th Session of the great Council of Chalcedon in 451 A.D., Bishop Ibas was pronounced, as well as the letter to Maris, to be " Orthodox," was declared " free from suspicion" by having subscribed Leo's Tome, and was reinstated in the Honour and Dignity of the Episcopate, and in " the Church from which he was so unjustly rejected."

END OF THE CAUSE OF IBAS.

(a) C. 7, 8, dist. 50. Rumpler Ueber die Laien Communion der älteren Kirche und über die Reduction der Cleriker zu derselben, Salzburg, 1807.
(b) C. 21, dist. 50. Born de Communione peregrina, Lips., 1742.
(c) Cf. Devoti Instit., can., L. I, tit. 8, sect. 4, § 19, not. 2.

DANIEL.

Daniel, the Bishop of Harran (Charran), or Charræ,[*] was nephew, on the Sister's side, to the Bishop Ibas of Edessa. The former City was near to, and a little to the South of, the latter and is now in ruins. It is remarkable only from a religious point of view as being, in former times, the place where Terah the Father of Abraham died, and whence that Patriarch departed to enter upon the land of promise, whilst Edessa's history in the latter days makes it ever memorable as being the City which the great persecutor, Julian, passed by in his conquering career, because it was hopelessly and wholly given up to the Christian Faith.

Asseman, in his dissertation on Harran, in his "Bibliotheca Orientalis," Tom. 2, does not allude to its Bishop, Daniel, still that Bishop's name, as well as that of Irenæus, Bishop of Tyre, and others, is distinctly mentioned by him, at Sect. 63 of the "Chronicle of Edessa," in words cited in the introductory note under Sophronius, and translated there.

Also in Asseman, B. O. I, 200-201, there is a long note, quoted on pp. 35-37 above, supplying observable details relating to Daniel, in Charges 5,[†] 12, 14-18, which are given thus:—

6. Quod Danielem, suum ex fratre nepotem,[‡] juvenem adhuc cumque luxuriosissimum, Charrensem Episcopum fecisset, &c.

THE "Crimina" in Mansi-Labbe (Sacror Conc. nova et ampliss. Collectio. Florent. T. vii, 1762) are given in *Greek and Latin*, and follow after the presentation of οἱ κατὰ τοῦ Ἴβα λιβέλλοι (Libellus Samuelis et aliorum presbyterorum Edessæ, ad Photium et ad reliquos episcopos, contra Ibam).

The division into "xviii" crimina is not marked in the Greek, but only in the Latin Text.

---

[*] In Mansi, VII, Daniel is called "Carrhenorum civitatis Episcopus" with the note referring to the Codices thus—"Paris. Carrinorum, Divion. Cyrinorum."

[†] The figure 5 ought to be 6 on page 35.

[‡] "Suum ex fratre nepotem" is an incorrect translation into Latin of the Greek word ἀδελφιδοῦς in Mansi; for, we find in Stephanus Thesaurus: sub voce ἀδελφιδοῦς, Nepos e fratre vel sorore: aut Sororis filius, inquit T. Poll. [3, 22] Exp. a Suider ἀνεψιός; and sub voce ανεψιος, Amitinus, Patruelis, Fratris vel Sororis Filius. Dicitur interdum ὁ πρὸς πατρὸς ἀνεψιός et ὁ πρὸς μητρὸς ἀνεψιός. The Syriac proves that in this case ἀδελφιδοῦς is = ὁ πρὸς μητρὸς ανεψιος.

The whole is part of Actio Decima Chalcedonensis Concilii.

(The following is the Greek and Latin of the 6, 12, 14—18.)

Col. 224. Ὅτι ἐχειροτόνησε Δανιῆλον * τὸν αὐτοῦ ἀδελφιδοῦν ἐπίσκοπον τῆς Ἑλλήνων πόλεως· ᾧ ποτε ἔδει [1] πνεῦμα ἅγιον γενέσθαι, οὗ ἠδύνατο τὰ ἔργα καταιδέσαι

[1] ποιμένα sive κατέρα ex veteri versione in c. Boh.

καὶ ὑποπεῖσαι, νῦν γοῦν εἰς ἐπίγνωσιν ἀληθείας ἐλθεῖν· αὐτὸν ἄτακτον ὄντα, καὶ ἀσελγέστατον, καὶ νεώτερον. οὐδὲ γὰρ ἠξίωσεν, οὐδὲ ἐνέχετό ποτε λαβεῖν. ἀλλὰ δι' ὅλου σχεδὸν τῇ ἡμετέρᾳ πόλει παραβάλλων διὰ Χαλλῶάν τινα ὕπανδρον, ἐκτοπίζων ταύτην, καὶ (col. 225) περινοστῶν τόπον ἐκ τόπου καὶ εἰς τρυφὴν ἑαυτὸν μετὰ ταύτης ἐκδιδούς.

Col. 223. VI. Quia ordinavit Danielem [2] filium sui * fratris episcopum [3] Paganorum [4] civitatis; cui oporteret sanctum Spiritum adesse, cujus possent opera adducere et persuadere, ut vel nunc ad cognitionem veritatis accederent; iste illic ordinavit inquietum, et

[2] Suum fratruelem.
[3] Hellenopolis.
[4] Qui erat ex paganorum civitate, dum oportebat patrem sanctum fieri cujus possent opera reverentiam facere.

juvenem existentem, et luxuriosissimum. Neque enim statuit aut passus est aliquando latere, sed pene semper in nostram adveniebat civitatem propter Challoam (col. 226) quamdam maritatam, circumducens eam per loca diversa, et in deliciis cum ea deditus.

Col. 225. [XII.] Ὅτι ὁ ἐπίσκοπος Δανιῆλός τινας τῶν μάλιστα τῆς ἀσελγείας αὐτοῦ ἐχειροτόνησε κληρικούς.

Col. 226. XII. Quia episcopus Daniel quosdam suæ maximæ intemperantiæ clericos ordinavit.

Col. 228. [XIV.] Δανιήλου δὲ τοῦ ἐπισκόπου διαθεμένου καὶ καταλείψαντος ἅπερ ἔσχε πλούσια πράγματα, καὶ κτήματα ἐκ τῶν ἐκκλησιαστικῶν τοῖς ἐγγόνοις τῆς αὐτοῦ φίλης, καὶ αὐτῇ Χαλλώᾳ, οὔτε ἠγανάκτησεν οὔτε ἐνεκάλεσεν.

Col. 227. XIV. Daniele autem episcopo testante, et relinquente quam habuit locupletem facultatem et prædia ex ecclesiasticis rebus nepotibus suæ amicæ et ipsi Challoæ, neque indignatus est, neque increpavit eum.

Col. 228. [XV.] Ὅτι Χαλλώα ἡ φίλη Δανιήλου τοῦ ἐπισκόπου, τὸ πρότερον μηδὲν ἔχουσα, ἀποκεχρημένη τοῖς ἐκκλησιαστικοῖς τοῖς παρ' αὐτῇ οὖσι πολλοῖς πράγμασι, νομισμάτων δανείζει ἀπὸ διακοσίων καὶ τριακοσίων ὡς δῆλον ἐντεῦθεν γενέσθαι, πόθεν ἡ συναγωγὴ τῶν πραγμάτων.

Col. 227. XV. Quia Challoa, amica Danielis episcopi, quæ prius

---

* This is a mistake of the Historian. See p. 151 and note ‡.

nihil habuit, multis rebus ecclesiasticis abutens, quæ apud ipsam sunt, ducentos et trecentos solidos feneratur: ut ex hoc manifestum fiat. unde fit harum rerum collectio.

Col. 228. [XVI.] Ἀβραάμιός τις ἦν διάκονος. οὖτος [6] ἀπ' αὐτῆς ἐτύγχανε τῆς ἡμετέρας ἐκκλησίας διαφόρως πραγματευσάμενος, ὃν πρότερον πένης, καὶ μηδὲν, σχεδὸν εἰπεῖν, ἔχων, τῆς ἡμετέρας ἐκκλησίας πολλὰ, καὶ ἀμύθητα πράγματα ἔσχεν ἅ τινα κατὰ ἀλήθειαν ἦν τῆς ἡμετέρας ἐκκλησίας. ὑποπείθει τοῦτον Δανιῆλος ὁ ἐπίσκοπος, εἰς αὐτὸν παραπέμψαι τὸν κλῆρον κατ' ἐγγράφους διαθήκας, ὀμόσας αὐτῷ, τοῖς πτωχοῖς αὐτὰ διδόναι μετὰ τὴν ἐκείνου ἀποβίωσιν· τοῦτο γὰρ καὶ αἱ διαθῆκαι περιέχουσι. τούτων ἐν καθέξει γενόμενος Δανιῆλος, οὐ μόνον, ὡς ἐχρῆν, καὶ ὤμοσεν, οὐ διῴκησεν, ἀλλὰ τῇ δουλούσῃ τῇ ἀσελγείᾳ αὐτοῦ Χαλλόᾳ τῇ γυναικὶ δέδωκεν αὐτά.

[6] ἐπ' αὐτῆς ἤ. ἐσ. ἀπαντητήι.

Col. 227. XVI. Abraamius fuit quidam diaconus. Hic [6]apantita [7]erat nostræ ecclesiæ, diversis negotiabatur temporibus: primitus pauper et nihil fere habens, ex nostra ecclesia multas et innumeras res habuit, quæ [8] pro veritate erant nostræ ecclesiæ. Suadet huic Daniel episcopus, ut sub scripto testamento in eum suam transmitteret hæreditatem jurans ei, hæc se post eius mortem pauperibus erogare. Hoc enim et testamento continetur. Et postquam hæc Daniel est adeptus, non solum (sicut oportebat, et sicut juraverat) non disposuit, sed luxuriæ suæ [9]servivit: Challoæ enim mulieri dedit.

[6] Ex ipsa vel in ipsa nostra ecclesia erat & diversis modis negotiabatur.
[7] Hæc dictio in codd. Bohieri et Jolyi reperitur.
[8] Revera.
[9] Mancipio Challoæ mulieri dedit.

Col. 228. [XVII.] Ὅτι παρὰ τῶν ἐμπιπτόντων Ἑλλήνων ἁμαρτήματι θυσίας λαμβάνων Δανιῆλος ἐπίσκοπος σπόρτουλα, ἀφίησι τοῦ ἐγκλήματος, πραγματευόμενος ἑαυτῷ κἀντεῦθεν κέρδος.

Col. 227. XVII. Quia a paganis [10]incidentibus in peccatum sacrificiorum, accipiens Daniel episcopus sportulam remittit crimen, negotians et hinc sibimet lucrum.

[10] Lapsis.

Col. 228. [XVII.] Ὅτι τῆς ἐκκλησίας Ἐδέσσης τοῦ κτήματος Λαφαργαρίθας ὕλας τεμόντες, ἀπένεγκαν εἰς τὸ κτήματα Χαλλέας τῆς φίλης Δανιήλου τοῦ ἐπισκόπου, καὶ ἔκτισαν ἃ ἠβουλήθησαν.

Col. 227. XVIII. Quia et ecclesiæ Edessenæ e prædio Lafargaritha silvas cædentes portaverunt [11] ad prædia Challoæ amicæ Danielis episcopi, et ædificaverunt quæ voluerunt.

[11] Sibi.

We will here subjoin the following also:—

Col. 241. Part of the Letter of Ibas to Maris is read before the

Council.

Col. 249. After this Ibas asked that also a letter of the Edessan Clergy (instructio et deprecatio, etc.) might be read, ut cognoscatis quia et ab his quæ mihi illata sunt, alienus existo et "violentiam sum perpessus." This being granted by the Judges, Beronicianus, the Secretary of the Consistory, reads the declaration of the Edessenian Clergy, that Ibas never spoke the word (said by Maras to have been spoken by him), οὐ φθονῶ τῷ Χριστῷ γενομένῳ θεῷ· ἐφ' ὅσῳ γὰρ αὐτὸς ἐγένετο, κᾀγὼ ἐγενόμην, or, ἐπειδὴ κᾀγὰ, εἰ βούλομαι, γίνομαι κατ' αὐτοῦ.

This declaration is subscribed by about sixty Presbyters, Deacons, Subdeacons and Lectors ; Fecidas, Ursicinus, Eulogius, Libanius, Rhodon, etc., and most of them, it is stated, subscribed in Greek and *in Syriac :* καὶ ἡ ὑπογραφὴ Συριακή.

Ibas was, doubtless, considered responsible to a certain extent for the irregularities of his nephew Daniel, not merely as uncle, but as the latter occupied a Suffragan See subordinate to that of his own, Edessa being the chief and Metropolitan City of the Eparchy of Osrhoene. The "Ordo episcoporum" of Leo the Wise and Photius, calls Edessa the Metropolis, and gives καραι as one of the fifteen subordinate dioceses ; and Dr. J. M. Neale, in his History of the Holy Eastern Church, in the "Notitia of the Ancient and Modern Sees of the Diocœse of Antioch," makes Charræ rank fourth after Edessa, Metropolis, under Osrhoene. Chap. vii, p. 135.

III.

THE DEPOSITION OF DANIEL, THE BISHOP OF HARRAN (CHARRÆ).

EULOGIUS, Presbyter of Edessa, said :—

When we presented to the Holy Archbishop Domnus Libels (bills of indictment) against Ibas, who has been excommunicated, we preferred charges also against his nephew,* Daniel, Bishop of Harran, of Adultery, of Sacrilege,¶ and of other crimes. The Clerks, too, of the same City of Harran, joined us in (this) his Incrimination (Impeachment). But, for the sake of not worrying Ibas, the Archbishop Domnus refused to investigate these charges against Daniel, but ordered that his Uncle (by his Sister) Ibas, should hear his case (as Judge). Subsequently, however, we troubled the Gracious Emperor (with the case), who despatched us to the Holy Bishops Photius, and Eustathius, and Uranius, (before whom) to state† our complaints about him (Daniel) ; and we did state them. I request, therefore, of those Bishops to speak upon those same matters into which (judicial) investigation was made in their presence.

---

* In l. 6 the term ܩܠܚܝܒ his *Nephew*, the Son of his Sister. In l. 12 ܠܡܐ is "*his Uncle* by the Mother's side ;" ܠܝܐ "is *Uncle* by "the Father's side." Eusebius was the Brother of Ibas, named in A twice.

¶ Or, "pillaging the Sanctuary."

† In Mansi (Concil. amplis. Collectio, VII, p. 209, &c.), we read of the Commission (commonitorium) being given—"Damascio specta- "bili Tribuno et Notario prætorianorum," of the Synod being held "in "Colonia Christi amica Beryti," of "presentibus Iba, Joanne, Dan-

(2) JUVENAL, Bishop of Jerusalem, said :—

Let the Holy Bishops Photius, and Eustathius, and Uranius declare what they are cognizant of in the affair about Daniel.

(a) PHOTIUS, Bishop of Tyre, said :—

¶Since that time, I have forgotten, whilst the God-fearing Bishop Eustathius has had exact knowledge of, what was discussed. I, therefore, request of your Piety to ask him to afford distinct information on the subject.

(b) DIOSCORUS, Bishop of the City of Alexandria the Great (Capital), said :—

Let the God-fearing Bishop Eustathius, supplying* the forgetfulness of the God-fearing Photius, and affording an explanation of his view (of the case) and his (formal) Statement, tell us what he knows of the affair relating to Daniel.

(c) EUSTATHIUS, Bishop of Berytus, said :—

After the matter relating to his Orthodoxy had

"iele," &c. Our Acts do not give us the decision come to on the matter, however, on that occasion.

¶ Thus, perhaps : " Because from the time (that has elapsed), I have "forgotten the matters under discussion ; but the God-fearing Eusta-"thius knows them exactly. . . ." In this short speech we have a happy instance of the difference between, ܡܳܕܰܥ, *sciens*, and, ܡܶܐܫܰܠ, *rogans*. The distinction, with a difference of meaning, in the word Deposition, which so often occurs in this English Version, has not been pointed out, it being thought unnecessary.

* *"Supplying the forgetfulness,"* and *"explaining his view."* ܡܰܫܠܶܡ is act. part., governing ܛܽܘܥܝܰܝ, and the Greek of it was no doubt

been mooted with respect to Jbas, the Venerable Clergy of the City of Harran preferred¶ a complaint against Daniel, their Bishop, on the ground of the disgracefulness of his morals. We made full enquiry, therefore, into that matter. For, he was accused (in open court) to his face, and so clearly convicted that he himself explicitly (by his own word) confessed it, although he tried by (using) much sophistry to explain the matter away. When, then, we were deliberating upon his Deposition, but in consequence of the sanctity (or nearness) of the (Lent) Fast, delayed doing this, because, living in

---

ἑρμηνείων, whilst ⲕⲥⲥⲕⲟ seems to be Pael part. of ⲕⲕ, actively governing ⲕⲟⲙⲕ and agrees with, ⲙⲟⲕⲕⲙⲟⲓ. The particle ⲙ introduces here, as constantly in Syriac, what were simply participles in Greek. The expression ⲕⲟⲙⲕⲕⲕⲟⲕ is harsh, as usually ‖ⲕⲟ; is inserted in the sense of supplying *the place* of something, but no other sense seems possible here.

¶ Or, "began an agitation against Daniel." In p. 103, l. 14 ‖ⲕⲙⲝⲕ or ⲕⲙⲝ is *narratio* in its original sense. In l. 17, the word ‖ⲕⲟⲙⲙ is *fæditas*, and ‖ⲝⲟⲣⲣ *morum*:—"*wickedness of his morals.*" It seems mere chance that שֵׁכָר is also in Syriac ‖ⲙⲙⲝⲣ, as also that ‖ⲙⲙⲝⲣ is *sugar*. In l. 20 ⲙⲝⲕ ‖ⲝⲟ has its equivalent το οὗτος. In l. 21 ‖ⲣⲟ is fut. Aph. Castell has ⲙⲟ‖ id. q, Heb. הוֹדָה *gratias egit, laudavit, confessus est.* Confitendi notionem ibi habet, verbo frequentissimam, cum ⲝ construitur, e.g., Matth., x, 32, to which add Matth., vii, 23, and Apoc., iii, 5. See p. 368 on the word (‖ⲣ). Here we have an instance of Castell's correctness. From this verb, too, he says, is ‖ⲕⲝⲟⲝ ⲝⲟⲕ ⲝⲕ ⲝ *templum Confessorum*, very similar to which is ‖ⲣⲝⲝ ⲝⲕ ⲝ which occurs more than once, in another form, in our MS. (A). In l. 21, ‖ⲝⲟ ⲝⲟⲙⲝⲕⲝ, in the Greek, was no doubt κατεσοφίζετο. In Judith, chap. v, ver. 11, "*dealt subtilly with them.*" It is constantly used for σοφίζομαι in a *bad* sense. The difficult word ‖ⲕⲟⲝⲙⲝ is, perhaps, equivalent to the Greek σεμνότης, *gravity, respectability.*

V

heathen cities, we were unwilling to scandalize them (by the fact) that a Priest had fallen into such crimes, he, on the pretext of our procrastination, drew up in writing the Resignation* of his Bishopric and presented it to his Metropolitan, as we have learnt from the letters of that Metropolitan himself, Ibas. And, after the discussion of the whole case had been gone into, it eventuated in its being remitted to your Holy and Œcumenical Synod. For your judgment, then, which is final (in appeal),

---

* In p. 104, l. 1, the verb ܐܘܚܪ is *to delay, to put off*, and ܡܫܟܬܐ ܕܡܘܚܪܢܐ the *putting off time, delay*. Also, ܐܬܬܠܝ ܡܢ is *to decline, refuse, withdraw from*, and so *to resign*, and ܡܫܟܬܐ ܕܐܬܬܠܝܘ *resignation*, in p. 104, l. 2. The word is certainly, ܡܛܪܘܦܘܠܝܣ, as elsewhere frequently. Malim, ܡܛܪܘܦܘܠܝܛܐ μητροπολίτης, but, as he identifies it with Ibas, the meaning is certain. In p. 104, l. 7, and second word, the ܙ must be taken otiose, I think, especially as ܒܬܘܠܬܐ is feminine. "*And when these matters were* "*discussed, it resulted in their being sent to this Holy and Œcumenical* "*Synod,*" but, if not, we would render it thus: "*Whilst all this was* "*passing, the papers relative to this Holy and Œcumenical Synod were* "*despatched to us.*" Since ܠܫܠܡܐ is τελειῶσαι and εἰς τέλος, in ܫܠܡܐ may distinctly be implied the fact that the Council was the final Court of Appeal, as in short it would have been, had it not so perverted Justice that common justice required it to be superseded by another Œcumenical Synod and Court, which took place at Chalcedon in 451 A.D., although S. Leo the Great wanted it to be in Italy. Still, the word may mean τέλειοι or τελειούμενοι, *the perfect*, because they were consummate Christians, who had a right to partake of the Holy Eucharist, τὸ τέλειον, that sacred Mystery that unites to Christ and gives us the most consummate perfection we are capable of in this world, as says Bingham. Perhaps the whole passage may best be rendered thus :—" They accused him " to his face, and pressed him so hard, that he confessed himself almost " beaten in argument, although he had conducted his defence with clever-" ness. We contemplated at once deposing him, but we deferred it on " account of (the nearness of) the Sacred Lent Fast; because, being

has the settlement of this affair been reserved.

(*a*) URANIUS, Bishop of Himeria, said :—

—(Liban[ius],* Deacon of Samosata, being interpreter for him)—I say the same as the God-fearing
Bishop Eustathius has deposed.   For, he (Daniel) was
accused of disgraceful immorality, and was convicted
in our presence.

3 (*a*) JUVENAL, Bishop of Jerusalem, said :—

Relying with confidence on the excellent name
(fame), of the Holy Bishops Photius, and Eustathius,
and Uranius, I (decree) determine the very same as
they do about him (Daniel), who as Judges heard
the case.†

(*b*) PHOTIUS, Bishop of Tyre, said :—

Daniel, having been charged with these vices by
the Venerable and God-loving Clergy of the
Church of Charræ, and having been convicted to

" in Pagan Cities, we wished to avoid scandalizing the heathens by show-
" ing them that a Bishop could misconduct himself to that extent.   Then
" he (Daniel), availing himself of the delay, framed in writing the Re-
" signation of his Bishopric, and presented it to his Metropolitan, as we
" learn from the letters of the latter, Ibas.   While all this was going on,
" the Documents, relating to this Holy Œcumenical Synod, were sent
" to us.   It is thus left to you, who are perfect, to terminate this affair."
    * If the Greek were ἑρμηνεύοντος Λιβανίου, then, before the verdicts
or sentences were given, Libanius read explanations, or a full report of
the proceedings, of the trial of Daniel, then ܐܡܿܪ ܐܢܐ, "I say. . . .
" for, he has been accused," &c.; but there seems no evidence of the
latter doing so, and Libanius must be considered as merely the interpreter
of Uranius's Syriac into Greek, though the word, ܐܬܟܣܣ, meaning *re-
dargutus est*, might seem to give countenance to the idea suggested above.
    † If ܡܬܕܝܢܢܘܬܐ is governed by ܕܫܡܥܘ, and not by ܕܝܢܐ,

his face,* it appears to me that he ought to be removed from the Throne of the Priesthood. For, it
is impossible that such a man should (be allowed to)
stand before the Holy Altar.

(c) URANIUS, Bishop of Himeria in the Eparchy of
    Osrhoene :—

(Libanius, Deacon of Samosata, being interpreter)—said, that it was iniquitous, as well as contrary
to (all) propriety and rectitude, that the Priesthood
should be disgraced by a man who, to his face, has
been (convicted) proved guilty of shameful immorality of conduct (dissolute habits), and therefore I vote
(decree) that Daniel be removed from the Priesthood.

Also, since a considerable amount of gold, belonging to the two Churches of Edessa and Harran, is
in his (Daniel's) possession, I think it only right and
just that he should restore that gold—restore to each
of these Churches severally (that which belongs to it).

(d) EUSTATHIUS, Bishop of Berytus, said :—

It is a subject worthy of tears,† for a Priest to be
accused of dissolute habits, far more than that of his

___

then it should be, " as they who heard (as Judges) the proceedings re-
" specting him."

* That is, " in the open Court." The term " the Throne of the
Priesthood " is an instance of the right to the Priests of the Church
of having a Throne, though a second one, as well as the first Order of its
Ministry. See Bingham, Book II, chap. xix, who explains the meaning of the terms ὁ ἐκ τοῦ δευτέρου θρόνου, and " corona presbyterii," and
τὸ τῶν πρεσβυτέρων συνέδριον.

† In p. 105, l. 14, it should be ܠܒܟܳܝܐ, worthy of *tears*, a subject

Deposition—(for a Priest) for one, the (special) property of whose Office it is, by his Purity of body and his Orthodoxy of Faith, to draw down the Holy Ghost, through the Consecration of the Pure Oblations, with which he has been entrusted for the benefit of mankind. Daniel, therefore, by reason of his having been convicted to his face of such crimes, should be removed from the Priesthood by a sentence (judicial) of your Holiness. For, the Holy Ghost left him because of his evil life, even before the tongue of the High Priests (or the Bishops pronounced his sentence), since the Holy Ghost flies from fraud and never dwells in a body that loves sin.

(e) DIOSCORUS, Bishop of Alexandria, said :—

To the verdict given by the God-fearing Bishops, Photius, and Eustathius, and Uranius respecting Daniel, I, likewise, for my part, give assent.

(f) THALASSIUS, Bishop of Cæsarea in the First Cappadocia, said :—

The man, who has occupied the Priesthood and, by worldly impurity, gets so contaminated as to bring contumely on the (Pure) Mysteries, affords proof against himself that he is unworthy of the Episcopate. For that reason let Daniel, having proved himself to be such, as also the Depositions of the God-fearing Photius, Eustathius, and Uranius make

---

deserving *grief.* The verb ܣܘܠ, in active voice, governs ܠܘܪ as its subject, indicated by the ܠ,

evident, be degraded from the Dignity of the Priesthood.

(*g*) STEPHEN, Bishop of Ephesus, said :—

What those persons who were ear-witnesses of the case about Ibas have adjudged, *that* I, also, in conjunction with them, pronounce to be my decision.

(*h*) EUSEBIUS, Bishop of Ancyra, said :—

Assuredly the Venerable God-loving Bishops Photius, and Eustathius, and Uranius, who have pronounced sentence on Daniel, are pious* men. To that sentence of condemnation pronounced by them, I, also, for my part, give assent. Let Daniel, then, be removed from the Priesthood : for, it is not seemly that he should serve the Holy Altar, who is addicted to disgraceful habits.

(*i*) CYRUS, Bishop of Aphrodisias, said :—

Seeing that Daniel, after having been charged with odious practices and tried before the God-fearing Bishops Photius, and Eustathius, and Uranius and convicted, has been sentenced to Deposition by those same Pious Bishops, as they have shown as well by Document as now they have also by their speeches, I am, too, entirely of the same opinion with your Holiness respecting him.

---

* In p. 106, l. 18, ܠܡܚ is the predicate, and ܐܬܒܚܡ in l. 24 may be translated *disgraced*, or *made contemptible by dissolute habits, immoralities*.

(*j*) DIOGENES, Bishop of Cyzicus, said :—

Accepting* the truth of those who have tried Daniel, I do, likewise, for my part, assent to the Condemnation pronounced on him by you.

(*k*) JOHN, Bishop of Sebastia in the First Armenia, said :—

I, on my part, assenting to what has been deposed to by the God-fearing Bishops Photius, and Eustathius, and Uranius respecting the Condemnation of Daniel, do also vote that this man be deprived of (removed from) the Priesthood.

(*l*) BASIL, Bishop of Seleucia in Isauria, said :—

If, according to the Sentence of the God-loving Bishops Photius, and Eustathius, and Uranius, Daniel, Bishop of Charræ, "took the members of "Christ and made them members of an Harlot,"† he has whetted against himself "the sword‡ of the "Spirit :" and it is right and just that he should be driven away, the Shepherd from his Flock, because he is the scab of the sheep.

(*m*) FLORENTIUS, Bishop (of Sardis) in Lydda (Lydia), said :—

To all, which those Pious Bishops have done who have already adjudicated upon the affair of Daniel, in everything it is right and just for us to assent,

---

* The part. ـٰجل is present, *following after*, i.e., *agreeing to, accepting the truth of*, must be the sense.

† See 1 Cor., vi, 15.   ‡ Ephesians, chap. vi, verse 17.

since verily he has already brought ignominy upon himself by his turning aside into that wicked folly.*
Let Daniel, therefore, be stripped of the Honour of the Priesthood, forasmuch as he avowed himself, in the presence of the Judges, to have been destitute of (all) gravity of conduct.

(*n*) MARINIANUS, Bishop of Synnada, said :—

I, also, assent to the Deposition of Daniel, since once already have the Pious Bishops Photius, and Eustathius, and Uranius justly condemned him.

(*o*) ATTICUS, Bishop of Nicopolis in Ancient Epirus, said :—

¶In accordance with the sentence of the Judges, let punishment, prescribed by the Canons and the (Definitions) Decisions of the Holy Fathers, be executed upon Daniel who has been condemned by them, inasmuch as he has made himself liable to such a sentence.

---

* In p. 108, l. 1, ܬܘܕܝܬܐ is properly *a begging off*; hence *a declining, turning away*—ܥ *from* a thing—ܒ *into* a thing. Perhaps it might be correct to translate—" by his own abdication (brought about) " by the atrocity of his offence," but not so naturally.   Dr. R. P. Smith informed me some years since, that he knew of one example ܐܪܙ, although he would have preferred ܐܪܙ = ܐܪܙ.

¶ Or, better :—" Let the punishment, prescribed by the Canons, over- " take Daniel in conformity with the sentence of the Judges, which they " have inflicted upon him, because he has fallen under the blow of the " prosecution of the Law and the Definitions of the Holy Fathers ;" or, " let punishment, according to the Canons and the Definitions of the " Holy Fathers, be pronounced upon Daniel, who has been condemned " by them, since he has fallen under—i.e., has made himself liable to— " such a sentence."   The ܬܘܕܝܬܐ ܥ belongs to the ܡܩܒܠ ܥ most probably.

(*p*) NUNECHIUS, Bishop of Laodicea Trinitaria, said:—

If the Judges themselves have accused Daniel, what (more) can we do in the matter (but agree with them)? I, for my part. pronounced it to be right that he should be removed from the Priesthood.

(*q*) LUKE,* Bishop of Dyrrhacium, said :—

In accordance with the Depositions of the God-loving Bishops Photius, Eustathius, and Uranius respecting Daniel, I, for my part, likewise assent to the Deposition (pronounced) upon the aforesaid Daniel.

The HOLY and ŒCUMENICAL SYNOD said :—

" We, all of us, say the same."

[END OF THE CAUSE OF DANIEL.]

---

* For ܠܘܩܐ, *Luke*, see 2 Tim., iv, 11. In l. 24 ܕܐܠܥܙ ܗܘ is *the above-mentioned* (Daniel).

W

IRENÆUS.

Irenæus was at first a Count of the Empire. In an unofficial capacity he attended the Great Œcumenical Synod of Ephesus in 431 A.D., accompanying Nestorius as a friend thither, with ten Bishops of the Church; whilst Count Candidian, Captain of the Imperial Guards, went expressly in an official one, serving the interests of the Emperor Theodosius II. Irenæus sympathized with the Easterns and John, Bishop of Antioch, and naturally upheld the cause of the friends of Nestorius, against whom, however, the Emperor after some hesitation declared himself, and banished Irenæus from Court. Now Historians say—it is an error—that Theodoret, "out of deference to "the Bishops of Phœnicia" and "because he knew his zeal, "his magnanimity, his love for the poor, and other virtues," consecrated him Bishop of Tyre. But in 448 A.D. a Law was made expelling from their Churches all Nestorians, if Bishops or Clerks, &c., mentioning Irenæus by name, and ordering him not to leave his country, but to remain there in quiet, without either the name or the dress of a Bishop. In this retreat Irenæus wrote a history of the Nestorian controversy under the title, "Tragædia, seu commentarii de rebus in Synodo Ephesia ac in Oriente gestis." The Greek Text of this work is lost; but there remain extensive fragments of an old Latin version, published by Charles[*] Lupus under the very inexact Title of "Variorum Patrum Epistolæ ad Concilium Ephesium pertinentes," Louvain, 1682. (From Nouvelle Biographie Generale, Tom. 25, Didot frères, Paris, 1858.) Baluze, in his "Nova Collectio Conciliorum," says the edition of Lupus is very incorrect, and proceeds to give us another, which he would have made more accurate, if the Monks who owned one of the two MSS. had allowed him to use it (fol. 663–940). He says it was written after the time of Justinian, was called "Synodicon," and against the books which Irenæus, the upholder of Nestorius, called "Tragædia," i.e., perhaps, "Pro-"phetia instantis Constitutionis," as Anastasius says of a similar work in Hist. Eccles., p. 51, after Theophanes," &c. This "Synodicon adversus Tragædiam Irenæi," comprises 225

---

[*] Sic for Christian. Another edition more complete has come out.

chapters, including numerous documents and extracts of importance to the student of Nestorian controversies. Among these are sundry letters from Theodoret of Cyrus, John of Antioch, &c., and some things by Irenæus himself. This Synodicon, with the editorial prefaces, notes, &c., occupies 275 columns of the folio of Baluze. From the same volume the following deserve special notice in reference to Irenæus and his character: A letter from the Ephesian Council (431 A.D.) to the emperors says: " Nos autem detenti rescribere vestræ potentiæ " latitudinem horum quæ passi sumus a magnificentissimo " Comite Irenæo, breviter non potuimus intimare, qui omnem " sanctam Synodum conturbavit, et terrorem imposuit sanctis- " simis episcopis per quosdam extraneasque concursiones, ut " etiam plurimi nostrorum circa ipsam periculum paterentur " vitam" (fol. 496). This is in Mansi also.

The "Synodicon" has a letter by Nestorius, in which the latter says to John of Antioch—" Ea enim quæ ad nos nuper " scripsistis, et ad magnificentissimum Christi amatorem " Irenæum filium nostrum," &c. (fol. 688). The epistle, alluded to, really contains only a message to Nestorius, or, rather, the notice of one, forwarded, it would seem, through Irenæus (fol. 445). An epistle from Memnon of Ephesus to the Constantinople Clergy, confirms what the Council reports as to the violent measures of Irenæus (fol. 524). Irenæus was banished with Photius to Petra, the decree for which appears in the Synodicon, and some indication of the mode of executing it (foll. 884, 885). The culprits were to be deprived of all their dignities and possessions, and exiled to Petra, " ut paupertate " perpetua et locorum solitudine crucientur." The directions for carrying out the decree are very curious :—Quæ sintque de Irenæo et Photio sunt sancita a divino et immortali vertice, præfulgens divinarum litterarum tenor ostendit, Magnificentia igitur tua his quæ sunt decreta divinitus absque mora obediens, ad loca quæ jussi sunt duci cum competenti solatio præparet veredos duos cum duobus parippis Oresti et Stephano, qui singulariter directi sunt ad peragenda quæ divinitus decreta sunt, quæque nostris præceptionibus continentur, coadjuvantibus eos ex Syria tam regionum judicibus quam provinciarum quarunque ordinibus, insuper et defensoribus et reliquo solatio vel auxilio, et decurionibus vel curialibus.

Baluse, N. C., fol. 1516, has this:—Irenæus comes, apertus Nestorii ac Theodoreti amicus, ab isto ordinatus episcopus. Bigamus autem dicitur, quia post secundas nuptias factus fuerat episcopus Tyriorum, contra canones, ut docet Theodosii constitutio adversus eum lata, quæ extat in tomo tertio conciliorum, pag. 1216. (From notes on the "Concilium Quintum," sub an. 553.) Much of the above from H. Cowper.

Now, it is a most important and remarkable feature characterizing our great MS., designated A, that it not only enables us to add an entirely new page to our long-received Histories, but it obliges us to make corrections of what have been regarded as historical facts recorded in their old pages. Here is a case in point. Fleury and others say that Theodoret consecrated Irenæus to the Bishopric of Tyre, but when we come to handle the cause of Theodoret, in this MS., we shall find that there is strong evidence, amounting to moral certainty, that the then Archbishop of Antioch, Domnus, consecrated and instituted Count Irenæus to the Bishopric of the Metropolitical City of Tyre. So we shall discover, also, from the same quarter, are to be attributed to this same Archbishop Domnus, and not to Theodoret of Cyrus, or to Flavian, the Archbishop of Constantinople, those memorable words, respecting the Apostle Peter, that have for centuries resounded in Western Christendom, viz., ὅς καὶ τοῦ μακαρίου Μάρκου διδάσκαλος 'ην, καὶ τοῦ χοροῦ τῶν ἀπόστολων πρῶτος καὶ κορύφαιος.

In addition to the above we may here quote Baronius, Tom. 7 (Lucæ, 1741), Pagius 448 A.D., ii. A num. ii ad xix Theodosius Imp. vetuit libros Porphyrii et contra Cyrilli scripta editos, decrevitque etiam, ut quicumque nefariam Nestorii doctrinam quovis modo sectarentur ex Ecclesiis expellerentur. Ac denique statuit, ut Irenæus qui Nestorio faverat, et contra Canones Tyriorum Episcopus ordinatus fuerat, Sacerdotio penitus execretur. Legitur edictum illud Tom. 3, Concil., pag. 1216, ubi hanc habet subnotationem . . Irenæus, qui pæfato Edicto deponitur successorem habuit Photium . . et quia Imperatoris jussu, non synodali sententia dejectus est Irenæus, id circo anno sequenti secunda Synodus Ephesina eum canonice deposuit. Ordinatus fuerat a Theodoreto Cyrensi Episcopo, sed contra ejus Episcopatum tria vitia ab adversariis objecta: quod hæreticus Nestorianus esset, quod Bigamus, quod ab alienæ Provinciæ Episcopo consecratus. Ejus sanctitatem, humanitatem, pecuniæ contemptum, eleemosinas, aliasque virtutes, Theodoret prædicat, etiam in Epistola XXXV. . . . . Verum in Concilio Ephesino et post ejus celebrationem semper Nestorianis favit, ut ex dictis liquet.

IV.

THE DEPOSITION OF IRENÆUS, THE BISHOP OF TYRE.

(1) JOHN, Presbyter of Alexandria and Proto-Notary, said :—

We lodge an information with your Blessed and Œcumenical Synod against Irenæus that he is indeed a firm maintainer* of the impious Doctrine of Nestorius and a well-known aider and abettor of his, so far even as (to merit) to receive the punishment of exile. Therefore it is that he has had to sojourn, and does now sojourn, at any place which suited the pleasure of our Victorious and Christ-loving Emperors (to assign to him). Further, when he became Bishop of Tyre—how, I know not—it appeared still more evident at Tyre† that he is a follower of the false Doctrine of Nestorius. For, true is the Divine Scripture that declared—" If the Indian can change "his skin and the leopard his spots, then will you

---

* The word ‏ܐܣܬܐܘܠܐ‎ is, doubtless, in the Greek ἑδραίωμα, which word is used by S. Paul in 1 Tim., iii, 15, where he calls the Church "the Pillar and Ground of The Truth,"—*firmamentum, basis—foundation* (of a wall), *pedestal* (of a column). It is a compound of ‏ܐܣܬܐ‎, the

stat. emph. of ‏ܐܣ‎, as ‏שֵׁת‎ is from a rad. ‏שִׁית‎=‏שָׁתַת‎, and, in accordance with the peculiar genius of the Syriac, may be rendered a *firm maintainer* or *supporter*. Nestorius was the *basement*, and Irenæus the *pedestal*, of Nestorianism, to use a pardonable metaphor.

† In p. 109, l. 12, ‏ܨܘܪ‎ should, probably, have been written ‏ܨܘܪ‎ in the original MS., as the former is never, and the latter always, elsewhere used for Tyre. It seems an impossible word. At line 16, too, ‏ܐܪܥܬܐ‎, feminine plural, seems preferable to ‏ܐܪܥܐ‎ (fem. sing.) in MS. and corresponds with ‏ܨܘܪܝܐ‎.

" be able to do good by having learnt (to do) evil."* Moreover,¶ the aforesaid is a man who had two wives and, in his other conduct, was impure.   For, in this way it is well to express oneself before so (Reverend) an Assembly as this, as well as before other similar ones.   But, being such a character (without going into particulars)—clad, moreover, in Lamb's clothing, he proved himself a tyrannous Wolf† to the people of Tyre—and, to omit‡ the intervening circumstances, inasmuch as he had received Consecration uncanonically, he was deposed in a just and righteous manner.‖   Thus it was that the God-loving Photius was consecrated to the Bishopric of Tyre, who also, at the present time, continues with your

---

* The quotation is from Jeremiah, xiii, 23, where, in Dr. Lee's Syr. O. T., the passage stands thus : ܘܐܡܪ ܒܟܠ ܥܟܡܚܣ ܣܘܦܗ

ܘܢܦܣܟ ܓܡܚܗ · ܘܢܓܢܐ: ܚܠܟܚܗ · ܘܐܦ ܐܢܠܘ̈ ܠܐ

ܥܚܓܣܝ ܐܢܠܘ̈ · ܠܦܠܠܐܚܗ : ܥܠܗܠ ܝܠܕܓܘܠܘ ܚܡܚܠܐ .

¶ " The man of whom we were making mention was married twice" (which is contrary to the canons), " and in the rest of his mode of life " is impure : for, so it is right to speak before this assembly and such " (an assembly)."   He means, it is right to generalize, and not go into the particulars of the immorality of the individual man.

† S. Matth., vii, 15.

‡ In p. 109, l. 23, ܘܟܚܚܐ, ܘܘܚܡܠ̈ is literally : " And, that I " may omit the medias res, inasmuch as he had received Consecration (the ܣܝܡ ܐܝܕܐ is *the Imposition of the hand* in Consecration) uncanoni-" cally, he went out (i.e., he was expelled) in a just and righteous way : " and thus Photius received the (imposition of the) hand for the " Bishopric of Tyre."   At 2 Tim., i, 6, we have this imposition of hands of the Apostle in the words διὰ τῆς ἐπιθέσεως τῶν χειρῶν μου, and *with* the accompaniment of the Presbyters' hands at 1 Tim., iv, 14, in the words μετὰ ἐπιθέσεως τῶν χειρῶν τοῦ πρεσβιτερίου.

‖ See introductory note.

Holiness. This, therefore, is what we urge* (viz.); that, in accordance with justice and propriety, a Synodical and Legal Sentence should be pronounced upon him (Irenæus), lest the bitter root bring the plant† to prove injurious, and many, by its means, be contaminated.

2 (*a*) Dioscorus, Bishop of Alexandria, said :—

This Holy and God-loving Synod has heard from the Deposition‡ of the God-fearing Presbyter and Prime Notary, John, what is in conformity to propriety and Law and in accordance with Ecclesiastical Canons. Let then that, too, be added‖ (to what has already been done), which is the duty of this Holy Synod with respect to the Deposition of Irenæus—a man who is a Bigamist and a Blasphemer, and who has omitted no kind§ of Impiety

---

* At p. 110, l. 5, the word ܠܐ should be ܠܐ. No doubt the Scribe made a mistake. The word ܠܐܐ is equivalent to πρέπον implying *fitness, propriety* rather than *duty.*

† The predicate in this sentence is ܐ, ܐ, and ܐ in 3rd per. sing. fut. of ܐ, or, perhaps, Aphel. "Lest the plant prove to "be a bitter root and noxious, and many, by its means, are defiled." Or, Ne amara radix sarculos progeminet nocivos, quibus multi comtaminentur : "lest the bitter root bring the plant to prove injurious," &c. The word ܐ, commonly occurring in the Psalms and elsewhere, means *grass.*

‡ The words, ܐ, κατάθεσις, *Deposition* or *statement,* and, ܐ, *Deposition* or *removal,* occur within a few lines and in this one short speech,

‖ At l. 14 of text, ܐ ܐ ܐ is an expression that implies the formal sentence of the Synod, which he required to be added to the Expulsion, by the Emperor, of Irenæus for his Nestorianism.

§ This, of course, means that Irenæus had committed all possible

X

against Christ—the man whom I first (of you all)
adjunge removed from all the Honour of the Priesthood and Communion with the Laity.

3 (b) JUVENAL, Bishop of Jerusalem, said :—

We, likewise, join in the Sentence of the Holy
and God-loving Archbishop Dioscorus of the Church
of Alexandria the Capital.*

(c) THALASSIUS, Bishop of Cæsarea, said :—

It is sufficient for Irenæus's expulsion from the
Episcopate that he is infected with the Doctrine of
Nestorius.   But, because there is added the fact that
he was found to be a Bigamist, also, which is a violation of the Canons, I think it right that he should
be deprived of the Priesthood and of Communion
with Christians.

(d) STEPHEN, Bishop of Ephesus, said :—

From the very first I have been opposed to Irenæus being a Bishop, because, in a manner contrary
to all (ecclesiastical) Law and Order, he had been
clothed in the habiliments of the Priesthood. Seeing,
then, it is fitting and proper, as the Venerable Presbyter and Proto-Notary John has required, that he
(Irenæus) should be deposed by a common Sentence
of this Assembly, let Irenæus, aforementioned, be

---

kinds of Impiety against Christ, (the word |¦¿¦ means *species, kind*) of
which the speaker gives a short recapitulation.

 * Alexandria the Capital is, perhaps, the more correct way of rendering this oft-repeated expression than Alexandria the Great.

condemned by our Humbleness also, and be not allowed to hold any Communion with the Laity.

(e) EUSEBIUS, Bishop of Ancyra, said :—

Let Irenæus, who took two wives and has been accused of holding the tenet of Nestorius, be deprived of the Honour of the Priesthood. .

(f) FLORENTIUS, Bishop (of Sardis) in Lydia, said :—

What has been affirmed by the God-loving Presbyter and Prime-Notary John makes manifest that Irenæus's sentiments belong to the Impiety of Nestorius. Irenæus ought, therefore, to be ejected from the Honour of the Priesthood, because, as it were, by him the sublimity of the Mystery of Christians has been lowered in subservience¶ to the Nestorian opinions.

(g) MARINIANUS, Bishop of Synnada, said :—

Let Irenæus, who, in a two-fold capacity, has attained communion* (fellowship) and has been proved to be an adherent of the Doctrine of Nestorius, be deprived of the Episcopal Dignity.

(h) EUSTATHIUS, Bishop of Berytus, said :—

¶It is through the wickedness of the rebellious

¶ Or, "by means of Nestorian opinion." The sublimest mystery of Christians is the Doctrine of The Incarnation.

* This may be taken, perhaps, in a two-fold sense, or translated, "elevated or advanced to the (position of receiving the) two-fold communion of bread and wine," as my friend Martin would have it.

¶ Or, "The wickedness of the rebellious Dæmon occasioned to the race of the sons of men that they be deemed worthy of the Advent of

Dæmon that mankind have been judged worthy of the Advent (of the Son) of God. That Dæmon intended to harm us, and it is entirely contrary to his intention that he has made us to be thought worthy of the Mercy of God. (In the same way) do evil and impious men furnish, at the present time, the Holy Churches of God with the means of finding shelter from Calumny; indeed, when these men have once become completely eradicated, the trees of God bear (abundant) fruit. Irenæus, therefore, being one of the Defenders of the Impious Doctrine of Nestorius, has been justly sentenced to the punishment of Deposition by your Blessedness, and should also be deprived of Communion in the Pure Mysteries, as having been indeed the cause of all kinds of misfortunes next after Nestorius.

(*i*) Sozonius, Bishop of Philippi, said :—

l, certainly, from the first have never been desirous that Irenæus should become a Bishop, for fear the wolf should get to live among the lambs; and, with great forbearance¶ of spirit, did I continue harshly to conduct myself towards those who were assenting parties to it. For, his work of Impiety is well known,

---

God. For, when he willed to work evil to us, it was contrary to his will that he caused us men to be deemed worthy of the mercy of God : and now the will of man has brought calamity and impieties upon the Holy Churches of God that they may be proved to be blameless. For, at a time when these evils should have been extirpated from their very roots, at this same time the trees of God should yield fruit."

¶ Perhaps it may be better rendered thus—"And I used to complain of the great forbearance of those who allowed themselves to be persuaded into it,"

as well as the trouble he gave himself on behalf of his fellow thinker, Nestorius, so that, in consequence of such Impiety as his, either he should not have become (Bishop) in the first instance, or he ought to have remained such, as most explicitly do the Canons of the Fathers determine. Therefore, let him who loves Nestorius be with Nestorius.

(j) The HOLY SYNOD said :—
  "These things we say—from the impious all of
"us turn our faces—from Heretics we all turn our
"faces. Great is the choice of the Emperors.
"What was done by Irenæus, in his capacity of
"Bishop, must be repudiated—every act of Irenæus
"the Heretic must be repudiated. Just is the Sen-
"tence of the Synod. Just is the Sentence of the
"Gracious Emperors. What has been done by the
"wicked must be repudiated. Who, then, will put
"up his hand for a Bigamist and a Blasphemer?"

[END OF THE CAUSE OF IRENÆUS.]

AQUILINUS.

Aquilinus, or Acilinus, was consecrated to the Suffragan Bishopric of Byblus by the Metropolitan Bishop of Tyre, Irenæus.

He is called Celenius of Bibulus, as Irenæus is called Renius and Sophronius Sphirion, in Addl. MS. in Brit. Museum, numbered 14,643,[*] in connection with the Second Synod of Ephesus. He was one of the degraded Bishops, and his See appears to have been occupied by Marinianus. There were fifteen Bishops whom the Schismatics from the first and Œcumenical Synod of Ephesus, in 431 A.D., reckoned as having lost their Sees, because they refused their assent to the peace and reconciliation[†] between S. Cyril of Alexandria and the Archbishop John of Antioch, as the happy result of the negotiations commenced by Bishop Paul of Emesa who was the representative of that Archbishop, in conjunction with Aristolaus representing the Emperor and the Court at Constantinople. Although Aquilinus was ejected from his Bishopric, yet he was afterwards restored to it on his communicating with John of Antioch, notwithstanding his refusal to give his assent and approval to the Deposition of the great Heretic Nestorius.

He is called, by Fleury, Aquilinus of Barbalissa (Barbalissus).

The "Synodicon," before alluded to and written against the "Tragædia" of Irenæus of Tyre, refers once and again to Acili-

---

[*] See Cowper's Syriac Miscellanies, p. 90.

[†] It was on the happy occasion of this peace and reconciliation being accomplished that S. Cyril penned one of his three grand Epistles which have become an Œcumenical heritage of Christians and "binding on the whole Church," the first paragraph of which is thus translated by P. E. Pusey, M.A. :—"*Let the heavens* "*rejoice and the earth be glad,* for, *the mid-wall of partition* is un- "done, and that which vexed been stopped and the cause of all our "dissension been taken away, Christ the Saviour of us all dispen- "sing peace to his Churches, the most pious and devoted Kings "calling us thereto, whose most excellent emulations of ancestral "piety, guard the right Faith both sure and unshaken in their "own souls, and take very special pains for the Holy Churches, "that they may have glory renowned for ever and render their "kingdoms most famous: to whom the Lord of Hosts Himself "imparts good things with wealthy Hands and gives to overcome "their adversaries, grants them the victory. For He would not lie "Who says, *I live, saith the Lord, for them that honour Me I will* "*honour.*" This letter is referred to above, in Ibas's Letter to Maris, at p. 118, and also in the cause of Theodoret further on.

nus, who in one place is called "Acilinus Barbalissi Euphra-
"tesiæ."

Baluze thinks he is the same as Aquilinus of Byblus, who is
mentioned by Evagrius, Book I, 10.

In Dr. Neale's Hist. of the Holy Eastern Church, Vol. I,
chap. vii, Notitia of the Ancient and Modern Sees of the Diocœse of Antioch; under Phœnicia Prima, Berytus is put 3rd,
and Byblus 4th, after Tyre, Metropolis, with this note on the
former place—"Theodosius junior made this a Metropolis, as-
"signing to it Byblus, Botris, Tripolis, Orthosias, Arce, Anta-
"radus, *Agathias*, iii, 51.   But this arrangement was shortly
"afterwards disallowed in a Council at Constantinople." In the
same chapter, at page 134, Barbalissus is put the 10th after
Hierapolis, Metropolis : under Euphratensis.

It will, probably, be found impossible to uphold the view
which identifies Barballissus with Byblus, as both sites are
known and far asunder.   "Rufinus episcopus civitatis Bybli,"
also, appears in the Chalcedon lists.   There was a wonderful
amount of making and unmaking Bishops in those days, and
transactions were too numerous.   The Roman Emperors made
themselves ordinarily, to all intents and purposes, except in
matters relating to The Faith, practical heads of the Church
in the Eastern Empire, and they were not unfrequently too
demented or prejudiced to rule the Church with discretion and
judgment.

V.

THE DEPOSITION OF AQUILINUS,* BISHOP OF THE CITY
OF BYBLUS.

(1) PHOTIUS, Bishop of Tyre, said :—

As regards Aquilinus, Irenæus, who has been
deposed (expelled), made him Bishop of Byblus.
While this man was more impious and a greater
heretic than Nestorius, and much more passionate
(violent) than Irenæus, full of contempt for the
Altar, and the Church, and the Communion of
Priests, he (yet) carried his crime so far as to prefer
to them the friendship of his companion in Heresy.
Though often summoned to appear before me and
the Pious Archbishop Domnus, he absconded (hid
himself), so that the Pious Archbishop Domnus gave
me licence, by a written document, to consecrate another Bishop in his place.   But it has happened that
this Consecration has been deferred only in consequence of our having been convoked to this Great,
Holy, and Œcumenical Synod.

2 (a) DIOSCORUS, Bishop of Alexandria, said :—

Aquilinus, formerly Bishop of Byblus, has, as has
been declared by the God-fearing Photius his Metropolitan, deprived¶ himself of the Honour of the
Priesthood, by refusing to observe the established
order of things, and by having chosen to attach himself to his fellow-Heretic Irenæus.

---

* Aquilinus or Acilinus.
¶ Literally, "estranged himself or been estranged from," as in the

Let him, then, share in the lot of one, of whom it is said—"(As) he delighted not in blessing, so let "it be far from him."[*]

Let him, therefore, have what he has desired, i.e., let him be removed from the Episcopate.

Be it also known that, if anyone of the other Bishops under the Jurisdiction of Phœnicia,—I mean of those who are Suffragans to the God-loving Bishop Photius,—should be found to be a Heretic and should be infected with the false Doctrine of Nestorius, such an one shall be expelled by his Metropolitan and the Synod acting along with him. For, it is the Metropolitan's office to be alive to the dangers which threaten him, and to watch over (superintend) the execution of the commands, issued by this Holy and Œcumenical Synod. Now, we request him (Photius) to declare, with his own voice, that he will do this, and that he will notify each particular case individually to the Exalted Thrones.[†]

(b) PHOTIUS, Bishop of Tyre, said :—

I will use all diligence so as not to permit that any Bishop or Cleric, infected with the (impieties) of Nestorius, remain in the districts of Phœnicia; and especially (do I expect) that the Holy Synod of my Province will second me in this, to the Glory of

---

many other instances in which the word occurs in this MS.

[*] Psalm, cix, verse 17. In Prayer Book Version it is, at 16th verse, —" he loved not blessing, therefore shall it be far from him."

[†] That is to say, to the Emperor Theodosius and his Government. The Provincial Synod, being a "perfect council" because of the presence and action of the Metropolitan President, could accomplish this.

Christ, and to the credit of this Blessed, Œcumenical, Synod.

(c) JUVENAL, Bishop of Jerusalem, said :—

The blessed Apostle has said—" If an unbeliever "depart, let him depart."‖   Because, then, when he was summoned two or three times, according as the God-fearing Bishop Photius has informed us, Aquilinus refused to go to his own Church, he has deposed (ejected) himself from the Honour of the Priesthood.   For, also, in another place, the same Apostle has said—" A Heretic, after the first and " second admonition, reject, knowing that he who is " such is subverted and sinneth, being condemned of " himself."§

(d) STEPHEN, Bishop of Ephesus, said :—

This Aquilinus, formerly Bishop of the City of Byblus, has brought the punishment of Deposition upon himself, because he forsook that Holy Church entrusted to him, and preferred to It the friendship of the Impious Irenæus, who ordained him Bishop. He, therefore, should, likewise, according to my

---

‖ 1 Cor., vii, 15. S. Paul's words are—Εἰ δὲ ὁ ἄπιστος χωρίζεται, χωριζέσθω· where he is arguing the question of a Christian man or woman married to a heathen, and the desertion of one from the other. Juvenal argues that, although a Christian may not put away or desert his wife when an unbeliever, yet, if she desert her husband, the guilt of desertion sets him free.   So Aquilinus, having deserted Christ's Spouse the Holy Church (at Byblus), to which he had been wedded in spiritual bonds, releases her and frees her to contract another bond.

§ Titus, iii, 10, 11, Αἱρετικὸν ἄιθρωπον μετὰ μίαν καὶ δευτέραν νουθεσίαν παραιτοῦ· εἰδὼς ὅτι εξέστραπται ὁ τοιοῦτος, καὶ ἁμαρτάνει ὢν αὐτοκατάκριτος,

judgment, be put under the same sentence of condemnation as Irenæus.

(e) THALASSIUS, Bishop of Cæsarea, said :—

Aquilinus, who is infected with the same impiety as Irenæus, since he forsook the Holy Church of the Orthodox and attached himself to the aforesaid Irenœus, as we have learnt from the speech of the God-loving Photius, has degraded himself from the Dignity of the Episcopate.

(f) EUSEBIUS, the Bishop of Ancyra, said :—

Aquilinus should be removed from the Episcopate : for, it is my opinion that, when* he fled from (abandoned) the Priesthood, he deprived himself of (its) Function and Honour.

(g) JOHN, Bishop of (Sebastia in) Armenia Prima, said :—

He, who has withdrawn himself from the Communion of Christ, especially from being disposed to Impious Doctrine, deserves to be removed from the Honour of his Grade, particularly since he has brought such a punishment upon himself. It is for this reason that Aquilinus, also, who has put his Church into a widowed state (by deserting it), should be removed from the Church which he has purified, though unintentionally, by (really) withdrawing

---

* If the word be meant for ‎ܡܬ̈ܐ‎, plural of ‎ܡܬܐ‎, it will be *conservi, socii ; compeers, colleagues,* then the rendering will be "before "being prosecuted by his colleagues," But this hardly seems feasible.

himself from it. Inasmuch as he clothed himself with blasphemies, it is only just and right that he should be deprived of his Priestly Office, another taking his place, who will be able to govern the people, entrusted to him, on the principles of the Orthodox Faith, and in all Virtues acceptable to God.

(*h*) PHOTIUS, Bishop of Tyre, said :—

Inasmuch as Aquilinus has separated himself from the Function of the Priesthood, it is with justice, also, that he be deposed by this Blessed and Œcumenical Synod. I, also, for this reason, give my assent to the Holy Synod in the sentence passed on him, and I, too, adjudge him deprived of the Honour of the Episcopate.

(*i*) EUSTATHIUS, Bishop of Berytus, said :—

" Every living creature loves that which is like " itself,"* says the Divine Scripture. Because, therefore, Aquilinus, who was formerly the Bishop of Byblus, has adhered to the blasphemous Doctrine of Irenæus, it is only just and right for him to be inflicted with a punishment of the same character (as that which Irenæus received).

The HOLY SYNOD said :—

" We all of us say the same—we all depose " Aquilinus."

————————

[END OF THE CAUSE OF AQUILINUS.]

———————————————————————
* Ecclesiasticus, chap. xiii, verse 15.

SOPHRONIUS.

Sophronius, undoubtedly, the Bishop of Constantia, or Constantina, is mentioned as Bishop of Tella or Thella, as well, in the following words, by the Author of "The Chronicle of Edessa," recorded by Asseman, in Tom. 1, p. 202, as by these Acts of the Second Ephesine Synod in the next few pages.

ܘܐܬܟܢܫܬ ܬܘܒ ܠܐܦܣܘܣ ܣܘܢܗܕܘܣ ܐܚܪܢܬܐ. ܗܢܐ ܐܣܪܗ
ܠܪܒܐ ܦܠܒܝܢܘܣ ܐܦܣܩܘܦܐ ܕܩܘܣܛܢܛܝܢܘܦܘܠܝܣ
ܘܠܕܘܡܢܘܣ ܕܐܢܛܝܘܟܝܐ: ܘܠܐܝܪܝܢܐܘܣ ܕܨܘܪ: ܘܠܗܝܒܐ
ܕܐܘܪܗܝ: ܘܠܐܘܣܒܝܘܣ ܕܕܘܪܘܠܐܘܢ: ܘܠܕܢܝܐܝܠ ܕܚܪܢ:
ܘܠܣܘܦܪܘܢܝܘܣ ܕܬܠܐ: ܘܠܬܐܘܕܘܪܝܛܘܣ ܕܩܘܪܘܣ.

"Item altera Synodus Ephesi coacta fuit (non anno 445, sed "449) in qua Dioscorus anathemate percutit magnum Flavianum "Episcopum Constantinopoleos, Domnum Antiochiæ, Irenæum "Tyri, Ibam Edessæ, Eusebium Dorylæi, Danielem Haran, So-"phronium Telæ (seu Constantinæ), et Theodoretum Cyri."

In Le Quien's "Oriens Christianus," Tom. 3, c. 967, under "Ecclesia Constantiæ," reference is thus made to Tella:— "Constantina . . nominabitur Tela recentioribus et indi-"genis, quia in colle posita erat."

The name of Sophronius of Canstantine appears in the Chalcedonian lists thus:—"Sophronius, Episcopus civitatis Con-"stantinæ, subscripsi Σωφρόνιος Κωνσταντίνος." (Binius, Vol. III, p. 278.) He was made by the Fathers of the Council of Chalcedon, as we find from the 8th Session—a session chiefly devoted to the cause of Theodoret—to anathematize, along with two other Bishops, the Arch-Heretic Nestorius.

Eusebius, in his life of Constantine (Book II, chap. xlv), speaks of two Laws being promulgated, of which one was intended to restrain the idolatrous abominations prevalent, and the other related to the erection of Oratories and Churches on a grander scale. The first provided that no one should erect images, or practice Divination and other false and foolish arts, &c. The allegations, directed against Sophronius, refer to the last-named practices.

VI.

DOCUMENTS DRAWN UP AGAINST SOPHRONIUS, BISHOP
OF THE CITY OF TELLA (CONSTANTINA).

JOHN, Presbyter and Prime Notary, said :—

Simeon, Presbyter, and Cyrus and Eustathius,
Deacons of Tella, present Libels (of Indictment) to
your Holiness, which I hold in my hand and will
read, if your Great and Blessed Synod will command it.

JUVENAL, Bishop of Jerusalem, said :—

Let them be read and be deposited along with
the Documentary Transactions.

And he (John) read :—

To the Holy, God-loving, and Œcumenical Synod
which, by the Grace of God, is assembled at
Ephesus the Metropolis, from Simeon, Presbyter, and Cyrus and Eustathius, Deacons, and
the rest of the Clergy of the City of Tella.

We, having learnt from the Holy Fathers to accept those who honour God and to reject those who
blaspheme Him, pray that the Libel (of indictment),
which we bear, may be accepted, and that the same
may be read before your Holy and Œcumenical
Synod.

Whereas, then, Sophronius, Bishop of our City
of Tella, who is nephew¶ of Ibas, Bishop of
Edessa, has put aside the fair name of Priest, be-

¶ Or, " son of the paternal uncle." See note at page 152.

Z

loved of God ; and whereas¶ it is befitting and proper for him to continue by night and by day in
prayer, with the view to obtain pardon not only for
his own personal sins but also for those of the lay
people—none of these things has he thought of
doing ; but,¶ on the contrary, he has been parti-
cipating in (been partner with) "the table of
Devils,"* (Dæmons' Tables) : (he has taken part) in
the numerical computations (of Astrology), and in
the motion of the Stars and in (their) variation, and

¶ Or, " and he ought to have persevered night and day in prayer."

¶ Or it may, perhaps, be translated as follows :—" Sophronius, we
" say, instead of this, has done quite the reverse, as (for instance, serve)
" at the table of Devils, devoted himself to forbidden Calculations (cy-
" phering), to Astrology, to the errors of Sorcery and Pagan Divina-
" tions.   He has not been satisfied (with being infected) with the
" false Doctrine of Nestorius which he has learnt from his relative Ibas ;
" he has thrown himself, moreover, into all these horrible things."

* S. Paul, in 1 Cor., x, seems to have been in the minds of the complainants against Bishop Sophronius (for the words are the same as his)
and the allegation against him to have been that he violated what is implied
in v. 20, from which verse we conclude, with Bishop Wordsworth, that
" Worship offered to any but the One True God is accounted by God
" to be offered to *Devils* who *do exist*, although it be offered by man to
" *idols* (e.g., Jupiter, Venus, Bacchus, &c.) which *do not exist*."
We quote Mat. Martin here :—Dæmon, δαιμων. Plato in Cratylo, dæmones
dictos ait, ὅτι φρόνιμα καὶ δαήμονες, quia *sapientes ac Scientes.*   Serv. in 3,
Æn. "*Corybantes, dæmones sunt, ministri deum.   Demones, quasi δαή-*
" *μορες, qui totum sciunt :*" nempe quum δαίμωι est θεός, alioqui dæmones
multa sciunt.   Sed more gentili loquitur Servius.   Macrob. Saturn, Lib. i,
cap. 23, "*Dii sunt dæmones, i.e., scientes futuri, ut Possidonius scribit*
" *in libris, quibus titulus est,* περὶ ἡρώων καὶ δαιμόνων, *quia ex æterna*
" *substantia partita atque divisa qualitas illis est. . . .*" Sciunt (δαίω
scio) autem multa, partem ex prima creatione, partim experientia et divina revelatione.   Multi autem spiritus sæpe falluntur et fallunt. at
æmulantur divinitatem, dum furantur divinationem, ut ait Tertul. in Apo-
loget.   Gentili sensu δαίμων aut δαιμόνιον alias est Deus et Numen, alias
spiritus Deo inferior. . . . .   In N. T. Græco semel est δαίμονες
Matth., viii, 30.   Alioqui δαιμόνια sunt impuri spiritus.   Vulgata Latina
Versio tamen pro hac voce alicubi vertit dæmones, Matth., ix, 24, et
x, 8, et xii, 24, 27, 28, Jacob, ii, 9.   Passim alioqui tum in canonicis

in Divination,* and in the vaticinative Art of the
Pagans. Not being satisfied with the miserable
Doctrine of Nestorius which he learnt from his
relative Ibas, he has in addition thrown himself into
all these miserable occupations. We, therefore, pray
of your Piety to deign to listen to the few words
we wish to say, in all humility, relative to the conduct of Sophronius.

Once upon a time as he was travelling, he happened to lose a considerable amount of gold; and
when his suspicion rested on certain persons and he
had made them take an oath upon the Evangelists
(in the matter),—not satisfied with this—he, further, testing them by the ordeal† of bread and cheese
like the heathen, compelled them to eat. And, when

---

tum in apocryphis literis est δαιμόνιον, semper de malo spiritu. LXX.
Interpretes etiam illud habent pro אֱלִיל Psalm xcvi, 5 pro נָד Esa., lxv,
10, quod aliter exponitur τύχη: sicut etiam Gen. xxx, 10, item pro
שָׂעִיר Esa., xiii, 21 (ubi Aquil. τριχῶν) et pro עַי Esa., xxxiv, 14 et
pro שֵׁד Deut., xxxii, 17, Psalm cvi, 35. Etiam Ps, xci, 6, pro יָשׁוּד.
אֱלִיל quidem est idolum, nihil, sive ex אַל non, nihilum; sicut idolum
est res ficta, aut enim nihil est, aut saltem hoc non est.

See at page 43 of Cureton's "Ancient Syriac Documents," where
Shabil (a High Priest the son of High Priests) calls himself "an
"obscure dead man, for whose death there is no hope of resurrection;
"for I have been slain by paganism and am become a dead corpse of the
"evil one," which is an English translation of the Syriac words—

ܡܰܝܬܳܐ . ܐ݇ܢܳܐ ܗܘ ܡܢ ܚܫܝܟܘܬܐ . ܘܗܘܝܬ ܠ ܥܠܡܗ ܕܒܝܫܐ .

* Mat. Martin says—"Mantia, μαντεία, divinatio, a μαντεύομαι
vaticinor. Isidorus, Lib. viii, ix. Varro dicit, divinationis quatuor
esse genera, terram, aquam, aërem, et ignem. Hinc geomantiam, hydro-
mantiam, aëromantiam, pyromantiam dictam constat." Under Mantia, p.
280, Tom. prim., Lexicon Philologicum, M,DCCI.

† Tyromantia, per caseum, cujus meminit Hesychius, nisi legendum
pyromantia. (Fabricius, cap. xii, p. 142, Bibliographica Antiquaria.)
To the kinds of Divination given by Fabricius and Martinius, we must
add phialo-mantia, as discovered and discerned by the Syriac term in our MS.

he still did not find (the money), he prepared himself (and used) a divining Cup,‡ affirming that "the money

---

* "Divining cup." Such cups are first mentioned in Gen., xliv (the Cyatho or κυλικο μαιτεια was adopted by many nations of antiquity) where, says Rev. J. M. Rodwell, in Transactions of the Biblical Archæological Soc., Vol. II, Part 1, נָחַשׁ, cognate with לָחַשׁ, means *to utter a low, whispering, hissing sound*, hence to *practice enchantment* by muttering magical formulæ, hence to *augur* and *divine*. It is thus twice used in Gen., xlv and Gen., xxx, 27, which should be rendered "I have "consulted divination and the Lord hath helped me for thy sake." He continues, "It was by a cup, or נָבִיע, that Joseph was in the habit of "divining: and it is remarkable that the Septuagint Translators should "have rendered the Hebrew נביע. or cup, by κονδυ, which Athanæus "(Deip., ii, 55) explains by ποτηριων ασιατικον and Hesychius by ποτηριον βαρβαρικον, &c." After the remarks on Mr. Rodwell's Patera Paper—a circular Terra-Cotta vase discovered at Hillah near Babylon, well represented in the opposite page with the characters—comes a note by S. M. Drach, the first part of which I here subjoin. The C'biah נביע (not כום), for Joseph's divination (נחש) cup, he says, is supposed, by Hebrew authorities, to have been (comp. נבעה and *dome*-shaped hills) of longish shape, which, by striking, indicated the birth-rank of Joseph's brothers (Gen., xliii, 33), but he does not give his authority for saying this, and calls it "a curious proof of the Rabbinical "antiquity of spirit-rapping"! It may be interesting to him and all Spiritualists and Physicists to be assured that, after "a prolonged and im-"partial enquiry" made by a Commission appointed by the Physical Society of S. Petersburg to examine the Phenomena of Spiritualism, it appeared at the conclusion that "those so-called spiritual manifestations "proceed from unconscious movements, or from a conscious imposture, "and the spiritual doctrine is a superstition." (Brit. Medical Journal, April, 1876.)

Mr. H. F. Talbot, Vol. II, Part 1 of the same Transactions, says that Sakru is Magician, סחר *Magus Præstigator* and sakri סחר or סאחר *magia, illusio, præstigiæ*. We may observe here he understands that the celebrated Egyptian Scholar de Rougé has lately ascertained that the much-disputed Title Pharaoh signifies "the great House," Phe-raah, having found it so written in hieroglyphic character. The Chaldee and Syriac כעמתא is juramentum from יִמָא jurare, which is the Assyrian Mamita (Matth., v, 33) or has a close analogy to it.

The learned Fabricius, Cap. xii, de divinationibus, Vatibus, miraculis, Magia, &c., in his "Bibliographica Antiquaria," at p. 419, says: "Ex "poculis divinatio vide Suidam in Κοτταβιζειν(a) et supra Cyathomantia,"

(a) Κοτταβιζειν. Mat. Martin, on this word, at p. 209 of Vol. I, writes thus: "Suid. "Cottabus latex, id est, ærea phiala, quam inter cœnandum ponebant vini plenam:

" is to be found with such and such a person,¶ whose
"name is so and so, and who is clothed in such and
"such a way." And many times the Dæmons,
wishing to confirm him in the imposture, pointed out
the thief, not because they wanted to convict him
(the thief), but because they were eager to plunge
(overwhelm) the Bishop in ruin.

On another occasion, too, he was guilty of this
same thing, and had recourse to the Divining-cup (or
phial-Divination), as we learnt from Simeon, who
used to act as Server to him at the Bishop's House:
for, he once took this man's son and introduced him
quite alone into his bed-chamber, with one Abraham,
Deacon, a relative of his, together; and, having
placed a table in the middle, they put under the
table Incense, destined for the Dæmons, but, upon
the table, a phial (dish) in which were oil and water;
and he placed the lad, in a state of nudity, at the side
of the table; and the whole was covered with clean

---

and at p. 413: "Cyathomantia. Vide Mandæum, cap. xv. Apologiæ
"pro Magis Gensii(*b*) victimas humanas, Tomo I, p. 353. Supplemen-
"torum Tomum ab(*c*) Observationes selectas Hallenses Observationes IV,
"Mich. Christiani Tierof diss. de sacris vinculis. Jen 1657, et inter-
"pretes ad Gen. xliv, 5, qui locus tamen nihil aliud significat, quam ex
"poculo illo ablato Josephum augurari de malo peregre adventantium
"animo."

¶ Or, it may be rendered thus :—" On what man will my gold be
"found? What is his name? What is his dress? The Demons, un-
"doubtedly wishing to lead him astray (into error), pointed out the thief,
"not that they had a desire of punishing him, but because they sought to
"lead the Bishop into perdition (aimed at overwhelming him in ruin)."

"deinde in parva pocula conjicientes de alto projiciebant (ἐρρίπτουν) ut strepitum
"ederent, qui cottabus vocabatur."
(*b*) Jac Gensium de victimis humanis Tomo 1, cap. xx, sq. Gensium is one of the
many Authors Fabricius refers to in his work "Bibliographica Antiquaria."
(*c*) Sic, but ἐδ must surely be meant.

linen (white sheet).   Then, the Deacon began inton-
ing words which the Bishop had formulated for him
from his wicked divining-art.   Then they questioned
the lad, saying to him—"What do you see in the
"Phial?" and he said, "I see flames (sparks) of fire
"going upwards out of it;" and again, after a little
while, he questioned him, saying—"What do you
"see yet?" and he said, "I see a man, sitting on a
"throne of gold, and clad in purple, and a crown
"upon his head."   They then dug near (behind) the
door and made there a deep hole (well), which they
filled with oil and water, and they made the lad
stand there, and said to him—"What do you see in
"the hole (well)?" and he said, "I see Habib" (for,
he was on a journey to Constantinople); "and I see
"him," the lad continued to say, "seated on a black
"mare-mule that is blind-folded; and behind him two
"men on foot."   Further still, they brought an
egg, and, when they had opened it, they threw away
what was the white of the egg, and left the yolk of
it; and they said to the lad—"What do you per-
"ceive in the shell of the egg?" and he said, "I
"perceive Habib proceeding on the road, on horse-
"back, and he has put a collar round his neck, and
"before him are going two men."   And on the
day after, the Bishop's son arrived from Constantinople, just as his father had divined.

This the lad confessed on oath upon the Evangelists, along with his Father and Mother, in the
presence of witnesses, who affirmed that the circum-

stance took place exactly as it was visioned to the lad. Moreover, the lad went on to say—"For eight "months, I used to be walking, (when) seven men, "dressed in white, constantly went in front of me.' And in the lapse of these eight months the lad was out of his mind, having been driven mad (lost his reason); and it was with difficulty that, after having brought him into holy places and anointed him with consecrated oil, they succeeded in curing his insanity.

Now, as regards these Astrological Writings of his (Sophronius), to what purpose is it to speak of them? There are those, too, who wrote them; the very scribes, who copied them, are at Tella; there is Maras, the Sub-Deacon, and there are Adesia and Stratonica, Deaconesses of the Church; there is Peter, the Chief Physician of the City; lastly, there is Uranius,¶ Deacon of the same, who con-

---

¶ This may be translated thus :—"And there is, last, the Deacon of "the same City, Uranius, who owned that he had read them, when he "went up to the Bishop's House to get him to subscribe his hand to "some alms-deed (receipt), when he saw the good Bishop moving the "brazen sphere, belonging to his evil Divination, and experimentalizing "with it. When he came down (from the Bishop's House), he made "known to his comrades all he had seen. And, as though all these "miserable affairs were not enough for him, Habib, his Son, brought "thither Hesychius, a Jew, and bid him step up to the Bishop's House, "and ate with him Jewish food in his Father's absence ; and in the "Week of the Pentecost, which is the time when *we* ourselves fast, he "was feasting with the Jew at the Bishop's House ; and, for about ten "hours, this man continued feasting with the Jew, up to the time when "he took him (the Jew) into the Church of the Apostles, whilst the "Service was proceeding. When, in consequence, the City had become "excited into a commotion, with the Clergy, it expelled the Jew as well "Habib ; but they, on being expelled, fled to the Prætorium of General "Florus ; and, on this impious and heathen Florus becoming irritated, he "and his rushed upon the City and murdered in it many persons, men and "boys, and wounded more than one hundred people ; whilst those who,

fessed to have read them when he went to the Episcopal Palace for the purpose of getting a ticket of Alms signed, and there saw the good (Reverend) Bishop carrying and inspecting the brass-sphere destined for his criminal incantations (divination) ; and, on coming out, he told his colleagues all he had seen. Not satisfied with giving himself over to these wicked practices, his son Habib introduced a Jew, (named) Housick, into the Bishop's House and ate with him, after the fashion of the Jews, in the absence of his Father. During the week of Lent, when we fast,‡ he feasted with this Jew, and kept him at table till ten o'clock ; and even carried his audacity (so far as) to bring him into the Sanctuary of the Apostles, at the time that Service was being held. The City and the Clergy, shocked by this

---

" in the confusion, had fled to the Holy Altar, there, and with the arrows " remaining unextracted from their persons, had their blood shed, some " of them before the Altar. And in this condition a multitude of them " died clasping the Altar."

§ The laws against corresponding and conversing too familiarly with Jews and Gentile philosophers forbade the Clergy, says Bingham (Bk. VI, chap. iv), to eat with the Jews under pain of suspension. And the Apostolical Canons prohibited them not only fasting or feasting with the Jews, but receiving even any of those portions or presents, which they were used to send to one another upon the Festivals.

In p. 123, l. 17 of the Text, the word may be rendered *pittacium*, or *pyctacium* quod videtur, ait M. Martinius (1) esse tabella pice illita ad scribendum, (2) est tabella quævis alia similis usus, &c.

Castell says of the Syriac word for *pulmentarium* :—" Secundum " Syros sunt Esculentorum deliciæ." Mat. Martin has—" Pulmentum " vocatur a pulte. Sive enim sola puls sive quid aliud ejus permixtione " sumatur, pulmentum proprie dicitur. Gen. xxvii, 4." (Vol. II, p. 569.) Again, at p. 570, he defines Puls thus :—" Cibus ex farina vel " lacte in olla coctus, liquidus ; etsi alius crassior, quam alius : non tamen " duratus in panem, et hæc quidem simplex puls : cui interdum et alia " junguntur, ut caseus, ova, &c."

conduct, chased both the Jew and Habib, who sought refuge in the Prætorium of the Commandant (Duke) Florus. The impious and pagan Florus rushed up-on the City, where (his people) laid violent hands on a great number of men and children—certainly more than a hundred. In despair, these took refuge near the Tabernacle ; but, then, the arrows reached their bodies, their blood was shed before the Altar, and many died in the act of embracing It.

We have, then, prayed this of your Holy Synod— to avenge us of this pestilent and murderous man, since all the Lay-people, and the company of the Monks have taken oath, declaring, " We will not for " the future receive this man any more, or hold com-" munication with him, or have any intercourse with " him at all ;" because they have seen that any con-nection (relation) with him is dangerous.

Already the Masters of the world have taken cognizance (of our complaints), and have ordered that they be reserved, until your Holy Synod has effected the Deposition of Ibas and Sophronius.

This is what we learnt when the City, the Clerks and Monks included, was assembled to commence proceedings (to draw up Documentary Acts) in the presence of the Defender (Procurator) of the City. From the persons belonging to the household (of Sophronius) we have our information. Others have heard it besides us.

Those Documentary Acts are in the custody of the Procurator of the same City.

AA

We, therefore, fall at the feet of your Holy Synod, entreating you to have compassion on us, and on our City, and on all the region that is scandalized by Sophronius, and to rid our Church of him, which, being filled with the arms and the blood of those who were slain in the very middle of the Sanctuary, has been closed for two months.

I, Cyrus, Deacon, present (this Libel) in conjunction with those of my Confraternity.

I, Eustathius, Deacon, present (this) with those of my Confraternity.

THALASSIUS, Bishop of Cæsarea, said :—

It is in accordance with justice and in conformity with the Laws Ecclesiastical that the enquiry should be reserved for him who is going to be appointed Bishop of the City of Edessa, so that he, with the whole Synod of his Province, will, when it is agreeable to them, accomplish that which is pleasing to the Lord God and is befitting His Glorious Name.

The HOLY SYNOD said :—

"This is a correct sentence—this we all approve "of—this we all determine."

JUVENAL, Bishop of Jerusalem, said :—

I, also, for my part, adjudge it just and right that, when there shall be an Orthodox Bishop at Edessa, he, together with the Orthodox Bishops of the Province, should take cognizance of the cause of

Sophronius; and whoever shall find Nestorians in the Province shall eject them, and (so) purify the Church.

[END OF THE CAUSE OF SOPHRONIUS.]

THEODORET.

BB

THEODORET.

This magnificent character of the 5th Century of our Era comes next to be arraigned at this lawfully-constituted Tribunal of the Church—lawfully constituted less from an ecclesiastical, than from a civil and imperial, point of view. But whether at its bar Justice is to have her due in the matter of ordinary procedure, and in the cause of one of the most self-sacrificing of the Sons of Men, or whether a mere travestie of her fair name, with the beam of her scales unset and eyes unblinded, is to be perpetrated will soon become apparent.

Theodoret, named Θεοδώρητος because, after several years of barrenness of his mother, he was "given of God" in answer to the "effectual, fervent prayer of a righteous" Anchorite, was a Native of Antioch, and was born of noble and wealthy Parents, who dedicated him to God from childhood, and left him a large inheritance which he literally gave away, leaving himself nothing. In Theodoret's Letter to Nomus, Ex-consul, as given by Baronius (Tom. 7, p. 618), "quâ ipse (says Baronius) totam vitam suam et res ab se in Episcopatu gestas brevi compendio narrat," Theodoret says of himself: "Illud quidem "adjiciam (quando quidem calumniatores hæc dicere me co- "gunt) quod ante conceptionem genitores me offerre Deo pol- "liciti sunt et ab incunabulis."

At Antioch he was ordained a Reader of the Church when very young. At the Monastery of Apamea he made the acquaintance of Nestorius and of John of Antioch. When about 35 years of age, he was, contrary to his wish, consecrated Bishop of Cyrus, situate in Syria Euphratensis, and said to have been built by the Jews, in honour of Cyrus, at their return from the Captivity. Although an inconsiderable city in itself (indeed, Pelagius, the Presbyter, calls it a *town, small borough*), the Diocœse embraced "800 Parishes among its dependencies." It was this Diocœse, suffragan to the Metropolitical City of Antioch, which, though it "on his accession had been one "mass of Heresy, became altogether free from that evil leaven," by reason of his indomitable labours on behalf of The True Faith. It had reason, too, to thank him for many great public works his indefatigable zeal for the temporal, as well as spiritual, good of his people enabled him to accomplish.

Notwithstanding, such was the opposition he met with, and
such the calumnies heaped upon him, and the trials he had to
go through, greatly from his being reputed to be a Nestorian
through his apparent complicity with the great fautors and
abettors, if not originators, of that form of Error, that in the
Letter, quoted above, he complains that, although he had lived
20 years without accusing any man and without being accused
by any man, &c., yet his endurances were very great indeed—
"et sæpe (he declares) ad inferorum etiam portas mortis
"perveni."

Of this noble Champion of the Church my friend, a Chap-
lain of the noted Church of Sainte Geneviéve, well says :—

His eventful life, his apostolic labours crowned with the
greatest success, his ardent contentions inspired by an honest
opinion and by an upright conscience, his numerous writings,
and, above all, the persecutions of which he was the object
have made him one of the most remarkable personages of those
troubled and unhappy times. His reputation and his authority
were immense in the East : he had fought Cyril with vivacity
for many years, but he had not hesitated to submit as soon as
he recognized The Truth ; he was regarded as an oracle by his
Colleagues in the Episcopate, and he himself teaches us that
his discourses at Antioch were frequently applauded by the
faithful. Everyone was pleased to hear him speak.

Theodoret had, nevertheless, many enemies, because he had
long supported the party of Nestorius and written violent dia-
tribes against S. Cyril. He also continued to be suspected by
all those who held for Eutyches and Monophytism; his letter
of congratulation to Dioscorus had been ill-received; the Emperor had withdrawn from him his good graces, and, in spite of
the powerful protectors whom the Bishop of Cyrus reckoned
at Court, Theodosius had given him repeated blows. First, he
had condemned him not to pass out of his Diocese (June–July,
448 A.D.); afterwards, he had forbidden him to come to the
Council, unless he was sent for ; and, as if a first prohibition
was not enough, a second Edict was issued on the eve of the
opening of the Synod (30th March, 6th August). Theodoret,
in one word, was a victim to the strokes of the conductors of
the Cabal of Ephesus. Thus, they did not fail to deal with
him, and in going through the Acts of this famous Council we

easily recognize that he was the most redoubtable adversary of the whole assembly.

It is, nevertheless, a strange thing and one of the finest tributes rendered to the memory of this great man, that he is the only one of the Bishops condemned or deposed on whose memory hovers no disquieting doubt. In spite of the hatred they bore him, and the pleasure they would have had in dishonouring him, they did not attempt to raise against him one accusation which could properly be defamatory. They had made Ibas a thief and a debauché, Daniel of Harran a Libertine and an unchaste man, Irenæus an impious person and a bigamist, Sophronius a Magician and a sorcerer: they dared not make Theodoret anything but a Heretic and a Nestorian. And for that, moreover, they were obliged not to rely on his more recent writings, on his solemn and reiterated declarations, quite orthodox and approved as such by S. Flavian, John of Antioch, and Domnus, they must rummage in his former pamphlets, in his treatises against S. Cyril or on the Incarnation. (Martin's Etude.)   Before the Council in Session the Assessor is made to quote extracts from one or two of Theodoret's works that are now lost. One of these works so used is designated AN APOLOGY ON BEHALF OF DIODORE OF TARSUS AND THEODORE OF MOPSUESTIA, WARRIORS OF THE (TRUE) RELIGION. The same seems, also, to quote directly from his, no doubt, splendid Commentary on the Psalter, now quite lost to the Church, or indirectly from some kindred writer on the Psalms, perhaps Theodore of Mopsuestia, his teacher.*   From these extracts we gather that the first work, the Apology, resembled, in its mode of treatment of the subject matter, that of his "Eranistes or Polymorphus," in which he upholds the great Truth of the Co-Existence of the Two Natures (of the Divinity and of the Humanity) in the One Person of Christ without confusion or commixture, and combats the different forms of error against It,

---

* Cave, in his "Historia literaria," p. 247, says Theodore had as his hearers Nestorius and Theodoret. Ἀνὴρ inquit Sozomenus (L. 8, c. vii) καὶ τῶν ἱερῶν βίβλων, καὶ τῆς ἄλλης παιδείας, ῥητόρων τε καὶ φιλοσόφων ἱκανὸς ἐπιστήμων. Theodoret, Soz. (L. 5, c. xl) πάσης μὲν* ἐκκλησίας διδάσκαλος, κατὰ πάσης φάλαγγος αἱρετικῆς ἀριστεύσας.

* See Dioscorus's Letter below and Appendix to this Vol.

by a catechetical and categorical form of reasoning, similar
to which, also, is the treatment adopted in his Great "Commentary on the Bible," in its early part.

The Synod did not spend too much time in judging him,
and the Bishops soon pronounced their formal Sentence. He
had been specially marked out by the Emperor, who, on the eve
of the assembling of this Œcumenical Council, and notwithstanding the strongly-marked censure of him in the formal
Document (a) convoking it, added another (β, p. 8), with
special reference to Theodoret, as we have seen. The Eutychian party had no difficulty in accomplishing their end, in
silencing and rendering him, to all appearance, useless to the
world and the Church. There is no doubt he had a leaning to
his old friend Nestorius as well as to Diodorus and Theodorus, the real originators of Nestorianism, but he can hardly,
with any great amount of justice, be branded as a Heretic, inasmuch as the wickedness of Heretics as such consists in the
wilfulness with which they cling to the Heresy as such.

At the Great Council of Chalcedon, summoned by the
Emperor Marcian in 451 A.D., in the 8th Session, the Bishops
were particularly urgent for Theodoret to anathematize the
Heresiarch, interrupting him in his address to the Council
with the exclamations—" Say plainly, Anathema to Nestorius
" and his Doctrines, anathema to Nestorius and his followers,"
when Theodoret replied, " Of a truth, I say nothing but what
" I think is pleasing to God. Be assured, first of all, that I
" feel no anxiety to be restored to my city, or recover my dig-
" nity; no! that is not what has brought me hither; but
" having been aspersed, I am come to convince you that I am
" orthodox, and that I anathematize Nestorius, Eutyches, and

We may here observe that two MSS. in London and one in Paris
ascribe the Headings of the Psalms to Theodore, which Headings,
be it observed, actually take the place of a brief Commentary, as
manifestly in Ceriani's magnificent Ambrosian Edition of the Pes-
chito, and of something more, when the Canons, that is, the literary matter that comes after each first verse, are taken into
consideration. Theodoret speaks of someone who dared to do
away with the Greek and Hebrew Headings on the Psaltery and
to make new ones of his own accord, trusting some Jewish
teachers whom he followed. So these headings are the more interesting since there can be little doubt that Theodoret speaks of
his teacher Theodore.

"all who affirm that there are two Sons." Again the Bishops
interrupt him, and again he said, "Anathema to Nestorius, to
"all who refuse to call the Virgin Mary 'Mother of God,' &c."
The issue was that the Magistrates said—"In accordance with
"the decision of the Council, Theodoret shall again be put in
"possession of his Church at Cyrus." (Oxford Fleury, p.
378).

Notwithstanding all that has been written about him by Dr.
F. H. Newman and others, I may, without much presumption,
fearlessly assert that the complete History, with information
derived from Syriac sources, of the Life and Labours, personal and literary, of the great Bishop of Cyrus, whom the
Latrocinium of Ephesus unintentionally honoured in condemning him, and that, also, of his Master, whom some in the real
and Orthodox Œcumenical Council, just quoted, openly and
without objection, described as "the Blessed Theodore of Mop-
"suestia, the Hero of The Truth and Doctor of the Church,"
have yet to be accomplished by some learned Scholar and
Son, or, it may be, literarily accomplished Daughter, of our
Zion.

Fritsche, in his "Dissertatio de Theod. Mops. vita et scriptis,"
has remarked that "Theodoretus, qui sæpius Theodorum, nomine
ejus non addito. impugnat, etiam ad Theodorum respexit," quoting
the following passages in Theodoret's προθεωρια of his ερμηνια
εις τους ψαλμους (p. 605, 606, of Migne. Patrol LXXX. 862, 863)
επειδη δε και τας επγραφας των ψαλμων ψευδεις τινες απεκαλεσαν,
αναγκαιον ηγεομαι και περι τουτων βραχεα διεξελθειν, εμοι δοκει
τολμηρον ειναι τας ανεκαθεν εμφερομενας επι Πτολεμαιου . . . . . .
ανατρεπειν επιγραφας.   If Esdras wrote the inscriptions on his
copy, and if the LXX προς δε ταις αλλαις θειαις γραφαις και τας
επιγραφας ηρμηνευκασιν· ταλμηρον οιμαι και λιαν θρασυ, ψευδει
ταυτας προσαγορευειν και τους οικειους λογισμους της του πνευ-
ματος ενεργειας σοφωτερους υπολαμβανειν.

There is much valuable and highly interesting information, relative to Theodoret and the Psalter, treasured up in MSS. not yet
brought to light by any Editor.

VII.

THE DEPOSITION OF THEODORET. THE BISHOP OF CYRUS.

PELAGIUS, Presbyter of Antioch, said :—

I have a Libel (Bill of Indictment) against Theodoret and Domnus, and I request that it may be
received and read.

JUVENAL, Bishop of Jerusalem, said :—

Let the Libel of Pelagius, Presbyter of Antioch,
be received and read.

And he (John, the Prime Notary,) read :—

To the Holy and God-loving Œcumenical Synod
assembled at Ephesus, the Metropolis, from
Pelagius the Presbyter :—

¶It is as the Source of all good, so to speak, to the
human race that the GOD of that race, The TRUE

¶ Hoffman gives, as a translation of this rather difficult exordium,
the following, anglicized :—" The GOD of Mankind and True Saviour
" Jesus Christ, Who is The Only True GOD and The Only Eternal
" Life, has, (so to speak), as a Fountain Head of all other good things
" for mankind, caused this your Godly, Blessed, and Œcumenical Synod
" to assemble, partly aforetime in Nicæa—for, I believe, I behold that
" and its successors in this one—partly twice here already.   This is the
" third Œcumenical Synod assembled at the end of ages ; and this is, I
" believe, the last of all Synods through The HOLY GHOST, since The
" HOLY GHOST, The All-PERFECTOR HIMSELF, has in a special manner
" assembled it, that it may be the last, so that here it may be fulfilled :
" ' On the mouth (evidence) of two or three witnesses every word shall
" ' stand,' and so that he who does not acquiesce in the Dogmas con-
" firmed by The HOLY GHOST through you shall be esteemed a Heathen,
" a Publican, and, in short, an anathematized man ; and whilst every sin
" and blasphemy is forgiven to men, this shall not be forgiven, either in

Saviour Jesus Christ, Who Alone is The True[*] God and Alone Eternal[†] Life, caused that your Divine and Blessed Œcumenical Synod to assemble, which took place in Nicæa.

I believe I perceive that Synod, and the one subsequent, united (in accord) at this moment.

God has already assembled you here twice; but, this third Œcumenical Synod, placed at the termination of ages, will be, I opine, the last of all the Councils convoked by The Holy Ghost.

That is the reason why The Holy Ghost, Who is The Perfector of all, has assembled it with special care, because it is the last; wishing to fulfil here again (what is written, viz.,) "by the mouth of two or three witnesses shall every word be established."[‡]

Whoever, then, will not yield himself to what The Holy Spirit shall decide, by your means

---

" this world, or in the world to come; because he has blasphemed against " The Holy Ghost. For; if, according to the Laws and the Holy " Scriptures, two or three men in number are to be believed, who, then, " would dare to contend in this against the three—the Trinity of wit- " nessing Synods, that is, indeed, against The Trinity Itself, Which " through you is Itself a witness,—without being justly condemned by " you? Whilst I, also, for my part, with justice, as well as everybody " else, desire this, I have recourse to this Petition, and I expect to re- " ceive help, in what I have suffered, from you who are devoted by God " to the general good." It may, likewise, be rendered, I think, as if the Synod were the origin of all Blessings to men, or of very many Blessings, if the word |ܐ‍ܝ‍ܒ‍ܘ‍ܛ‍ܐ| be taken as signifying *many, very many*.

* John, xvii, 3,—or, "in His One-liness is Very GOD" is a very literal, but very exact, rendering.

† John, vi, 33.

‡ Deut., xvii, 6; Mat., xviii, 16; &c. Or, "upon the evidence of " two or three witnesses shall every truth be established." "Every truth" is the rendering of an ancient concordance in my possession, which I think is an exact and true one.

and mediation, let him be regarded "as an heathen "man and a publican;"* let him, in fact, "be "excommunicated." And, whilst every sin and (all) blasphemy will (can) be forgiven unto men, this will not be forgiven unto them, either in this world or in the world to come, because it is Blasphemy against THE HOLY GHOST.†

For, if two in number, or three persons,‡ bearing witness (to a certain matter) are to be believed, according to the Law‖ and the Divine Scripture§— when three Synods (bear witness) pronounce, by the the help of The TRINITY, that is to say, when The TRINITY ITSELF (bears witness) pronounces, through their (the Synods') mediation, who would venture to dispute your (Synodical) Judgments by alleging that they are not with justice determined ?¶

Convinced myself, as everybody must be, that this is true and excellent, I have come with this Petition to you; and I hope to be deemed deserving of your support, in my sufferings, seeing that you are appointed of GOD for the purpose of enhancing everybody's weal.

I am of Syrian origin, and of the City of Antioch, situate in the East. From my childhood I have loved solitude and to be secluded from the bustle of

---

* Matthew, xviii, 17.   † Matthew, xii, 31 and 32.
‡ Matthew, xviii, 16.   ‖ Deut., xvii, 6; and xix, 15.
§ 2 Corinthians, xiii, 1, &c.
¶ Or, perhaps, very literally—" Who (being arraigned) will dare to " (contend with) contest those matters you determine, (saying) that they " are not justly condemned ?"

business, to pass my life like the Monks, and to feed¶ on the Profane Sciences.   I have acquired human wisdom enough, seeing men in the world believe in being wise, not to be astonished at their discoveries. I aimed, too, at the acquisition of the knowledge of those Doctrines that are sublime and (exceptionally) perfect—I mean, the Doctrines only of the Holy Scriptures.

Whilst still a youth, not yet hirsute, I enter the Monastery.   I found my happiness in entire quietude, poor and sinful being as I am, but I was allowed continually to search into the all-Holy and Divine Books, whereby to attain to that wisdom, which is hidden in Divine and ineffable Mysteries and comparable with which, since tasting it, I have found nothing, nor (comparable with which) anything in the world do I know worthy of love.   Wholly devoted to this work, I kept reflecting how I could be useful to myself and, through my instrumentality, to others, whilst by night and by day I used (continually) to be making a Collection of Doctrines, precious to The Truth; brewing, all the while, in meditation over them,

---

¶ The word ܡܩܪܐ is *lectio*. Food in external reading doubtless means that he studied the works of Plato, &c. See below. Literally, "The (mental) diet of the Monks and (other) food in reading, external to it, I have been fond of from my youth up; and I have acquired a small fund of human wisdom as great as that of those whom men of the world deemed wise. I was aware that I should not admire their inventions(*a*) and I, therefore, made advance that I might specially obtain knowledge of the most sublime and perfect Doctrines—I mean those of the Holy Scriptures."

(*a*) That is, the inventions, discoveries, of the worldly wise.

without so* much despairing, in the least, of my insufficiency, as strengthened by love towards GOD. He, however, who is ever wont to envy what is good and excellent (viz., Satan) permitted it not (to continue).

Everyone has heard speak of Theodoret, and everyone knows him as an Adversary of GOD. He and Domnus, Bishop of Antioch, are pronounced Impious Persons, at the City of Alexandria the Capital, by every mouth of the Christ-loving people, and that at a City greater than all others under the Sun, and which, in Religion more than in greatness, is superior to those others. Now this man, who is really a hater of GOD, supercilious and proud, although he had (only) attained to (the post of) Bishop† over a small city, that is, a town—this man Theodoret (I say) has brought upon himself a just resentment (indignation); for, he has tired the Emperor's ears with the cries of all the people and the complaints (brought in on his account)—this man and Domnus, the Bishop of Antioch aforesaid,

---

* In the Syriac Text, at p. 129, ll. 26 and 27, ܠܐ ܗܘ is τοσοῦ-τος and ܡܣܒܪ is *to despair.* In p. 130, l. 1, the word ܐܬܠܒܟ, or ܐܬܠܒܟ, answers to *corroboratus,* and l. 3, ܣܒܕ to *pertulit,* and l. 6, ܟܘܠܐ is from ܢܨܐ, *to quarrel,* on which see Castell's Lexicon, p. 562.

† In p. 130 of Syriac Text, at l. 17, ܩܣܛܪܐ is *castra* Romana, or, rather, *Castrum.* Mat. Martin says, p. 198, *Castrum* onomast. vertit ἔρυμα. Magn. Etym. κάστρον, ὀχύρωμα, id est, munimentum. Perot. *Castrum* significat locum, muris munitum : et castello majus est, minus oppido. *Castrum* a casa deducitur, quod sit conjunctio quædam casarum. In l. 18, the word ܐܦܣܩܘܦܐ is *Bishop.*

who favours the troubles the other originates, out of a culpable love for the mischievous and impious Doctrine of Nestorius, occupied themselves with war against my peaceful self: and, having filled me with the dread of terrible dangers (impending), they obliged me to a compulsory silence. They made and composed Declarations of Faith, whereby they tormented (annoyed) certain persons of my acquaintance.¶ They even had the audacity to draw up (a Formulary of Faith) a Creed, according to their own fancy, without the slightest regard for the Synod* preceding this your Holy one, the which, however, has clearly forbidden anyone to presume to write, expound, or compose any Formula† of Faith other than that of the Holy and Blessed Fathers. And they added that I must not discourse on the subject of The Faith openly in the presence of anybody, and that I must not venture in secret to teach (It to) those who are desirous of learning. Theodoret said (to me, in so many words), without

---

¶ Or—" For, they made and dressed up those documents on Oath, in " which they brought charges against some of those persons who were in " acquaintance with me."

* The Synod (431 A.D. of Ephesus), ܠܘܣܘܕ, commanded that no man should be permitted either to write, expound, or compose ܟܕܒܥܝ beyond the Faith of the Fathers. See Canon vii of this Œcumenical Council.

† In p. 131, l. 14, the word ܐܘܡܘܣ looks back to ܐܥܒܝܣܘ in l. 7, and ܐܠܟܟ, or ܐܠܟܟ, in l. 15, which is first person sing., to ܠܘܕܐ in l. 3, and is exegetical of this last word. Also, judging from what follows in the text, the second word in l. 16, if the scribe had written with vowels, the full and correct reading would be ܐܥܒܝܣܘ, first pers. fut. Aph. of ܚܒܝܣ.

writing it, among the Bishops who were present,—
" Expound the treatises of Plato and Aristotle, and
" of the Physicians, but by no means approach (touch)
" the Scriptures."   And, in accordance with this,
they said something of this sort to me—" We
" straitly command you not to speak in the Name of
" Jesus."*   And when they could not incrimi-
nate me by any queries of theirs in any accusation
—(they did) what nobody ever ventured upon, even
in Pagan times—they concerted (conspired) together to
force me to sign (their) document with my own hand,
and they constrained me, besides, to confess that 1
had done so without any compulsion.

They managed† all this with tolerable adroitness
—anyone would have said so—so that nobody ever
could be able to blame them much.—[How so ? it
may be asked.]—Did they fear, on this point, any of
those who were able to recognize the Error which
Nestorius had thrown into the bosom of the Church,
and were competent to refute the Impieties he had
spread ?   I do not know ; yet [I do know one thing]:
(viz., this,) that I am conscious of a ready and powerful will to do (what is right and good).¶

---

* Acts of Apostles, Chap. iv, 18.   They silenced him, he means
to say, on religious subjects.

† In p. 132, l. 4, the expression ܐܘܪܒܥܬܐ implies the being guilty of
acting *fraudently*, or with great *chicanery*, ܠܬܘܠܐ ܐܘܡܒܠܐ, the being
able to rashly *reprobate* or *condemn*.   The word ܠܒܥܐ is in stat. con-
struct. no doubt.   The passage is to me not very easy satisfactorily to
translate in a literal sense.

¶ Perhaps—" As regards myself, I am aware of nothing but a ready
" and vigorous will (to do what is required)."

I, therefore, pray you, and supplicate you, on my knees, O Holy Men !*

(Now) as regards these Bishops who, when once assembled together, overwhelmed me with torments, and indignities, and dangers well-nigh exposing me to death, I forgive them, I am silent about them, I pray for them who thus behaved. For, of what use (need) can human vindictiveness be to Christians,—to those, to whose honour nothing so much redounds as to suffer for Christ's sake ?

¶Now I ask only one request—one that is suitable and appropriate for your Holy Synod to grant and befitting and proper for me to receive. And what is that ?—(that you) maintain and uphold The Faith of the Holy Fathers, Which (Faith) these men and many more, through their instrumentality, have, in my opinion wanted to deprave, and that you will not allow any Novelty, contrariant to It, to be introduced into It. Loose my tongue for the confession of The Truth, which they, referred to above, out of envy at my peacefulness, have gagged ; and open my mouth for the exposition of Divine Truth (God's Words), seeing that it is a misfortune that I should be doomed to silence, and that my voice on behalf of Orthodoxy be extinguished (suppressed). If the Holy Fathers were jealous† for the Lord, according to what is

---

* In l. 12, if ܣܥ is by the scribe meant for ܣܥ, the passage had better be rendered thus : " For this reason I beg and supplicate that you would investigate the conduct of those who assembled some time since."

¶ " And all I pray is that only which is suitable."

† At 1 Kings, xix, 10, it is *jealous for*. At 1 Maccab., ii, 27 and

written; Take* unto you now, more so than they did in old time (formerly), the armour of GOD, and transfix¶ manfully, with the (spear) lance† of the Spirit, the yoke (or the neck) of these false Shepherds, I mean, of those malicious and fierce (devouring) wolves who, under the mask of Shepherd, have corrupted the Flocks, in their unwariness, of the Good Shepherd.   Effectually smite them who have introduced strange Doctrine into the Church and have contaminated the Elect and Precious Race; and spare not those who have hewn in pieces many Churches, with the sword of Impiety, like Agag.‡   Be like unto Elijah, who, though alone, contended (made war) against so many Priests of Baal and was crowned (victorious) over them by the sentence of fire from Heaven.‖   Do you, who are so great and worthy an assembly, and a mighty body of Priests, and a holy Battalion—you whose war is against two or scarcely more than two, that have sprung from two; armed, too, with tongues of Fire and of

---

26, and 30, it is *zealous of*.   * Eph., vi, 12 and 13.

¶ Perhaps we may translate this sentence thus—"Transfix manfully, "with the sword of the Spirit, the couple (Domnus and Theodoret) of "these false Shepherds." The Syriac word for couple means *neck* literally, but my friend Martin says it can signify *soc* (plough-share) et *plaine ou champ labouré* (field worked in). But this appears to me not to harmonise with the metaphor used.

† Eph., vi, 17.

‡ The same word for "hewn in pieces," in p. 133, l. 19, is used in 1 Sam., xv, 33, in Syriac O. T, to which reference is made.

‖ 1 Kings, xviii, 19-40. In l. 24, ܐܘܕܝ, or ܐܘܕܝ, was "pronounced victorious by the heavenly sentence of fire that fell "upon them."

the Holy Spirit which came down from Heaven*—
do you burn those who have dared to mix strange
fires and error, those who hold the Doctrine of
Nestorius and who give licence, though an unsound
one, to like-thinkers with him.   Burn him who
surreptitiously concealed letters, (Synodical) that
treated of matters relating to The Faith, of the
Church of Alexandria and the (Presiding) head of
this Holy Synod, when the bearers of them had
been sent to him; and although the guardians of them
reminded him that it was only right and proper for
him to read them out in the Church, (yet) he refused
to do this, but demurred, through attachment to
the Impious Irenæus; and reluctantly did he, after
compulsion by the Imperial Authority, consecrate another in his (Irenæus's)† place by the Imposition of
hands, so that the Vine of Sodom might perpetually
sprout and many drink of the deadly wine which
these artful Cultivators manipulate for the destruction (of mankind).

However, the anger of God did not wait long;
for, beholding them who, having so drunk, became
undone and lost, He commanded that there should
take place (this) your Assembly who are true
Cultivators, so that, when you apply the true

---

* See Acts, ii, and 2 Kings, i, 5-12. In p. 134, l. 6, ܡܟܣܝܢ
. . . . . . ܪܚܡܝܢ, we may render thus—(Yes, burn) those who are
taken up with the Doctrine of Nestorius, and inspire a false confidence
in those who think like them.

† It is clear from this that Irenæus was consecrated Bishop by the
Archbishop Domnus. More about this further on.

energy of love, you may accomplish the work of purification for Him, Who has put you in trust, not only when you cut off branches, but also when you utterly remove from the very root all this death-clad vine, by the exercise of the power entrusted to you by the Lord "to root out"* and to "set free."* For, by this means, you "build up and plant"* trustfulness in believing Nations (Peoples).

That is the wish† (object) of this your Holy Synod.

With this intent you have been convoked by GOD to be a company (battalion) of The HOLY SPIRIT.—The Body of the Church has need of the help (hand) of the Lord, because of having been sorely devoured by evil (the wicked).

For this purpose have you all been gathered together in this place : (viz.) in order that you may establish One "Glorious Church, having neither spot "nor blemish."‡

Thus you will, for a second time, deliver and purify It by the power of The Truth, whereby you will present It to the whole earth under Heaven, not as disgraced¶ and calumniated by Heretics, but as One invested with the Heavenly and Apostolic Glory—the Doctrine of the Alone True Religion.¶

Now we have witnesses to prove the Innovation

---

* Jeremiah, i, 10.

† This is what should have been the object of the great Eutychian and other parties connected with the Council.

‡ Cicatrix, *scar.* See Ephesians, Chap. v, 27.

¶ Or, " as still reviled."

¶ Literally, " The Doctrine of The Religion in one (only) Form."

upon The Faith, made by those mentioned above ; and, if your Holy Synod command it, we can at once produce (some of) them, although we could not possibly trouble many of them to come hither in consequence of the great distance (length of time).

PELAGIUS, Presbyter of Antioch, said :—

We have, likewise, a Volume written by Theodoret against the first Holy Œcumenical Synod held in this place, and against a former Treatise composed by the Blessed Cyril : and, with it, another Book, also, which he (Theodoret) wrote against him afresh, after he had communicated with the Blessed Cyril.*

DIOSCORUS, the Bishop of Alexandria, said :—

Let Pelagius, the Presbyter, produce the Volume, and the Book lately written by Theodoret, that he has offered to show.

JOHN, Presbyter and Proto-Notary, read :—

Copy of a Letter to the Monks against the God-fearing Bishop Cyril and against the Holy and Œcumenical Synod of Ephesus† :—

When I survey the present condition (order) of the Church, and the tempest that has (so) lately risen upon the pure Bark, and the fierce storms of the winds, and the violence of the waves, and the profound darkness ; and, along with these, the

---

* See Vol. I, p. 320, and Appendix H in this Vol.
† See the end of this celebrated Letter.

quarrels, also, of those on board,* and the contentions
of persons appointed to serve as Priests,† and the
insobriety of the Pilots—in fine, (when I survey)
the entire blackness of the calamity, I am reminded
of the Lamentations of Jeremiah, and with him I
exclaim—"My inside pains me, and my heart's
"affections try me, and my soul is dissolved with
"my heart, and I eagerly implore and desire, by the
"means of the tears of my eyes, to drive away the
"magnitude of grief."‡   For, whilst it is befitting
and proper that, in this cruel winter, the crew (sailors)
should be watchful and contend with the storm, and
that they should be anxious for the safety of the
Ship, and that the sailors should desist from contentions with each other, and, by prayer and by skill, aim
at averting the evil (misfortunes), and the passengers sit peacefully, quarrelling neither with each other
nor with the sailors, but should supplicate the Lord of
the sea to change, by His will, the sad state of affairs,
none of these things, forsooth, is anybody willing to
do ; but, as if it were a battle in the night, we throw
one another into confusion and, leaving our adversaries, we both turn all these weapons against
ourselves and kill our own comrades as if they were
the foes in (actual) antagonism with us, whilst parties
standing in our very neighbourhood laugh at (the

---

* In p. 137 of Syriac Text, l. 1, the word ܪܕܝܢ *those who are
sailing, the passengers,* not the crew, as we learn from l. 15, where it
occurs with ܬܠܒܘܢ, which future verb is used at Matthew, xx, 21.

† It is ἐρέττειν in the Greek, *remigare.*

‡ Lamentations, iv, 19.

mode of) our warfare, and are delighted at our misfortunes, and rejoice as they witness our ruination of one another (our mutual destruction).*

Now, the cause of these misfortunes are persons who have striven to deprave The True and Apostolic FAITH and have dared to add to the Doctrines of the Gospel any teaching whatsoever† antagonistic to It, and have received those Impious Chapters, with the Anathematisms, of Cyril,‡ which they sent to the Imperial City after having confirmed them, as they supposed, by their own subscriptions.

These (Chapters and Anathematisms) have manifestly sprung from the bitter root of Apollinarius. They are, moreover, participative of the Blasphemies of Arius and Eunomius.‖   Further, whoever chooses to investigate the matter with accuracy will perceive that they are not far removed from the Impiety of Valentinus, and Manes, and Marcion.

For; in the 1st Chapter, he (Cyril) repudiates the INCARNATION, Which took place for our sake, by teaching that GOD did not assume HUMAN NATURE, but was changed into Flesh, affirming that the INCARNATION of our REDEEMER existed only in appearance and fantasy, and not in reality, which

---

* In l. 27, ܣܝܦܐ, *cut with a sword.*

† Literally, ܗܘܝ ܐܝܕܐ is *whatever it be*, in l. 4, but ܐܝܕܗܘܢ or ܐܝܕܗܘܢ is *their hand.*

‡ For S. Cyril's Chapters see p. 112.

‖ This is the great Heresiarch who denied that "Jesus Christ is "God of God, VERY GOD of VERY GOD, &c.," and was condemned at the Council of Nicæa in 325 A.D., and Eunomius, made Bishop of Cizycum in 360 A.D., was a great supporter of Arianism.

notions, however, are the offspring of the Impiety of Marcion, and Manes, and Valentinus.*

But in the 2nd Chapter and the 3rd, as if forgetting what he put at the beginning, he introduces an Hypostatic (Personal) Union and a Concursus, constituting a Physical Union ; teaching by these terms a commixture and a con-fusion of the Divine Nature and of the Likeness of a Servant.†

Now this is the offspring of the HERESY of Apollinarius.

But in the 4th Chapter he rejects the distinction of the terms of the Gospel and of the Apostles, and does not suffer us to take those terms according to the teaching of the Orthodox Fathers, and apply to His Nature those which are proper to GOD, but (he wants) that we should attach to the Human Nature, assumed by Him, those of a humble kind, and that are spoken by Christ in a human way.¶

Hence, then, persons of a sound way of thinking become able to (trace) discern the Relationship of the Impiety.‡ For, Arius and Eunomius, in speaking of the Only-Begotten Son of GOD, as a

---

* These were great Heresiarchs in the Second and Third Centuries.

† In p. 139, l. 1, possibly the right reading is, ܠܚܒܕܐ, a *servant, slave.* But the word ܠܚܒܕܐ occurs again in line 14, and is *effectum, a thing made.* " A fusion of the Divine Nature and of the Form of a Slave. This, " then, has its origin in the Heresy of Apollinarius."

¶ Or, perhaps,—" According to the teaching of the Orthodox " Fathers, he does not allow us to take those terms and to apply those " concerning His Nature which are proper to God, and to attach to the " Human Nature assumed by Him those of a humble kind and that are " spoken in a human way."

‡ Namely, that it sprang from Arius.

" creature"* and as " that which once was not"* and
as "a thing made,"* dared to apply to the Divinity
of Christ* those mean, humble, properties belonging
to Humanity and spoken of as (proper to) Man,
making thereby a diversity of Essence and a Dissimilarity.

Besides, to be brief, he (Cyril) affirms of
the DIVINITY of Christ,—Impassible and Immutable — that IT both suffered and was crucified and died, (which is) a doctrine that surpasses
even the folly of Arius and of Eunomius.   For,
they who venture to call the Maker and Framer of
the Universe a Creature never proceeded to such
a height of Impiety (as that).

He (Cyril), likewise, blasphemes against the HOLY
GHOST, when he affirms that HE does not proceed
really from the FATHER, according to the word of our
Lord, but that He derives His Essence from the
Son.

Now this is fruit, produced from the seed of
Apollinarius, whilst it also approaches the evil work
of Marcion.

SUCH are Egyptian products—in truth, the more
evil offspring—of an evil Sire.

Now those, whose business† is exercised in the
healing of the soul, ought either to have rendered

---

* See Appendix K.   Perhaps better—" those humble expressions,
" and which were spoken by Christ in a human way."

† "*Those*," that is, the Chief Pastors of the Church who are the soul-
healers, or, rather, the under Physicians or Healers of men's souls
who act with authority from the Chief Physician and Healer.

these things abortive when conceived, or, when brought forth, to have destroyed them, because they corrupt and (bring) a deadly poison into our Nature.   (Instead of that, however,) they keep nurturing* them and deeming them worthy of immense solicitude, to their own injury and to that of those who are induced to give ear to them.   But, so far as we are concerned, we do our endeavour to preserve the Inheritance of the Fathers intact, and The Faith we have received (inviolate), with which (Faith) we do baptize and have been baptized and which we do keep spotless and pure; and we confess our Lord Jesus is PERFECT GOD and PERFECT MAN,† of a reasonable Soul and Body subsisting: Who, as to His Divinity, was begotten of The Father before the Worlds; but, in the latter times, the Same was, as regards His Humanity, for us and for our Salvation, born of the Virgin Mary —Co-essential with the Father as to His DIVINITY, and Con-substantial with us as to His HUMANITY.   For, a Union took place‡ of the Two Natures.

For this reason we acknowledge ONE CHRIST, ONE SON, ONE LORD; for, we do not dissolve the Union, but we believe the Union was made

---

* The Metaphor adopted in the first clause is continued, and the word ܡܬܪܣܐ is Pa., from ܪܒܐ, *nutrivit, educavit.* "*They with great power*
" *bring them up and deem them worthy of great care..*

† These are the same words as appear in the Quicunque vult.

‡ *Took place* is the rendering of the Syriac equivalent to γίγνομαι, *factus sum,* in the third person.

without confusion, being assured (of this) by the Lord, Who said to the Jews:—" Destroy this Temple " and the third day I will raise It up again."* But, if commixture had taken place, and confusion, and One Nature formed out of those two, then it had been fitting and proper for him to have said:—" Dis- " solve Me, and the third day I will rise again."

But now, in order to show that the One is GOD by Nature and that the Other is the Temple, and that the two constitute ONE Christ, He said:—" Dissolve " this Temple, and the third day I will raise It up " again;"* clearly indicating that it is not GOD, but the Temple that was subject to dissolution, and that the Nature of the ONE was compatible with dissolution; but, as to the Other, (it was) His Power that raised up what was dissoluble. So, we confess Christ to be GOD and Man, following (therein) the Divine Scriptures. For, that our Lord Jesus Christ is GOD, the Blessed Evangelist St. John pro- claims (thus) :—" In the beginning was The Word, " and The Word was with GOD, and The Word was " GOD. He was in the beginning with GOD. All " was made by Him, and without Him was not any- " thing made."† And again:—" He is the True " Light, enlightening every man that cometh into the " world."‡ But the Lord Himself manifestly teaches (this), when he says :—" Whosoever sees Me, sees " My Father;"‖ and:—" I and My Father are

---

* John, ii, 19.   † John, i, 1
‡ John, i, 9.   ‖ John, xiv, 9.

"ONE;"* and :—"I am inThe Father and The Father
"is in Me."† And the Blessed Paul, in his Epistle
to the Hebrews, said :—"Who is the Brightness of
"His Glory and the Image (Impress) of His
"Being (Essence), and Who upholds all things by
"the power of His Word."‡ And in that to
the Philippians (he said) :—"Let this mind be
"in you which was, also, that of Jesus Christ
Who, although He was the Form of GOD,
"(yet) He did not think it robbery to be the counter-
"part of (equal with) GOD ; but emptied (divested)
"Himself, taking the Form of a Servant."‖ And,
in that to the Romans, he said:—"Whose are the
"Fathers, of whom, according to the Flesh, is Christ,
"Who is over all, the Blessed GOD."§ Also, in
that to Titus:—"Hoping for the announcement of
"the Blessed Revelation of the Great GOD and our

---

* John, x, 30.   † John, x, 38 ; xiv, 10, 11 ; xvii, 21, 23.

‡ Heb., i, 3. Bishop Andrews, I think, translates this verse in the
Greek N. T., thus :—"The brightness of His Father's glory, the very
"character of His substance, the Heire of all things, by Whom Hee
"made the world." Brightness, splendour, effulgence of His Father's
Glory, as a ray is of the Sun, helps to explain the description—Light of
Light—in the Nicene Creed ; and the Image of His Essence, or the
Impress or character of His Being, destroys the Anomæan notion of
Eunomius and his Co-thinkers who denied the Likeness of the Second
Person to the First of The Trinity, as well as His Consubstantiality.
Bishop Wordsworth, in his Greek N. T., at p. 380, points out that
in this passage the Apostle declares the co-eternity and consubstantiality
of the Son.   ‖ At Phil., ii, 5, 6, 7, it is in N. T —
pre-existent in the form or condition of God.

§ Rom., ix, 5. Bp. Wordsworth, at p. 247 of his N. T., shows
that this passage distinctly asserts our Lord's *Incarnation*, His *Existence
from Everlasting*, His *Supremacy*, His *Divinity*, and His claim to be
called *The Blessed One*, and provides "a safeguard, not only against So-
"cinianism and Arianism, but also against Nestorianism, by declaring
"that God and Man are One Christ."

EE

"Saviour Jesus Christ."* Isaiah, too, exclaims: —"A Child is born to us and a Son is given to us, —"He Whose power is upon His shoulder; and His "Name shall be called the Messenger of the Great "Covenant, the Wonderful, the Counsellor, the "Mighty GOD, the Powerful ONE, the Prince of "Peace, the Father of the future world."† And elsewhere he said:—"After Thee shall they walk— "they who are bound with chains: and unto Thee "shall they pray, because GOD is in Thee and there "is no GOD beside Thee; for, Thou art truly GOD "and we knew it not,—GOD the Redeemer of "Israel."‡ But the Name of Immanuel signifies GOD and Man; for, it is explained, according to the Doctrine of the Gospel, as "GOD with us,"‖ that is, GOD in Man, GOD in our Nature.

Also, Jeremiah, the Divine prophet, proclaims it, when he says:—"He is our GOD, and no others are to "be regarded in comparison with Him. He hath dis- "covered all the way of knowledge and hath deliv- "ered it to Jacob His Servant and to Israel His "Beloved. Afterwards was He seen upon the "earth and held converse with the sons of men."§

And thousands of other expressions any one may cull from the Divine Evangelists, and from the Writings of the Apostles, and from the Prophecies of

---

* Titus, ii, 14.   † Isaiah, ix, 6.

‡ Isaiah, xlv, 13. The variations, great and small, between such passages as this, or rather their translation from Syriac into English, and the English Version of the Bible will be observed.

‖ Mat., i, 23.   § Baruch, ii, 36-38.

the Prophets, proving that our Lord Jesus is VERY
GOD.   But that He is, also, named Man after the
INCARNATION, the Lord Himself teaches, when
discoursing with the Jews, and exclaiming—" Why
" do ye want to kill Me—a Man Who hath spoken to
" you true things ?"*   And the Blessed Paul, in
the first Letter to the Corinthians, (teaches it), when
he says:—" Since through man (came) death, through
" man also came the Resurrection of the Dead."†
And, in showing concerning Whom he is speaking,
he explains what has been spoken, after this manner:
—" As in Adam all men are dead, so in Christ all
" of them live."‡   In writing to Timothy, also, he
said:—"There is only ONE GOD—ONE Mediator, also,
" of GOD and Men—The MAN Christ Jesus."‖   In
the Acts of the Apostles, also, when he is addressing the Athenians, (Paul says):—" GOD, then, having
" over-looked the times of ignorance, now commands
" us all, in every quarter, to repent, since He has
" appointed a time when He will judge the world
" in righteousness by That Man Whom He hath
" appointed, affording good faith thereof to all men
" in that He hath raised Him from the Dead."§
The Blessed Peter, too, in preaching to the Jews,
said:—" Men of Israel ! hear these words : Jesus of
" Nazareth, a Man that appeared (is revealed) from
" GOD among you by signs, and wonders, and powers
" which GOD wrought by Him."**

---

* John, vii, 19, and John, viii, 40.   † I Cor., xv, 21.
‡ I Cor., xv, 22.   ‖ I Tim., ii, 5.
§ Acts, xvii, 30, 31.   ** Acts, ii, 22.

And the Prophet Isaiah, predicting the sufferings of Christ, Whom a little before he had named GOD— HIM he calls a man, thus speaking:—" A Man Who " is one of stripe and knows how to bear sickness, " Who bears our sins and hath suffered for our " sakes."*

But many other similar expressions to these testimonies I should continue to cull from the Divine Writings, and insert the min this letter, were I not¶ persuaded of your Piety, that your mode of life in this world consists in meditation on the Divine Scriptures, like the man who, by the Psalmist, is designated " Blessed."

Leaving, then, to your industry the collecting of the proofs, I pass on to my subject (to that which is set before me).

We confess our Lord Jesus Christ to be VERY GOD and VERY MAN, not dividing the ONE (Christ) into two Persons, but we believe that the Two Natures are united without confusion.

By that means are we easily able to refute the many vain Blasphemies of the Heretics; for, manifold and varied is the error of those who have opposed The Truth, as we, also, forthwith (now) show.   For, Marcion, and Valentinus, and Manes deny that GOD The Word took the Nature of Manhood; nor do they believe that our Lord Jesus Christ was born of the Virgin, but that GOD The

---

* Isaiah, liii, 3.   ¶ Literally—" had not been persuaded of " the piety that is in you, that its mode of life in this world consists in " meditation in the Divine Scriptures."

Word was born in the manner (Form) of the *semblance* of Man and appeared as Man in Phantasy rather than in reality.* [   ] But Sabellius, the Libyan, and Photinus, and Marcellus of Galatia, and Paul of Samosata, affirm that a mere man was born of the Virgin, since they evidently deny that Christ is, also, GOD before the worlds.   Arius and Eunomius, likewise, contend that GOD The Word took body only from the Virgin, but Apollinarius, also, adds to the body an irrational soul, just as if the INCARNATION of GOD The Word took place for beings destitute, rather than for those possessed, of reason ; but the Doctrine of the Apostle teaches us that PERFECT MAN was assumed by PERFECT GOD.   For, this sentence reveals it—(viz.,) "He Who is the Form of GOD "assumed the Form of a Servant,"† because Form or figure is here substituted for Nature and Essence. That sentence indicates, then, that, whilst he had the Nature of GOD, He took the Nature of a Servant. Therefore, when speaking of the Prime Inventors of Impiety—Marcion, and Manes, and Valentinus— we are anxious to prove, from the Divine Scriptures,

---

* According to Migne's Patrologiæ Cursus, a paragraph, contained in the original Letter of Theodoret, must be omitted by the Scribe here. It is this :—

Valentinianus et Bardesanes nativitatem quidem admittunt, sed negant nostræ nàturæ assumptionem, et aiunt Filium DEI tanquam canali aliquo Virgine usum esse.

† Philip., ii, 6, 7.   Pre-existing in the manner or form of GOD.

that our Lord Jesus Christ is not only GOD, but Man also.   On the other hand, when we would refute the Impiety of Sabellius, and Marcellus, and Photinus, and of Paul, should we not have recourse to the testimony of the Scriptures to show that our Lord Christ is not Man only, but GOD before the worlds and Co-essential (Consubstantial) with the Father?

As regards, again, the Doctrine of Arius, and Eunomius, and Apollinarius on the subject of the IN-CARNATION, we prove It to the uninitiated (ignorant) to be imperfect, by showing, by the words of the Holy Ghost, that a Perfect Nature was assumed by The Word.   For, that He took a reasonable soul our Lord Himself teaches, where He says:—" Now " is My Soul troubled !" and in what He said:—" O, " My Father! deliver Me from this hour, but to " this hour have I come for this.*   .   .   .   My Soul " is sorrowful, even unto death ;"† and in another place:—" I have the power of laying down My Soul, " and I have the power of taking It again.   No man " taketh It away from Me."‡   The Angel, too, said to Joseph:—" Take the Lad and His Mother " and go into the land of Israel ; for, they are dead " who sought the Soul of the Lad."‖   And the Evangelist, likewise, said:—" And Jesus continued " to increase in stature and wisdom, and in favour " with GOD and man."§   Now, *THAT* did not in-

---

* John, xii, 27.   † Mat., xvi, 38.
‡ John, x, 18.   ‖ Mat., ii, 20.
§ Luke, ii, 52.

crease in stature and wisdom Which is perfect at all times, but That Human Nature which took being in time, and increased, and came to perfection. And, therefore, all those properties of Humanity in reality appertain to our Lord Jesus Christ—I mean hunger, thirst, and fatigue, and sleep, and sweating, and prayer, and want of knowledge, and fear, and all similar things—things such as we speak of as specially appertaining to ourselves, to which, on GOD The Word accepting them, He appropriated to Himself, when purchasing our Redemption; but the giving ability to the lame to walk again, the raising of the dead, and the multiplication of bread, and the changing water into wine, and all those other wonderful works we believe to be works proper to the power of GOD, so that This Same Christ our Lord could, I affirm, suffer and dissolve (those) sufferings: He could, in truth, suffer, and in that which was visible (to us) : and He could in truth dissolve these sufferings by That Divinity, Which, in a manner ineffable, dwelt in Him.

Now, this, also, the narrative of the Holy Evangelists distinctly declares : for, we learn from them that, when He was lain in the crib, whilst confined in swaddling clothes, by the star He was announced, by the Maji worshipped, and glorified by the Angels.* It is with reason that we make a distinction (between these things, some from others) : His being¶ The Infant, and the swaddling clothes, and the

---

* Matthew, ii; Luke, ii.　　¶ (The fact of) His being.

meanness of the bed, and all the (circumstances of) poverty—*these* we have as things proper to His HU-MANITY : whilst the journeying of the Maji, and the guidance of the star, and the Choir of the Angels proclaim the DIVINITY of Him, " Who hideth "Himself."*

In the same way He flees into Egypt, and, by the flight, escapes the wrath of Herod ;† for, He was Man.   But it was as GOD that He shakes the Idols‡ of Egypt ; for, He was GOD.

Being circumcised he observes the Law, and offers the sacrifices of Purification ;‖ for, from the root of Jesse§ did He spring, and He was under the Law** as Man ; but, afterwards dissolved the Law and gave the New Covenant : for, He was the Law-Maker, and, by His Prophets, had promised to give the Law.

He was baptised by John, and *that* argues His being one of us.   But He was testified to, from Above, by the Father, and was manifested by the Holy Spirit, and *that* proclaims Him to be before the worlds.   He hungered, but He also satisfied many thousands with five loaves of bread—*this* is a property of DIVINITY and *that* of HUMANITY. He thirsted and asked for water, but He was the Foun-tain of Life.   *The one,* indeed, appertained to Human infirmity, but *the other* to Divine Power.   He slept in the ship, but He also quelled the storm of the sea—*that* belonged to a suffering nature, but *this*

---

* Isaiah, xlv, 15; liv, 8; &c.   † Matthew, ii, 14, 15.
‡ Isaiah, xix, 1.   ‖ Luke, ii, 21-24.
§ Isaiah, xi, 1, 10.   ** Galatians, iv, 4.

to a creative and formative Power that bestowed upon
every man his existence. He was wearied with
exertion in walking, but He, also, caused the lame to be
swift* of foot, and He raised† the dead from the grave
—*this* is, ¶ indeed, a Power above (over) the worlds, but
that is¶ proper to our infirmity. He feared death,
but he abolished‡ (loosed) death—*the one* was an indication of mortality; *the other* of immortality, besides being an indication that He gives Life. " He
" was crucified,"‖ according to the Doctrine of the
Blessed Paul, " through weakness, but He lives by
" the power of GOD." That term "weakness" should
teach us that not He, Who is Omnipotent, and Incomprehensible, and Invariable, and Immutable, was
affixed (to the Cross) by nails, but That Nature
Which, by the power of GOD, took being in life, according to the Doctrine of His Apostle.   He died
and was buried—two characteristics *these* of the
Form of a Servant.   " The gates of brass He
" crushed into pieces, and brake the bars of iron,"§ and
overthrew the Empire of Death, and, on the third
day, caused the Temple (of His Body) to rise again
—*these* are proofs of the Form of GOD, according to
the teaching of our Lord when He said: "Destroy this
" Temple, and the third day I will raise It up again."**
    Thus in Christ, by means of the Passion,
we perceive, indeed, HUMANITY ; but, by means

---

* Lit. *swift of leg.*   † John, xi, 44.
¶ In these lines, " is " I prefer to " was," as also in the previous page,
the expressions " He is circumcised," l. 11, and " a Law-Maker," l. 15.
‡ 2 Tim., i, 10.   ‖ 2 Cor., xiii, 4.
§ Isaiah, xlv, 2 ; Psalm, cvii, 16.   ** John, ii, 19.

of his wonderful works, we descry His DIVINITY (DEITY), not that we divide the Two NATURES into Two CHRISTS; but we discern the Two NATURES to exist in ONE CHRIST, and are persuaded, as well, that GOD The WORD was begotten of the Father, as that He, Who is our beginning, is derived from Abraham and David. For this reason, also, it is that the Blessed Paul said, in discoursing about Abraham :—"He said not of " Thy seeds (descendants), as of many, but as of one, and of Thy seed (descendant) which is Christ."* And, in writing to Timothy, he said:—"Remember " that Jesus Christ, of the seed of David, rose from " the dead, according to my Gospel."†   And, in writing to the Romans, he said:—"Concerning His " Son, Who was born of the seed of David according " to the flesh."‡   And again:—"Whose are the " Fathers, of whom is the Christ according to the " flesh."‖   And the Evangelist (says):—"The " Book of the Generation of Jesus Christ the Son " of David, the Son of Abraham."§   And the Blessed Peter, in the Acts :—"A Prophet truly " (he said) was David; and, knowing that GOD " had sworn to him with oaths that of the " fruit of his loins, according to the flesh, He would " raise up Christ and cause Him to sit upon His " Throne, he foresaw and spake concerning His Re- " surrection."**

---

* Gal., iii, 16.   † 2 Tim., ii, 8.
‡ Rom., i, 3.   ‖ Rom., ix, 5.
§ Mat., i, 1.   ** Acts, ii, 30.

And GOD spake to Abraham:—" In thy seed, in-"deed, shall all the nations of the Earth be "blessed."*

And Isaiah (says):—" There shall come forth a "Rod out of the root of Jesse, and a Sucker shall "grow up out of his root, and the Spirit of GOD "shall rest upon Him, the Spirit of Wisdom and "Understanding, the Spirit of Counsel and Might, "the Spirit of Knowledge and of the Fear of the "Lord. The Spirit of Godly Fear shall fill him."†

‡*AND A LITTLE AFTER:—*

"There shall arise a Root of Jesse, and He that shall "stand for a Head to the Gentiles, and in Him shall "the Gentiles hope ; and His rest shall be glorious."||

It is, therefore, evident from what has now been said that Christ, according to the flesh, is the Son of Adam and David, and that He is clothed with their nature; but that, by reason of His Divinity, He existed before the worlds, as the Son of GOD and The WORD, Who was, in a manner ineffable and beyond human ken, born of THE FATHER, and is Co-eternal with Him, as (His) Brightness, as (His) Image, and (as His) Word. For, as word is united with mind and brightness with light, from which it cannot be separated, so is The Only Begotten SON, also, (united) with HIS FATHER.

We, therefore, affirm of our Lord Jesus Christ that He is The Only Begotten of GOD, and

---

* Gen., xxii, 18. † Isaiah, xi, 1, 2, 3.

‡ These words in the MS. are in red, as if the Notary in reading the Letter to the Synod had purposely omitted something. || Isaiah, xi, 10.

The First Begotten — The Only Begotten, assuredly, before the INCARNATION and after the INCARNATION; but The First Begotten after being born of the Virgin.   For, to The Only Begotten The First Born¶ seems to be the contradistinction, because The Only Begotten is (so) named Who Alone is born of any substance (essence), and The First Born is He Who is the first of many brethren.   Now, as regards GOD The WORD, Who Alone was born of the Father, the Holy Scriptures teach that The Only Begotten became, also, The First Born when He took our nature of the Virgin and deemed them worthy of being called His brethren who believed in Him, so that the same (person) could be in reality The Only Begotten in that He was GOD, and The First Born in that He was Man.

It is thus that we, confessing the Two Natures, worship The ONE Christ and offer up the One Worship to Him; for, we believe that the Union (of the Two Natures) was effected, by the Conception Itself, in the womb of the Blessed Virgin: and, therefore, we speak of the Holy Virgin, as being both Mother of GOD and Mother of Man; for which reason, also, our Lord Jesus Christ is called, by the Divine Scriptures, GOD and Man: but does not (the name of) Immanuel, in this way, proclaim the Union (One-ness) of the Two Natures?

If, then, we designate Christ GOD and Man, who is so stupid as to cry out against the term

---

¶ Or, perhaps,—The first begotten.

"Mother of Man" when put in juxtaposition with that of "Mother of GOD?" For, if we assign two names to our Lord Jesus Christ, on Whose account the Virgin is honoured and is called Blessed among women, what person is there, of a proper state of mind, who would refuse to call the Virgin by the appellatives of our Redeemer, seeing that it is on His account that She is honoured by Believers? for, not HE, Who (was born) of Her, is, for Her sake, worshipped; but She, on account of HIM Who is of Her, is exalted by most lofty appellations.

If, however, Christ is GOD only and received from the Virgin a Beginning of His Essence, from that circumstance the Virgin should be named and called the Mother of GOD only, since in that case she brought forth GOD only.

But, if Christ is both GOD and Man—and He was indeed ever that (the first); for, He had no beginning, since He is Co-eternal with His Father, whilst the other (Man), in the last days, He took from human nature—a person, who would teach from these two, must weave appellatives for the Virgin, indicating which is proper and appropriate to the Nature, and which to the Union of the Two Natures. If, however, any person is desirous of giving utterance to panegyrics, and of spinning out encomial sentences, and pronouncing orations of Praise, and wants only to make use of magniloquent terms, not in disputation, as we said, but in panegyrizing, let him, astonied, as is possible, at the magnitude of the Mystery, call her whatever he likes, let him use the very highest, let him praise, let him wonder. For, many expressions, similar to these, have I found in Orthodox Doctors. Everywhere, however, let moderation be preferred; for, I highly regard the man who asserts moderation to be best, and that, although he may not be of our flock.

This is the Confession of the Church's Faith. This is the Doctrine of The Faith of the Gospel and Apostles. For this we refuse not three times and many times, by the aid of the Grace of GOD, to die. These things we have been ready to teach even to those now in error; and frequently have we challenged them to discussion, being anxious to show them THE TRUTH, but they have not consented; for, fearing their evident refutation, they have refused the contest. For, truly weak is (falsity) Error, and it is conjoined with Darkness, as it is said that:—"Everyone "that doeth evil cometh not to the Light, lest his "deeds should be made manifest by the Light."*

In consequence, then, of our not inducing them, after having made great exertions for it, to acknowledge The Truth, we returned to our Churches saddened and gladdened—gladdened, inasmuch as we acted inerrantly, and saddened because of the corruption of (some of) our members.

I, therefore, pray your Holiness with all your soul to supplicate our Merciful Lord, and to exclaim to Him:—"O Lord! spare Thy people, and give not

---

* John, iii, 20.

" Thine Heritage to reproach."*   " O Lord ! feed us
" as (our) Shepherd lest we come at last to be
" what we were at first, when we acknowledged
" no Head and Thy Name was not invoked over
" us.   O Lord ! behold us a scorn to our neigh-
" bours, a derision, and a by-word to those that
" are round about us;"† because depraved teachings
have entered into Thine Inheritance and have
polluted Thy Holy Temple ; and the daughters
of strangers rejoice over our calamities, because
we are divided into many tongues—we who, heretofore, have been of one tongue (language).   O
Lord ! our GOD ! grant us a tongue¶ which we have
lost through neglecting Thy commandments.   O
Lord ! our GOD ! take possession of us.   O Lord !
beside Thee we know no other—we call on Thy
Name.   Make of us two one, and dissolve the middle
wall of partition, even the Impiety which has arisen.
Gather us together, one by one, even The New Israel
which is Thine.   Build up Jerusalem and assemble
(reunite) the dispersed of Israel.   Let there be again
only One Fold and let us all be fed of Thee; for, "Thou
" art the Good Shepherd,—He Who laid down His life
" for His sheep."‡   " Awake, why sleepest Thou, O
" Lord?   Arise and reject (cast off) us not for ever!"‖
" Rebuke the winds of the sea, and give Peace to Thy
" Church, and the stilling of the waves."§

¶ Or, "the peace which, &c.," if the right reading be the word ܡܚܝܠ with
ܠ for its object.   * Joel, ii, 17.   † Psalms, xliv, 13, 14; lxxix, 4.
‡ John, x, 11.   ‖ Psalm, xliv, 23.
§ Mat., viii, 26; Psalms, cvii, 29; lxv, 7; lxxxix, 9.

These prayers and similar ones I beseech your Piety to utter to the GOD of All; for, since He is Good and Merciful, and ever desirous of granting the prayer of those who fear Him, He will hear your Petition, and disperse this darkness (now) imminent, which is even blacker than (that of) the Egyptian plague, and will bestow that Peace which from Him is so gracious, and will gather together the dispersed, and will receive the outcast.

Then, again shall be heard "the voice of Praise and Salvation" "in the dwelling of the Righteous." Then, we, too, shall exclaim to Him—"Thou hast made us "glad by reason of the days of our humiliation and "the years when we experienced these afflictions."*

You, likewise, having obtained your request, in praising Him, will say—"Blessed is GOD Who hath "not disregarded our Prayer, nor (withheld) His "Grace from us."†

---

* Psalm, xc, 15.   † Psalm, lxvi, 20.

Compare this magnificent specimen of Catholic Theology with the celebrated Anathemas of S. Cyril, at p. 112, and the difference will appear, I think, infinitesimal, except on one point. But the fact of Theodoret's having written against Cyril—the pregnant expression of the latter about there being only one Nature of our Incarnate Lord, without any explanation of it, would warrant both Theodoret and Bishop Ibas in writing against him—sufficed alone for his enemies to accuse and arraign him. See Appendix H, in Vols. I and II.

The Greek Letter will be found in Migne's Cursus (Paris, 1859), beginning thus :—Θεοδωρήτος πρὸς τοὺς ἐν τῇ Εὐφρατησίᾳ, καὶ Ὀσροη-νῇ, καὶ Συρίᾳ, καὶ Φοινίκῃ, καὶ Κιλικίᾳ μονάζοντας.

Ὁρῶν τὴν ἐν τῷ παρόντι καιρῷ τῆς Ἐκκλησίας κατάστασιν, &c. Respicienti mihi præsentem Ecclesiæ conditionem, et procellam quæ nuper in divinam navem surrexerit, &c. (From Col. 1,415 to Col. 1,434. Series Græca, Tom. 83. Theodoretus Cyr. Epis. IV.)

See, also, Mansi's Nova et amplissima Collectio, Tom. 5, p. 1,023, seq.

[4] (a) John, Presbyter and Prime-Notary, said :—

The book, presented by Pelagius, the Presbyter, bears upon it the following Title : —" *An Apology of* " *Theodoret, Bishop, on behalf of Diodorus and* " *Theodorus, Warriors for the (True) Religion.*"

The Holy Synod said : —

That alone suffices for his Deposition, for which the Great Emperor has already given orders, so that, if anything were said relative to Theodoret against his deposition, it would be possible for even Nestorius to find an abetter.*

(b) John, Presbyter and Prime-Notary, read (extracts) from a Book (Treatise) of Theodoret :—

" And what shall I say about the Athenians, (so) " particularly addicted to the worship of Dæmons ? " The Divine Peter himself, when discoursing to " the Jews, did not designate our Lord Jesus Christ " (as) GOD, whilst he even extended his† address " about Him in reference to His being MAN."

---

* The undue bias and readiness of the Synod to return a verdict unfavourable to the person at the bar is remarkable : for, no sooner does the Assessor say that the MS. of Pelagius bears this Inscription— " Bishop Theodoret's Apology of Diodore and Theodore, Champions " of God"—than the Assembly cried out :—" That is enough to get " Theodoret deposed ; for, the Emperor has said that to refuse to depose " him would be to support Nestorius." In this sentence, probably, allusion is made to the Imperial Document (β) above, p. 8.

† The pronoun in, ⲟⲏⲗⲥⲟⲥ, *his* word, p. 159, l. 3, shows that ⲡⲗⲥⲟ cannot mean The Divine Word (for He is not Peter's Word) but his discourse to the Jews. Literally :—*but even he also (Peter) put forth his word of Him (i.e., spake of Him) as of a man.*

GG

(*c*) Another extract from the same Treatise :—

"As regards the entire Deed (writing) of Arraign-
"ment, he has filled it with expressions like these,
"(viz): 'He (Christ) did not take (upon Himself) Man.'
"'He did not (actually) become Man, but acted in
"the manner of Man.' 'The Only Begotten suffered,'
"and 'He (The Only Begotten) tasted of death.' "*

(*d*) Again, from the same Treatise :—

"Show, then, what there is against Diodorus.
"But you have nothing (to show).   If, however, you
"stumble at the term PURPLE (Vestment);—for,
"this you signified in what follows, when you said
"that it is a proof of dissimilarity; and you carped
"at the name of TEMPLE—"†

(*e*) Again, from the same Treatise :—

"Therefore GOD The WORD is not a Lamb, but
"as a Lamb¶ (of sacrifice) he offered (sacrificed) the
"Nature which He had assumed, and is called 'the
"Lamb‡ (of God) ;' and that in consequence of the
"Union (of the Two Natures)."

---

* These sentences, forming this second Extract, cited by, and now arrainged against, Theodoret, are excerpted from a work of S. Cyril named—" De eo quod unus Christus contra Theodorum."

† The words Purple and Temple were commonly used by Nestorius and his followers to describe the Body in which God The Word took habitation.   Also, the Nestorians were accused of " corrupting the " Divine Writings and of removing the Landmarks of the Holy Fa-"thers," in order to attribute the Incarnation only to the Flesh ; saying that the birth and death of Christ belong simply and merely to the Temple of God, &c.

¶ Or, better, perhaps—He offered (sacrificed) the Nature He had as-sumed as a Lamb (of sacrifice).   Isaiah, liii, 7 ; 1 Peter, i, 19; &c.

‡ S. John's Gospel, i, 29.

(*f*) Again, from the same Treatise :—

"How, then, do you fail to perceive this, that
"when you arraign Diodorus for having affirmed
"that the Nature which was assumed was the Son
"of Grace, you implicate yourself (in the charge)?
"because you have blamed him for not having
"affirmed Him to be the Very Son of the Father,
"Who is the seed of David; for, how is that Nature
"which was derived from David truly the Son of
"the GOD of All? For He, Who was begotten of
"Father before the worlds, owns this name."

(*g*) Again, from the same Treatise :—

"Subsequently he exhibits a certain work (creed)*
"which was written by himself. And he arraigns it.
"But I have fallen in with the writings of the giant.†
"This nowhere have I seen, and I have not considered
"that it would be deserving of arraignment. How-
"ever, I am of opinion¶ that, as regards this subject,
"people who are willing to examine the sense of what
"is written come to entertain the same sentiments.
"For, so the writings of the Holy Gospels and Apos-
"tles draw (lead on) to it every one who wishes for
"Eternal Life. There are, however, myriads of people
"who, while looking upon them in (different) various

---

* Probably ‏ܩܢܘܡܐ‏ means here, as it does so frequently, *a Formulary of Faith, a Creed.* At p. 160, l. 10, it should be ‏ܦܓܥܬ‏, *I have met with*—that is the correct word and its translation.

† Theodore of Mopsuestia, probably.

¶ "But, as regards this, I am of opinion that those can understand
"these views who wish to examine the sense of what is written. .
". . all who wish for Eternal Life are led on to it by the writings," &c.

" senses and diversely, run in an opposite direction,
" and are drawn into the outer darkness.   But not on
" that account, however, do we blame the Holy Scrip-
" tures—no!—but we do reprehend the idiotcy of
" those who entertain false notions (will not think
" with wisdom).¶   In this way and at this place
" (passage) have we acted, showing what is the mean-
" ing of those things which have been written with
" just intent.   The meaning, then, of the Treatise is
" so and so."

    " Further,* it is only just and right to know, also,
" about the Œconomy for our Redemption that GOD
" consummated that Œconomy by our Lord Christ."

    " GOD he (Theodorus) here calls the GOD of
" All, the Father of our Lord Jesus Christ; and
" Christ (he calls) GOD The WORD, Who became
" INCARNATE, The Only Begotten Son of God.
" For it is, by His means, that the GOD of All pur-
" chased our Redemption.   Thus, too, the Blessed

¶ Or it may be rendered with Martin, whose note we subjoin, thus:
—" The same have we done in this actual case.   We show that all that
" has been composed with a good intention.   See here, then, what is his
" idea (of Theodorus or Diodorus)? in this writing.(a)   We must
" know concerning the matter of our salvation that GOD has accom-
" plished it through our Lord Christ."(b)   " The things that have been
written" would be what was put into the ‎ܠܣ݂ܡܐ, probably.

  * In p. 161, Martin considers that lines 2, 3, and 4 may be a quotation from Diodore or Theodore, and Hoffman as the quotation from the
Creed, the ‎ܠܣ݂ܡܐ, which is to be explained.

   (a) The preceding and the following are not without difficulty. One does not know
of whom, and of what, there is a question here. However, as it is an extract from a
work destined to defend Theodorus against S. Cyril (Mansi, *Conciliorum omnium amplis.
Coll.*, IX, 230-255), one has a right to suppose, that it is a reply to the objections which
Cyril raised against the writings of Theodore of Mopsuestia.
   (b) It is probably a citation from Theodore of Mopsuestia which S. Cyril had in-
criminated.

" Paul said that 'God was in Christ, having recon-
" ' ciled the world to Himself.' "*

"Now notice, likewise, what (he says) afterwards:—
" GOD The WORD took Perfect Man, who is of
" the seed of Abraham and David, according to the
" announcement of the Divine Scriptures :—'Who
" ' was by Nature that which they also were, being
" ' of their seed, (that is to say) Man, Perfect in
" ' Nature, of a reasonable (intelligent) Soul, and
" ' human flesh subsisting.' "†

(*h*) Again, from the same Treatise :—

" What novelty has Theodorus (advanced)· in
" affirming that a 'beginning‡ was (by Christ) as-
" sumed of a reasonable (intelligent) Soul and
" human Body,' and that this 'beginning came from
" Abraham and David,' and that 'in Nature He is
" what they are.' " .

(*i*) Again, from the same Treatise :—

" Here attend‖ to the change of tenses: He said not
" 'I am His Father and He is My Son,' but 'I *will*
" *be* to him a Father and he *shall be* to Me a
" Son.' "

(*j*) Again, from the same Treatise :—

" For, One (and the same) is the Son, Who in

---

* 2 Corinth., v, 19. The verb is in the past participle.
† It would seem that the verse in the Quicunque vult, or Creed called after S. Athanasius, originally came from Theodore of Mopsuestia.
‡ The word is ﺍﻟﻤﻌﻲ, *primitia.*
‖ "Attend or set thy mind upon." See S. John's Rev., xxi, 7.

" Nature is The Only Begotten (and) Who (clothed " Himself with) put on our Nature."¶

(*k*) Again, from the same Treatise :—

" Wherefore He took that which He had not, " Flesh* proper ; and although It was at first Mortal, " It was deemed worthy of Immortality by (virtue " of) the power of GOD The WORD That took it ; " and, through the means of It, the whole race of " men rejoiced in the benefit."

(*l*) Another (extract) from the same (Theodoret's) Book :—

¶" Let him say, if, in consequence of the Nature, " the Worship is paid to It, which is paid by every " one to the Nature which is assumed, and not in " consequence of the Union with that ? It is entitled " to this from (his being) GOD The WORD. But if, " by reason of this, It is worshipped by all creation " as that which is united to GOD The WORD, and " is called His Temple, and because the Flesh of

---

¶ Or, " One in Essence is the Son, Who," &c.

* In p. 162, l. 10, the word in the text is ܡܟܐܙܢܠ which is of a rather doubtful character, but seems to be a sort of adjective to ܡܢܝܡܚ or ܣܡܐܙܠܣ, *Mary.* The sense would bear it—*He, the Flesh of Mary.* It was the Flesh that was *mortal,* not HE, Christ. Martin suggests ܡܟܐܙܡܡܠ.

¶ Or, perhaps, it may be better rendered in Martin's way :— " Let him say, then, if it is by (reason of) nature that He receives (possesses) the homage which every man renders to the Nature that has been assumed (adopted) and whether it is not rather in consequence of the Union contracted with GOD The WORD, that He has been deemed worthy of this honour. If, then, the Creation adores Him (the assumed, adopted, Nature) on account of His adhesion to GOD The WORD, and if, (for this reason,) He has been called The Temple and The Flesh of The Only Son, his opposition is superfluous and inspired by a quarrelsome spirit.

" The Only Begotten, then there is the solution of
" the great difficulty stated above. On the other
" hand, the Psalmist in that case is a Blasphemer and
" very presumptuous, and thou hast often said what is
" agreeable to Him, and hast said it a little while
" ago.

(*m*) Again, from the same Treatise : —

" If, therefore, The GOD of All raised the Flesh
" (from the dead) by the means of GOD The WORD,
" (then) there was a real verification (manifestation) ¶
" of the word of our Lord which was made to the
" ' Jews ; and He raised the Temple which was dis-
" ' solved by them.'*

" But it was the Lord Jesus Who rose from the
" dead."

" Dost thou then, also, name the Flesh the Lord
" Jesus ? "†

(*n*) Again, from the same Treatise :—

" The Likeness, therefore, of a Slave is associated ¶
" with GOD The WORD, and, as you say, ¶ (is
" associated) with HIM in honour and glory, and in

Moreover, the Psalmist is an impudent Blasphemer. That these ideas
please you, you have often declared, and you will even soon repeat it."
It probably refers to some quotation from the Psalms, putting the fine
argument of his opponent out of court. About Theodoret and Theodore, in connection with the Psalms, see Introductory Note, page 205.

¶ The word, (The Truth,) of our Lord which was stated to the
Jew was verily made manifest (exhibited).

* Reference is made to John, ii, 19.

† In p. 163, l. 8, it should undoubtedly be ܐܘ, not ܐܘ, in both cases.

¶ Or, better, perhaps :—" Has communion with."

¶ Literally,—"According to thy words."

" all other prerogatives. Not because of the Nature,
" but, by reason of the Union, does It attain to these
" things."

(*o*) Again, from the same Treatise : --

" How is He, then, Very MAN, Who is GOD
" in Nature, and is Very GOD? For, the Name of
" GOD is proper for Him, seeing He is so in
" Nature and in Truth ; but to Him, likewise, is
" (the name of) Man (appropriate), since* it, indeed,
" belongs to the Form of a Servant which (He is)
" in Truth. But, when applied to GOD The
" WORD, He is that only Œconomically,¶ since
" the Nature assumed is Man in Verity, whilst He,
" That assumed (It), is, indeed, Very GOD. But be-
" cause of the reason of the Œconomy, He is also
" Man, not as having been changed into this, but
" because He assumed the Human Nature."

(*p*) Again, from the same Treatise :—

" But again forgetting† these words, and having,
" also, abandoned the other‡ Teaching, he turned to
" the evil peculiarly his, and covertly advanced the
" Blasphemy of Apollinarius, and exclaimed that¶

---

* At p. 163, in lines 19 and 20, the word ܟܠ must have the same meaning.

¶ Or, perhaps, equally as well—"By the Incarnation" in l. 21, and, in l. 24, "by reason of the Incarnation." "He is also Man, not that The Word was changed into, but that He assumed, the Human Nature."

† Or, "Having forgotten," ܟܠ, *oblitus est.*

‡ *Other* (ܐܚܪܝܢ) teaching, apparently, was right teaching, and, therefore, *old,* which he had abandoned.

¶ Or, perhaps,—"he said again and again."

" we speak of One (Only) Son, just as the
" Fathers did, and of 'One (Only) Nature of The
" 'WORD INCARNATE.' Look at the bitterness
" of Orthodox Teaching. For, having postulated¶
" what is evidently confessed by the Just, 'ONE
" 'SON,' he introduces after it 'ONE NATURE,'—
" a thing which grew out of the Blasphemies of Apol-
" linarius. But he added this—'INCARNATE'*
" —being apprehensive of a disclosure of his Blas-
" phemy.† He must tell us, however, what Fathers

¶ " For, after having previously laid down (ܡܩܕܡ ܣܐܡ) from these
words, which are clearly confessed by the Just, that there is One Son,
he brings forwards (ܡܥܠ is Aphel) after it that there is One Nature,
which (doctrine) grew out of." At p. 164, l. 11, ܢܦܩ, prodiit, germi-
navit, is the correct word.

* The word ܡܬܒܣܪ is in the present tense and therefore means—is
made flesh, is Incarnate.

† "Of One (Only) Son and of One (Only) Nature of the INCARNATE
" WORD." Similar is the expression, if not identical—viz., " We
" must not, then imagine Two Natures, but One INCARNATE Nature of
" GOD THE WORD." This sentence, involving, at first sight, an heretical
sentiment about the Person of Christ, Dr. Neale, in his History of the Holy
Eastern Church, suggests may have been cited by Cyril " simply because
" he believed it to come from S. Athanasius who employed the word
" φύσις in the sense of Person." (See Vol. I, p. 294.) But we should
look at the occasion, which, I think, the following gives:—Cyrille répond :
" Nestorius a tout à fait raison d'enseigner les deux natures : car dans le
fait, la nature dù Logos est toute autre que celle de la chair : mais il a
tort en ce qu'il ne veut pas reconnaitre avec nous l'ἕνωσις des natures.
Pour nous, nous les unissons, et c'est ainsi que nous professons un seul
Christ, un seul Fils, une seule nature of Dieu devenue chair (μίαν τὴν
τοῦ Θεοῦ φύσιν σεσαρκωμένην). We cannot do better service for
this celebrated and controverted sentence of S. Cyril than quote extracts
expository of it from the 2nd Imperial Edict against the Three Chapters. The simple words of Héfélé, as given by Delarc, will suffice :—
" Celui qui est né de Marie est un de la sainte Trinité, de même sentence que
le Père quant à la divinité, de même substance que nos quant à l'humanité,
passible dans sa chair, impassible dans sa divinité, et aucun autre que le
Logos de Dieu ne s'est soumis à la souffrance et à la mort. Il ne faut
pas dire que c'est le Logos que a opéré les miracles et que c'est un au-

" brought up this expression. For,* the very contra-
" dictory to this we can discover among the Holy
" Fathers, since in their Sermons they have perfected
The Two Natures.   Dost† thou name Apollinarius,

tre Christ qui a souffert : car c'est le même Seigneur Jèsus Christ, Logos
de Dieu, qui a pris chair et s'est fait homme. . . . En disant que
le Christ est composé (σύνθετος) de deux natures, de la divinité et de l'humanité, nous n'introduisons cependant aucun mélange (σύγχυσις) dans
cette unité (ἕνωσις), et en reconnaissant dans chacune de ces natures le
seul Seigneur Jésus-Christ, le Λόγος divin devenu homme, nous n'étab-
lissons ni séparation, ni division, ni déchirement dans la seule et même
hypostase ; mais nous désignons la différence des natures par ce dont elles proviennent ; et cette différence n'est pas anéantie par l'ἕνωσις,
puisque chacune de ces deux natures existe dans cette unité. . . . .
La nature divine n'est pas métamorphosée en la nature humaine, et la
nature humaine n'est pas métamorphosée en la nature divine : mais chacune de ces natures reste dans les limites, le Logos a opéré l'unité de
l'hypostase.   Cette unité hypostatique prouve que le Dieu Logos, cette
hypostase de la Trinité, de s'est pas uni avec un homme existant antéri-
eurement, mais qu'il s'est créé une chair due sein de la sainte Vierge, de
la propre hypostase de la sainte Vierge, et qu'il a animé cette chair d'une
âme raisonnable,—et c'est là la nature humaine.   Cette union hypostatique du Logos avec la chair nous à été aussi enseignée per l'apôtre S.
Paul. . . . . Aussi professons-nous une double naissance du
Logos : l'une immatérielle ayant en lieu du sein du Père avant toute éter-
nité, l'autre dans les derniers temps, lorsqu'il a pris chair de la sainte
Mére de Dieu et qu'il est devenu homme. . . . . Il est Fils de
Dieu par la nature, tandis que nous, nous ne le sommes que par grâce ; il
est, à cause de nous et κατ' οἰκονομίαν, devenu fils d'Adam, tandis que
nous, nous sommes par nature fils d'Adam . . et, après l'incarnation,
il y en a un de la sainte Trinité, le Fils unique de Dieu, notre-Seigneur
Jésus-Christ, que se trouve composé de deux natures unies entre elles (σύνθετος).   Telle est la doctrine des Pères. . . . . Tout en profes-
sant ces doctrines, nous acceptons l'expression de Cyrille disant qu'il n'y
a qu'une φύσις τοῦ Λόγου σεσαρκωμενη. . . . car, toutes les fois
qu'il s'est servi de cette expression, le mot φύσις a pour lui le sens de
ὑπόστασις... &c. (Histoire des Conciles par Mgr. C. J. Héfélé, tome
troisiéme, Paris, 1870.)

   * Perhaps—" Everything contrary to this we can discover among the
Holy Fathers ; for, in preaching The Two Natures, they teach that The
Two Natures were Perfect." But, if ܐܠܨܐ were a constr., it must
precede the dependent noun.

   † At p. 164, l. 20, ܠܡܩܪܐ (part., as the ܡ shows) is equiva-

" and Eunomius, and Asterius, and Ætius ?*   For,
" it was they who gave birth to this Blasphemy.

Dioscorus, Bishop of Alexandria, said :—

Theodoret, who has been aforetime, and is at
present, Impious, who has not desisted from his
Impiety, but, even up to the present time, has per-
sisted in his Blasphemies, so much so as to give
umbrage to the ears of the Gracious and Christ-
loving Emperors, and to move them justly to withdraw their countenance from him, because they nauseate
these pernicious Doctrines—Theodoret, who is bent
on the destruction of souls without number, who has
brought trouble on all the Churches of the East,
and who has planted the seed of false Doctrine, and,
as far as he could, has (thereby) drawn the simple-
minded into his Impiety; who, moreover, has ventured to hold tenets and write in opposition to those
Positions which have been laid down by our very Blessed Father and Bishop Cyril,—must be (estranged)
removed from the whole Function of the Priesthood
and its Honour and Rank, and be also interdicted
Communion with the Laity; all the God-loving

---

lent to ܐܠܘܣܩܘܤ, *dost thou name.*

* The salient point of Error in the system of Apollinarius was that
he taught the Λόγος, or Divine Word, took the place of the νοῦς, or
rational Soul, in the Human Nature of Christ, subduing the ψυχή.
He denied the Blessed Virgin to be the Mother of The Incarnate Word.
Eunomius, the voluble disciple and secretary of Ætius, was the head of
the extreme Arians; and Ætius, the most odious of them, was the first
to affirm that the Son was *unlike* the Father in *essence*, as well as in
will. Asterius (says Canon Bright) was the Arian " Sophist " who
placed the Son, as " a Power of God," in the same category with the
locusts.

Bishops and Clerics in the world being aware that whosoever shall venture, after this judgment and synodical condemnation, to receive him anywhere, or to be with him, or to communicate at his table, or to exchange the merest conversation with him, will of necessity render himself liable to be put on his defence, in the Divine Court of Judgment, before the Tribunal of God ; and he will have, too, to give justification of himself on the charge of * having dared to set at nought what has been decreed by this Holy and Œcumenical Synod.

Now we will convey† (the account of) all these transactions of to-day to the Gracious and Christ-loving Auditory (audience) of the Victorious Emperors in order that their Clemency may command these Treatises of the impious Theodoret, so replete with all Impiety and mischievous Doctrine, to be committed to the burning of the fire.

(*b*) Now let the Notaries Demetrius, and Flavius,

------

* In p. 165, l. 20, the ܒ is omitted before ܐܝܟ, according to the usual practice in Syriac. See Dr. R. P. Smith's Thesaurus Syriacus, Fasciculus 1, on ܒ being omitted before ܐܝܟ.

† In p. 165, l. 24, ܢܣܒ must be *we have reported*, or *we report;* but, if the right reading be ܢܣܒ (Aphel), *we will report.*

Let the Reader note here the bearing of the President of the Council. Not satisfied with his own sentence being pronounced, and pronounced as sufficient for the condemnation of the criminal, he affects to intimidate, and he does intimidate, other Bishops who are to follow, and to settle any wavering voters, besides consigning, in the manner of Councils, the books of Theodoret to the flames, to say nothing of taking upon himself the part of despatching envoys to Archbishop Domnus to ascertain his opinion on the day's transactions, which, however, we might in charity perhaps regard, from an

and Primus proceed to the God-loving Domnus, Bishop of Antioch, and read to him all the transactions of to-day, so that he may unreservedly declare his opinion on those transactions.

(c) The HOLY SYNOD said :—

"That is a just Judgment."

———

JUVENAL, Bishop of Jerusalem, said :—

As regards Theodoret, who has dared to write what is contrariant to The Faith of The True Religion and to the Definitions established at the former Holy and Œcumenical Synod of Ephesus, I too, give my decision that he be removed from the Rank of the Priesthood and from Communion* in the Holy Mysteries. I, also, (adjure) call all men to witness that not even a single communication between him and them ought to take place, nor ought they to offer salt, or (address even) a mere word, to him.

THALASSIUS, Bishop of Cæsarea of the First Cappadocia, said :—

Theodoret, who has become the (Foster) Father and the writer of the impious Doctrine of Nestorius, and who, from his childhood even to a protracted old age, has been trained¶ in Blasphemies against our

———

ecclesiastical point of view, as a piece of courtesy due to one who occupied the Patriarchal Throne of entire Christian Asia.

  * See note at p. 145.

¶ Or, "brought up." The word ܪܒܝ is a Pass. part. of Pa., *educatus, nutritus.*

Lord Christ, I give order to be deprived of the Rank of the Priesthood; and I refuse him all communion with Christians whatever.

EUSEBIUS, Bishop of Ancyra in the First Galatia, said:—

Theodoret, who dared to write in opposition to the affirmations (Chapters) of Cyril of Holy memory, is known* for his aversion for the exactness of our Orthodox Faith. I, therefore, adjudge him deserving of being deprived of the Dignity of the Priesthood and of Communion with the Laity, seeing that, by reason of his being infected¶ (sick) with affinity to the Doctrine of Nestorius, he has cut himself off from the Honour of the Episcopate.

JOHN, Bishop of Sebastia, in the First Armenia, said:—

Theodoret, who is infected with the same pernicious Doctrines as Nestorius, it is only right and just should receive the same judicial sentence; and, seeing that he returns to the vomiting of his Blasphemy, or, rather, since he has never desisted from it, it is fitting and proper, also, that he should be discarded from the Honour of the Priesthood and be interdicted all communion with Christians. He who neither the teaching of the Fathers, nor the Divine Scriptures, nor anything else of what has been divinely spoken, has put to no better use, ought to have been regarded as a man long since excommu-

---

* Or, " is known as one who is without love for the Catholic Faith."
¶ Literally: Ex eo enim quod ægrotavit.

nicated and condemned. ¶For, it is hateful that those who have once allowed themselves to be comprehended within the mesh (snare) of Blasphemy should assume, in old age, Orthodoxy of Faith.

BASIL, Bishop of Seleucia, said :—

Him who disputes the writings of the Very Blessed Cyril, the late Archbishop of the Great City of Alexandria, 1 reckon just as Impious and condemned as a person who is opposed to the Holy Gospel. I, therefore, follow your Piety in what is above indited against Theodoret; and all matters that have been determined on I approve as just and excellent; and I adhere to the judgment of those who have adjudged that he (Theodoret) be deposed from the Honour of the Priesthood and (deprived) of Communion in the Mysteries.

DIOGENES, Bishop of Cyzicus, said :—

Assenting, as I do, for my part, to the judgment

¶ This little sentence presents some difficulty of translation. Castell, p. 447, notes on the word ܠܒܟ—Peculiariter *prehendi* est *in carcerem duci, in vincula conjici*, and on ܚܢܩ (strangulavit, suffocavit, from which is derived ܚܢܘܩܝܐ, laqueus), at p. 305—Verbum non de strangulatione solum ponitur, sed de omni suffocationis genere, ut, quæ fit per *submersionem:* And the word ܟܣܝ is in the subjunctive mood, and means *to cover over*, ܠܡ is *pro*, and ܣܝܒܘܬܐ *senectus.* Martin renders it thus :—Il est bien difficile, en effect, de pûter dans la vieillesse des sentiments orthodoxes à ceux qui se sont une fois laissés dominer par le blasphême. And Hoffman thus :—Es ist freilich (geir) hässlich, auf solche, die einst (in ihrer jugend) von dem galgenstrick (mathat has proceeded from the Holy Fathers against Theodoret, being entirely with them, I pronounce him (Theodoret) to be deposed from all the Function of the Priesthood and (deprived) of Communion in the Holy Mysteries.

FLORENTIUS, Bishop (of Sardis) in Lydda (Lydia), said :—

It would have been better for Theodoret not to have been born rather than that, as is the case, his writings prove him to be a Blasphemer. For, it were better for him not to have been in existence than that he should, as of himself, be so wicked as act in antagonism with the Lord of All, Christ. Because, then, he has armed his tongue against the Priesthood which he once assumed, let him be deposed from the Dignity of the Episcopate and from Communion with the Laity, seeing that he has proved himself to be a Teacher of a deadly poison to the people.

SELEUCUS, Bishop (of Amasia), said :—

In following, as I do, the correct Decision of the Holy Fathers, Theodoret, who attempted to alter the Definitions which our Fathers established from of old, and to subvert the Faith established by the Holy Fathers at Nicæa, I dismiss from the Dignity of the Episcopate and pronounce deprived of Communion with the Laity.

---

hnōquītā) der lästerung gepackt sind, im alter die korrektur für den glauben auszudehnen (nkassē cal).

MARINIANUS, Bishop of Synnada,* said :—

Let Theodoret, who has been known, up to the present time, to entertain opinions beyond,† and in excess of, the Creed of the CCCXVIII Fathers assembled at Nicæa, be deprived of the Rank of the Episcopate and of Communion with the Laity.

EUSTATHIUS, Bishop of Berytus, said :—

We, all of us Bishops of the East, render thanks to God the Saviour of All, and to our Gracious and Christ-loving Emperors, for having assembled here this Holy and Œcumenical Synod. For, on behalf of the liberty of the East, was this Holy Assembly appointed¶ (to take place) ; and a man devoid of honour having been expelled, a man of integrity¶ can now, with freedom of speech, proclaim the Words of God; and there remains now no (place for any) Calumniator against the East, as we believe will (actually) be the case, when, Theodoret having been rooted out, as well as those who have already been ejected from the Church, there will also be (substituted) others in their stead —men of the Orthodox Faith—for the teaching of The True Religion to the Flocks of Christ. Let Theodoret, therefore, be adjudged, in pursuance

---

* No doubt the Scribe means ܣܘܢܕܐ, Synnada, but he has written ܣܘܢܕܐ in the MS.

† The frequent expression ܠܥܠ ܡܢ does not here mean strictly *adverse* or *contrary to*, but, rather, that Theodoret held opinions *beyond* or *outside* of the authorized Creed.

¶ Or, "established." See Imperial Documents at pp. 3 and 39.

¶ Or, "a just man."

II

of your Sentence, as among those who have been ejected; having henceforth no permission whatever, either to teach, or to address, or trouble the (inerrant) sound sheep of God, and being made to desist, too, from communicating in the Pure Mysteries.

The HOLY SYNOD said :—

"That is a just sentence—cast out the Heretic. "We all declare for this—all of us agree to the

"DEPOSITION OF THEODORET."

[END OF THE CAUSE OF THEODORET.]

Thus we see condemned by the Sentences of the Bishops, and by the unanimous vote, of the Synod, without a hearing even on that point of Doctrine in which we may reasonably consider him to be not faultless, a man of the purest and most innocent life, as well as possessed of the grandest virtues that can adorn humanity, a Bishop whose saintly memory, alone of all the Chiefs tried is stainless, and whose deeds place him in the very van of the noblest representative personages that figure so differently during the frightfully disquieting and unhappy epoch of the fifth period of the Church.

In looking back upon this case of Theodoret, and on this Version of it, I would desire to make a few reflections. In the first place I must express a hope that some *English* Scholar, by means of Dr. W. Wright's three-volumed Catalogue of the Syriac MSS. deposited in the British Museum—more rechercher and splendid than any Library in the world possesses—which *Foreign* Scholars so frequently visit, may, by carefully overhauling those MSS. one by one, be fortunate enough to discover, not only many more treasures-trove, but the very treatise or treatises of Theodoret, in which the above, some of them very difficult, Extracts appear. And this is not chimerical or visionary. For, what may we not hope for after the discovery of the Epistles of S.

Clement of Rome by Bryennius,(a) Metropolitan of Serrhæ, and the Syriac MS. of those same Epistles lately sold to the Syndics of the University of Cambridge (I tried hard myself to purchase the MS.) at the sale, at Paris, of the Library of the great Oriental Scholar Jules Mohl. Already has Dr. Martin printed some Syriac MSS. the contents of which are very germane to our subject. In a journal published at Leipzig very lately, he has given to the world " Lettres de Jacques de Saroug aux moines du Couvant de " Mar Bassus, et à Paul d'Edesse relevées et traduites." And, from the correspondence between Jacob of Sarug and these Monks, which appears to have taken place not later than 473 A.D., that is, full eighty years before our great MS. (14,530) was written—for the Scribe says he wrote it in the Month of May, 553 (see the end of this translation)— and certainly not a quarter of a century after the Second Synod of Ephesus was held, I here subjoin an Extract, from the Zeitschrift alluded to, as translated at page 225 :—

III. Quelque temps plus tard, il m'est tombé entre les mains des dis-cours de Diodore, de Théodore, et de Théodoret et j'ai vu que tous avaient bu le fiel amer du Dragon. J'anathématise donc, avec l'impie Nestorius, que je viens de nommer, Diodore, Théodore, et Théodoret, ses compagnons, car il est évident pour moi que tous ces hérétiques, enivres par le fiel du serpent ancien, divisent l'Emmanuel en deux fils, l'un fils unique de Dieu et l'autre fils de la Vierge Marie.(b) C'est pourquoi je répète ce que j'ai dit dès long-temps : J'anathématise Nestorius, Euty-chès, et quiconque accepte leur doctrine impie ; Diodore, Théodore, Théodoret, quiconque lit leurs livres en partageant leur idées, quiconque ne confesse point que Dieu le Verbe est entré par l'oreille de la Vierge, sans qu'il y ait eu de péché commis, pour s'incarner et pour se faire pro-clamer par l'Ecriture fils de David, fils de Abraham. Or, lui, seul fils unique, a été engendré de deux manières, l'une du père, sans corps, et sans commencement, l'autre de la Vierge Marie, corporellement, suivant ce qui est écrit, Dieu a été vu dans la chair,(c) et Dieu a envoyé son fils, lequel est né de la femme.(d) L'Eglise vierge a été fiancée a celui qui était et qui est, à Jésus-Christ ; à *celui qui était hier qui est aujourdhui et qui sera toujours*.(e) C'est à cet époux veritable qu'est fiancée la fille de la lumière et c'est pourquoi, pendant la célébration des Mystères, elle lui adresse les paroles des Séraphins, comme à son Père ; car, de même qu' elle célèbre un père saint, elle célèbre aussi un fils saint. Ceux donc qui *divisent en deux le seul Christ indivisible*, et qui *placent en lui des nombres* et *des noms, qui proclament Dieu le Verbe* et *qui parlent de l'homme qui a été pris : ceux-là, l'Eglise les anathématise*. (Zeitschrift der Deutschen Mogenländischen Gezellschaft. Drisssigster Band, II. Hezft. Leipzig, 1876).

(a) His Edition and learned Volume, by M. Nicholas Damalas, just published at Athens, containing the Introduction to a Commentary on the New Testament most ably and favourably reviewed in *The Academy* (Oct. 28th, 1876), "are an evidence of " activity in the theological Schools of the Oriental Church for which Western Scho- " lars have not been prepared."

(b) Le second membre de l'énumération est omis.

(c) Cfr. à Timothée, iii, 16.   (d) Aux Galates, iv, 4.   (e) Psaume, ii, 6.

At page 226, following immediately after the above extract, this paragraph occurs:

IV. Ceux encore qui prétendent que Dieu le Verbe ne s'est pas incarné de la Vierge, mais qu'il en est sorti et qu'il s'est montré seulement en apparence, comme un fantôme et sans réalité, ceux-là aussi l'Eglise qui est pleine de la vérité du fils unique, les anathématise, parceque la bénédiction a été promise aux nations dans la semence d'Abraham. Or, cette semmence, c'est Jésus-Christ, qui s'est incarné dans le sein de la Vierge, fille de David, fille d'Abraham, appelée pour cela mère de Dieu. *Ceux également qui competent et classent les natures après l'union, qui reconnaissent leurs propriétés et leurs singularités, ceux-là l'Eglise les déclare étrangers à sa communion,* parceque le Christ ne doit pas se deviser en deux. C'est un seul et même qui est Dieu en verite, par son incarnation dans la Vierge Marie, suivant ce qui est écrit : *Le Verbe s'est fait chair ; il a opéré des marveilles et a supporté des douleurs volontairement.* Les choses elevees sont siennes et les choses humbles sont siennes encore, comme les choses elevees. Le fils unique est seul ; il est insondable, inaccessible, inexplicable, indivisible, inscrutable, ineffable. A lui, à son Père, au Saint Esprit, gloire dans les siècles des siècles !

Again, at pp. 247, 248 :—

Dans les lettres cependant que Votre Saintete a lues et qu'elle a trouvees infirmes ou mortes, "j'anathematisais Nestorius et Eutychès, "Diodore, Theodore et Theodoret, quiconque reçoit leur doctrine, qui-"conque ne confesse point que Dieu le Verbe est entre par l'oreille de la "Vierge afin d'habiter dans ses entrailles saintes et de s'y incarner, après "quoi il a ete vu revêtu de chair, tout en etant Dieu ; quiconque ne re-"connait point qu'un seul fils unique a ete engendre de deux manières, "l'une du père sans corps et sans commencement, l'autre de la Vierge "Marie corporellement ;" quiconque ne croit pas qu'uue personne seule de la Trinite s'est incarnee et que cette personne est celle du fils unique, egal à son père en toutes choses. D'où vient qu' avec lui et comme lui il participe aux glorifications des Seraphins. "*Ceux donc qui divisent en* "*deux le seul Christ indivisible et qui placent en lui des nombres et des* "*noms, qui, en confessant Dieu le Verbe, parlent aussi de l'homme qui a* "*ete pris: ceux encore qui pretendent que Dieu le Verbe ne s'est pas incarne* "*de la Vierge, mais qu'il en est sorti* et qu'il s'est montre seulement en "apparence, comme un fantôme sans realite ; ceux qui comptent et qui "classent les natures après l'union, qui reconnaisen leurs proprietes et leurs "singularites, ceux qui ne confessent pas que celui qui etait Dieu "en verite est devenu homme en verite, par son incarnation dans le sein "de la Vierge Marie, ceux-là l'Eglise les anathematise." Voilà les paroles que Votre Paternite a dit être infirmes et mortes.

Soon after the above was put into type came (with " Les facultés de "Théologie et les futures Universités Catholiques," in which Dr. Martin as "Aumonier de l'Ecole Monge" will, I doubt not, distinguish himself very considerably) the Syriac Text, the French translation, &c., kindly despatched to me by himself, from which I extract some more matter, so opportunely brought to light, in connection with Theodoret.

Again, at p. 250:—

J'anathematise egalement ceux qui, *après l'union, divisent, distinguent ou comptent, dans un seul Christ, les natures, avec leurs particularites et leurs operations pour donner à Dieu ce qui est de Dieu* et à l'homme ce qui est de l'homme ; car le Christ est un ; c'est Dieu fait homme, le Verbe fait chair, le cache devenu manifeste, l'invisible rendu visible dans la chair, et qui, en etant tout cela, demeure toujours Dieu.   Or, quand on anathematise toutes les personnes qui ont combattu cette verite et qui ont donne naissance à une infinite de disputes et de scandales, il est evident qu'on anathematise aussi tous ceux qui pensent comme elles.   Elles ont toutes, en effet, developpe les idees de Nestorius.   Mais Nestorius est anathematise, lui, sa doctrine et tou ceux qui pensent comme lui, qu'ils aient vecu avant ou après lui.

X. Ce sont les disciples de Simon le Magicien qui ont mis au jour cette heresie ; Paul de Samosate l'a enseignee ensuite sous diverses formes, et après lui, Diodore et Theodore l'ont consignee par ecrit, avec tout l'art et toute la pompe de la philosophie grecque.   Nestorius n'en a ete que l'interprète et le vulgarisateur ; il l'a revêtue des charmes du style.   Theodoret enfin et ceux qui ont partage les mêmes opinions l'ont soutenue dans leur temps, de tous leurs efforts.

I will now add to the foregoing some indications that refer to a preferable and, some of them, far more exact rendering of the Syriac Text. That at p. 217 is the following:—

The Body of the Church has the need of the hand of the Lord—(the right reading, at l. 13, p. 135 of the Text, is ܘܢܬܒ ܐܝܕ)—because it is sorely devoured by evil.   For this purpose have you all been gathered together in this place : (viz.) in order that you may establish for CHRIST One Glorious Church, having neither spot nor blemish,(a) and that you may, having thus for a second time saved and purified It by the power of The Truth, present it to the whole earth under Heaven, not as reviled and calumniated by Heretics, but invested with the Heavenly and Apostolic Glory of the Doctrine of The Alone True Religion.

At page 218, it should be put thus, before the beginning of Theodoret's Letter :—John, Presbyter and Proto-Notary, read :—

Copy of the Letter of Theodoret to the Monks (directed) against, &c.

Also, at foot of page 219, the reference is to the Prophecy of Jeremiah, chap. iv, verse 19 ; whilst, however, the long Citation itself, or rather Citations, would seem to be composed of a sort of cento of terse and laconic Jeremiads culled out of the writings of the Prophets.

(a) See Eph., v, 27 (the Church glorious); S. John's Rev., xii, 2, 9 (the Church glorified), and xix, 7.

At p. 221, and l. 13, it would be better thus :—And he does not allow us to take these terms, and to apply those which are proper to God (the Divine predicates) to His Nature—to attach those which are of a humble kind and are spoken humanly (i.e., spoken of Christ as a human being) to the Human Nature assumed by Him.   The words, *by Christ*, should be put thus—(*of Christ*).

— l. 19.   Perhaps it should be " well-meaning persons," as οἱ εὐφρονουντες generally has that signification.

At p. 222, l. 5 :—Stating the (their well-known) Diversity of Essence.   " Alienum paternæ substantiæ et dissimilem inde eum osten-" dere festinantes," are the words of Garner of his " Beati Theodoreti, Ep. Cyri Operum," Tom. 5 (Opus postumum, 1684) in the Auctarium, p. 62.

— l. 21 :—The noxious culture, or noisome toil (and soil), of Marcion.   In (Garner it is " malignæ culturæ," and " Macedonius.")   Some suchexpression is wanted to correspond with the word " seed " and " fruit."

At p. 223, l. 9 :—; and The Faith, which we have received, with which we do baptize and have been baptized, we do keep spotless.

— l. 24 :—for, on the one hand we do not dissolve the Union and we believe on the other hand——

At p. 224, l. 3 :—For, if commixture and con-fusion had taken place and One Nature was (had been) formed out of those two, then, &c.

— l. 14.   Perhaps it would be better :—experienced the dissolution, but the Power of the other raised up what was dissolved.

At p. 226.   Foot Notes—Titus, ii, 13, and Isaiah xlv, 14.

At p. 230, l. 4, it should be, as in Migne, thus—(and of Paul).

At p. 231, l. 8 :—such things as we speak of as belonging to our original or, perhaps, first-fruit, which woɪd is used by S. Paul at Rom. xi, 16, in that sense.   At p. 234, l. 7, the same word occurs.   In the Greek it is ἡ ἀπαρχη ἡμων, corresponding to the Syriac.

At p. 236, the expressions μονογενής and πρωτότοκος must be distinguished, and the distinction finds expression in the terms—Only Begotten and First-Born.   So translate thus—Now that God The Word was Alone Born (the Only Begotten) of the Father the Scriptures teach us.   But the Only Begotten became, also, the First-Born.

At p. 237, l. 20, it would be better :—*grew* from Human Nature.

— l. 21 :—a Dogmatic writer (or teacher) must weave appellatives from these two (must write these two in one texture).

At p. 238, l. 1 :—" he may enjoy his desire " is the proper rendering.

— l. 6 :—who asserted moderation to be best, which is an allusion, doubtless, to the well-known saying, μέτρον ἄριστον, of one of the Seven Wise Men of Greece.

At p. 240, l. 5 :—this present darkness, or, read *prevailing* instead of *imminent*.

To appreciate Theodoret's Letter, and its Theological terminolgy, we must read the Original in Greek.   For, it is impossible to convey in a translation the full meaning of those dogmatical expressions contained in it.

The refined terms and predicates belonging to dogmatic theology, τὸ Θεῖον δόγμα, can most adequately if not only, be expressed by the delicate shades of meaning attached to Greek words, such as ἀσυγχύτω ἀτρεπτως, ἀνομοιος, ἑνωσις, σύγχυσις, φύσις, πρόσωπον, ἑτερούσιος Hence it will be best to study them in the original letter Theodoret wrote, which is subjoined according to the text as produced by Hoffmann, together with some of the Syriac words, corresponding to the Greek ones, indicated by anglicised characters.

THEODORET'S LETTER.

—o—

Ὁρῶν τὴν ἐν τῷ παρόντι καιρῷ τῆς ἐκκλησίας κατάστασιν καὶ τὴν ἔναγχος ἐπαναστᾶταν τῇ ἱερᾷ (dkītā) νηὶ ζάλην, καὶ τὰς σφοδρὰς καταιγίδας, καὶ τῶν κυμάτων τὴν προσβολὴν, καὶ τὴν βαθεῖαν σκοτομήνην, καὶ πρὸς τούτοις τῶν πλωτήρων τὴν ἔριν καὶ τῶν ἱερεύειν [l. ἐρέττειν] λαχόντων τὴν μάχην, καὶ τὴν τῶν κυβερνητῶν μέθην, καὶ ἁπαξαπλῶς τὴν τῶν κακῶν ἀωρίαν· τῶν Ἱερεμίου θρήνων ἀναμιμνησκόμαι καὶ μετ' ἐκείνου βοῶ [Ier. 4, 19]. Τὴν κοιλίαν μου, [τὴν κοιλίαν μου] ἐγὼ ἀλγῶ καὶ τὰ αἰσθητήρια τῆς καρδίας μου μαιμάσσει, ἡ ψυχή μου σπαράσσεται καὶ ἡ καρδία μου, καὶ πηγὰς [δακρύων] ἐπιζητῶ, ἵνα ταῖς λιβάσι τῶν ὀφθαλμῶν τὸ πολὺ τῆς ἀσθενείας ἀποσκευάσωμαι (ꜱedhoq) [νέφος]. Δέον γὰρ ἐν οὕτως ἀγρίῳ χειμῶνι [καὶ] τοὺς κυβερνήτας ἐγρηγορέναι καὶ τῷ κλύδωνι μάχεσθαι καὶ τῆς τοῦ σκάφους σωτηρίας φροντίζειν· καὶ τοὺς ναύτας τῆς κατ' ἀλλήλων ἔριδος ἀποστάντας, εὐχῇ καὶ τέχνῃ τὰ δεινὰ διαφυγεῖν (neghōn men)· καὶ τοὺς πλωτῆρας ἡσυχῇ καθῆσθαι, καὶ μήτε ἀλλήλοις μήτε τοῖς κυβερνήταις ζυγομαχεῖν· τὸν δὲ τῆς θαλάττης ἱκετεύειν δεσπότην, ἵνα νεύματι μεταβάλῃ (p. 123) τὰ σκυθρωπά· τούτων μὲν οὐδεὶς οὐδὲν ἐθέλει ποιεῖν· ὡς ἐν νυκτομαχίᾳ δὲ ἀλλήλους ἀγνοήσαντες καὶ τοὺς ἐναντίους καταλιπόντες, καθ' ἡμῶν αὐτῶν πάντα δαπανῶμεν (nappequan) τὰ βέλη, καὶ τοὺς ὁμοφύλους ὡς πολεμίους τιτρώσκομεν (qattelnan), οἱ δὲ πλησίον ἑστῶτες γελῶσιν ἡμῶν τὴν μέθην, καὶ τοῖς ἡμετέροις ἐπεντρυφῶσι (metbassmīn) κακοῖς καὶ χαίρουσιν ὑπ' ἀλλήλων ἡμᾶς ὁρῶντες δαπανωμένους· αἴτιοι δὲ τούτων οἱ τὴν ἀποστολικὴν διαφθεῖραι πίστιν φιλονεικήσαντες καὶ τοῖς εὐαγγελικοῖς δόγμασιν ἀλλόκοτον διδασκαλίαν ἐπιθεῖναι τολμήσαντες, καὶ τὰ δυσσεβῆ κεφάλαια (Κυρίλλου), ἅ μετὰ ἀναθεματισμῶν εἰς τὴν βασιλίδα πόλιν ἐξέπεμψαν, δεξάμενοι, καὶ ταῖς οἰκείαις ὑπογραφαῖς, ὡς ᾠήθησαν, βεβαιώσαντες· ἅ σαφῶς ἐκ τῆς πικρᾶς Ἀπολλιναρίου βεβλάστηκε ῥίζης, μετέχει δὲ καὶ τῆς Ἀρείου καὶ Εὐνομίου δυσσεβείας· εἰ δέ τις ἀκριβῶς κατιδεῖν ἐθελήσειεν, οὐδὲ τῆς Οὐαλεντίνου καὶ Μάνεντος καὶ Μαρκίωνος ἄμοιρα δυσσεβείας τυγχάνει. Ἐν μὲν γὰρ τῷ πρώτῳ κεφαλαίῳ τὴν ὑπὲρ ἡμῶν γεγενημένην οἰκονομίαν (mdabbrānūtā) ἐκβάλλει· οὐκ ἀνειληφέναι τὸν Θεὸν [λόγον] φύσιν ἀνθρωπείαν, ἀλλ' αὐτὸν εἰς σάρκα μεταβληθῆναι διδάσκων· καὶ δοκήσει (masbrānūtā) καὶ φαντασίᾳ τὴν

1

τοῦ σωτῆρος ἡμῶν ἐνανθρώπησιν, ἀλλ' οὐκ ἀληθείᾳ γεγενῆσθαι δογμα-
τίζων : ταῦτα δὲ τῆς Μαρκίωνος καὶ τοῦ Μάνειτος καὶ (p. 124)
Οὐαλεντίνου δυσσεβείας ὑπάρχει γενιήματα. 'Εν δὲ τῷ δευτέρῳ καὶ
τρίτῳ κεφαλαίῳ, ὥσπερ ἐπιλαθόμενος, ὧν ἐν προοιμίοις ἐξέθετο, τὴν
καθ' ὑπόστασιν ἕνωσιν εἰσάγει·ᵃ καὶ σύνοδον καθ' ἕνωσιν φυσικήν, κρᾶσιν
τινα καὶ σύγχυσιν διὰ τούτων τῶν ὀνομάτων γεγενῆσθαι διδάσκων τῆς τε
θείας φύσεως καὶ τῆς τοῦ δούλου μορφῆς : τοῦτο τῆς αἱρετικῆς 'Απολλιναρίου καινοτομίας (heresiōtūtā) ἐστὶ κύημα. 'Εν δὲ τῷ τετάρτῳ κεφαλαίῳ ἀπαγορεύει τῶν εὐαγγελικῶν καὶ ἀποστολικῶν φωνῶν τὴν διαίρεσιν·
καὶ οὐκ ἐᾷ κατὰ τὰς τῶν ὀρθοδόξων πατέρων διδασκαλίας τὰς μὲν θεοπρεπεῖς φωνὰς περὶ τῆς θείας ἐκλαμβάνεσθαι (d neṣqol wnessab) φύσεως·
τὰς δὲ ταπεινὰς καὶ ἀνθρωπίνως εἰρημένας τῇ ἀναληφθείσῃ προσάπτειν
ἀνθρωπότητι· καὶ ἐντεῦθεν τοίνυν ἔστιν εὑρεῖν (ἰδεῖν l') τοὺς εὐφρο-
νοῦντας, τὴν τῆς ἀσεβείας συγγένειαν. Ἄρειος γὰρ καὶ Εὐνόμιος :
κτίσμα, καὶ ἐξ οὐκ ὄντων, καὶ δοῦλον, τὸν μονογενῆ υἱὸν τοῦ Θεοῦ εἶναι
φάσκοντες, τὰ ταπεινῶς (ḥālein mākkātā) ὑπὸ τοῦ [δεσπότου]
Χριστοῦ καὶ ἀνθρωπίνως εἰρημένα τῇ θεότητι αὐτοῦ προσάψαι τετολμή-
κασι· τὸ ἑτεροούσιον (ḥāi dōitjā ḥrīnā) ἐντεῦθεν καὶ τὸ ἀνόμοιον
κατασκευάζοντες· πρὸς τούτοις, ἵνα συνελὼν εἴπω, αὐτὴν τὴν ἀπαθῆ καὶ
ἄτρεπτον τοῦ Χριστοῦ θεότητα καὶ παθεῖν καὶ σταυρωθῆναι καὶ ἀποθανεῖν (p. 125) [καὶ ταφῆναι] διαγορεύει: τοῦτο δὲ καὶ τῆς 'Αρείου καὶ
Εὐνομίου μανίας ἐπέκεινα· οὐδὲ γὰρ οἱ κτίσμα τολμῶντες ἀποκαλεῖν τὸν
ποιητὴν τῶν ὅλων καὶ δημιουργὸν (gābolā) εἰς ταύτην ἐξώκειλαν
(ṣreku l) τὴν ἀσέβειαν. βλισφημεῖ δὲ καὶ εἰς τὸ ἅγιον πνεῦμα· οὐκ ἐκ
τοῦ πατρὸς αὐτὸ λέγων ἐκπορεύεσθαι (nfaq), κατὰ τὴν τοῦ κυρίου
φωνήν, ἀλλ' ἐξ υἱοῦ τὴν ὕπαρξιν ἔχειν. καὶ οὗτος δὲ τῶν 'Απολλιναρίου
σπερμάτων ὁ καρπός· γειτνιάζει δὲ καὶ τῇ Μαρκίωνος πονηρᾷ γεωργίᾳ.
Τοιαῦτα τοῦ Αἰγυπτίου τὰ κύηματα πονηροῦ πατρὸς ἀληθῶς ἔγγονα
πονηρότερα. Ταῦτα δὲ, δέον ἢ ἀμβλωθρίδια ποιῆσαι (l mauḥātū)
κυοφορούμενα, ἢ [εὐθὺς] τεχθέντα διαφθεῖραι τοὺς τῶν ψυχῶν τὴν
ἰατρείαν ἐγκεχειρισμένους: ὡς ὀλέθρια καὶ τῆς ἡμετέρας φύσεως δηλή-
τρια ἐκτρέφουσιν οἱ γεννάδαι, καὶ πολλῆς ἀξιοῦσι σπουδῆς ἐπ' ὀλέθρῳ
σφῶν αὐτῶν καὶ τῶν τὰς ἀκοὰς αὐτοῖς ὑπέχειν ἀνεχομένων (mettpīsin).
Ἡμεῖς δὲ τὸν πατρῷον κλῆρον ἄσυλον φυλάττειν σπουδάζομεν, καὶ ἣν
παρελάβομεν πίστιν, μεθ' ἧς καὶ ἐβαπτίσθημεν καὶ βαπτίζομεν, (p. 126)
ἀνέπαφον (dlā tolṣā) καὶ ἀκήρατον διατηροῦμεν· καὶ ὁμολογοῦμεν
τὸν κύριον ἡμῶν 'Ιησοῦν Χριστόν, Θεὸν τέλειον, καὶ ἄνθρωπον τέλειον
ἐκ ψυχῆς λογικῆς καὶ σώματος, πρὸ αἰώνων μὲν ἐκ τοῦ πατρὸς γεννη-
θέντα κατὰ τὴν θεότητα· ἐπ' ἐσχάτων δὲ τῶν ἡμερῶν δι' ἡμᾶς καὶ διὰ
τὴν ἡμετέραν σωτηρίαν ἐκ Μαρίας τῆς παρθένου τὸν αὐτὸν κατὰ τὴν
ἀνθρωπότητα· ὁμοούσιον τῷ πατρὶ κατὰ τὴν θεότητα, καὶ ὁμοούσιον ἡμῖν

(a) Καὶ σύνοδον καθ' ἕνωσιν φυσικήν is, according to the Syriac text, to be
construed with the preceding accusative, τὴν καθ' ὑπόστασιν ἕνωσιν, not with
the following, κρᾶσιν τινα καὶ σύγχυσιν.

2

κατὰ τὴν ἀνθρωπότητα· δύο γὰρ φύσεων ἕνωσις γέγονε· διὸ ἕνα Χριστόν, ἕνα υἱόν, ἕνα κύριον ὁμολογοῦμεν· οὔ τε γὰρ τὴν ἕνωσιν λύομεν, καὶ ἀσύγχυτον αὐτὴν γεγενῆσθαι πιστεύομεν, τῷ κυρίῳ πειθόμενοι λέγοντι τοῖς Ἰουδαίοις· [Io. 2, 19] Λύσατε τὸν ναὸν τοῦτον, καὶ ἐν τρισὶν ἡμέραις ἐγερῶ αὐτόν. Εἰ δὲ κρᾶσις ἐγεγόνει καὶ σύγχυσις, καὶ μία φύσις ἐξ ἀμφοῖν ἀπετελέσθη, ἐχρῆν εἰπεῖν· Λύσατε μὲ, καὶ ἐν τρισὶν ἡμέραις ἐγερθήσομαι· νῦν δὲ δεικνὺς, ὡς ἄλλος μὲν ὁ Θεὸς κατὰ τὴν φύσιν, ἄλλος δὲ ὁ ναός, εἷς δὲ Χριστὸς ἀμφότερα, Λύσατε, φησὶ, τὸν ναὸν τοῦτον, καὶ ἐν τρισὶν ἡμέραις ἐγερῶ αὐτόν· σαφῶς διδάσκων, ὡς ὅτι οὐχ ὁ Θεὸς ἦν ὁ λυόμενος, ἀλλ᾽ ὁ ναός, καὶ τοῦ μὲν ἡ φύσις τὴν λύσιν ὑπεδέχετο· τοῦ δὲ ἡ δύναμις ἤγειρε τὸ λυόμενον. Θεὸν δὲ καὶ ἄνθρωπον τὸν Χριστὸν ὁμολογοῦμεν ταῖς θείαις ἀκολουθοῦντες γραφαῖς. Ὅτι [μὲν] γὰρ Θεὸς ὁ κύριος ἡμῶν Ἰησοῦς Χριστός, ὁ μακάριος Ἰωάννης, ὁ εὐαγγελιστής, βοᾷ· [1, 1] Ἐν ἀρχῇ ἦν ὁ λόγος καὶ ὁ λόγος ἦν πρὸς τὸν Θεὸν καὶ Θεὸς ἦν ὁ λόγος· οὗτος ἦν ἐν ἀρχῇ πρὸς τὸν Θεόν· πάντα δι᾽ αὐτοῦ ἐγένετο, καὶ χωρὶς αὐτοῦ ἐγένετο οὐδὲ ἓν [ὃ γέγονε]. καὶ πάλιν [1, 9] Ἦν (lies dōïtauhi hwā) τὸ φῶς τὸ ἀληθινὸν ὃ φωτίζει πάντα ἄνθρωπον ἐρχόμενον εἰς τὸν κόσμον. [καὶ] αὐτὸς δὲ ὁ κύριος διαρρήδην διδάσκει λέγων· [Io. 14, 9] Ὁ ἑωρακὼς ἐμὲ ἑώρακε τὸν πατέρα [μου]. καί, ἐγὼ καὶ ὁ πατὴρ ἕν ἐσμέν· κἀγὼ ἐν τῷ πατρὶ καὶ ὁ πατὴρ ἐν ἐμοί. καὶ ὁ μακάριος Παῦλος ἐν μὲν τῇ πρὸς Ἑβραίους ἐπιστολῇ [1, 3] φησίν· Ὃς ὢν ἀπαύγασμα τῆς δόξης αὐτοῦ καὶ χαρακτὴρ τῆς ὑποστάσεως αὐτοῦ, φέρων τε τὰ πάντα τῷ ῥήματι τῆς δυνάμεως αὐτοῦ (l ḥailā d mellteh). Ἐν δὲ τῇ πρὸς Φιλιππησίους· [2, 5] Τοῦτο φρονείσθω ἐν ὑμῖν, φησίν, ὃ καὶ ἐν Χριστῷ Ἰησοῦ, ὃς (fol. 65ʳ) ἐν μορφῇ Θεοῦ ὑπάρχων, οὐχ ἁρπαγὴν ἡγήσατο τὸ εἶναι ἴσα Θεῷ, ἀλλ᾽ ἑαυτὸν ἐκένωσε μορφὴν δούλου λαβών. Ἐν δὲ τῇ πρὸς Ῥωμαίους [9, 5] φησί· Ὧν οἱ πατέρες καὶ ἐξ ὧν ὁ Χριστὸς [τὸ] κατὰ σάρκα, ὁ ὢν ἐπὶ πάντων Θεὸς εὐλογητός. Ἐν δὲ τῇ πρὸς Τίτον [2, 13] Προσδεχόμενοι τὴν μακαρίαν ἐλπίδα (lsabrā dtūbā) τῆς ἐπιφανείας τοῦ μεγάλου Θεοῦ καὶ σωτῆρος ἡμῶν Ἰησοῦ Χριστοῦ. [καὶ] Ἡσαίας δὲ βοᾷ [9, 6] Ὅτι παιδίον ἐγεννήθη ἡμῖν, καὶ υἱὸς ἐδόθη ἡμῖν, οὗ ἡ ἀρχὴ ἐπὶ τοῦ ὤμου αὐτοῦ, καὶ καλεῖται τὸ ὄνομα αὐτοῦ μεγάλης βουλῆς ἄγγελος, θαυμαστός, σύμβουλος, Θεὸς ἰσχυρός, ἐξουσιαστής, ἄρχων εἰρήνης, πατὴρ τοῦ μέλλοντος αἰῶνος. καὶ πάλιν· [45, 4] Ὀπίσω σου, φησίν, ἀκολουθήσουσι δεδεμένοι χειροπέδαις (b sotmē) καὶ ἐν σοὶ προσεύξονται, ὅτι ἐν σοὶ Θεός [ἐστι], καὶ οὐκ ἔστι Θεὸς πλήν σου. Σὺ γὰρ εἶ θεός, καὶ οὐκ ᾔδειμεν, Θεὸς τοῦ Ἰσραὴλ σωτήρ. [καὶ] τὸ Ἐμμανουὴλ δὲ ὄνομα, Θεοῦ καὶ ἀνθρώπου τυγχάνει σημαντικόν, ἑρμηνεύεται γὰρ κατὰ τὴν τοῦ εὐαγγελίου διδασκαλίαν, μεθ᾽ ἡμῶν ὁ Θεός, τουτέστιν, ἐν ἀνθρώπῳ Θεός, ἐν τῇ ἡμετέρᾳ φύσει Θεός. καὶ ὁ θεῖος [δὲ] Ἰερεμίας ὁ προφήτης προθεσπίζει λέγων· [Baruch 2, 36] Οὗτος ὁ Θεὸς ἡμῶν, καὶ οὐ λογισθήσεται ἕτερος πρὸς αὐτόν, ἐξεῦρε πᾶσαν ὁδὸν ἐπιστήμης, καὶ ἔδωκεν αὐτὴν Ἰακὼβ τῷ δούλῳ αὐτοῦ, καὶ Ἰσραὴλ τῷ ἠγαπημένῳ ὑπ᾽ αὐτοῦ (page 129), μετὰ ταῦτα ἐπὶ τῆς γῆς ὤφθη, καὶ τοῖς ἀνθρώποις

8

συνανεστράφη. καὶ ἄλλας ἄν τις μυρίας εὕροι φωνὰς ἔκ τε τῶν θείων
εὐαγγελίων καὶ τῶν ἀποστολικῶν συγγραμμάτων καὶ ἐκ τῶν προφητικῶν
θεσπισμάτων, δεικνύς, ὅτι Θεὸς ἀληθινὸς ὁ κύριος ἡμῶν Ἰησοῦς Χριστός.
Ὅτι δὲ καὶ ἄνθρωπος μετὰ τὴν ἐνανθρώπησιν προσαγορεύεται, διδάσκει
μὲν αὐτὸς ὁ κύριος Ἰουδαίοις διαλεγόμενος καὶ βοῶν· [Io. 8, 40] Τί με
ζητεῖτε ἀποκτεῖναι, ἄνθρωπον, ὅστις τὴν ἀλήθειαν ὑμῖν λελάληκα ; καὶ ὁ
μακάριος Παῦλος ἐν τῇ πρὸς Κορινθίους προτέρᾳ ἐπιστολῇ [15, 21]
λέγων· Ἐπειδὴ γὰρ δι᾽ ἀνθρώπου ὁ θάνατος, καὶ δι᾽ ἀνθρώπου ἀνά-
στασις νεκρῶν. καὶ δεικνὺς περὶ τίνος λέγει, ἑρμηνεύει τὸ εἰρημένον,
οὑτωσὶ λέγων· [ibidem 22] Ὥσπερ γὰρ ἐν τῷ Ἀδὰμ ἀποθνήσκουσι
πάντες οἱ ἄνθρωποι, οὕτως [καὶ] ἐν τῷ Χριστῷ πάντες ζωοποιηθήσονται.
καὶ Τιμοθέῳ δὲ γράφων [ὁμοίως] φησίν· [II. 2, 5] εἷς Θεός, εἷς καὶ
μεσίτης Θεοῦ καὶ ἀνθρώπων· Χριστὸς Ἰησοῦς. καὶ ἐν ταῖς πράξεσι
τῶν ἀποστόλων [17, 30] ἐν Ἀθήναις δημηγορῶν· Τοὺς μὲν οὖν χρόνους
τῆς ἀγνοίας ὑπεριδὼν ὁ Θεός, φησί, τὰ νῦν παραγγέλλει πᾶσι, παιταχοῦ
μετανοεῖν· καθότι ἔστησεν ἡμέραν, ἐν ᾖ μέλλει κρίνειν τὴν οἰκουμένην
ἐν δικαιοσύνῃ ἐν ἀνδρὶ ᾧ ὥρισε, πίστιν παρασχὼν πᾶσιν, ἀναστήσας
αὐτὸν ἐκ νεκρῶν. [καὶ] ὁ μακάριος δὲ Πέτρος Ἰουδαίοις διαλεγόμενος·
[Acts 2, 22] Ἄνδρες, φησίν, (semar: gabīē, lam,) Ἰσραηλῖται,
ἀκούσατε τοὺς λόγους τούτους· Ἰησοῦν τὸν Ναζωραῖον, ἄνδρα ἀπὸ τοῦ Θεοῦ
ἀποδεδειγμένον εἰς ὑμᾶς (θethzī bkōn) σημείοις καὶ τέρασι καὶ δυνάμεσιν
οἷς ἐποίησεν ὁ Θεὸς δι᾽ αὐτοῦ. (ca. p. 130) [καὶ] ὁ προφήτης δὲ Ἡσαΐας
τοῦ [δεσπότου] Χριστοῦ τὰ πάθη προαγορεύων, ὃν πρὸ βραχέων ὠνόμασε
Θεόν, τοῦτον ἄνθρωπον ἀποκαλεῖ, οὑτωσὶ λέγων· [53, 3] Ἄνθρωπος ἐν
πληγῇ ὢν καὶ εἰδὼς φέρειν μαλακίαν· οὗτος τὰς ἀνομίας ἡμῶν φέρει,
καὶ ὑπὲρ ἡμῶν ὀδυνᾶται (hašš)· καὶ ἄλλας δ᾽ ἂν ὁμοφώνους μαρτυρίας
συλλέξας ἐκ τῶν θείων γραφῶν, ἐνέθηκα ἂν τῇ ἐπιστολῇ ταύτῃ, εἰ
μὴ τὴν ὑμετέραν θεοσέβειαν ἠπιστάμην βίον (dobbārāh dabcālmā
hānā) ἔχειν τὴν τῶν θείων λογίων μελέτην (hergā), κατὰ τὸν ἐν
ψαλμοῖς μακαριζόμενον ἄνθρωπον. Τῇ ὑμετέρᾳ τοίνυν φιλοπονίᾳ κατα-
λιπὼν τὴν τῶν μαρτυριῶν συλλογήν, ἐπὶ τὰ προκείμενα βαδιοῦμαι. Θεὸν
[τοίνυν] ἀληθινὸν καὶ ἄνθρωπον ἀληθινὸν τὸν κύριον ἡμῶν Ἰησοῦν
Χριστὸν ὁμολογοῦμεν, οὐκ εἰς δύο πρόσωπα διαιροῦντες τὸν ἕνα, ἀλλὰ
δύο φύσεις ἀσυγχύτως ἡνῶσθαι πιστεύομεν· οὕτω γὰρ καὶ τὴν πολυσχεδῆ
τῶν αἱρετικῶν βλασφημίαν ῥᾳδίως διελέγξαι δυνησόμεθα : πολλὴ καὶ
ποικίλη τῶν ἐπαναστάντων τῇ ἀληθείᾳ ἡ πλάνη, ὡς καὶ αὐτίκα δηλώ-
σομεν. Μαρκίων μὲν γὰρ καὶ Οὐαλεντῖνος καὶ Μάνης οὔτε ἀνειληφέναι ἀνθρωπείαν φύσιν τὸν Θεὸν λόγον φασίν, (p. 131) οὔτε ἐκ
παρθένου τὸν κύριον ἡμῶν Ἰησοῦν Χριστὸν γεγεννῆσθαι πεπιστεύκασιν
(mhaimnīn). ἀλλ᾽ αὐτὸν τὸν Θεὸν λόγον χρηματισθῆναι εἰς εἶδος
(ḥezwā) ἀνθρώπειον καὶ φανῆναι ὡς ἄνθρωπον, φαντασίᾳ μᾶλλον ἢ
(wlau) ἀληθείᾳ χρησάμενον· Οὐαλεντῖνος δὲ καὶ [Βαρδισάνης τὴν μὲν
γέννησιν δέχονται· τὴν δὲ ἀνάληψιν ἀρνοῦνται τῆς ἡμετέρας φύσεως,
οἷόν τινι σωλῆνι χρήσασθαι τῇ παρθένῳ λέγοντες τὸν υἱὸν τοῦ Θεοῦ.]·
Σαβέλλιος [δὲ] ὁ Λίβυς (Lībājā) καὶ Φωτεινὸς καὶ Μάρκελλος ὁ

4

Γαλάτης καὶ Παῦλος ὁ Σαμοσατεὺς ἄνθρωπον ψιλὸν ἐκ τῆς παρθένου γεννηθῆναι λέγουσι, τὸ δὲ (geir) καὶ Θεὸν εἶναι τὸν προαιώνιον Χριστὸν
διαρρήδην ἀρνοῦνται· Ἄρειος δὲ καὶ Εὐνόμιος σῶμα μόνον ἀνειληφέναι
ἐκ τῆς παρθένου τὸν Θεὸν λόγον φασίν· Ἀπολινάριος δὲ τῷ σώματι
προστίθησι καὶ ψυχὴν ἄλογον, ὡς τῆς ἐνανθρωπήσεως τοῦ Θεοῦ λόγου
ὑπὲρ ἀλόγων, οὐχ ὑπὲρ λογικῶν γεγενημένης· ἡ δὲ τῶν ἀποστόλων
διδασκαλία τέλειον ἄνθρωπον ὑπὸ τελείου Θεοῦ ἀνειλῆφθαι διδάσκει·
τὸ γὰρ [Phil. 2, 6], Ὃς ἐν μορφῇ Θεοῦ ὑπάρχων μορφὴν δούλου ἔλαβε,
τοῦτο δηλοῖ: ἀντὶ φύσεως γὰρ καὶ οὐσίας (oïtjä) ἡ μορφὴ πρόκειται·
δηλοῖ γὰρ ὅτι φύσιν ἔχων Θεοῦ, φύσιν ἔλαβε δούλου· διὸ τοῖς μὲν
πρώτοις τῆς ἀσεβείας εὑρεταῖς Μαρκίωνι καὶ τῷ Μάνεντι καὶ
Οὐαλεντίνῳ διαλεγόμενοι ἀποδεικνύναι σπουδάζομεν (p. 132) ἐκ τῶν
θείων γραφῶν, ὅτι οὐ μόνον Θεὸς ἀλλὰ καὶ ἄνθρωπος ὁ δεσπότης
Χριστός. Σαβελλίου δὲ καὶ Μαρκέλλου καὶ Φωτεινοῦ [καὶ Παύλου]
τὴν ἀσέβειαν ἐλέγχομεν, μάρτυρι τῇ θείᾳ γραφῇ κεχρημένοι καὶ δεικ-
νύντες, ὡς οὐκ ἄνθρωπος μόνον, ἀλλὰ καὶ Θεὸς προαιώνιος καὶ τῷ πατρὶ
ὁμοούσιος ὁ δεσπότης Χριστός. Ἀρείου δὲ καὶ Εὐνομίου καὶ Ἀπολι-
ναρίου τὸ περὶ τὴν οἰκονομίαν ἀτελὲς δῆλον ποιοῦντες τοῖς ἀγνοοῦσι,
τελείαν εἶναι τὴν ληφθεῖσαν ἀποφαινόμεθα φύσιν ἐκ τῶν θείων λογίων
(melle) τοῦ ἁγίου πνεύματος. Ὅτι γὰρ καὶ ψυχὴν ἀνέλαβε λογικήν,
αὐτὸς ὁ κύριος διδάσκει λέγων· [Io. 12, 27] Νῦν ἡ ψυχή μου τετάρακται,
καὶ τί εἴπω; πάτερ σῶσόν με ἐκ τῆς ὥρας ταύτης, ἀλλὰ διὰ τοῦτο ἦλθον
εἰς τὴν ὥραν ταύτην. καὶ πάλιν [Matth. 26, 38] Περίλυπός ἐστιν ἡ
ψυχή μου ἕως θανάτου· καὶ ἑτέρωθι· [Io. 10, 18] Ἐξουσίαν ἔχω πάλιν
λαβεῖν αὐτήν· οὐδεὶς αἴρει αὐτὴν ἀπ᾽ ἐμοῦ. καὶ ὁ ἄγγελος πρὸς τὸν
Ἰωσήφ, [Matth. 2, 20] Παράλαβε, φησί, τὸ παιδίον καὶ τὴν μητέρα
αὐτοῦ καὶ πορεύου εἰς γῆν Ἰσραήλ, τεθνήκασι γὰρ πάντες οἱ ζητοῦντες
τὴν ψυχὴν τοῦ παιδίου. (p. 133) καὶ ὁ εὐαγγελιστὴς πάλιν φησί·
[Luk. 2, 52] Ἰησοῦς δὲ προέκοπτεν ἡλικίᾳ καὶ σοφίᾳ καὶ χάριτι παρὰ Θεῷ
καὶ ἀνθρώποις. προκόπτει δὲ ἡλικίᾳ καὶ σοφίᾳ, οὐ [θεότης] ἡ ἀεὶ τελεία, ἀλλ᾽
ἡ ἀνθρωπεία φύσις, ἡ χρόνῳ [καὶ] γινομένη καὶ αὐξομένη καὶ τελειουμένη.
οὗ χάριν τὰ μὲν ἀνθρώπινα πάντα τοῦ δεσπότου Χριστοῦ: πεῖναν, φημί,
[καὶ] δίψαν, καὶ κόπον, καὶ ὕπνον, καὶ ἱδρῶτας, καὶ προσευχήν, καὶ
ἄγνοιαν, καὶ δειλίαν, καὶ ὅσα τοιαῦτα τῆς ἡμετέρας ἀπαρχῆς εἶναί
φαμεν, ἣν ἀναλαβὼν ὁ Θεὸς λόγος προσῆψεν (saqqef) ἑαυτῷ, τὴν
ἡμετέραν πραγματευόμενος (mettaggar) σωτηρίαν. τὸν δὲ τῶν χωλῶν
δρόμον, καὶ τῶν νεκρῶν τὴν ἀνάστασιν, καὶ τὰς τῶν ἄρτων πηγάς
(nebcē), καὶ τὴν ἐξ ὕδατος εἰς οἶνον μεταβολήν, καὶ πάσας τὰς ἄλλας
θαυματουργίας· τῆς θείας εἶναι δυνάμεως ἔργα πιστεύομεν. ὡς τὸν αὐτόν,
φημὶ [δὴ] τὸν δεσπότην Χριστόν, καὶ πάσχειν καὶ πάθη λύειν: πάσχειν μὲν κατὰ τὸ ὁρώμενον, λύειν δὲ (man) τὰ πάθη κατὰ τὴν ἀρρήτως
οἰκοῦσαν θεότητα. δηλοῖ δὲ τοῦτο σαφῶς καὶ τῶν ἱερῶν εὐαγγελιστῶν
ἡ ἱστορία (ʜsūrtä) μανθάνομεν γὰρ ἐκεῖθεν, (p. 134) ὡς ἐν φάτνῃ
κείμενος καὶ σπάργανα περιβεβλημένος, ὑπὸ ἀστέρος ἐκηρύττετο, καὶ
ὑπὸ μάγων προσεκυνεῖτο καὶ ὑπὸ ἀγγέλων ὑμνεῖτο, καὶ διακρίνομεν

ϐ

εὐσεβῶς, ὅτι τοῦ νηπίου [τὰ ῥάκη] καὶ σπάργανα καὶ τῆς κλίνης ἡ
ἀπορία καὶ ἡ πᾶσα εὐτέλεια, τῆς ἀνθρωπότητος ἴδια. ὁ δὲ τῶν μάγων
δρόμος καὶ τοῦ ἀστέρος ἡ ποδηγία (haddājūtā) καὶ ἡ τῶν ἀγγέλων
χορεία (djūsnā) κηρύττει τὴν τοῦ κρυπτομένου θεότητα. οὕτως ἀποδι-
δράσκει μὲν εἰς Αἴγυπτον, καὶ τῇ φυγῇ τῆς Ἡρώδου μανίας ἀπαλλάτ-
τεται: [καὶ] γὰρ ἄνθρωπος ἦν. Συσσείει δὲ κατὰ τὸν προφήτην
(mistake of MS.: θεὸν) τὰ χειροποίητα Αἰγύπτου: Θεὸς γὰρ ὑπῆρχε.
Περιτέμνεται καὶ φυλάττει τὸν νόμον καὶ καθαρσίους προσφέρει θυσίας:
ἐκ γὰρ τῆς Ἰεσσαὶ βεβλάστηκε ῥίζης. Καὶ ὑπὸ νόμον ὡς ἄνθρωπος
ἦν. καὶ ἔλυσε τὸν νόμον μετὰ ταῦτα καὶ δέδωκε τὴν καινὴν διαθήκην:
νομοθέτης γὰρ ἦν· καὶ ταύτην αὐτὸς δώσειν διὰ τῶν προφητῶν
ἐπηγγείλατο. Ἐβαπτίσθη ὑπὸ Ἰωάννου: τοῦτο δείκνυσι τὸ ἡμέτερον.
Μαρτυρεῖται ἄνωθεν ὑπὸ τοῦ πατρός, καὶ ὑπὸ τοῦ πνεύματος δείκνυται:
τοῦτο κηρύττει τὸν προαιώνιον. Ἐπείνησεν· ἀλλὰ καὶ πολλὰς χιλιάδας ἐκ
πέντε ἄρτων ἐκόρεσε: τοῦτο θεῖον, ἐκεῖνο ἀνθρώπινον. Ἐδίψησε καὶ ᾔτησεν
ὕδωρ, ἀλλὰ πηγὴ ἦν ζωῆς: (p. 135) καὶ τὸ μὲν ἦν τῆς [ἀνθρωπίνης]
ἀσθενείας, τὸ δὲ τῆς θείας δυνάμεως. Ἐκάθευδεν ἐν τῷ πλοίῳ, ἀλλὰ
καὶ τῆς θαλάττης τὴν ζάλην ἐκοίμησε: τοῦτο [sic!] τῆς παθητῆς
φύσεως, ἐκεῖνο [sic!] τῆς ποιητικῆς καὶ δημιουργικῆς [καὶ τῆς] τοῖς
πᾶσι τὸ εἶναι δωρησαμένης. Ἐκοπίασε βαδίσας, ἀλλὰ καὶ χωλοὺς
ἀρτίποδας εἰργάσατο, καὶ νεκροὺς ἐκ τῶν τάφων ἀνέστησε: καὶ τὸ μὲν
ἦν τῆς ὑπερκοσμίου δυνάμεως, τὸ δὲ τῆς ἡμετέρας ἀσθενείας. Ἐδει-
λίασε θάνατον, καὶ ἔλυσε θάνατον: καὶ τὸ μὲν τοῦ θνητοῦ δηλωτικόν,
τὸ δὲ τοῦ ἀθανάτου, μᾶλλον δὲ (bram dein) ζωοποιοῦ τυγχάνει σημαντικόν. Ἐσταυρώθη, κατὰ τὴν τοῦ μακαρίου Παύλου διδασκαλίαν,
ἐξ ἀσθενείας, ἀλλὰ ζῇ ἐκ δυνάμεως Θεοῦ. τὸ τῆς ἀσθενείας ὄνομα διδα-
σκέτω οὐχ ὡς ὁ παντοδύναμος καὶ ἀπερίγραφος, καὶ ἄτρεπτος καὶ
ἀναλλοίωτος προσηλώθη, ἀλλ᾽ ἡ ἐκ δυνάμεως Θεοῦ ζωοποιηθεῖσα φύσις
κατὰ τὴν τοῦ ἀποστόλου διδασκαλίαν ἀπέθανε καὶ ἐτάφη: ἀμφότερα
τῆς τοῦ δούλου μορφῆς. Πύλας χαλκᾶς συνέτριψε (shaq) καὶ μοχ-
λοὺς σιδηροῦς [sic!] συνέθλασε καὶ κατέλυσε τοῦ θανάτου τὸ κράτος·
καὶ ἐν τρισὶν ἡμέραις ἀνέστησε τὸν οἰκεῖον ναόν (l haikleh): ταῦτα
τῆς τοῦ Θεοῦ μορφῆς τὰ γνωρίσματα κατὰ τὴν τοῦ κυρίου διδα-
σκαλίαν· φησὶ γάρ· [Io. 2, 19] Λύσατε τὸν ναὸν τοῦτον καὶ ἐν τρισὶν
ἡμέραις ἐγερῶ (mqīm) αὐτόν. Οὕτως ἐν τῷ [ἑνὶ] Χριστῷ διὰ
μὲν τῶν παθῶν θεωροῦμεν τὴν ἀνθρωπότητα, διὰ δὲ τῶν θαυμά-
των νοοῦμεν αὐτοῦ τὴν θεότητα. οὐ γὰρ εἰς δύο Χριστοὺς τὰς
δύο φύσεις μερίζομεν, ἀλλ᾽ ἐν τῷ ἑνὶ Χριστῷ νοοῦμεν τὰς δύο
φύσεις· καὶ ἴσμεν, ὅτι μὲν ἐκ τοῦ πατρὸς ὁ Θεὸς λόγος ἐγεννήθη, ἐκ τοῦ Ἀβραὰμ δὲ καὶ Δαβὶδ ἡ ἡμετέρα ἀπαρχὴ προσε-
λήφθη. Διὸ καὶ ὁ μακάριος Παῦλος φησί, περὶ τοῦ Ἀβραὰμ διαλεγό-
μενος· οὐκ εἶπε· [Καὶ] τοῖς σπέρμασί σου, ὡς ἐπὶ πολλῶν, ἀλλ᾽ ὡς
ἑνός· Καὶ τῷ σπέρματί σου, ὅς ἐστι Χριστός. Καὶ Τιμοθέῳ δὲ γράφων
[II, 2, 8], μνημόνευε, φησίν, Ἰησοῦν Χριστὸν ἐγηγερμένον ἐκ νεκρῶν
ἐκ σπέρματος Δαβὶδ, κατὰ τὸ εὐαγγέλιόν μου. καὶ Ῥωμαίοις ἐπιστέλ-

6

λων [1, 3], Περὶ τοῦ υἱοῦ αὐτοῦ, φησί, τοῦ γενομένου ἐκ σπέρματος
Δαβὶδ κατὰ σάρκα. καὶ πάλιν [9, 5]· Ὧν οἱ πατέρες καὶ ἐξ ὧν ὁ
Χριστὸς τὸ κατὰ σάρκα. καὶ ὁ εὐαγγελιστής [Matth. 1, 1]· Βίβλος
γειέσεως Ἰησοῦ Χριστοῦ υἱοῦ Δαβίδ, υἱοῦ Ἀβραάμ. Καὶ ὁ μακάριος
Πέτρος ἐν ταῖς πράξεσι [Acts 2, 80], Προφήτης, φησίν, ὑπάρχων ὁ
Δαβὶδ, καὶ εἰδὼς ὅτι ὅρκῳ ὤμοσεν αὐτῷ ὁ Θεὸς ἐκ καρποῦ τῆς ὀσφύος
αὐτοῦ [MS. σαυτοῦ!] ἀναστήσειν τὸν Χριστὸν καὶ καθίσαι ἐπὶ τοῦ
θρόνου αὐτοῦ· προειδὼς ἐλάλησε περὶ τῆς ἀναστάσεως αὐτοῦ. Καὶ ὁ
Θεὸς τῷ Ἀβραὰμ φησί [Gen. 22, 18]· Ἐν τῷ σπέρματί σου ἐνευλογη-
θήσονται πάντα τὰ ἔθνη τῆς γῆς. Καὶ ὁ Ἡσαΐας [δὲ]· [11, 1]
Ἐξελεύσεται ῥάβδος ἐκ τῆς ῥίζης Ἰεσσαί, καὶ ἄνθος ἐκ τῆς ῥίζης αὐτοῦ
ἀναβήσεται, καὶ ἐπαναπαύσεται ἐπ᾽ αὐτὸν πνεῦμα θεοῦ, πνεῦμα
σοφίας καὶ συνέσεως, πνεῦμα βουλῆς καὶ ἰσχύος, πνεῦμα γνώσεως καὶ
εὐσεβείας, πνεῦμα φόβου θεοῦ ἐμπλήσει αὐτόν. καὶ μετ᾽ ὀλίγα, [11, 10]
Καὶ ἔσται, φησίν (lam), ἡ ῥίζα τοῦ Ἰεσσαὶ καὶ ὁ ἀνιστάμενος ἄρχειν
ἐθνῶν ἐπ᾽ αὐτῷ ἔθνη ἐλπιοῦσι· καὶ ἔσται ἡ ἀνάπαυσις αὐτοῦ τιμή.
Δῆλον τοίνυν ἐκ τῶν εἰρημένων, ὡς τὸ μὲν κατὰ σάρκα ὁ Χριστὸς τοῦ
Ἀδὰμ καὶ Δαβὶδ ὑπῆρχεν ἀπόγονος, καὶ τὴν αὐτὴν αὐτοῖς περιέκειτο
φύσιν, κατὰ δὲ τὴν θεότητα τοῦ θεοῦ προαιώνιός ἐστιν υἱὸς καὶ λόγος,
ἀφράστως τε καὶ ὑπὲρ ἄνθρωπον (l cel men haunā) ἐκ τοῦ πατρὸς
γεννηθείς, καὶ συναΐδιος ὑπάρχων, (p. 138) ὡς ἀπαύγασμα πρὸς τὸ
φῶς ἀχωρίστως ἔχει· οὕτως ὁ μονογενὴς υἱὸς πρὸς τὸν ἑαυτοῦ πατέρα.
Φαμὲν τοίνυν τὸν κύριον ἡμῶν Ἰησοῦν Χριστὸν υἱὸν εἶναι μονογενῆ τοῦ
θεοῦ καὶ πρωτότοκον· μονογενῆ μέν, [καὶ] πρὸ τῆς ἐνανθρωπήσεως
καὶ μετὰ τὴν ἐνανθρώπησιν· πρωτότοκον δέ, μετὰ τὴν ἐκ παρθένου γένε-
σιν (jaldā)· τῷ γὰρ μονογενεῖ τὸ πρωτότοκος [ὄνομα] ἐναντίον [μὲν
εἶναί πως] δοκεῖ, διότι μονογενὴς μὲν ὁ μόνος ἔκ τινος γεννηθεὶς
προσαγορεύεται, πρωτότοκος δὲ ὁ πολλῶν ἀδελφῶν πρῶτος. τὸν δὲ
Θεὸν λόγον μόνον ἐκ τοῦ πατρὸς αἱ θεῖαι γραφαὶ γεννηθῆναι λέγουσι.
Γίνεται (hwū) δὲ καὶ πρωτότοκος ὁ μονογενής, τὴν ἡμετέραν φύσιν
εἰληφὼς ἐκ τῆς παρθένου, καὶ ἀδελφοὺς τοὺς εἰς αὐτὸν πεπιστευκότας
προσαγορεῦσαι καταξιώσας· ὡς εἶναι τὸν αὐτὸν μονογενῆ μέν, καθὸ
Θεός· πρωτότοκον δέ, καθὸ ἄνθρωπος. οὕτως ἡμεῖς τὰς δύο φύσεις
ὁμολογοῦντες τὸν ἕνα Χριστὸν προσκυνοῦμεν, καὶ μίαν αὐτῷ προσφέρομεν
τὴν προσκύνησιν. Τὴν γὰρ ἕνωσιν ἐξ αὐτῆς τῆς συλλήψεως ἐν τῆς
ἁγίας παρθένου νηδύϊ γεγενῆσθαι πιστεύομεν. Διὸ καὶ θεοτόκον καὶ
ἀνθρωποτόκον τὴν ἁγίαν παρθένον προσαγορεύομεν. Ἐπειδὴ καὶ αὐτὸς
ὁ δεσπότης Χριστός, Θεὸς καὶ ἄνθρωπος ὑπὸ τῆς θείας καλεῖται γραφῆς.
καὶ ὁ Ἐμμανουὴλ δέ, τῶν δύο φύσεων κηρύττει τὴν ἕνωσιν. Εἰ δὲ τὸν
Χριστὸν Θεὸν καὶ ἄνθρωπον (p. 139) [ὁμολογοῦμεν καὶ] λέγομεν, τίς
οὕτως εὐήθης, ὡς φυγεῖν τὴν ἀνθρωποτόκος φωνήν, μετὰ τῆς θεοτόκου
τιθεμένην· εἰ γὰρ τῷ δεσπότῃ Χριστῷ τὰς δύο τιθεμεν προσηγορίας, δι᾽ ὃν ἡ
παρθένος τετίμηται καὶ εὐλογημένη ἐν γυναιξί [Luk. 1, 28] προσηγο-
ρεύθη, τίς [οὖν] εὖ φρονῶν παραιτήσαιτο ἀπὸ τῶν τοῦ σωτῆρος
ὀνομάτων ἀποκαλέσαι τὴν παρθένον, ἢ δι᾽ ἐκεῖνον παρὰ τῶν πιστῶν

7

γεραίρεται: οὐ γὰρ ὁ ἐξ αὐτῆς δι᾽ αὐτὴν σεβάσμιος, ἀλλ᾽ αὐτὴ διὰ τὸν
ἐξ αὐτῆς ταῖς μεγίσταις προσηγορίαις καλλύνεται (metqallkā). Εἰ
μὲν οὖν Θεὸς μόνον ὁ Χριστός, καὶ ἐκ τῆς παρθένου τοῦ εἶναι τὴν ἀρχὴν
εἴληφεν, ἐντεῦθεν μόνον ἡ παρθένος ὀνομαζέσθω καὶ καλείσθω θεοτόκος,
ὡς Θεὸν φύσει γεννήσασα. Εἰ δὲ καὶ Θεὸς καὶ ἄνθρωπος ὁ Χριστός,
καὶ τὸ μὲν ἦν ἀεί· οὔτε γὰρ ἤρξατο τοῦ εἶναι, συναΐδιος (bar mtom-
mājūtā) γὰρ τῷ γεννήσαντι· τὸ δὲ ἐπ᾽ ἐσχάτων τῶν καιρῶν ἐκ τῆς
ἀνθρωπείας ἐβλάστησε φύσεως: ἑκατέρωθεν ὁ δογματίζειν (d nēolaf)
ἐθέλων πλεκέτω τῇ παρθένῳ τὰς προσηγορίας, δηλῶν, ποῖα μὲν τῇ φύσει,
ποῖα δὲ τῇ ἑνώσει προσήκει· εἰ δὲ πανηγυρικῶς (ḥaggājat sic = ḥaggājat
τις λέγειν ἐθέλοι, καὶ ὕμνους ὑφαίνειν (nezqor), καὶ ἐπαίνους διεξ[ι]έναι,
καὶ βούλεται τοῖς σεμνοτέροις ὀνόμασιν ἀναγκαίως κεχρῆσθαι, οὐ δογ-
ματίζων, ὡς ἔφην, ἀλλὰ πανηγυρίζων (mhaggē) καὶ θαυμάζων ὡς οἷόν
τε τοῦ μυστηρίου τὸ μέγεθος: (p. 140) ἀπολαυέτω (nqaddē) τοῦ
πόθου (hau mā dmahheb), καὶ τοῖς μεγάλοις ὀνόμασι κεχρήσθω, καὶ
ἐπαινείτω καὶ θαυμαζέτω· πολλὰ γὰρ τοιαῦτα παρὰ ὀρθοδόξοις διδασκάλοις
εὑρίσκομεν. Πανταχοῦ δὲ τὸ μέτριον τιμάσθω. Ἐπαινῶ γὰρ τὸν εἰρηκότα,
ἄριστον εἶναι τὸ μέτριον, εἰ καὶ τῆς ἡμετέρας ἀγέλης οὐκ ἔστιν. Αὕτη τῆς
ἐκκλησιαστικῆς πίστεως ἡ ὁμολογία. Τοῦτο τῆς εὐαγγελικῆς καὶ ἀποστολικῆς διδασκαλίας τὸ δόγμα (jullfānā d haimānūtā). Ὑπὲρ ταύτου
τρὶς καὶ πολλάκις ἀποθανεῖν τῆς τοῦ Θεοῦ δηλονότι χάριτος συνεργούσης
οὐ παραιτησόμεθα. Ταῦτα καὶ τοῖς πλανωμένοις διδάξαι προεθυμή-
θημεν· καὶ πολλάκις αὐτοὺς εἰς διάλεξιν (nianillā) προυκαλεσάμεθα,
ὑποδεῖξαι αὐτοῖς σπουδάζοντες τὴν ἀλήθειαν, καὶ οὐκ ἐπείσθησαν. Ὑφο-
ρώμενοι γὰρ τῶν ἐλέγχων τὸ προσφανές, ἔφυγον τοῖς ἀγῶνας· σαθρὸν γὰρ
ὡς ἀληθῶς τὸ ψεῦδος, καὶ τῷ σκότει συνεζευγμένον (kdinā cam). Πᾶς
γάρ, φησίν (oamīr) [Io. 3, 10], ὁ φαῦλα πράσσων, οὐκ ἔρχεται πρὸς τὸ
φῶς, ἵνα μὴ φανερωθῇ ὑπὸ τοῦ φωτὸς τὰ ἔργα αὐτοῦ. Ἐπειδὴ τοίνυν
πολλὰ πεπονηκότες, οὐ πεπείκαμεν αὐτοὺς ἐπιγνῶναι τὴν ἀλήθειαν, εἰς
τὰς οἰκείας ἐπανήλθομεν ἐκκλησίας ἀθυμοῦντες (mcāqin) καὶ χαίροντες·
τὸ μέν, διὰ τὸ ἡμέτερον ἀπλανές, τὸ δέ, διὰ τὴν τῶν μελῶν ἡμῶν
σηπεδόνα (tamsōtā). Διὸ τὴν ὑμετέραν ἁγιωσύνην παρακαλῶ, εὐθύμως
τὸν φιλάνθρωπον (mraḥmānā) ἡμῶν ἱκετεῦσαι δεσπότην, καὶ πρὸς αὐτὸν
βοῆσαι (tegcōn) [Ioel 2, 17]· Φεῖσαι, κύριε, τοῦ λαοῦ σου καὶ μὴ δῷς τὴν
κληρονομίαν σου εἰς ὄνειδος· ποίμανον ἡμᾶς κύριε, ἵνα μὴ γενώμεθα ὡς
τὸ ἀπαρχῆς, ὅτε οὐκ ἦρχες ἡμῶν, οὐδὲ ἐπεκέκλητο τὸ ὄνομά σου ἐφ᾽
ἡμᾶς. Ἰδέ, κύριε, ὅτι [Ps. 78 (79), 4] ἐγενήθημεν ὄνειδος τοῖς γείτοσιν
ἡμῶν, μυκτηρισμὸς καὶ χλευασμὸς τοῖς κύκλῳ ἡμῶν· ὅτι εἰσῆλθε δόγματα πονηρὰ εἰς τὴν κληρονομίαν (p 141) καὶ ἐμίαναν τὸν ναὸν τὸν
ἅγιόν σου· ὅτι εὐφράνθησαν θυγατέρες ἀλλοφύλων ἐπὶ τοῖς ἡμετέρας
κακοῖς· ὅτι ἐμερίσθημεν εἰς γλώσσας πολλάς οἱ πρώην [ὁμοφρονοῦντές
τε καὶ] ὁμοφωνοῦντες. κύριε, ὁ Θεὸς ἡμῶν, εἰρήνην (lege lĕainā) δὸς
ἡμῖν ἣν ἀπωλέσαμεν, τῶν σῶν ἐντολῶν ἀμελήσαντες. κύριε, ὁ Θεὸς ἡμῶν,
κτῆσαι ἡμᾶς [Is. 26, 13]. κύριε, ἐκτός σου ἄλλον οὐκ οἴδαμεν· τὸ
ὄνομά σου ὀνομάζομεν. ποίησον τὰ ἀμφότερα ἕν, καὶ τὸ μεσότοιχον

8

[τοῦ φραγμοῦ] λῦσον καὶ τὴν ἀναφυεῖσαν ἀσέβειαν· συνάγαγε ἡμᾶς ἕνα
καθ᾽ ἕνα, καὶ τὸν νέον σου Ἰσραήλ, οἰκοδομῶν Ἰερουσαλὴμ καὶ τὰς
διασποράς Ἰσραὴλ ἐπισυνάγων· γενοίμεθα πάλιν μία ποίμνη (cānā),
καὶ πάντες ὑπὸ σοῦ ποιμανθείημεν· σὺ γὰρ εἶ ὁ ποιμὴν ὁ καλός, ὁ τὴν
ψυχὴν αὐτοῦ τεθεικὼς ὑπὲρ τῶν προβάτων. ἐξεγέρθητι, ἱνατί ὑπνοῖς,
κύριε· ἀνάστηθι καὶ μὴ ἀπώσῃ ἡμᾶς εἰς τέλος· (p. 142) ἐπιτίμησον
(Ps. 43, 2) τοῖς ἀνέμοις καὶ τῇ θαλάττῃ· καὶ δὸς γαλήνην τῇ ἐκκλησίᾳ
σου, καὶ κυμάτων ἀπαλλαγήν (ghājtā). Ταῦτα καὶ ὅσα τοιαῦτα παρακαλῶ τὴν ὑμετέραν θεοσέβειαν βιᾶν πρὸς τὸν τῶν ὅλων Θεόν· ἀγαθὸς γὰρ
ὢν καὶ φιλάνθρωπος καὶ τὸ θέλημα τῶν φοβουμένων αὐτὸν ποιῶν ἀεί,
τῆς ὑμετέρας δεήσεως ἐπακούσεται, καὶ τὸν παρόντα ζόφον ἀποσκεδάσει
τὸν τῆς Αἰγυπτιακῆς πληγῆς ζοφωδέστερον, καὶ τὴν αὐτοῦ φίλην χα-
ριεῖται γαλήνην, καὶ συνάξει τοὺς διεσκορπισμένους καὶ τοῖς ἀπωσ-
μένους εἰσδέξεται. καὶ ἀκουσθήσεται πάλιν φωνὴ ἀγαλλιάσεως καὶ
σωτηρίας ἐν σκηναῖς δικαίων. τότε καὶ ἡμεῖς βοήσομεν πρὸς αὐτόν·
(Ps. 89, 15), Εὐφρανθείημεν ἀνθ᾽ ὧν ἡμερῶν ἐταπείνωσας (jaumātā
dmokkākan) ἡμᾶς, καὶ ἐτῶν ὧν εἴδομεν κακά· καὶ ὑμεῖς δὲ τῆς αἰτή-
σεως ὑμῶν τυχόντες (teŭwōn), ἀνυμνοῦντες αὐτὸν ἐρεῖτε· [Ps. 69, 20
(19)] Εὐλογητὸς ὁ Θεὸς ὃς οὐκ ἀπέστησε τὴν προσευχὴν ἡμῶν, καὶ τὸ
ἔλεος αὐτοῦ ἀφ᾽ ἡμῶν. [Αὐτῷ ἡ δόξα εἰς τοὺς αἰῶνας. Ἀμήν.]

9

THE SENTENCE OF DOMNUS
Made known to the Notaries on their arrival at his domicile.

We left Domnus at p. 25.   The Envoys, commissioned by the Council to urge his attendance on its sittings, reported that they had found him perfectly unable, through bodily debility, to join in the Council's deliberations in person.

The President, at this stage of the proceedings, despatches Notaries who apprize him of all the transactions of the day, of which Domnus is made to say that he thoroughly approves.   But these Notaries are apparently not commissioned to announce to Domnus that he himself is soon, or perhaps the next, to be tried at the bar of Justice.   For, they are positively and perfectly silent as to the approaching fact of the Chief Bishop of Christian Asia being for one moment the subject of this Œcumenical Synod's formal adjudications.   The Acts, we say, give no instruction of his being at all, or in any way, apprized of this circumstance, and this is in the case of a Patriarch of the Church.   Can anything be more contrary to all principles of justice and fair dealing?   "It is of itself enough to justify "the Anathema which fourteen centuries have cast upon the "celebrated Cabal of Ephesus."

VIII.

[HIS SENTENCE DESPATCHED BY DOMNUS.]

Now when the Notaries, who had been despatched to Bishop Domnus, had read to him (an account of) what had been transacted,

DOMNUS, Bishop of Antioch, (replied) :—

I was wishful, had I enjoyed my usual health, to have assembled with your Piety and, together with your Holiness, to have heard all that was said relative to Ibas, and Daniel, and Irenæus, and Aquilinus, and Theodoret, but, in consequence of great bodily debility, I was prevented from doing this.

It has, however, been thought right and just by your Piety that he, who in body has been disabled¶ from going, should (learn) be informed of those matters that are already on a fair way for justice, by your judgment, O holy (Fathers)! at the hands of those who have been despatched from your Holy Synod— the Venerable Notaries, Demetrian, Flavian, and Primus.

After having heard at one (and the same) time* the whole of your holy commands and just decision concerning all of them (the accused) one by one, I

¶ Better, perhaps—" He who, on account of bodily sickness, could not come, should learn all that has been (already) accomplished in a right manner—or put in the right path—by your just judgment, O holy Fathers."

* In p. 171, l. 13, the Jud in the word ܗܘܡܪܘܣ is a mistake of the Scribe, no doubt. In the next line the word ܐܚܡܕ is *simul, at one time.*

(can only) bestow great praise (on you), being brought to the same opinion as yourselves in all these matters: and I pronounce the (same) decision with you, and I adhere to (join you in) the same commands as you, in regard of all those men who have been justly deposed (expelled) by you, whilst I differ from you in nothing and would make no alterations in what has been ·effected, but to all those transactions that have been apostolically* conducted and accomplished by your Blessedness, I, with all readiness (possible) on my part, do give my confirmation and assent.

[END OF THE "SENTENCE OF DOMNUS."]

----

* In l. 24, ܐܠܗܐܝܬ means, of course, in an Apostolic manner, or, rather, in accordance with "the Apostolic Canons." "The Canons, " commonly called Apostolical or Ecclesiastical," number at most 85, which were drawn up by the Church's Synods held at the end of the Second and beginning of the Third Centuries, and added to afterwards, and collected, not all at once, but as they were made, some after others, and they were the Rule of Discipline, or the Code of CANONS, OF THE PRIMITIVE CHURCH, or, however, for the Eastern Part of It. (See Johnson's Vade-Mecum, Vol. II.)   They are referred to expressly by the Great Councils of Nicæa and of Constantinople : and the fifth and sixth Holy General Councils, says Sparrow, held 700 years, more or less, after Christ's passion, ordained that, for the government of the Churches and a preventive against disorder, eighty-five Canons of the Apostles, which had been delivered to the Church by Clemens, the disciple, companion, and perpetual follower of the Apostles themselves and the successor of Peter, should by the faithful be diligently observed." He cites the Admonition of the Apostle at 2 Thess., ii, " Stand fast, and hold by our traditions, whether (given) by word or letter."   See A Collection of Articles, Injunctions, Canons, &c., by Bishop Sparrow. Imprinted at London, 1675.

RELEASE OF

;ERTAIN CLERKS.

[REMOVAL OF ECCLESIASTICAL CENSURE.]

The spiritual power, or Discipline, of the Church, entrusted to Her by Her Divine Head, seems here to have received practical illustration of what it was in the 5th century, to "bind" and to "loose," and in the exercise of the Lesser Excommunication called ἀφορισμὸς, *separation* or *suspension*; the greater being "the total separation, and anathema, *the curse*," which was the greatest curse that could be laid upon men—παντελὴς ἀφορισμὸς. The former mode of punishment consisted, says Bingham, "in excluding men from the participation of the Eucharist and prayers of the faithful, but did not expel them the Church; for, still they stay to hear the psalmody, and reading of the Scriptures, and the Sermons, and the prayers, of the catechumens and the penitents, and then depart with them, when that first service, called the service of the catechumens, was ended." (Bk. XVI, Chap. xi, Sect. 7. See also Note at the end of the cause of Ibas, p. 145.)

Now four members of the Christian Church, of whom three were Deacons and the other a Reader, had been prohibited participation in the greatest privilege to membership, for some misdemeanour not named, by the exercise of the power of "binding" by no less a person than the Archbishop of that See that was soon to rise to be the second in Christendom—viz., that of the Royal City of Constantinople; and, using this Œcumenical Tribunal as the Appellate Court in the last resort they prayed for the removal of the interdict or censure, under which they had been put by that Archbishop.

The Presiding Judge of the Council, doubtless, glad of a small opportunity of doing somewhat towards crushing the rising power of New Rome as well as of defeating the influence of Old Rome at this Synod, over which he had shown his own power to be supreme, had no sort of hesitation in "loosing" those whom his Rival at Constantinople had "bound."

IX.

[RELEASE OF CERTAIN CLERKS.]

Then Theosebius, and Epiphanius, and Theophilus, Deacons, and Eudromanus, Reader, approached the Holy and Œcumenical Synod, and said :—

Flavian, formerly Bishop of Constantinople, put us under an Interdict from appearing here (at this Tribunal). We pray your Piety to release us from the (bond of) censure.

The HOLY SYNOD said :—
It is right and just that they should be received.

DIOSCORUS, Bishop of Alexandria, said :—
Well-known matters has Theosebius mentioned, with Epiphanius and Theophilus, Deacons, and Eudromanus, Reader; but they have not alluded to the cause of Inhibition. This God-fearing, Holy, and Œcumenical Synod, however, having a regard for The True Religion, has released them from their Interdict. Let, therefore, the persons named above be admitted to Communion, as formerly.

The HOLY SYNOD said :—

" We all say the same. We, all of us, give our " assent to this with one common voice (unani- " mously)."

———

[END OF THE "RELEASE OF CERTAIN CLERKS."]

It is probable that during this part of the Synod's proceedings, or somewhere after the trial of Theodoret, another important one took place, that of the Deposition of Athanasius from the Bishopric of Perrha in Syria, and the Consecration of Sabinian to it, the discussion of which formed the 14th Session, and between which two Bishops Dijudication was effected by the Magistrates, of the Council of Chalcedon, in 451, A.D.

So, also, might have come on at this stage of the business the examination of Candidian's case, who was Bishop of Antioch, in Pisidia, referred to by Theodoret in one of his letters, and against whom several complaints were vainly submitted to this Council.

And the same may be said of Athenius whose name, it would seem, appears nowhere but in one of Theodoret's Letters.

But this, we repeat, is only a probability. The certainty of the matter could be ascertained from a discovery of the three lost leaves of the original MS., if those leaves contained information respecting the order of the Sessions and arrangement of the proceedings, and the absence of which marks the first of the Lacunæ remarked upon above, at foot of p. 27.

It will not be inappropriate or inopportune to offer in this place a few observations and references relative to the Bishops, Candidian, Athanasius and Athenius.

A graphic description of the proceedings at Ephesus, and some particulars not mentioned elsewhere, we read in one of the Letters of Theodoret, addressed to John of Germanicia.[a]

De præsenti rerum statu nihil sperare licet, Theodoret begins, defectionisque absolutæ initia hæc esse arbitror; and he goes on to complain, that even those who declare their abhorrence of the violent proceedings at Ephesus ($\mu\epsilon\tau\grave{a}$ $\beta\acute{\iota}\alpha\varsigma$), now acquiesce in what was done there; while the promoters of it show more and more their insolence, actually affirming that no innovation was made in the dogma ($\mu\eta\delta\epsilon\mu\acute{\iota}\alpha\nu$ $\gamma\epsilon\gamma\epsilon\nu\hat{\eta}\sigma\theta\alpha\iota$ $\pi\epsilon\rho\grave{\iota}$ $\tau\grave{o}$ $\delta\acute{o}\gamma\mu\alpha$ $\kappa\alpha\iota\nu\sigma\tau\sigma\mu\acute{\iota}\alpha\nu$), as if he, Theodoret, had been expelled because of an immoral life (ob cædes et maleficia)! while even $\beta\acute{a}\rho\beta\alpha\rho\sigma\iota$ clearly see, that they expelled him as well as others on account of the Dogma. $K\alpha\grave{\iota}$ $\gamma\grave{a}\rho$ $\tau\grave{o}\nu$ $\kappa\acute{\nu}\rho\iota\sigma\nu$ $\Delta\acute{o}\mu\nu\sigma\nu$, he continues, $\dot{\omega}\varsigma$ $\tau\grave{a}$ $\kappa\epsilon\phi\acute{a}\lambda\alpha\iota\alpha$ $\mu\grave{\eta}$ $\delta\epsilon\xi\acute{a}\mu\epsilon\nu\sigma\nu$ $\kappa\alpha\theta\epsilon\hat{\iota}\lambda\sigma\nu$ $\sigma\grave{\iota}$ $\beta\acute{\epsilon}\lambda$-$\tau\iota\sigma\tau\sigma\iota$, $\pi\alpha\nu\epsilon\acute{\nu}\phi\eta\mu\alpha$ $\tau\alpha\hat{\nu}\tau\alpha$ $\kappa\alpha\lambda\acute{\epsilon}\sigma\alpha\nu\tau\epsilon\varsigma$ $\kappa\alpha\grave{\iota}$ $\dot{\epsilon}\mu\mu\acute{\epsilon}\nu\epsilon\iota\nu$ $\tau\sigma\acute{\nu}\tau\sigma\iota\varsigma$ $\dot{\sigma}\mu\sigma\lambda\sigma\gamma\acute{\eta}\sigma\alpha\nu$-$\tau\epsilon\varsigma$ ($\dot{\epsilon}\gamma\grave{\omega}$ $\gamma\grave{a}\rho$ $\alpha\dot{\nu}\tau\hat{\omega}\nu$ $\tau\grave{a}\varsigma$ $\kappa\alpha\theta\acute{\epsilon}\sigma\epsilon\iota\varsigma$ $\dot{a}\nu\acute{\epsilon}\gamma\nu\omega\nu$)· $\dot{\epsilon}\mu\grave{\epsilon}$ $\delta\grave{\epsilon}$ $\dot{\omega}\varsigma$ $\tau\hat{\eta}\varsigma$ $\alpha\acute{\iota}\rho\acute{\epsilon}\sigma\epsilon\omega\varsigma$ $\dot{\epsilon}\xi\acute{a}\rho\chi\sigma\nu$ $\dot{a}\pi\epsilon\kappa\acute{\eta}\rho\nu\xi\alpha\nu$ $\kappa\alpha\grave{\iota}$ $\tau\sigma\hat{\iota}\varsigma$ $\dot{a}\lambda\lambda\sigma\iota\varsigma$ $\dot{\omega}\sigma\alpha\acute{\nu}\tau\omega\varsigma$ $\delta\iota\grave{a}$ $\tau\grave{\eta}\nu$ $\alpha\dot{\nu}\tau\grave{\eta}\nu$ $\alpha\acute{\iota}\tau\acute{\iota}\alpha\nu$ $\dot{\epsilon}\xi\acute{\epsilon}$-$\beta\alpha\lambda\sigma\nu$. For that it was not a question of the moral life and conversation ($\dot{\eta}$ $\pi\rho\alpha\kappa\tau\iota\kappa\grave{\eta}$ $\dot{a}\rho\epsilon\tau\hat{\eta}$): $\alpha\dot{\nu}\tau\grave{a}$ $\beta\sigma\hat{a}$ $\tau\grave{a}$ $\pi\rho\acute{a}\gamma\mu\alpha\tau\alpha$. $K\alpha\tau\grave{a}$ $\gamma\grave{a}\rho$ $K\alpha\nu\delta\iota\delta\iota\acute{a}\nu\sigma\nu$, $\tau\sigma\hat{\nu}$ $\Pi\iota\sigma\iota\delta\acute{\iota}\sigma\nu$,[b] $\lambda\iota\beta\acute{\epsilon}\lambda\lambda\sigma\nu\varsigma$ $\dot{\epsilon}\pi\acute{\epsilon}\delta\nu\sigma\acute{a}\nu$ $\tau\iota\nu\epsilon\varsigma$, $\mu\sigma\iota\chi\epsilon\acute{\iota}\alpha\varsigma$ $\alpha\dot{\nu}\tau\sigma\hat{\nu}$

---

[a] This Letter, bearing the number 125 in the MSS., left out by *Sirmond* in the collection of Theodoret's Letters, but given in the Appendix to vol. iv., was numbered 147 by *Garnerius*, and stands under the same number in *Migne*, Series Græca, vol. lxxxiii., col. 1409 ff.

[b] Candidianus is mentioned as member of the Synod, vol. i., 10, 22 (ii. 16, no. 24), and 99, 17 ff. (ii. 144. no. 19), speaking judgment against Ibas.

κατηγοροῦντες πολλὰς καὶ ἑτέρας παρανομίας, καί φασιν εἰρηκέναι· εἰ δογμάτων κατηγορεῖτε, δεχόμεθα τοὺς λιβέλλους· οὐ γὰρ ἤλθομεν μοιχείας δικάσαι. Διά τοι τοῦτο καὶ Ἀθήνιον καὶ Ἀθανάσιον[c] ὑπὸ τῆς ἀποστολικῆς ἐκβληθέντας συνόδου τὰς οἰκείας ἀπολαβεῖν ἐκκλησίας ἐκέλευσαν : as if our Saviour no commandment had given as to life, but only ordered to preserve the δόγματα, ἃ πρὸ τῶν ἄλλων διέφθειραν οἱ σοφώτατοι. Let them therefore not cloke their godlessness, which they have proved by tongues and fists (μὴ . . . κρυπτέτωσαν τὴν ἀσέβειαν, ἣν καὶ ταῖς γλώτταις καὶ ταῖς χερσὶν ἐβεβαίωσαν).

Theodoret goes on to disavow the chapters, which they had so often rejected, and which they have accepted at Ephesus. But they change their minds according to the time, like the polypus, according to the colour of the rock it lives upon, and the chameleon to the surrounding leaves ; and having formerly applauded my preaching as apostolic, now they condemn it (τὴν διδασκαλίαν

---

* The moral weight of the argumentative power manifested by the great Eutychian intriguers in this deliberative assembly must have been, in the first session, whatever it may have been afterwards, infinitesimally small, whilst the physical power appertaining to their position in the Empire they brought to bear upon its members in a terrific manner. The above words of Theodoret if used here as indicating instruments of conveying terror inadequately describe the scene. "When Dioscorus began to pronounce sentence against Flavian, Onesiphorus, Bishop of Iconium, rose with several others and seized his knees entreating him not to proceed, Dioscorus rose from his throne, and, standing on his footstool, declared, that although his tongue were to be cut out he could not say otherwise ; and as the Bishops continued to entreat him, holding him by his knees, he cried out ' where are the Counts!' which brought in the Proconsul, with a great number of soldiers, armed with swords and clubs, and bringing chains with them. By this means the greater part of he Bishops were compelled to affix their signatures to a' carte-blanche ; being shut up in the church till evening, and prevented from taking either rest or refreshment, &c." (From the Oxford Fleury, p. 310). On the carte-blanche referred to, it is thought was afterwards indited the long address to the Emperor, discovered in the magnificient MS, (No. Add. 12156,) in British Museum, of Timothy Ælurus, reproduced in my Vol. 1, and translated in Vol. 2, in Appendix D.

We may add here, that according to Breviculus Hist. Eutych. (Labbe, t. 4 p. 1080, B) as given in the same page of the Oxford Fleury, it was *three days after the session* in which Flavian was deposed, that the President of the Synod managed to effect the deposition of Archbishop Domnus. "Dioscorus produced some letters before the Council,—(these very interesting letters are also given in our MS, as will appear further on)—which Domnu[a] had written to him, charging St. Cyril's 12 Articles with being obscure, and the Council were thus prevailed upon to depose him as suspected of Nestorianism, though he was absent and laid up with sickness" The session in which Flavian was deposed was *the first*, and the motive assigned to Dioscorus for deposing him, and using an artifice in the accomplishing of his object, is that Domnus had retracted his forced subscription to the condemnation of the Archbishop Flavian.

[c] Athenios is not mentioned in the List of the Members, but two of the name of Athanasios, one Bishop of Opus in Achaia (i. 2, 14 ; ii. 17, 49), the other of Busiris (i. 12, 16 ; ii. 19, 99) ; whether one or which of those can be identified with the Athanasios mentioned by Theodoret, I cannot say—perhaps the latter.

ἡμῶν ἀποστολικὴν ὀνομάζοντες· ταύτην ἀνεθεμάτισαν), and the man whom they accused of Valentinianism and Apollinarism, ὡς νικήφορον περιεῖπον τῆς πίστεως καὶ τῶν τούτου προεκυλινδοῦντο πόδων καὶ συγγνώμην ἐζήτουν καὶ πατέρα πνευματικὸν ἐκάλουν.[a] Theodoret comforts himself with the righteous judgment of the Lord; hopes to be forgiven, because of this endurance of injustice (διὰ τὴν ἀδικίαν); expects that the coming election of the Patriarch of the East will make the views of everyone apparent; and asks for the prayer of John, that he might be able to stand against the plots of his enemies.

In the famous Letter Theodoret sent to the Bishop of Rome Leo (numbered 113),[b] he gives the following account of the proceedings at the Synod (*Migne*, 83 col. 1316 *b*).

Ὁ γὰρ τῆς Ἀλεξανδρείας δικαιότατος πρόεδρος οὐκ ἠρκέσθη τῇ ἀνόμῳ ταύτῃ καὶ ἀδικωτάτῃ καθαιρέσει τοῦ ἁγιωτάτου καὶ θεοφιλεστάτου τις Κωνσταντινουπολιτῶν ἐπισκόπου τοῦ κυρίου Φλαβιανοῦ οὐδὲ ἐνέπλησεν αὐτοῦ τὸν θυμὸν τῶν ἄλλων ἐπισκόπων ἡ παραπλησία σφαγή, ἀλλὰ κἀμὲ τὸν ἀπόντα ὁμοίως καλάμῳ κατέσφαξεν, οὔτε καλέσας εἰς κριτήριον οὔτε παρόντα κρίνας, οὐκ ἐρωτήσας, τίνα φρονῶ περὶ τῆς τοῦ θεοῦ καὶ Σωτῆρος ἡμῶν ἐνανθρωπήσεως. καὶ τοὺς μὲν ἀνδροφόνους καὶ τυμβωρύ χους καὶ τοὺς τὰς ἀλλοτρίας συλήσαντας εὐνὰς[c] οὐ πρότερον κατακρίνου σιν οἱ δικάζοντες, ἕως ἂν ἢ αὐτοὶ τὰς κατηγορίας ταῖς ὁμολογίαις κυρώ σωσιν, ἢ παρ' ἑτέρων ἐναργῶς ἐλεγχθῶσιν. ἡμᾶς δὲ ὁ τοῖς θείοις νόμοις ἐντεθραμμένος, πέντε καὶ τριάκοντα σταθμοὺς ἀφεστηκότας κατέκρινεν ὡς ἠθέλησε.

In this letter also Theodoret acknowledges the superiority of the See of Rome and sounds the praises of S. Leo, and as to the celebrated Letter Leo wrote to S. Flavian, Archbishop of Constantinople, which, rejected at Ephesus and accepted at Chalcedon, has now become the common heritage of the Church, Theodoret says he admires it as the very language of the Holy Ghost. He speaks of his labours for the Church during the 26 years of his Bishopric, and in the 800 Parishes of his diocese, and enumerates the several works he wrote in 20 years, from which to ascertain whether he had kept The Faith or not.

He asks the advice of Leo as to whether he ought to acquiesce in his unjust deposition or not, awaiting his decision.

---

[a] We find these acclamations almost verbally in the Syriac text of the Acts: cp. vol. ii., p. 126 f. note, a proof that Theodoret did read, as he says, the depositions of the Synod.

[b] Lxiii. in *Martin*, Le Pseudo Synode, p. 65, note 4, is a misprint.

[c] This is apparently an allusion to *Candidianus*, *Athenius* and *Athanasius*, mentioned in Epistle 147, where Theodoret places himself in contraposition to these men: Quænam ob cædes et maleficia *ego* expulsus sum? quænam hic adultera commisit? quæ sepulcra ille perfodit, etc.?

DOMNUS.

DOMNUS.

Last, but by no means least, on the list of the arraigned
stands the cause of Domnus II; and very singular does it appear. Indeed, the whole position of this Bishop among his
Fellows and members of this Council is perfectly unique.
For, whereas he was Patriarch* of the probably first formed See
of Christendom, next after that of Jerusalem—seeing that he
exercised Patriarchal Jurisdiction and occupied, in regular succession from S. Peter, the Overseership of Antioch the Great
Capital, it is no anachronism, nor incorrect, to speak of him and
his as such—and Patriarch, too, of the then certainly Apostolic
Throne that held the third rank, and therefore, in moral right

---

* Bingham, who informs us (Book II, chap. xvii) that Patriarchal Power had come to its height about the time of the
Councils of Ephesus and Chalcedon, when writing on the
subject of Patriarchs and referring to Domnus, says:—"Next
in order to the Metropolitans, or primates, were the patriarchs; or, as they were at first called, archbishops and
exarchs of the Diocese. For though now an Archbishop or a
Metropolitan be generally taken for the same, to wit, the primate of a single province; yet anciently the name Archbishop
was a more extensive title, and scarcely given to any but those
whose jurisdiction extended over a whole imperial diocese, as
the Bishops of Rome, Alexandria, Antioch, &c. That this was
so appears evidently from one of Justinian's Novels, where,
erecting the bishopric of Justiniana Prima into a Patriarchal
See, he says, ' Our pleasure is that Justiniana shall not only be
a Metropolitan, but an Archbishop?'* Here the names are
clearly distinguished, and an archbishop superior to a metropolitan. And hence it was that, after the setting up of patriarchal power, the name Archbishop was appropriated to the
Patriarchs. Liberatus† gives all the Patriarchs the title of
Archbishops. So does the Council of Chalcedon frequently,
speaking of all the Patriarchs of Rome and Constantinople‡
under the name of Archbishops also. These were otherwise
called ἔπαρχοι τῆς διοικήσεως, exarchs of the Diocese, to distinguish them from ἔπαρχοι τῆς ἐπαρχίας, the exarchs of a
single province, which were only metropolitans. Thus Domnus, Bishop of Antioch, is styled exarch of the eastern dio-
cese,|| by the Councils of Antioch and Chalcedon.

---

* Justin. Novell., II. Volumus, ut non solum metropolitanus,
sed etiam archiepiscopus fiat.
    † Liberat. Breviar., c. xvii.   ‡ Con. Chalced., Act. 16. It.
Act. 4, et can. 30.
    || Con. Antioch. in Act. 14. Con. Chalced.

and importance, able and entitled to claim the President's
chair, he was consigned to the least dignified, nay, to the
lowest position of all, and, through the powerful influence of
the "Facinorosus Eutyches" with the Emperor and the Court,
"Synodalis Presidentiæ apud Ephesum *Invasor*" was appointed.
Equally unique, too, was afterwards his situation at Chalcedon
in 451 A.D.; for, according to Christianus Lupus (1681), p. 827,
"Non solus Dioscorus Alexandrinus, sed etiam Juvenalis Hie-
"rosolymitanus, Thalassius Cæsaræensis in Cappadocia,
"Basilius Seleuciensis, et cæteri, Primates, immò omnes La-
"trocinali Judicio co-operati Episcopi, in retractatoria apud
"Chalcedonem Synodo fuerunt demutati in reos, compulsi ad
"suorum operum rationes, et solemnem pœnitentiam." But
Domnus took no such step and appears in no such character
at Chalcedon. Again, all the other Victims to the violence of
Eutychian partizanship, who were condemned and excommunicated at this Robber Council, repaired without delay to the
Judges of the succeeding and superseding one for justice to
be done to them, but Domnus alone not only put in no appearance but employed no representative at Chalcedon; and these
same Judges awarded to these same Bishops the restored Dignity, Rank, and Authority attaching to their Office, whilst
a doubt, or a half conviction, evidently hung over the judicial
mind as to the innocence or criminality of the Bishop Domnus.
Nor is his noble act of moral courage in retracting his condemnation of Flavian to be omitted from the category of facts that
render him solitaire among the many, on which subject of re-
traction Lupus writes thus, at p. 841:—"Infelix Domnus, ut
"suam pellem a Dioscori furore redimeret, condemnavit non
"solum modo innocentissimum, sed insuper sibi amicissimum
"Antistitem. Manifestè contra conscientiam Divina atque
"humana prevaricatus. Isto intento, Dioscorus larvam depo-
"suit, resumpsit odia, et ipsum etiam Domnum, quod duode-
"cem Cyrilli Capitula nuperrimè damnasset, degradavit. Et
"ejus in sedem intrusit, aut intrudi curavit Maximum, Diaco-
"num et Archi-Mandritam, fidelem amicum S. Cyrilli. . . .
"Domni damnationem nequaquam propter damnata S. Cyrilli
"Capitula, sed propter adjutam S. Flaviani damnationem
"stabilivit atque ita hominem quasi de novo damnavit. Solus
"hanc causam retractavit ac definivit. Et omnis Orientalis

Ecclesia comprobavit.   Eodem igitur suæ sedis Privilegio solus
. . . retractavit ac definivit caussam S. Flaviani.

THE FORMAL PROCESS OR INDICTMENT AGAINST DOMNUS CONSISTS OF

1. A Libel presented by Cyriacus, the Presbyter   (172–177)
2. Various heads or counts of indictment by the same (177–180)
3. A Letter of Domnus to Archbishop Flavian   (180–184)
4. A Libel of Marcellus Presbyter of Antioch and of
    others written out by him   (185–190)
5. The Petition of Heliodorus, Deacon, and Abraham
    and Gerontius, Monks   (190–195)
6. The Profession of Faith extorted from Pelagius,
    the Presbyter   (195–198)
7. Information furnished by Theodosius, the Monk,
    to the Patriarch of Alexandria   (198–200)
8. Some letters in a correspondence between the
    Patriarchs of Antioch and Alexandria (Inclusive) (201–229)
    After which follow
9. The opinions formulated by separate Bishops of
the Synod, (inclusive)   (233–237)
    (The figures indicate the pages in my Syriac Text.)

Now, as to these accusations against Domnus, besides involving complaints about amicable relations with Bishops Theo-
dcret, Irenæus, and Ibas, the Libels pretend that the Patriarch had manifested opposition to the Decrees of Theodosius
II against Bishop Irenæus, and had even courted the friendship of the Archbishop Flavian, besides recommending Theodoret to him, so that Theodoret and Domnus were as
representatives of that Archbishop in the East.   He was,
likewise, charged by them with having attempted to alter the
Form of the Sacrament of Baptism, with having extorted frcm
the Priest Pelagius a Nestorian confession of Faith, and with
having removed from the Church of Emesa Peter, who had been
canonically elected, in order to give it to another Priest of
doubtful morality but of undoubted leaning and bias towards Nestorianism.   They, moreover, affirmed that he had been appointed
Patriarch of Antioch through the good offices of a Pagan
Quæstor Isocacius, that the said Patriarch had consecrated
persons to Bishoprics without observing the prescribed cere-
monial, and that he had removed Bishop Alexander from the
See of Antarados in order to put Paul in his place, besides
other objectionable acts more or less plainly advanced.

As regards the very interesting and important correspondence between the Archbishops of Antioch and Alexandria, the Great Capitals, the letter of admonition, issuing from the latter to the former, complains of the tendencies shown by Domnus towards the enemies of the Orthodox Faith—i.e., of the favour manifested towards Nestorianism,—naming in particular Bishops Irenæus and Theodoret. The date of this Epistle will be found to be, as we shall see in the note in its place, between the issuing the Imperial Decree, whereby Irenæus was removed from the Metropolitan City of Tyre, and the appointment to that City of Photius, on 9th of September, in the year 448.

Domnus replies by a circular Letter in which, unfortunately, occur two Lacunæ. He complains that his calumniators should have been attended to, and professes his faith in the General Councils, and adheres to the terms of peace negotiated by Bishop Paul of Emesa with S. Cyril of Alexandria. Domnus urges him to put an end to false reports and rightly to inform the Faithful of Alexandria about those of the East. He sends a verbal message, through the envoys despatched to him by Dioscorus, in relation to the Bishopric of Tyre. This Epistle was probably written at the end of April or the beginning of May, 448 A.D., about which time Theodoret was preaching some of his eloquent Sermons at Antioch. It would naturally be shewn to Theodoret, as he was a principal party concerned in it, who, doubtless, forthwith then wrote on behalf of himself and his Colleagues to the Archbishop of Alexandria.

It was about this time, too, that the Archbishop of the East pronounced Sentence at the Synod at Antioch in favour of Ibas, Bishop, and against the Clerks, of Edessa, which Sentence gave such mortal offence to the great Eutychian party as to determine them to aim a second blow in order to break down the power of the Orientals by issuing an Imperial Edict against Theodoret, as the first, directed against the Bishop of Tyre, had not had the desired effect. See the speech of Samuel, p. 95.

All the time that Dioscorus was exchanging letters with Domnus, he seemed desirous of crushing all obstacles to the attainment of the victory of the League to which he lent himself so willingly and successfully. He sends a final communication to to the Archbishop of Antioch—we gather it from the latter's reply—in which he makes sundry complaints of well-intentioned parties, (the chief person is intimated in no enigmatical terms) by their preaching and teaching, having become disturbers of the Peace, as well as impugners of the Faith, of the Church, &c.

In all probability, likewise, he added something relative to S. Cyril and his Twelve Anathemas against Nestorius. At the conclusion he expresses a wish for his letter to be read, in their assemblies, to the Faithful.

Domnus rejoins, and steadfastly resolves to abide by the peace effected by Paul of Emesa, and refuses to rake up old grievances. He complains grievously of the conduct of certain monks connected with Alexandria. He had not openly read Dioscorus's letter, as he wished, for fear of the consequences. He makes profession of his Orthodoxy [here occurs a hiatus in the MS.].

These were the last two Letters that passed between the two Archbishops, and how distressing and painful the correspondence had become to Domnus appears from a very important Letter, hitherto attributed to Theodoret, which he (Domnus) wrote to S. Flavian, Archbishop of Constantinople.

After viewing this last cause of the arraigned, Dr. Martin writes as follows:—"Thus was deposed Domnus, Patriarch of Antioch, against all the laws of the Church and against all the forms of human justice. Knowing beforehand that he was condemned, he did not dream of protesting against the iniquity of which he was the victim. Strong in his innocence, he appealed to the Tribunal of God, and, disgusted with all terrestrial grandeur, he rejoined the Convent* whose sweet

---

* The following from Asseman, in his "Acta S. Simeonis Stylitæ," Adnotationes, p. 401, seems a strong confirmation of this opinion :—(18) *Domnus*, hujus nominis secundus in Serie Patriarcharum Antiochenorum apud laudatum le Quien, quadragesimus primus recensetur. Johanni avunculo successit, exeunte anno Christi 441, quum Theodoreti testimonio constet septimum ejus annum in Christi 448 incidisse. Antiocheno autem Pontificatu privatus est à Dioscoro, subrogato Maximo, circum annum 449. De Eo Evagrius initio Capitis Decimi tertii hæc scribit : *Hic* (Simon) *primus stationem super columna instituit, cujus domicilii ambitus vix duorum erat cubitorum: quo tempore Domnus Antiochenæ urbis Episcopatum administrabat. Qui quum ad Simeonem venisset, stationem ejus ac vivendi rationem admiratus, secretiora quædam concupivit. Ambo igitur in unum convenerunt, et quum immaculatum corpus sacrificassent, vivificam Communionem sibi mutuo impertierunt.*

solitude the agitations of public life had often made him regret. After having been witness of all the horrors which fanaticism could commit by men clothed with a sacred character, he declined to occupy the world with his name and his complaints, and, burying himself before the time in the silence of the tomb, he wished to be dead to all below. If once again History speaks to us of him, some years later, it is because his succesor to the See of Antioch troubled the repose due to his memory, out of compassion for his misfortunes."

X.
DOMNUS.
DOCUMENTS BROUGHT UP AGAINST DOMNUS, THE BISHOP OF ANTIOCH.*

(*a*) JOHN, Presbyter and Proto-Notary said :—

The Venerable Presbyter Cyriacus has remitted Libels to your Holy and Œcumenical Synod, which I will read, if your Piety command it to be done.

JUVENAL, the Bishop of Jerusalem, said :—

Let the Libels be received and read.

(*b*) JOHN, Presbyter and Proto-Notary, read :—

To the Holy, and God-loving, Œcumenical, Synod, assembled by the Grace of God at Ephesus, the Metropolis, from Cyriacus the Presbyter.

We have learnt from your Holiness to receive those who glorify God, and to repudiate those who blaspheme Him.

This, therefore, we now pray of your Piety—that you would repress Blasphemy and uphold the Doctrine of those who love at all times to glorify Christ.

Now the circumstances relating to the case in hand (we will) with all brevity (subjoin).

Domnus, the Bishop of Antioch, by strenuously advocating† the Tenet of him, has, from the begin-

---

* Or, " Procedure directed against Domnus, the Bishop of Antioch." The word used in the text is the usual Greek term Syrianized—viz., ‏ܗܘܦܪܟܣܝܢ‎.

† It is no easy matter to give a satisfactory translation of line 16 on p. 173. *Martin* suggests that there may be an allusion to the sentence of Domnus despatched to the Synod by the Notaries (comp. p. 264) and renders it—Domnus combat son propre sentiment.

ning, manifested the fruit of his partiality for Theodoret, the Bishop of the city of Cyrus, in that he has
continually lived with him, and he encouraged him so
far as to assist his Impiety, openly, instead of re-
vering God ; and, what is worse than all, whilst seated
on the (Episcopal) Throne*, he is continually
clapping† his hands in Church at the Blasphemies
(uttered by Theodoret) against the Lord of all,
CHRIST. And, by fulsome praises, he has
rendered him presuming and arrogant in his
Impiety—whilst, by assigning him a house in the

---

* At p. 173, l. 23, ﻼﻤﻜﻋ, which Castell renders Sedile (Sug-
gestus, locus excelsior, *ubi sacerdos ad aram stabat*), doubtless implies,
and refers to, the Bishop's throne ; and ﻼﻤﻗ is *colaphus, maxilla,* and
ﻼﻤﻗ *perculsit, tetendit, plausit* manibus, Ps., xlvii, 2, and xcviii, 8.
In his absence, or *when at a distance,* is the meaning of ﻼﻤﻗﻮﻤﺑ.
Possibly |ﻼﻤﻗ| may refer to Literæ formatæ, of the different kinds of
which Bingham gives a description in Bk. II, chap. iv.

† Theodoret, in his letter to Dioscorus, who had, truly or not,
complained of Theodoret for dividing Christ into two Sons, says in his
reply, justifying himself for what he did—"I taught thirteen years
under the Blessed John (of Antioch) who was so delighted with my
discourses that he often rose up and clapped his hands." Public applause of the Preacher in church and elsewhere was called κρότος by
the Greeks, as we have seen at p. 44, note †. Sometimes it
was done by the assembly, similarly to the Synodical acclamations, e.g.,
when Paul of Emesa, in delivering a Homily in the presence of Cyril
of Alexandria, "used this expression, agreeing with Cyril's Doctrine
" that had been preached before—' Mary the Mother of God brought
" ' forth Emmanuel'—the people immediatley cried out, 'O Orthodox
" ' Cyril, the gift of God, Thy Faith is the same ; this is what we de-
" ' sired to hear,. if any man speak otherwise, let him be anathema.' "
Sometimes they added other indications of their applause, as clapping of
their hands, &c. Thus S. Jerome tells Vigilantius—"The time was,
when he himself had applauded him with his hands and feet, leaping by
his side, and crying Orthodox, for his Sermon upon the Resurrection."
Many other instances of this κρότος are given by Bingham, Bk. XIV,
chap. iv, sec. 27. It seems to us a strange custom, but we must remem-

Church*, he causes his residence there instead of in his own City (Metropolis)—by calling him at all times " Father" (when present), and when absent by bestowing on him " The Blessing," and by upholding and supporting him in Letters written to other persons.

Further, he (Domnus) was in Communion with the man, in consequence of whose false faith the Gracious Emperor had determined, by Royal Orders, that he should confine himself entirely within his own City†.

Also, at the time when it was resolved (by the Emperor) to depose that Irenæus of Tyre from the Ministerial Function, this aforenamed Domnus did not eject Irenæus from his Communion.   On the conrtary, he showed himself adverse to, by question-

---

ber the force of habit, by which τὰ μὴ καλὰ καλὰ πέφανται. S. Chrysostom "probably, saw the system in its more outrè forms (see the account given by Eusebius, E. H., VII, 30, of Paul of Samosata) and very frequently and strongly spoke against it," &c. Fleury's Ecclesiastical History, Oxford, p. 56, note. In his 83rd Letter Theodoret, refers to it himself, for which see Migne's Cursus Completus.

* Under the general term "the Church" here would be included various buildings, comprehending all the οἶκοι or exedrae of it. Domnus would assign for Theodoret's residence part of the *Pastophoria*, which Bingham believes included the *Diaconicium* and the *gazophylacium*, or treasury, and the habitations of the Bishops and Clergy and *Custodes* Ecclesiae.—The word pastophorium is a name taken from the Septuagint translation of Ezek. L, 17, where it is used for the chambers in the inner Court of the Temple.   Hence Bingham thinks that the Pastophoria of the Christian Church were places put to the same use as in the Jewish Temple, from which the name is borrowed (Bk. VIII, Chap. VII, Sect. 11).

† See 79th and 82nd Epistles of Theodoret.

This enforced interment was an act of very great injustice on the Emperor's part, and filled mens' minds with consternation ; "on ne luy put pas ne anmois, (says Tillemont) persuader qu'il fust heretique,

ing, the divine (royal) Commands that had been issued by the Christ-loving Emperor, inasmuch as he did not ratify the Deposition of Irenæus, which had been decreed by the Emperor's good pleasure.

And, as for Theodoret, it was at the instance of this man that he (Domnus) betook himself to the Impious Flavian for an aider and abetter*.

Now, what subsequently (and consequently) happened, even if we were not to speak of it, the facts clearly proclaim ; (viz.,) the agitation of the Churches —the commotion among the flocks—your troubles, O Holy Priests !—the turning upside down of the whole world together, which, according to the vulgar

---

seulement qu 'il troubloit la province par les assembléses qu'il tenoit à Antioche : et sur cela il écrivit de sa main un billet au General des armées Romaines (dans la Syria) qui portoit, que puisque l'Evesque de Cyr assembloit sans celle des Synodes, et que cela troubloit les Orthodoxes, cet officier auroit soin qu'il demeurast à Cyr, sans aller en d'autres villes, et qu'il le feroit avec sagesse et precaution, [afin que cela ne causast point de bruit dans la province.] Ce General estoit Consul en 448.

Theodose avoua et confirma le 30 mars 449, l'ordre qu'il avoit donnée à Theodoret de ne point sortir de Cyr.

Il se retira donc à Cyr pour obéir à l'Empereur et il accepta cette espéce d'exil avec joie, parce qu'il luy procuroit le repos qu'il aimoit tant. Il esperoit que le traitement injuste que luy faisoient les enemis de la verité, luy obtiendroit le pardon d'une partie de ses fautes. Il regardoit la honte de son exil comme un honneur, et comme la verification de ce que dit St. Paul, que tous ceux qui veulent vivre avec pietè souffriront persecution. Ainsi quelque tort que luy fissent ses ennemis, il ne croyoit pour luy souffrit aucun tort. Cependent la relegation estoit la terreur et l'affliction commune de tout l'orient.

Tous les Saints et tous les solitaires estoient dans les larmes, et dans toutes les assemblées des personnes de pieté, on entendoit plus de soupers que de paroles.

Le temp de sa promotion nous oblige de ne mettre la relegation de Theodoret qu'à la fin de 447, ou en 448, avant Pasque (Vol XV, p. 273-5).

* Most probably an allusion is implied here to the Letter Domnus wrote to Flavian—given further on—in the month of Eloul (Sept.), 448.

custom, they thought took place, when the impious Flavian aforesaid despatched (information) of what he had done against The Faith at Constantinople, to those his two friends (Doctors) in the East, and, by their hands, to other persons, our enemies, there*.

But all that the same Theodoret has ever done in opposition to The Faith, since the Great Synod (held there) previously to this present one, which confirmed that of Nicæa—who is competent to relate?

For, he never† desisted assembling the followers of his own opinion, and confirming them in Impiety by his writings; and, in opposition to the legislative Determinations, of the Holy Fathers, he has advanced against The Faith novel and depraved statements, some parts (extracts) of which statements are in our possession carefully preserved; and by another treatise of Theodoret, which proceeded from him previously to that Synod which on a former occasion assembled in this place, the Determination of all the Holy Fathers he presumed to sit in judgment upon, but who can describe the Profanity of those who are now so audacious in it, that the hearing of it alone suffices to defile the hearts of the Faithful?

At one time, for instance, he, Theodoret, ventured

---

* He alludes to the documents (Acts) of the Synod at Constantinople, in Nov., 448 A.D., being sent to the Eastern Bishops, according to the suggestion of Sabbas, Bishop of Paltus in Palestine, for signature. Domnus himself declared afterwards that he had received and signed them. Comp. Mansi, Concil. Tom. VI, 693, B. 836, A.

† The Emperor and Enemies of Theodoret constantly harped upon this accusation.

to affirm that it was obligatory (on our part) to baptize in a manner other than in conformity with the Holy Tradition (Doctrine) of our Redeemer.

When the Presbyter, however, who was near, and has now come into the Metropolis, in order to give information of these matters to your Holiness—when he showed him (a copy of) the book which contained the Decrees of the CCCXVIII Holy Fathers, and the Definition of the Holy Fathers who (on a former occasion) assembled here, that there was nothing whatever of that kind there which they enjoined, this great and wonderful Theodoret, snatching the book out of the hand of the Presbyter, bade one of his own party throw it into the fire.

And there was a bath in the neighbourhood of the spot where the book was given to be committed to the flames. Now attentively consider, I beseech you, by the Holy and Everlasting Trinity, if what happened is not worthy of grief. For, as soon as the book fell into the fire, the flame suddenly elevated itself from thence, and consumed the cauldron, liquifying the brass belonging to it with the the lead ; and the water was spilt all over the fire, —a (fit) representation of the Impiety of the man we have been mentioning, which, before God and man, will not be obliterated.

This circumstance, too, moved those who were present, at the time, to no little grief at it.

Now we entreat your Piety not to hesitate, by reason of the insignificance of the tale, but to attend to the wickedness of the act committed.

Among our adversaries—I mean the heathen people, or Jews, or Heretics—has any man ever dared to perpetrate such a deed against the Church? Now do you have mercy together with God, upon the East—no small part of the world that is submerged in wickedness—and do you decree and decide in matters pertaining to God and having relation to The Holy Faith impugned.

> I, Cyriacus, Presbyter, present this Libel, having written it with my own hand.

The Presbyter CYRIACUS said :—

I request, likewise, that these Heads (of Accusation) be read.

THALLASSIUS, Bishop of Cæsarea, said :—

Let them be read.

(c) JOHN, Presbyter and Proto-Notary, read :—

> Heads (of Accusation) from the Homiletical Expositions of the Bishop Domnus.

Three days after they had seized the Venerable Presbyter Pelagius, and struck him, and dragged him along in order to exact of him, in writing, an impious Profession of Faith, during the time when Service was (proceeding) in the Church of Paul, and whilst Theodoret was expounding and saying that Thomas touched Him*, Who was raised from the

---

* John, xx, 26, 27. This sentence seems elsewhere to be attributed to Theodore, Bishop of Mopsuestia.

dead, and worshipped Him Who caused Him to rise,
the Bishop Domnus ascended (the Bema) after Him.

After having praised him (Theodoret)—for, *that*
he made a practice of doing (in the Church)—and
spoken a good deal about him, he uttered, likewise,
the following :—" He (God) spoke to the " Blessed
Peter—' Arise, Peter, ! slay and eat,'* and " nobody
commits a sin in repeating to thee, Theodoret !
" ' Arise, slay, and eat.' "

Again, when the Bishop Domnus was giving
Expositions (Homiletical)—it was the Wednesday of
the Week which is the Great Week, during the
course of his† catechizing—and was preparing those
who, after three days, had to draw nigh to be baptized ; after having spoken a little, he added the
following. Raising his left hand high, and with his
right pointing to it, he went on and expressed him ·
self in this way :—" Likeness and likeness.   The
" likeness of God was not changed into the likeness of
" a servant, and the likeness of a servant was not
" changed into the likeness of God‡.   This did eat :
" that did not eat.   This was wearied : that was not
" wearied.   This did sleep : that did not sleep.   This

---

* Acts, x, 13.

† In p. 177, l. 25, ‎‎, "during the course of his catechizing on the Thursday of the Great Week (μεγάλη τετάρτη) when
preparing to offer for Baptism those who were baptized three days after."
This seems to prove that, on Easter Eve, or the day of the Burial of our
Lord, the Sacrament of Baptism was administered in the Primitive
Church, the other solemn times appointed by the Church for that purpose
being Pentecost, Whitsuntide, and the Epiphany.

‡ See Appendix, B.   In p. 178, l. 3, the Scribe meant to write ‎‎.

did walk : that did not walk." And (he added)
yet :—" For me to say these things to you it is not
" grievous, whilst for you it is safe*. The property
" of the (likeness) Nature of God is that He is
" Un-variable,—Unchangeable,—Incomprehensible*
" — Invisible, — Intangible**—Impassable, — Un-
" knowable. But the property of the form (nature,
" likeness) of a Servant is that he is variable,—
" changeable, — comprehensible*** — visible,—tan-
" gible,—passable,— mortal, —subject to injury."

And after a second short interval he yet said :—

" Do not confuse the duality of the Natures,"
" whilst those impious Nestorians, Pepirius, and
" Eutyches, and Theosebius, cried out against Him
" and demanded that he should say so."

Also, when an Edict of the Gracious Sovereigns
was affixed at Antioch against the impious Nestorius, and against Irenæus who received the Imposition of hands (in Ordination) from Domnus, although
he was a man who had had two wives, and for twelve
years did not communicate with the Holy Church of
God, (viz.,) from the time when Nestorius was exiled until he became Bishop,—on that day (we say)
when he was giving Expositions in the Church, and
whilst the Copiatæ and the Lecticarii and other Nes-

---

* See Pilip. iii, I. ܗܢܘ ܗܢ ܗܢܝܢ ܝܐܘܕܘܬ ܠܚܘܢ ܠܐ ܩܐܢܝܐ
ܘܠܗܘܢ ܕܠܚܘܢ ܠܟ ܥܠܝܟ .ܩܕܡܘܗܝ Tὰ αὐτὰ γράφειν ὑμῖν ἐμοὶ μὲν οὐκ
ὀκνηρὸν ὑμῖν δὲ ἀσφαλές. Ce que je vais dire ne me nuira pas et pourra
vous instruire.

* Or—Inaccessible.   ** Or, Impalpable.   *** Or—accessible.

torians were vociferating—"Cast out the Edict!"
—Domnus, in the course of his Exposition, said :—
" I accept your zeal, by which you, like Naboth,*
" will not hesitate to contend for the inheritance of
" your Fathers. Fear not. The billows of the sea
" are they, and they shall be dissolved in foam."

Again, too, in the Pascal Week, as he was delivering a Homily on the Resurrection, when he came
to our Lord (His Resurrection), he said :—" The
" Man died, but God The Word raised Him from
" the dead."

And again, in the Church (Martyrium)† of the
Holy Stephen, he said this—(viz.,) " I admire the
" patience of the Holy Martyr Stephen who, when
" he was being stoned, prayed for those who were
" doing it, being made like unto our Lord Christ ;
" for, although the persons were different, yet the
" grace was the same."

And, after the Heads (of Accusation) had been
read,

The HOLY SYNOD said :—

" Ibas never said that. This man is a teacher of
" him (Ibas). Anathema to the Blasphemer!
" Anathema to Domnus! Ibas never said that."

(d) The Presbyter CYRIACUS said :—
I request that this letter be, likewise, read.

EUSEBIUS, Bishop of Ancyra, said :—
Let it be received and read.

---

* 1 Kings, xxi.   † See p. 24.

John, Presbyter and Prime-Notary, read :—

To the Holy and God-loving Lord our Brother and
fellow-Minister Flavian, Domnus sends greeting
in our LORD.*

We have been of late braving the brunt of many
storms, O man, who art in every respect a lover of
God ! and are now appealing to the Governor of the
Ark to direct the tempest that is come upon us.†

---

* This well-known letter was for centuries thought to have been composed by Theodoret, whereas its true Authorship, our Acts inform us, is
to be attributed to Domnus II., Patriarch of Antioch. It is given in
full, varying considerably from this, as Epistle LXXXVI of Theodoret in
Migne's Patrologiæ cursus completus (vol. 83, 1859), and appended
in the original at the end of this translation. It occurs in our
Vol. I at p. 180, l. 10. My friend L'Abbé Martin says : "Cette lettre
" a été attribuée jusqu'ici à Théodoret, quoique beaucoup d'indices eussent
" pu faire soupçonner qu'elle n'était pas de lui.   On ne comprend pas, en
" effet, pourquoi il y est tant question des prérogatives du siege d'An-
" tioche, si Théodoret l'a composée, mais on s'explique parfaitement toutes
" ces particularités, quand on sait que Domnus en est l'auteur.   Un pa-
" triarche d'Antioche ne pouvait parler autrement." (Voir Fleury,
Histoire Ecclésiastique, Liv. XXVII, 16, cfr. XVIII, 28.—
Garnier, Historia Theodoreti, dissertatio prima, VIII, 10. Patrol,
grecque, 84, col., 130-131.—Henrion, Histoire Ecclésiastique, in 4°-
Paris, 1859, XV, col. 1404.—Dom Ceillier, Histoire Générale des
Auteurs Ecclésiastiques, in 4°, Paris, Vivès, Tom. 10, chap. iv, sur
Theodoret, § viii, p. 71, etc.)

In p. 181, from ܐܚܕ, in l. 15, to ܠ, in l. 22, the whole passage
is omitted in the Letter as given by Migne, as well as the words corresponding to the sentence—"so worthy in all points of the Doctrine of
" the Church," or, very literally, "which is not deficient (wanting) in
" any of all those points appropriate to the Doctrine of the Church."

Again, after the word ܐܠܗܘ, in l. 2, at p. 184, to end, i.e., to l. 17,
the Syriac Letter altogether differs from that in Migne, which concludes
as given below.   But the chief, and most interesting, difference appears
in the last sentence of, or rather the post-script appended to, the Syriac
Letter, which letter must have been written in the month of September,
448 A.D., as that month had not elapsed.   The month ܐܝܠܘܠ is September, or, rather, part of August and September.

† I somewhat differ from Martin in the rendering of the first part of the

What, however, has now become imminent over us through (a man's) daring, in my estimation, baffles all description.   For, at the time when we calculated that we had in my Lord, the God-loving Dioscorus, Bishop of Alexandria, a helper and fellow-worker against all who conspired in antagonism to The Faith of the Apostles, we sent, as a matter of obligation, one of the Venerable Presbyters that are with us*— an honoured man, distinguished in The Faith and for wisdom —with two Synodical letters, informing His Piety that, to the articles of the (covenant) Agreement drawn up in the days of Cyril of Blessed memory†, we held ourselves bound in all propriety and rectitude to assent, as well as to his letter so worthy in all points of the Doctrine of the Church : and as regards the letter of that Blessed man whose memory lives among the Faithful, Athanasius, which he wrote to the Blessed Epictetus, *that* also we received with (all) welcome, but, above all, we accepted and assented to The Faith, as defined at Nicæa in Bithynia by those Holy and very Blessed Fathers (who assembled there).

We prayed his Piety to compel those, who refused

Letter, as will be seen by comparing the following with my English Version :—" Dans ces derniers temps, nous avons subi l'impétuosité des " nombreux orages, ô homme ami de Dieu ; nous avous invoqué Celui " qui gouverne toutes choses et nous avons pu resister à la tempête qui a " fondu sur nous."

Governor *of the Ark* is translation of the reading in the MS. ܩܘܒܐܠ, but this is perhaps an old mistake (though it gives a very good meaning) for ܩܘܠ, of the *Universe*, as the Original has in this place τοῦ παντός.

* Eusebius.

† The agreement of Cyril and Paul of Emesa, in the year 443, A.D.

to hold to it (the agreement), to subscribe to it.
But one of ours*, one of those who think differently
from us and have caused these troubles, hurried (to
Alexandria) and led into error several parties well-
known there.   By raising calumnies against us, he
succeeded in exciting cries in the Church without
end against the God-loving Oriental Bishops.   My
Lord the pious Bishop Dioscorus, acting excellently,
imposed silence upon them promising to write to us
and to send Venerable Presbyters to us who should
inform us of the talk of which we were the object.
This is what he did, but he wrote letters which he
ought never to have addressed to us, as one who
knows the Word of God—"Lend not ear to vain
rumours."†   For, he gave credence to all that was
said against us, as he might have a right to do,
if he had discussed everything to the bottom
and had long recognized the justice of the accusations.   Here is the injustice of which Dioscorus
has been guilty towards us ; but we, who have suffered this injury, replied to him boldly, although in
friendly terms.   We assured his Piety that all these
rumours were destitute of foundation, and that none
of the God-loving Oriental Bishops held opinions
contrariant to Apostolic Doctrine.   Moreover, the
Venerable Presbyters whom he sent were convinced by examination into the facts.   But as to him,

---

* "One of ours"—most probably would be the Monk Theodosius of
whom mention is made further on.
† Exodus xxiii, 1.

without going any further into the matter, and giving
ear to all those who calumniate us, he did a thing
which we could not have believed, had not the entire
Church (assembly) of the Faithful been a witness of
it. For, yielding to the counsels of those who
anathematised us, he rose (from his seat) and pro
nounced his adhesion to their cries. Still further,
he despatched to the Royal City, as we learnt, certain Bishops who depend upon him, to excite, as he
hoped, fresh troubles against us.

We, however, prior to every (other) consideration,
have our Defender in the all-seeing ONE, since it is
for the Doctrines of GOD that we are contending.

And in the second place we now make appeal, also,
to your Holiness and urge you to contend and fight
for The Faith (so violently assailed) and on behalf of
the Canons (so grievously) trampled upon.

For, when in the Royal City the Holy and very
Blessed Fathers of the Church were assembled, they
confirmed, with one consent, and justified the arrangements of those who assembled at Nicæa concerning the Governors of Diocœses (Provinces),
assigning to each Governor that (province) which
appertained to him, and repudiating as contrary to
all order (the idea) that any one Governor should
infringe upon the others, but that the Bishop of
Alexandria should have jurisdiction over the
Egyptians only. Thus, each Governor has to ad-

minister his own particular Province.*   But this man

* The decision here alluded to of the Council of Nicæa is to be
found in its sixth Canon, and that of the Synod of Constantinople
in its second.   It seems to be worth while to give the original
Greek of both in full, because of their importance and the many
questions which have been raised about them.

CANON VI. OF NICÆA.

Τὰ ἀρχαῖα ἔθη κρατείτω τὰ ἐν Αἰγύπτῳ καὶ Λιβύῃ καὶ Πενταπόλει,
ὥστε τὸν Ἀλεξανδρείας ἐπίσκοπον πάντων τούτων ἔχειν τὴν ἐξουσίαν,
ἐπειδὴ καὶ τῷ ἐν τῇ Ῥώμῃ ἐπισκόπῳ τοῦτο σύνηθές ἐστιν· ὁμοίως δὲ
καὶ κατὰ Ἀντιόχειαν καὶ ἐν ταῖς ἄλλαις ἐπαρχίαις τὰ πρεσβεῖα σώζεσθαι
ταῖς ἐκκλησίαις· καθόλου δὲ πρόδηλον ἐκεῖνο, ὅτι εἴ τις χωρὶς γνώμης
τοῦ μητροπολίτου γένοιτο ἐπίσκοπος, τὸν τοιοῦτον ἡ μεγάλη σύνοδος
ὥρισε μὴ δεῖ εἶναι ἐπίσκοπον· ἐὰν μέντοι τῇ κοινῇ πάντων ψήφῳ, εὐλόγῳ
οὔσῃ καὶ κατὰ κανόνα ἐκκλησιαστικὸν, δύο ἢ τρεῖς δι' οἰκείαν φιλονεικίαν
ἀντιλέγωσι, κρατείτω ἡ τῶν πλειόνων ψῆφος.

Héfélé gives an interpretation of this Canon in the first volume
of his great work on th · Councils of the Church (French edition,
1869, pp. 378—393), and in the course of it he quotes (on
p. 385) the above passage of this Letter of Domnus, then still
supposed to be one of Theodoret's.   In J. Johnson's *The Clergyman's Vade-mecum*, containing the Canonical Codes of the Primitive
and Universal Church (London, 1723, third edition), occurs the
following English translation (Vol. II., p. 48) :—

" Let Ancient Customs prevail (as for Instance), those in *Egypt,
Lybia,* and *Pentapolis:* That the Bishop of *Alexandria* have
Power over all these, since the same is customary for the Bishop
of *Rome.*   Likewise in *Antioch,* and other Provinces, let the Privileges be secured to the Churches.   This is manifest as anything
at all, that if any be made a Bishop, without consent of his Metropolitan, this great Synod has determin'd that such a one ought
not to be Bishop.   If any two or three out of Affectation of Dispute
do contradict the Suffrage of the Generality, when duly pass'd
according to Ecclesiastical Canon, let the Votes of the Majority
prevail."

CANON II. OF CONSTANTINOPLE.

Τοὺς ὑπὲρ διοίκησιν ἐπισκόπους ταῖς ὑπερορίοις Ἐκκλησίαις μὴ ἐπιέναι,
μηδὲ συγχέειν τὰς Ἐκκλησίας· ἀλλὰ κατὰ τοὺς κανόνας τὸν μὲν Ἀλεξανδρείας ἐπίσκοπιν τὰ ἐν Αἰγύπτῳ μόνον οἰκονομεῖν, τοὺς δὲ τῆς ἀνατολῆς ἐπισκόπους τὴν ἀνατολὴν μόνην διοικεῖν, φυλαττομένων τῶν ἐν

(Dioscorus), as events prove, refused to conform to these decisions, and (exceeding) violating them, obtrudes on our notice the Throne of the Blessed Mark, and that, whilst he knows evidently that the great city of Antioch possesses the Throne of Peter[*], who was, too, the teacher of Blessed Mark and of all the first

τοῖς κανόσι τοῖς κατὰ Νικαίαν πρεσβείων τῇ Ἀντιοχέων Ἐκκλησίᾳ, καὶ τοὺς τῆς Ἀσιανῆς διοικήσεως ἐπισκόπους τὰ κατὰ τὴν Ἀσίαν μόνην οἰκονομεῖν, καὶ τοὺς τῆς Ποντικῆς τὰ τῆς Ποντικῆς μόνον, καὶ τοὺς τῆς Θράκης τὰ τῆς Θρᾳκικῆς μόνον οἰκονομεῖν. Ἀκλήτους δὲ ἐπισκόπους ὑπὲρ διοίκησιν μὴ ἐπιβαίνειν ἐπὶ χειροτονίαις ἤ τισιν ἄλλαις οἰκονομίαις ἐκκλησιαστικαῖς. Φυλαττομένου δὲ τοῦ προγεγραμμένου περὶ τῶν διοικήσεων κανόνος, εὔδηλον ὡς τὸ καθ᾽ ἑκάστην ἐπαρχίαν ἡ τῆς ἐπαρχίας σύνοδος διοικήσει, κατὰ τὰ ἐν Νικαίᾳ ὡρισμένα. Τὰς δὲ ἐν τοῖς βαρβαρικοῖς ἔθνεσι τοῦ Θεοῦ Ἐκκλησίας οἰκονομεῖσθαι χρὴ κατὰ τὴν κρατήσασαν συνήθειαν παρὰ τῶν πατέρων.

Compare *Héfélé*, Op. cit. Vol. II., 202—204, and Johnson's *Vademecum* II., 124 s., where the following translation of this Canon is given :—

"Let not Bishops go out of their *Diocese* to Churches out of their Bounds ; but let the Bishop of *Alexandria*, according to the Canon, administer the affairs of *Egypt*, and the Bishops of the East the Affairs of the East only, with a Salvo to the ancient Privileges of the Church of *Antioch*, mention'd in the *Nicene* Canons. Let the Bishops of the *Asian* Diocese administer the *Asian* Affairs only, and they of *Pontus* the *Pontic*, and they of *Thrace* the *Thracian*. And let not Bishops go out of their Dioceses to Ordination, or any Administrations, unless they be invited. And by the aforesaid Canon, concerning Dioceses being observed, 'tis evident that the Provincial Synod will have the Management of every Province, as was decreed at *Nice*. The Churches amongst the Barbarians must be govern'd according to the Customs which prevail'd with their Ancestors."

[*] Bishop Pearson says that He built His Church upon one to show the Unity, and upon many to show the Universality, of It. St. Cyprian says that upon one He builds His Church ; and, though he gives to all the Apostles an equal power, and says—"As my Father hath sent Me so "send I you," yet, in order to manifest unity, He has, by His own authority, so placed the source of the same unity as to begin from one. Certainly the other Apostles also were what Peter was, endued with an equal fellowship both of power and honour ; but a commencement is made from unity, that the Church may be set before us as one. . . . Let no one deceive the Brotherhood by falsehood, no one corrupt the

Apostles together, as well as their (head) leader. As for ourselves we are assured indeed of the exalted character of this Apostolic Throne, but we know also and measure ourselves; for, we have learnt from above to practice the Apostolic humility.

We supplicate your Holiness, then, that you would not allow the Holy Canons to be (with impunity) trampled upon, but readily to contend* for The Faith, since in This is our hope of Salvation, as likewise you yourself are persuaded; and through It (alone) can we hope to be thought worthy of Mercy and Grace, and look forward to †stand before the dread Judgement-seat of God and our Redeemer, our Lord Jesus Christ. Be induced, my Lord who art holy in every way, [to afford us help and to pray on our behalf.]

---

truth of our faith by a faithless treachery. The Episcopate is one, of which a part is held by each without a division of the whole. (De Unit. Eccl., c. iv.)   In the great Synod at Constantinople in 553 A.D. it is said that the Grace of the Holy Ghost was abundantly given to every single Apostle, so that he needed not the advice of another in what was to be done, yet they did not like to decide on the point in question. . . . before every one of them had supported his sentence with Scriptural Authority. · S. John Damascenus calls all the Apostles " The twelve-corded Lyre of the Holy Ghost. But neither " Peter alone is this Lyre, nor Andrew, but all the Apostles together. " If anyone declares Peter to be this Lyre, he is a Liar." S. Chrysostom says—" Paul went to Jerusalem to see Peter. Is there anything " more humble than this soul? He did not need Peter, but was his " equal. Still he goes to him, as if he were his superior and senior." And again—" He shows himself equal to the other Apostles, but he " does not compare himself with the others, but with the first of them, " showing thereby that every one of them had the same dignity. (On Gal., i, 11, and ii, 3). The above is from a long catena of Latin and Greek authors to the same effect as given in Overbeck's Orthodox Review.

* Romans xiv, 10.   † Jude iii.

I and those who are with me desire to offer much salutation to you and all the Brethren with you.

Further, let your Charity take notice that to Tyre the Metropolis was assigned a Bishop on the 9th of Eloul (September) now instant; (viz.) the Venerable Presbyter Photius.*

* This passage is the Postscript, referred to in note on p. 298, of this celebrated Epistle, of which the immediately preceding paragraph is in all probability the termination. It is one of those passages in the MS. numbered 14,530 in the British Museum, which enable us to correct what has passed as matter of history, and which will justify an attempt at a Dissertation on the subject of the corrections which our previous information must receive about the Second Synod of Ephesus from these newly discovered Acts contained in the MS. alluded to, as well as about other historical points. At the quaternian Centenary of the University or Tübingen in the Kingdom of Würtemberg to be commemorated in August next (1877), such a theme is formally to be proposed as a Prize Essay by the distinguished Professor—all honor to that University for the honor shown to Divinity—who has just been elected by the Deans of all the Faculties to be the Rector of the University and Presiding Genius of the University proceedings and has ordered the medal to be struck shall bear the proud inscription—QUINTUM SECULUM SUPERIORIBUS CLARIUS SURGIT—for the Jubilee year.

Historians have recorded much about various characters who occupied the See of Constantinople, but it is remarkable how little history gives us of S. Flavian. One of the chief objects of the Second Synod of Ephesus was to settle the controversy between him and Eutyches. The Orientals anathematized the one in their writings in which the other, however, is hardly mentioned. How strange to us appear events! "There is Eutyches who founds monophysism and the monophysists anathematize him! Ibas, Theodoret, and Flavian contend against Eutyches, and the memory of the first two is perpetuated from age to age to be an object of horror and malediction, while that of the third is completely effaced and disappears in eternal oblivion! Of Flavian not a word is there in Philoxène of Maboug, in Severus of Antioch, in John Sabas, &c. The tomb has swallowed him whole. The Holy Martyr is dead for ever to the Christians of Asia."

In his Martyrologium (1603), Baronius, on Februarii 18, writes thus:— De eodem Graeci agunt in Menologio hac die; ubi testantur Flavianum actum in exilium, and cō-fectum aerumnis obiisse, idque ex sententia Marcellini Comitis in Chron. sub Protogene et Asterio Conss. ubi ait eum exulasse factione Dioscori et Saturnini. Sed haec quidem omnia repugnare

Pray, then, I beseech you, that Apostolic Peace in the Holy Churches may everywhere abound and extend.

Pray, my Lord—a lover of God in truth—that we may have health in our Lord.

---

videntur Actis sacrosancti Concilii Chalced. in actione etenim prima et tertia Euseb. Episc. Dorilaei, et in Actione 4. Archimādritae Catholici, oblato S. Synodo libello, cōclamarunt adversus Dioscorum, S. Flavianum factione Dioscori necatum esse : id ipsum etiam Liberatus diaconus in breviar. haeres. Nestor. et Eutych. exactè describit cap. 12. factumque refert, antequam Epheso recessissent Episcopi. Id etiam Evagrius Scholast hist. libr. 2. cap. 2. Id denique Nicephorus (ut praeteream recentiores) pluribus testatur libr. 14. cap. 47. Caeterùm contigit utrumque esse verum : nimirum Flavianū á Dioscoro ita ut aiunt malè habitum, sicque affectum continuò missum esse in exilium, et tertia die vita functum. Confirmantur haec ex libro manuscripto qui habetur in Bibliotheca Vatican, num. 1855. In quo descriptæ habentur complures Epistolæ Roman. Pontiff. ubi inest libellus incerti auctoris . .
. . . In eo igitur haec de Flaviano leguntur : Ducitur in exilium Flavianus, et apud Epypam, quae est civitas Lydiae . . . . .
quā Ptolomaeus Hypepam vocat &c. Contigit obitus Flaviani sub Consulàtu Asterii et Protogenis . . . . Celebratur hac die solēnis translatio, quando venerandum corpus ejus per Marcianum Augustum, et S. Pulcheriam conjugem summo cum honore Constantinopolim translatum est &c. . . . . . . Mirificis laudibus S. Flavianum prosecuti sunt Patres, ij praesertim, qui Chalcedonem ad Concilium convenerunt ; ubi inter alia ejus praeconia, haec in Actione ii. sunt acclamata : Flaviano æterna memoria :ecce ultio, ecce veritas : Flavianus post mortem vivit, martyr pro nobis exorat : Flavianus post mortem fidem exposuit &c. Secundus Abel appellatur á Sebasteno Episcopo . . . . . De restituendo nomine ejus in diptycha, et abolenda memoria Eutychij, extat l. quoniam. C. de Episc. et cleric. Cæteras autem ejus res gestas, tam synodicas, quám privatas, intexuimus in Annal. Ecclesiasticis, per annos singulo servata temporum ratione. (P. 131. on the words—S. Flaviani Episcopi, qui cùm fidem Catholicam Ephesi propugnarit, ab impij Dioscori factione pugnis atque calcibus percussus, atque in exilium actus, post triduum vitam finivit.)

Note that on p. 304, at l. 1, "Leader" (Coryphaeus) ends the passage referred to at p. 170, that the brackets in l. 15 and 16 should be removed, and note marks * and † interchanged. Also, at note † on p. 299, the date should be 433, A.D.

Now ,when the Letter had been read,

The Holy Synod exclaimed :—

" He, who calumniates thee (Dioscorus!), is a Here-
" tic—He who calumniates thee, is a calumniator of
" the Synod—He who calumniates thee, is a calumni-
"ator 'of Cyril—He who calumniates thee, is a
"blasphemer of God.—We did not know all that.—To
" the Bishops long life—to the Emperors long life—to
" the Holy Synod long life.—Through thee God has
"spoken—the Holy Spirit has spoken in thee.
"Speak, my Lord! it becomes you—speak, my Lord!
"and Christ will speak.   Cut away this root—Be full
" of zeal for the Lord, Orthodox Teacher! and cut (off)
" this root, Orthodox Teacher! the posterity of Nes-
" torius shall not continue.   Always victorious, the
" Christ will be victor—the victorious Cross will
" always be victor.—To the Emperors long life—to
" the Patriarchs long life.—Victorious is The Faith of
" the Emperors—Victorious is The Faith of the
"Orthodox--Those who remain silent are Heretics*—
" Cut off this root—Let the root have its *quietus*—
" By your endeavours The Faith stands sure and
" stedfast."

---

* Very valuable is this little sentence, since it shows that there were
some Members of the Synod who were far from agreeing with its proceedings.   Terrified, no doubt, by the terrible scene in connection with
the first Session when Flavian, Archbishop of Constantinople, was so
mercilessly handled by the President ; conscious of the injustice as well as
violence of the Eutychian leaguers, &c., they remained taciturn rather than
be participators in other men's atrocious deeds, and preferred to submit to
be branded as Heretical to the charge of depraving That Deposit which
the whole Church of Christ had received, by a right Tradition, from the
Apostles themselves.

John, Presbyter and Proto-Notary, said :—

I have, likewise, other Libels against the God-fearing Bishop Domnus, which are presented to your Synod, as well as a Confession of Faith, from the Venerable Pelagius, Presbyter of Antioch ; and I bring this circumstance (now) to your knowledge.

Stephen, Bishop of Ephesus, said :—

Let them, likewise, be read and deposited among the Acts (Documentary).

John, Presbyter and Proto-Notary, read :—

TO THE Holy, Great, Œcumenical Synod which, by the grace of God and the God-fearing zeal of the Gracious and Christ-loving Emperors, is here assembled, the Petition and Complaint of Marcellus, Presbyter and Monk*, and of the Brethren that are with me.

A heavy storm has overtaken the Holy Churches in the East, O Holy (Fathers !) and from a small spark a great fire has been interminably kindling ; and little by little the evil, insinuating itself into the Churches, has introduced there a pernicious malady. For, those Heads of the Church,† who adhere to the

---

* If the printed text p. 186, l. 2 ܐܝܟ gives the correct reading, we must translate with Abbé Martin :—" complaint of Pelagius Presbyter, *and of my monastery* and etc." ; but, probably, we must read ܠܕܝܪܝ as in the Subscription p. 189, l. 27.

† At p. 186, l. 9 the word ܪܝܫܝ *Principes Ecclesiae*, i.e. Episcopi, Princes of the Church, to distinguish them from secular Princes, applying to them that prophecy of Isaiah, lx, 17, which, according to Jerome's

Doctrines of the false Faith of Nestorius, persecute the Orthodox Doctors and vex the peoples catholically minded by preaching among them the opinions of that Beast. .

Now, the source of all these calamities and the cause of the ruin in the East is the Venerable Domnus, the Bishop of Antioch, who consecrated them,[*] and Theodoret, who is full of all Impiety, receiving such from him (Domnus), as it were, by a sort of tradition, and who has, like some ferocious swine, dispersed the sheep of Christ.

---

translation, is: " I will make thy Princes peace, and thy Bishops right-eousness." In the Greek writers they are styled ἄρχοιτες ἐκκλησιῶν (Bingham).

[*] In " Domnus, who ordained them " (the Nestorian-minded Heads of the Church or Bishops by Consecration), Abbé Martin thinks, there is undoubtedly an implied allusion to the ordination of Irenaeus of Tyre. That fact, affirmed more clearly elsewhere, would tend to show that the Epistle 110, attributed to Theodoret is, in reality, that of Domnus. This opinion which occurred to him immediately on reading the 110th Epistle of Theodoret, he thinks capable of irrefragable proof, and he shows it to be correct in the following manner.

The author of the Letter, after having spoken of the ordination of Irenaeus by himself, although the latter was a Bigamist, adds : *Quod vero ad digamiam attinet, majorum vestigiis inhaesimus. Nam et beatae sanctaeque memoriae Alexander, qui apostolicam hanc sedem rexit, una cum sanctissimo Acacio Beroeae episcopo, beatae memoriae Diogenem digamum ordinavit, etc.*

It is very evident that the Author of the Letter speaks first of his pre-decessor in this See, secondly of his See as an Apostolical one, thirdly of Alexander as one of his predecessors. Now all this is applicable to the Bishop of Antioch and not at all to the Bishop of Cyrus. Alexander of Antioch was contemporary with Acacius of Beroea and was living at the commencement of the fifth century, [vie-siècle in Martin, le brigandage p. 145, note *b* is a misprint]. What seems strange, is, that authors, in borrowing details from the letter attributed to Theodoret, should not have perceived that the letter ought to be ascribed to Domnus. (Baronius, *Annales, ad ann.* 408, 31-32, 441, 71.—Tillemont, *Mémoires pour servir à l'Histoire eccl.,* xiv, 802, au mot *Acace,* 813, au mot *Alexandre* d' Antioche, et pages 174, 224-225 ; xv, 265, 868.—Dom Ceillier,

However, not for ever will God, whom these men (persecute) vex, extend His patience ; for, moving by Divine zeal our Gracious and Christ-loving Emperor, He has assembled in this place this your Holy, and Œcumenical Synod, in order to reduce the tempest to a calm : and He has lopped off the holders of the Doctrines of Nestorius, in order that you might lopp off branches belonging to him, and at once administer consolation to the wearied Churches of the East, and restore peace to the Orthodox Doctors (so) persecuted, the Holy Spirit granting assistance to your Piety (for that purpose).

Moreover, the Venerable Bishop Domnus upset the Church of Emesa* and handed over its property (possessions) to the Treasury (of the Mother-Church). For, whilst the God-loving Bishops of Phœnicia Libanensis (secunda)† were, according to the Canons,

---

Histoire générale des Auteurs Ecclésiastiques in 4o, Ed. Vivès, x, ch. iv, § vii, p. 72.)—*Suivant nous* (says Martin at the end of his note p. 145), *L'épître* 110 *est une lettre de Domnus à Théodoret et l'épître* 112 *en est la réponse.*

* Emesa (the modern *Homs*), reckoned the Metropolis of Phœnicia Secunda, in the *Notitia* of Hierocles, is situated near the river Orontes. Here Constantine built a splendid Church, renowned for its beauty, in rivalry perhaps to the magnificent Temple of the Sun, the youthful Priest of which, Bassian, was raised to the imperial purple by the Roman Legionaries in Syria A.D. 218, which under the name of Heliogabalus he wore for less than four years. No doubt, in this same Church, the Ordination took place, which is here spoken of as so irregular and disorderly. The great Mosk of Homs is built on the site of this Church, about which see Rev. G. Williams' introduction to Neale's *Patriarchate of Antioch*, p. xxii ff.—At Homs Husseyin Pasha was defeated by Ibrahim Pasha in 1832.

† The expression ܐܦܣܩܘ̈ܦܐ ܕܝܪ̈ܝ ܕܒܠܒܢܘ seems to me to include no *and*, as Hoffmann supposes—Phœnicia (prima) *and* (Phœnicia)

imposing hands (in Ordination) on the God-fearing Bishop Peter, a certain Uranius, a man of corrupt life, who had been several times publicly reprimanded for his dissolute habits, ventured to seize the Throne of the Church aforesaid in violation of the Canons, —no prayer at the time being made or invocation for Divine Grace—Jews and Pagans and Mimics having helped him for that purpose and placed simply the Holy Gospel on his head, while the God-fearing Bishops of the Province suffered violence.   But, after having escaped thence, they despatched while on their way an Inhibition in writing to the whole Clergy (of the Diocese), forbidding them to communicate with Uranius or to regard him as their Bishop; and they adjudged and assigned a punishment for the case of his affecting to act the Bishop.   Likewise, they wrote to Valerius, Bishop of Laodicea, who is a Nestorian, to caution him against communicating with him (Uranius), and, since he did not comply, they notified the same thing to the Clergy, and addressed an Inhibition to the Laity, of the city (of Laodicea).

Matters having, then, eventuated in this way, all the Monasteries of those parts and many of the Clergy and Laity withdrew from Uranius; whereupon this man without delay repaired to Theodoret and forced his Brother, while yet a lad, to receive Imposition of hands from himself for the Diaconate.

Libanensis (secunda). His reasons, however, for removing the *and* are quite correct; compare his note 287, and Le Quien II, 834, the *Notitia*, of Hierocles, ed. Parthey 715,5, 717,1.

He, likewise, wasted the Church's Treasure. Subsequently, he betook himself to the God-fearing Domnus, the Bishop of Antioch who, overcome by the witchery, so to speak, of Theodoret, imagined he could make a Bishop of a man so despicable, by means of mere Letters, whereby the Monasteries of the East felt scandalized, being well aware of the corrupt bringings up (education) of the man.

I also, therefore, having before my eyes the fear of God, and witnessing the ruin of this Church and the violation of the Canons of the Blessed Fathers,—I have left, at the age you see me, my Monastery with my Brethren and hastened (to fall) at the feet of your Sanctity, all the Orthodox Monks, who are very numerous, supplicating your Piety, through my means and mediation, to order the Letters of the Province to be read, whose Metropolitan, now here present, (viz) the God-fearing Theodorus of Damascus, will be able in person to confirm what he has written or what we have said, whereby your Piety will be able to ascertain to how great an extent the Venerable Bishops Domnus and Theodoret have trampled under foot the Canons, and will effectually rid the flock of Christ of the Nestorian Uranius who, we may add, subscribed to the unlawful Deposition of the God-fearing Presbyter and Archimandrite Eutyches, although he was not a Bishop. Further, he (Uranius) imposed hands, as one and as if intent on injury, creating confusion and trouble in the Churches ; and he handed over Strategius, who for twenty-two years had been a Reader of the same Church, to the Curial Authority, in consequence of his assenting to the Letters written against him by the Bishops of the Province.

Further, not long ago he (Domnus) located the Venerable Timothy in the city of Arcai,* in another Province, who ought to have been ordained by our Holy Father Juvenal, Bishop of Psalton* (Salton) in Palestine, whom (Timothy), in violation of all Canonical Order, the God-fearing Domnus translated to Arcai, having given orders for Uranius to do nothing more than to lay hands on him (in Ordination).

I, Marcellus, Presbyter and Monk, present these Libels to the Holy, Great, and Œcumenical Synod, which, by the Grace of God and the God-fearing zeal of our Clement and Christ-loving Emperors, is assemble at Ephesus the Metropolis.

---

* Arcai was, it seems, in Palaestina Prima, and Psalton nowhere. The Patriarchate of Jerusalem, formed out of that of Antioch, had three Provinces, says Bingham, assigned for the limits of its jurisdiction— Palaestina, Prima, Secunda, Tertia, but it never had quite fifty Bishops at the same time. In 451 A.D., Juvenal and Maximus agreed as a settlement of a long dispute that " S. Peter's See of Antioch should have the two Phœnicias and Arabia " and " the Holy Resurrection of Christ the three Palestines." Assemanus says :—" avulsis ab eadem (Hierosolym.) Metropoli nonnullis Arabiae Ecclesiis, quae tertiam Palaestinam constituerunt, Petra urbs, Bostrenae quondam subjecta, Metropoliticis juribus ornata est, quum id Maximus Antiochenus Juvenali Hierosolymitano permisisset, ut liquet ex his Liberati Diaconi verbis in Brevario cap. 13, *Septimo Secretario* (loquitur de Con. Chalced.) *tres actae sunt causae propter quod tres ejus computantur actiones. Prima est, qua firmata sunt, quae convenerunt inter Maximum Antiochenum, et Juvenalem Hierosolymitanum Episcopos, ut duae Phœniciae et Arabia dependerent Sedi Antiochenae ; Hierosolymitanae verò tres Palaestinae provinciae,* quarum primae metropolis Caesaraea, secundae Scythopolis, tertiae Petra. (Tom. iii, pt. 2, p. 594.)

(6) THE PETITION AND COMPLAINT OF THE DEACON HELIODORUS, AND OF THE MONKS, SIMON AND ABRAHAM AND GERONTIUS.

All peace and tranquillity did the Churches of God in the Eastern parts enjoy in the days of John of pious Memory and of those Blessed Fathers who preceded him.   But lo ! as soon as the God-fearing Domnus had, by the contrivance of the Pagan Iso-cacius and of others attached to theatricals, become Bishop, without any* election (or any meeting) of Bishops who, according to custom, should assemble (at Antioch) for his Consecration†—as soon as he had been made such, contrary to all Laws and Canons, at the 10th hour of the day‡—for, there was neither any assembly for (Divine) Service (held) on his account, nor Communion in the Mysteries, from

---

* Bingham gives the usual order of the Church in all the circumstances alluded to in this passage.   Assemanus on "Numerus Electorum Patriarchæ " at p. 678, of Tom. iii, writes :—*Metropolitarum unusquisque secum adducit tres Episcopos ex sua Provincia.*
De numero Electorum apud Graecos haec Codinus : Episcopi qui Constantinopoli versantur, tametsi plures adsint conveniunt ; saltem verò duodecim : alii etiam ex vicinis Ecclesiis evocati. Si verò neque ex iis qui peregrè advenerunt, neque ex vicinis Ecclesiis duodecim Episcopi reperiantur : tunc pro necessitate in loco electionis, quotcumque reperti fuerint, consident.

† Every Bishop, by the laws and customs of the Church, had to be ordained in his own Church in the presence of his own people, the Metropolitan or Primate and the Bishops of the Province meeting there for his Election and Ordination.   St. Augustine, of Hippo, is an instance of this almost universally acknowledged rule.

‡ In l. 17 of p. 190 ܟܐ ܟܚܡܣ (not ܟܐ as printed) *at the* 10th *hour* i.e. 4 p.m., an uncanonical hour ; for, Ordination usually took place at the time of the Oblation at the Morning Service, when the Ordained either celebrated or partook of the Eucharist, whether of Bishops, Priests or Deacons.   This was one of the irregularities against this ancient rule of the Church, urged against Novatian.

which circumstance, also, irregular proceedings
can be proved—(ever since, we say) all has become
(and is still) full of trouble and confusion.   For, precisely because he began in this way, did he (Domnus)
upset the Churches of the East, by delivering them
over, through treachery, to Theodoret the Blasphemer, Nestorian, and Oppressor*, in conjunction with
whom he put up a number of Nestorian Bishops of
the same sentiments as himself.   What, however, constitutes the chief mischief is this;—that to the
prejudice of the Faithful, he made Pompeianus
Bishop of Emesa and Uranius (Bishop) of it after
him, as well as Paul Bishop of Antaradus, by mere
Letters, and without any Invocation for Divine
Grace ; shewing thereby that the Imposition of hands
on himself (in Ordination) was (attained) for his
abolishing with impunity the Canons of the Fa-
thers†.   Further, as regards the God-fearing Bishop
Alexander, who can be (favourably) testified to for
rectitude of conduct and for conversation and for Orthodoxy, which fact, we opine, he (Domnus) himself
would not call in question—although he was

---

* At p. 190, l. 26, the original Syriac Noun, derived from the Verb
(signifying *deglutivit, devoravit, absumpsit*), may designate a *devourer* of
food and drink, or of men. The term *iniquus absorbet justum* i.e.
oppressit, indicative of the signification of the same verb, gives the
third appellative to Theodoret.

† "The Canons of the Fathers." This refers probably to "the Book
of Canons," very frequently quoted in the Council at Chalcedon, in 451
A.D. and composed of the Canons of the Primitive Church, containing the
Apostolical Canons, and the Code of the Universal Church i.e. the Ni-
caene, Ancyran, Neo-Caesarean, Gangran, Antiochean, Laodicean and
Constantinopolitan, Canons, to which were afterwards added those of
Ephesus and Chalcedon ; making in all 207 Canons.

examined, selected, and ad-judged by our Father S. Cyril, and by the Pious Proclus, and by the Holy Synod* assembled by them at Constantinople, for the purpose of occupying (the See of) Antaradus, as also the Letters despatched by them to the God-fearing Domnus certify, and (although) he had been received by them and communicated with them at Alexandria, at Ephesus, and at Constantinople, and the Blessed Cyril had addressed him as a Fellow-Minister,—(notwithstanding all this) he .(Domnus) ejected him from Antaradus, because he does not hold the opinions of Nestorius, and in consequence of his having resorted, in a time of trouble, to the Blessed Cyril ; and he presented, through Letters, Antaradus to Paul as recompence for having gone to the Oasis to Nestorius, and for having preached his Impieties in the Church, disturbing and agitating the Faithful there.

Refusing, moreover, to yield in this matter to the Blessed Bishops and to the Synod that assembled with them, on having learned that the Very Blessed Cyril had departed to the Lord, he seized the God-fearing Alexander in the Bishop's Hall†, (Court) when Theodoret and Pompeianus, originators of all these violent proceedings, were present with him, and ex-

---

* This was no doubt a σύνοδος ἐνδημοῦσα, similar to the one held in Nov. 448, A.D. at Constantinople, at which Eutyches was condemned.

† This might be the Secretarium or Diaconicium magnum without the Church, which was reckoned one of its exedrae. The consistory or tribunal was here, and it was large enough to hold a provincial and sometimes general Council. (Bingham).

torted from him a Document, which Theodoret had drawn up, (to the effect) that he (Alexander) would act (only) as a Presbyter and would not exercise the Power of the Episcopate. Then, completing all these violent proceedings, Domnus compelled Alexander to add, that he would not carry his complaints to the Holy Synod or to our Christ-loving Emperor, nor ever enter the house of the latter.

Now, this man labouring under these restrictive burdens is unable to get to your Holiness by reason of the document which was extorted from him contrary to (all) Law, and in consequence of the punishment which, contrary to all Justice, has been inflicted upon him.

It is for this reason, then, that we in our own persons, moved by zeal and wishful that the Districts of Aradus and Antaradus in conjunction with the Churches of the East should have pity bestowed upon them, have hastened to come as supplicants, falling at the feet of your Great, Holy, and Œcumenical Synod, in order to proffer this information, touching the God-fearing Domnus and regarding the way in which he has brought ruin upon the Cities through reposing confidence in Theodoret ; and we entreat your Holiness to order, that what we have presented in writing as proof of our (oral) statements should be read, and also to order that Paul, the Nestorian and Blasphemer, who journied as far as the Oasis, be removed from Antaradus and Aradus, and the God-loving Alexander be reinstituted thereunto, who for seven years has been detained at Antioch And (we further entreat you) to make null and void the document, which, contrary to Order, was extorted from him, so that he may occupy again these places (as his own) in the same manner as heretofore.   For, he (Alexander) is acceptable to all the people living at those places, as (the documentary proof of) their Election of him, addressed to the Blessed Proclus, attests; a copy of which he (Proclus) despatched* to the Bishop Domnus, as well as to the then Bishop of the Metropolis, Tyre.   It is in consequence of this that people without end have not, up to the present time, communicated with, but have even suffered persecution from, Paul as a Nestorian.

Finally, those sentiments, relating to the same Venerable Alexander, which were decided upon (pronounced) in an appropriate and canonical way by the Very Blessed Cyril and the Pius Proclus, as well as by the Synod that was assembled by their means, should be confirmed by your Holiness.

I, Heliodorus, Deacon and (we) Simon, Abraham and Gerontius, Monks, have presented this Libel, after having subscribed it by the hands (means) of the Venerable John.

---

* This and other acts of Proclus, referred to in this instrument, are in keeping with his fidelity to the Regimen and Discipline, as his first great Sermon on the Theotokos preached in the presence of his Patriarch, (afterwards pronounced the Arch-heretic Nestorius), and other instances of his title to a great Doctor in Divinity, were in keeping with his fidelity to The Faith and Doctrine, of the Catholic Church of Christ.

(7) CONFESSION* OF FAITH OF THE PRESBYTER PELAGIUS,

To my Lord, the Holy and God-loving Archbishop Domnus, and to the God-loving (men) Domnus, Theoctistus, Gerontius, Sabbas, Theodoret, Julianus and Julianus, Damianus of Sidon, Eustathius of Aegea, Meletius, the Presbyter Pelagius (sends) greeting in our Lord†.

Because some of those, who are continually in familiar intercourse with me, have appeared to your Holiness to entertain and affirm Doctrines contrariant to (those of) the Church—for, they contend that GOD THE WORD became Flesh by change, and that the Flesh of our Lord was changed into the Nature. of the DIVINITY, and they aim at proving that the DIVINITY and the HUMANITY of our LORD CHRIST constitute One only Nature—Your Holiness, moved by this consideration, has made me come, demanding of me some apology (explanation) relative to these False Doctrines. Moreover, some God-fearing men, Presbyters, have informed your Holiness, that I called the Doctors of the Church Jews.

In consequence of this, I have drawn up this Book of Confession of Faith in order that, by means of it, I might make confession in conformity with the Doctrine

---

* Or "Profession." See 2 Tim., vi, 13. † As Hoffman remarks, this address does not seem to be quite complete or correct.

of the Holy Fathers,—that ONE indeed is the SON of GOD, Who became INCARNATE—GOD The WORD —just as GOD the FATHER is ONE, and the HOLY GHOST ONE.   I, furthermore, confess the DIVINITY of Him, Who became INCARNATE, as well as His HUMANITY, and that, after the Union, they (the DIVINITY and the HUMANITY) remained without confusion—not that GOD The WORD by (any) change whatsoever became Flesh, nor that the Flesh was changed into the NATURE of DEITY—, but (I confess) that, after His Resurrection, our Lord's Flesh was not subject to suffering or corruption or death, but was made glorious in the Glory of the DIVINITY as being the BODY of GOD The WORD.   Notwithstanding, it abides within the properties (limits) of that (Human) NATURE and preserves also the (appearance) impress of the HUMANITY according to that voice of the Holy Angels* viz. "Assuredly this Jesus, Who has been taken up from you into Heaven, shall so come in like manner as you have seen Him go into heaven." In the same way He, our Lord, said to (His) Disciples after His Resurrection† :—"Touch me and perceive that a Spirit has not Flesh and Bones, as ye see that I have."

I anathematize, therefore, those who affirm that there is ONE NATURE (only) of the DIVINITY of CHRIST and of His HUMANITY, and those also who attribute suffering to the DIVINE NATURE, and

---

† Luke xxiv., 39.—See Matthew xxiv, 30, and Daniel vii, 13.
* Acts i, 11.—See John xx, 20 and 27.

do not confess the Properties of the Two Natures—viz., that of Impassibility of the DIVINITY and that of Passibility of the HUMANITY.

I thus confess One Only SON—the same to be GOD before the world, (but become also) Man in these last days—Son of GOD, even the FATHER, in His capacity as GOD, and Son of David in his capacity as MAN, Who is certainly designated the Son of David according to the Flesh, but the Son of GOD as to the DIVINITY*, Who was born of the Virgin Mary as to the Flesh. So, further, I call the Holy Virgin the Mother of GOD; because, in the conception, GOD The Word united to Him The NATURE, which was assumed by Him, that is, PERFECT MAN.

Thus I believe, thus I confess; but those, who hold opinions contrary to these sentiments and speak of these Two NATURES of our LORD CHRIST as One NATURE, which (Natures) were possessed (by Him) without confusion, I anathematize and pronounce strangers to (the True) Religion.

If, however, I am proved, after this Confession written in this book, to hold opinions other than this, or to speak differently in discussion, or to teach (differently) in private—since your Holiness has commanded that we must be content with the instructions given in the Church without any disputations—I confess that I ought to be removed from the Dignity of the Priesthood, to be anathematized as an Heretic, and to be handed over to the Laws.

---

* Romans, Chap. i, verses 3 and 4.

RR

Now, that by my own free will I have written this, and not under compulsion, I take Oath by the Holy Trinity and by the Clemency of the Victorious Lords of the World.

Dioscorus, Bishop of Alexandria, said :—

You have listened to those documents that have been read. It is (now) befitting, that the Venerable John, Presbyter and Proto-Notary, should also inform us whether he has anything else in his hands.

John, Presbyter and Proto-Notary, said :—

Some time ago (or last year), there came to Alexandria a certain Monk, Theodosius by name*, who attracted with him other Monks as well. He said a good deal against Theodoret, who was Bishop of Cyrus, and against the God-fearing Bishop Domnus of Antioch.

---

* After the great Council of Chalcedon, this Monk Theodosius went to Jerusalem, and so excited the monks there against their Bishop Juvenal (who had subscribed to the Council), that they would not receive him any more on his return, but raised Theodosius himself to the Episcopal Throne. But with the help of the Emperor Marcian, (several letters written by him and by the Empress Pulcheria, on this matter, to the Monks, Nuns, and other inhabitants of Jerusalem, and Sinai and Palestine; are given in *Mansi's* Tom. V.) Juvenal was reinstated by the army of the Comes Dorotheus; and Theodosius had to flee. A minute account of this, with some interesting anecdotes, (a blind Samaritan restored to sight, by applying the blood of the killed Monophysites; a zealous Monk throwing a basket full of dust and ashes on the head of Juvenal; an apparation of Christ to Petrus Iberius, whom Theodosius had made Bishop of Gaza; etc.) is to be found in the Ecclesiastical History of *Zacharias* Bishop of Meletina in Armenia. Already *Assemanus* had given some extracts of this work from an incomplete Vatican Manuscript, in Tom. II of the *Bibl. Orient.* p. 54-62, esp. p. 55: and A. Mai printed the whole with a Latin translation in 1838, (Vol. x, Script. Vet. Nova Collectio). But as late as 1870, J. P. N. LAND published from a more

He, also, produced papers containing Homilies and
Exclamations made at Antioch.   And, after there had
been (consequent on the recital of these papers) much
agitation at Alexandria, and all these Monks had
gone and appeared (stood) before the Holy, God-
loving Dioscorus, our Archbishop, and when, though
with difficulty, the Monasteries were kept in order by
the skilful management of him, their Chief, it seemed
good to his Blessedness to write to the God-fearing
Domnus, the Bishop of Antioch.

He wrote a first letter and despatched it by the
hands of Clerics.   The God-fearing Bishop, above-
mentioned, made reply to it, when he wrote a second
letter, and he (Domnus) replied to that also.   Now
we hold all these letters (in our hands) and notify the
fact, in order that you may give what orders you
please (on the subject).

---

complete MS. of the British Museum (Add. 17202), the whole of the
work of *Zacharias Rhetor* in the third Volume of his *Anecdota Syriaca*.
Book iii, Ch. 3—10 treats of Theodosius.   Chap. 9 informs us, that, after his
flight, Theodosius wandered about in the dress of a soldier, confirming
the Monophysites, till he was recognised somewhere near Sidon, and was
taken up and shut up in a small room of a cloister, where he had many
discussions with his opponents, the Eutychians, who wished to consider
him as one of their party, as well as with the Adherents of the Council
of Chalcedon, who tried to win him over to their side.   Towards the
end of his life he was troubled by reason of the Heresy of John Rhetor of
Alexandria, who published several writings under the name of Theodosius
and his friend Petrus of Gaza.   On p. 342-345 of the book quoted,
Land prints, from another MS. of the Brit. Mus. (12174,) another account
of the last days of the "Bishop, Confessor, and Martyr, Theodosius,"
which is also (probably) by Zacharias, who seems to be connected with
Theodosius and his friends, not only through their common belief, but still
closer as a native of Gaza.   There are, however, some slight differences
between these two accounts.   According to the latter, Theodosius went
first to Egypt after his expulsion from Jerusalem, then he desired to get

Thalassius, Bishop of Caesarea, said :—

Let the papers be read and deposited among the accredited Documents.

John, Presbyter and Proto-Notary, read :—

When the Bishop Theodoret was giving Homilies, and said " that GOD assumed (the Form of) MAN, even although it was not pleasing to men," and, again, that " Thomas touched Him Who rose, but worshipped Him Who raised Him (from the dead)," the people shouted these exclamations :—" That is the " Faith of the Apostles—that is The Orthodox " Faith — that is the Faith of Diodorus and " Theodorus—just as Diodorus and Theodorus (be- " lieved), so do we believe.   No man is a believer in

---

to Antioch, to unite his fellow-believers there, but particularly (as some say), to see the holy Simeon, who stood upon a Column in these regions. But before the doors of Antioch he was recognised, as he had lived there some time in the monastery of Mar Bassus.   He was to have been sent to Constantinople by order of the Emperor, but he left him afterwards in charge of the Abbat of a Cloister, named in the Syriac, who tried to convert him first by flattering, then by cruelty.   In consequence of ill treatment, he died on his way to the Capital of the Emperor Leo.   His friends sailed with his body to Cyprus, where it was deposited in a Monastery of the " Orthodox."   His Commemoration was kept on the thirtieth of the first Canun, soon after that of Jacob, the Brother of our Lord; and marvellously, says the writer, it happened, that the Commemoration day of the first Bishop of Jerusalem and that of Theodosius her orthodox Bishop fell together."   On the night of his death, the writer adds, Peter (of Gaza), who was at that time in Alexandria, saw in a vision Theodosius triumphantly accompanied by a host of angels, dressed in the white robe which the Archbishop of Jerusalem used to wear when baptising, and so he was carried into heaven.

We have given this note, as one proof more, how much information, elucidatory of Church History, can be gathered from Syriac sources, especially from the rich Collection in our British Museum. Abbé Martin, notwithstanding, in no enigmatical terms, states that nobody knows what became of this wonderful Monk.

" an Edict—no man receives his faith from an Edict.
" We are servants of the Apostles.   Turn out the
" enemies of the Church—turn out Heretics—him who
" makes (believes) God to suffer, turn out—turn out
" calumniators—turn out Eutyches and Maximianus
" —turn out Heretics.   Let Anathemas rest upon
" those two.   Let the Monastery of Maximianus
" be instantly burnt; let us make him go thither now
" (for that purpose).   He is Satan and not a Monk."

Also, at the time when the *Copiatæ* and *Lecticarii* and the *Laborantes** and some other Brethren
were shouting out these exclamations among the
people, Theodoret in the course of his Homily said
to the people :—" Naboth, the Jezreelite, because
" he would not deliver up the inheritance and
" vineyard of his Fathers, was stoned with stones,
" exclaiming—' I will not deliver up the inheritance
" of my Fathers†.'   Do you, likewise, be zealous for
" the Doctrines of your Fathers, saying—'We will
" not deliver up the inheritance of our Fathers.'
" Now there is nothing strange in this, that they who
" labour for (the true) Religion should suffer evil
" (persecution) ; for, from Above the Blessed Paul

---

* In p. 200, l. 4, ⳡⲟⲡ *Laborantes*. The Syriac word is rendered into this general term which, however, by no means accurately represents
the meaning, nor does any English expression that I am acquainted with do so. We give only an approximation to it. It is
given by Martin, as equivalent to *Ordonnateurs*, apparently ; though he
seems not to wish to indicate that their functions were the same as those
of modern French Ordonnateurs (at Funerals).   Hoffmann, who
consulted a MS. Lexicon of the Library at Halle, translates the Syriac
word into a German one that signifies *Layers of the Table-cloth*.

† Kings xxi, 6.

" teaches (this) when he says :—' all those who will
" live godly in Jesus Christ must (will) suffer persecu-
" tion.   But wicked men and deceivers (seducers)
" will add to (their) wickedness, being deceived and
" deceiving '."*

Again the people cried out—" Magicians to the
Stadium—the attributers of suffering to God to the
Stadium—O Thou, The Alone GOD ! strike them."

And many other such exclamations did they continue to shout out, when provoked to it by expressions of the Homilist.†.

---

* 2 Timothy, iii, 12, 13.   The Text and Syriac N.T. vary from
the Greek.

† In p. 200; l. 25, ܡܦܫܩܢܐ is *the Homilist*, or *the Interpreter*.   At p.
116, Note ‡, it is rendered by Assemanus *Commentator*, seu interpres.
See Bingham iii, Chap. xii, 4.   I have translated it *Homilist*, because it
seems to refer to the deliverer of the Homilies or Conferences—Theodoret.   But, if interpreter is the correct word, then it implies that just as
the reading of the Hebrew Scriptures, after the Dispersion of the Jews,
when that language ceased to be vernacular, required the interpretation or
explanation afforded by the Syriac Targums, or as Uranius Bishop of
Himeria used an interpreter into Syriac of addresses (see page 159) delivered in Greek, so the delivery in Greek of Theodoret's Homilies was
attended by a Syriac Interpreter in order to render their meaning in
telligible to the audience.
Hoffmann in his note refers to Bingham and to *E. A. Frommann, de
hermeneutis veteris ecclesiae, Altdorf* 1747, 4° (which dissertation has been
republished in the Author's *Opusculorum philologici atque historici argumenti
Tomi duo.   Coburgi* 1770, 8°).   It appears from both, that very little is
known about the Office of an Interpreter or *Hermeneuta* in the Ancient
Church.   The most explicit statement is that of Epiphanius (Expos. Fid.
n. 21, i, p. 1104), who ranks him together with the exorcista (ἐπορκιστής,)
and before the *copiata* ; this is confirmed by a passage of Eusebius, *de Mart.
Palaest.* p. 172 (comp. the notes of Valesius) and one of Procopius.
Of course the office was only wanted in Churches where different
languages were used, and it would be interesting to know, whether the
sermons of Theodoret in Antioch were, sentence by sentence, after they
were pronounced by him in Greek, translated by the Interpreter into
Syriac.   We should then have here an Analogon to a similar praxis in
the Synagogue.   (Note from a Syriac Scholar).

COPY OF A LETTER WRITTEN BY THE HOLY ARCHBISHOP
DIOSCORUS, BISHOP OF ALEXANDRIA, THE GREAT (CAPITAL),
TO THE GOD-LOVING DOMNUS, BISHOP OF THE CITY OF
ANTIOCH.

I have been brought to admire the Divine Scripture which exclaims—" If it be possible, as much as lieth on you, make peace with all men,"* but particularly do I admire, O God-loving man ! the Word —" I am at peace with those who hate peace"†— ; and, I judge, I can repeat it with truth ; since, learning it from the Psalmist, I have it constantly impressed on my mind, and, although people should scoff at me, I refuse and fear to return their infamy and scoffing. Yea, even when they show an audacious inclination to strike me and, by act, give proof of their intention, it is not mine to punish (for such acts) ; they must all be borne with, and no great attention ought to be paid to them.

That is my will to occupy myself in matters which concern our Community—(e.g.) that CHRIST is the ONLY BEGOTTEN SON OF GOD and THE FIRST BEGOTTEN, in Whom and by Whom are all things, Who, for our sakes, became INCARNATE and Who has, in no respect whatever, undergone (even) the shadow of a change‡.

With any of those, who, through ignorance or a false belief, have been pushed so far¶, that statements

---

* Rom. xii, 18.   † Ps. cxix, 6.

‡ In the Codex Vaticanus (Vercellone and Cozza, 1871) to which I have easy access, the exact words are—ΠΑΡѠΟΥΚΕ ΝΙΠΑ ΡΑΛΛΑΓΗΗΤΡΟΠΗϹΑΠΟ ϹΚΙΑϹΜΑΤΟϹ.

¶ Or, perhaps, " into (the position of) Dignity, and have advanced statements, &c."

have been advanced by them embodying Blasphemy, which lead to what is unbefitting (the character of) the Great and Profound Mystery of the (Divine) Œconomy—with any of those people, because it is a necessity, and impossible for me to escape it, I do find myself in direct (manifest) antagonism, being reminded of the only wise man who indicates this in saying*—"Everything is good in its season"— "there is a time for war and a time for peace"—"a time to serve and be zealous for the Lord." "Be clothed in the armour of God," Paul never ceases to cry out to us†. Too short would be the time for me, if I wished to quote and point out Sentences of the Divine Writers, which stimulate us‡ to the propriety and duty of resisting manfully, and of turning our faces from, and of hating, those who hate our Lord.

But it is time now for me to disclose the reasons tor, and to show the object of, this letter.

(Some) people give out—and the number of these I believe to be considerable and of an irreproachable life—that all, so to speak, of the Eastern people, zealous and Christ-loving as they are, feel at the present time scandalized and distressed. And, what is of still more importance, (they say) that those persons, who in reality ought to have steered skilfully through,—according to (the laws of their) art—and to have silenced the turmoil of, the approaching

---

* Eccles. iii, 11, and 8. † Eph. vi, 13.

‡ In. p. 202. l. 16 ܡܣܟ would seem to be the correct word, but the original MS. has ܡܣܟ.

waves, are in fact the very parties, who raised the storm through having drunk the poison of the Impious Nestorius, which they do not hesitate to vomit, by their teaching, in the Church, after having given their assent and consent to the Holy and Œcumenical Sy-nod* that took place of old at Nicaea, as well as to its Sister and Consentient one—I refer to that of Ephesus—and after having anathematized the Beast†, that contended with Christ, and all his Impious and unclean Doctrines.

Let any one say, in reference to those of whose acts an explanation has thus been intimated, who they are—and let him dart against them the affixing arrow of the true parable (viz.) "the dog that re-turns to his own vomit and the swine, that was washed, to her wallowing in the mire‡"—(who they are) that are labouring, after having destroyed the middle wall (fence of separation)§, to raise it again, without perhaps paying the matter proper attention, or without saying to themselves, as propriety sug-gests,—" if I build up again what I have pulled

---

* To the decisions, etc., of the 318 Fathers at the Council of Nicæa in 325, A.D., and to those of the Fathers at the General Coun-cil at Ephesus in 431, A.D., those of the Council of Constantinople in 381, A.D., being most probably included.

† Meaning the Heresiarch Nestorius.

‡ ii Peter, ii, 22—We find this expression frequently used. Bingham, Bk., xvii, ii, 3, speaks of an Order of a Council, "that if Clergymen, who are once corrected for their offence, shall relapse, and return to their vomit again, they shall be deprived of their dignity, etc."

§ The Peshitto-text in St. Paul's Epistle to the Ephesians (ii, 14) is . ܠܐܪܓܝܡܒ ܗܘܐ ܩܐܡܕ ܗܘ ܡܨܥ ܐ̈ܣܝ

At p. 203, l. 19, it should be ܠܐ̣ܟܝܢ, l. 21 ܦܠܐ, l. 25 ܠܡܐܘ

down, I am a transgressor of the command."   And
the fact of their having considered it at all and
speaking of it incorrectly, who have undertaken the
office of Priest and Teacher, renders them liable to
the charge of folly, and to be the subject of laugh-
ter.

Now, if in that great Church of Antioch in which
were found assembled a vast concourse of people,
these persons uttered Blasphemous expressions,
without anybody reproving them, who is there to
heal (the wound expressed by) the tears of those
scandalized thereby ?   And who is there that would
not consequently feel heaviness and sorrow, if, at the
very place of healing where it is right and proper for
them to be healed, they should there wither away*,
whilst yet your Piety possessed the power of curing,
yea the power to heal the lame† by word and deed ?

So, I was astonished on learning that, upon an
occasion when an assembly was taking place there
(at the Church in Antioch), that wise Bishop of
Cyrus took authority upon him—whence I know
not—to assert, and that in the presence of your
Perfection, that he was not dividing Immanuel by
affirming that "the mere Man only was palpable to
(touched by) Thomas, and that God only was
worshipped" (by him), "speaking such things out of
his own heart, not out of the mouth of the Lord," as it

* Meaning, " If they should find no remedy."
† Meaning, probably, " the power to apply a perfectly efficacious
remedy."

is written* ; of whom it is time to ask—"what have you been saying ?" or this—" whither are you going ?" and "you walk not circumspectly in forsaking† the Royal Road." " Cease to struggle in opposition to the Divine Scriptures." " Put a door upon, and a bridle, into your mouth." " Be in awe for the voice of the Father, which came from Heaven saying, "This is My Beloved Son in Whom I am well pleased‡." " Do not divide our One Lord Jesus Christ into Two Sons." For, although He became (to be in the Flesh), (derived) from a woman, yet, in the Assumption of the Flesh with a reasonable Soul, He continued to remain what He was before, that is, God. And hear the Philospher Paul, asking you and saying—" Is Christ divided§ ?" No, you will reply, if you do not suppose Two Sons and Two Christs and Two Lords ? Further, immediately meets you the Prophet, who restricts you by saying —" This is our God, and no other is to be compared "with Him. He has discovered all the way of "knowledge and has imparted it to Jacob His "servant, and to Israel beloved of Him. After- "wards, He appeared upon Earth and held converse " with the Sons of Men‖."

In order, too, that the Holy Virgin might be called the Mother of GOD, and the Evangelist be confirmed who writes—" The WORD be-

---

* Jeremiah xxiii, 14.   † Ephesians v, 15.

‡ Matthew iii, 17.   § 1 Corinthians i, 13.   ‖ Baruch iii, 35 and 36.

came Flesh and dwelt among us*," The (One) Who was worshipped by the Cherubin and adored by the Seraphin†—This Same One became like us, for our sake, sate upon a colt the foal of an ass, and, when the servants smote Him upon His cheeks, endured it patiently ¶ in order to fulfil all Righteousness.

These things they have handed down to us, "who from the beginiug were eye-witnesses and ministers of‡ The Word." These are the Doctrines of the Ancient and the Modern Synod. In these, John of Blessed memory, who was the Bishop previously to your Piety, (was consentient) and concurred with us completely.

But once more I turn to you, O God-loving Priest of Antioch and my Brother! and (I pray) you for his sake who never ceased from supporting (upholding§) that Concord (Peace) of the Church common to us and you, which he rendered powerless for men to dis-sever.

(I mention this) because they (alluded to above) are disturbers (of Concord) and highly reprehensible in speaking against a time of peace, not knowing how great a boon it is to live in peace.

Moreover, they composed treatises exceedingly reprehensible inasmuch as these are, according to their

---

* John i, 14.   † Isaiah iii, 2 and 3.
¶ Conformably to the Laws of the Incarnation.
‡ 1 John i, 11.
§ Included, perhaps, is the sense of " drawing closer the bonds of the Concord, Union. "

own statement, in direct antagonism to the
writings of our Blessed and Famous Father and
Bishop, Cyril. This proves beyond doubt that they
are highly reprehensible and not in accord with Holy
Scriptures. *For, our wise and distinguished Father
became the Teacher of the whole world, seeing that
he wrote in a more Catholic and enlightened manner
than all the world besides. He was not only
skilful in speech¶—for, that nature bestowed on
him from early youth—but, being richly endowed
with gifts from Above, he gave an exact Exposition, as It admitted of it, of the MYSTERY of
THE INCARNATION of THE ONLY BEGOTTEN SON
of GOD. And nothing proceeded from him, in which
he did not excel to admiration. Whether a treatise be
named, or a letter, or a set exposition, (Commentary),
or an address (discourse) to a Community, or Chapters,
or Anathematisms, all was exact, and accurate, neat,
and what might be inferred from the Divine Words, so
that it would be truly not inappropriate to say of them—
" Who is wise ? He shall understand them ; and the
" foolish ? and he may know them¶—that the ways of
" the Lord are right and that the Righteous will walk
" therein, but the transgressors shall fall thereby‡."

Now such a commotion, as at present exists in

---

* See one of the extracts in Appendices G, in Vols. 1 and 2.
¶ Or, perhaps, " an excellent Rhetorician." Literally, " elaborator
of words."
¶ Or, " and who the intelligent ? and he will know them."
‡ Hosea xiv, 9.

the Churches, will not stamp out even those members of them that are true Christians¶, although some persons change those (right ways of the Lord), or repudiate them according to their pleasure ; although they silence the Orthodox, and subject them to severe toils, and demand their manuscripts, and compel them to silence ; even although they reverse, so to say, the new order of things, by silencing, (though) in vain, those to whom our Redeemer ordered—"Go and teach all nations* "—whilst allowing those to speak, without let or hindrance, to whom our Master and Redeemer nevertheless† said—"Peace, be still‡." For, "if thou hast "wisdom, give reply to thy neighbour," says the Holy Scripture ; "and if not, let thy hand be upon thy mouth§ "

Besides, however, the above-mentioned circumstances, there is this one, which has occasioned grief to us and to the Egyptian Synod‖,— for, it is only right and just that, when I write to your Holiness, I should, with a frankness and a love befitting Brothers, make known all matters to you openly and without reserve, particularly those that make for the service of and are of utility to the fair name

---

¶ Or, perhaps, "separate (sever) those who are true Christians from the Churches."

* Literally, " necessarily."   † Matthew xxviii, 19.

‡ Mark iv, 39.   § Ecclesiasticus v, 12.

‖ The Church's Synod there.

of the (your) Community as well as to the spiritual* flocks of Christ.

(The matter I refer to is this)—Our Serene and Christ-loving Emperor, the Great Theodosius, being a source of Piety as he is, and that a perennial one, not long ago agreed to make certain Decrees, whereby he delighted the whole earth under Heaven and completely exhibited it as replete with enjoyment and gladness, and wherein he issued distinct orders respecting the writings of Porphyry and Nestorius, and respecting people, who entertain like opinions and make affirmations similarly to them and (so) stand in direct opposition to the Decisions of the Two Supreme and only Synods; to wit, those held at Nicæa and at Ephesus.

Moreover, he further issued a pious and holy Decree against Irenæus the Blasphemer, who had two wives and was unclean and impious and a fellow-believer in Nestorius's profane Doctrine, and removed the man who was without God from the Church of Tyre into exile, (thereby) ridding that Church of the cur that was incessantly barking at and worrying (teasing) the sheep. Now, whereas it is befitting and proper that this Church should have, *forthwith,*

---

* Literally, " reason-endowed," or rational.

See page 169 for quotations and information made about Irenæus from Lupus and the Synodicon.

adorned herself with, and have received, a Priest who knows how " rightly to divide The Word of Truth*," and is competent to administer the means of (spiritual) healing to the people there who have been so situated as if lacerated by some wild animal, a prey to savages, and abandoned to the preverse will of a false Shepherd, we have learnt that she has been in (widowed) sorrow up to the present time, and that many have (been scandalized) taken umbrage at that fact, and that they make mention of your Perfection in no flattering terms, fearing¶ lest there should indeed be, through this so protracted delay, a way for the second time achieved for the Wolf, which, though God permitted it, we cannot desire ; lest the bitter root, germinating afresh, should again occasion trouble, and (so), by its means, many be contaminated.

I therefore pray your Piety, who are not, I think, devoid of that wisdom which yields to the kind requests of Brethren, to rise up now and stop every mouth that utters iniquity against God. But par-

---

* 2 Timothy, ii, 15, ܘܥܕܢܐ ܠܐܡܝܢܐܠ .... ܗܟܢܐ
ܡܢܕܐ ܕܡܪܙܐ.

¶ Or perhaps we may translate it, " fearing the termination of this " wearisome delay (ἀναβολη) will be a second betrothal to that wolf : " the which, supposing God would allow it, we do not hope, lest wolf's " bane might spring up anew, contaminating many."

ticularly do I instruct (counsel) you to cry out to the Orthodox and exhort them to put out (their) silver to the money-changers*. Concede, then, to the Church of Tyre a Bishop. Forthwith ordain, by Imposition of hands, one whom you will test and examine by (the exercise of) that power and authority entrusted to you by God†. For, we are, in this way, participators in your Orthodox acts, God-loving man! if they be (those correspondent to) The Faith. It is true, assuredly, that when one member is honored, all the members are honored with it, and when, on the contrary, one member suffers, the others suffer with it.

---

* Matthew xxv, 27. Metaphorical allusion seems often made in our Syriac MSS. to this text. See Vol. 1, p. 314, (ܫܝܕ) of Dr. W. Wright's "Apocryphal Acts of the Apostles," ܟܣܦܟ ܕܝܗܒܬ ܠܝ ܐܪܡܝܬܗ ܥܠ ܦܬܘܪܟ ܒܚܘܪܝܗܝ. ܘܗܒܝܗܝ ܠܝ ܥܡ ܪܒܝܬܗ ܐܝܟ ܕܐܫܬܘܕܝܬ. which, at p. 280 of Vol. 2, "The Acts of Judas Thomas," is thus rendered: "Thy silver, which Thou gavest me, I have cast down upon Thy table; try it, and give it to me with its usury, as Thou hast promised."

Compare, also, Wright's "Aphraates" p. ܗܐ, 21f., as well as "The Doctrine of Addai" by Dr. G. Phillips, (Trübner, 1876) where occurs this sentence:—ܐܝܟ ܕܦܩܕ ܠܝ ܡܪܝ. ܗܐ ܡܟܪܙ ܐܢܐ ܘܡܫܡܥ ܐܢܐ— ܘܟܣܦܗ ܥܠ ܦܬܘܪܐ ܗܐ ܪܡܐ ܐܢܐ &c. which in the English Translation is thus rendered by Dr. Phillips at p. 22, "As my Lord commanded me, behold, I preach and publish. And his silver on the table, behold I cast before you, and the seed of His Word I sow in the ears of every man."

The term, ὁ τραπεζίτης, *the money-changer* was given to Theodotus who followed the great one of that name, viz. ὁ σκυτεύς *the currier*, the first who asserted Christ to be a mere Man and taught Monarchianism, and who was excommunicated by Victor, in the second Century.

† This passage and other similar ones in our Document imply that Imposition of hands and prayer form the first essential of Ordination and that Episcopal presupposes Sacerdotal Ordination. On this subject we may quote Courayer on the Validity of Orders in the English Church. He says the Scripture does not clearly and distinctly determine the

May this (last alternative), however, be far off on account of the love and affection which we entertain towards each other in Christ!

Now, this letter is communicated to you by my dear friends, Isaiah and Cyrus, Presbyters, whom your Piety will (we hope) regard with pleasure and will be pleased to send back to us immediately. No doubt you will favor us by writing a reply and will pray for us.

---

matter and form of Ordinations but it at least names imposition of hands and prayer, and names nothing else. He continues thus :—

This indication is supported by the testimony of Fathers and Councils, represented in the ancient Pontificials and other Ecclesiastical Books, being found to be conformable to these testimonies, does not leave the least probability of the necessity of any thing else. Nor is the judgment of the Catholic Church so incompetent a tribunal as is supposed. It is not the cause of the Anglicans that is concerned herein ; it is that of the whole Church : and even if the question did concern only the English who reject her infallibility, yet in a matter of this kind, the practice of the Ancient Church alone forms a proof, to which they have always professed to be willing to conform. To reduce then this whole answer to a few words, it is certain that the Scripture implies the sufficiency of the imposition of hands and of prayer, and implies nothing else ; that the Fathers and Councils support it uncontestably ; and that the practice of the Church demonstrates it.

Allowing the Sacrifice to be the Priesthood's Chief Function, on p. 222 we find this: it is certain, says Grabe, that St. Irenæus and all the Fathers, as well those who had seen the Apostles, as those who succeeded them, regarded the Eucharist as the Sacrifice of the New Law, and that they offered the bread and wine as sacred offerings : offering them to God before the consecration, as the first fruits of His creatures, to acknowledge His sovereign dominion over all things ; and after the consecration, as the Body and Blood of Jesus Christ, in order to represent the bloody Sacrifice offered on the Cross, and to obtain the fruits of His death for all them for whom it is offered. This is not, says he, the Doctrine of one particular Church or Doctor, but of the Church Universal. The Church had received it from the Apostles and the Apostles from Jesus Christ. And that this was not the private doctrine of a particular Church or Doctor, but the public doctrine and practice of Church Universal which she received from the Apostles, the Apostles received as the teaching of Christ Himself, Irenæus teaches distinctly, and before him Justin Martyr, and Clement of Rome, Ignatius, Tertullian, Cyprian, and others·

THE LETTER OF DOMNUS THE BISHOP OF THE CITY OF ANTIOCH, WHICH HE WROTE TO THE PIOUS AND HOLY DIOSCORUS THE BISHOP OF THE CITY OF ALEXANDRIA THE GREAT (CAPITAL).

To the Holy Lord and our God-loving Brother and Fellow-minister Dioscorus, Domnus (sends) greeting in our Lord :—

Your Piety's Letter I have read with great pleasure, God-loving man! wherein are exhibited many manifestations of your fraternal affection for me, and indications of the Spiritual nobleness of your God-loving soul.

Now assuredly your Piety learnt the concord subsisting in Evangelical Doctrines, between the God-fearing Bishops of the East and the Holy Fathers who assembled at Nicæa, at the time when many Synodical Tomes used frequently to be despatched from hence to you in the days of the Pious Bishop Cyril of Blessed Memory. Nor was there anything contrary to The Faith in what we wrote to you just lately through the God-fearing Presbyter Eusebius. For, we have demanded of those who have affirmed Doctrines contrariant to The Truth to receive instruction at the hands of your Piety, in order that they may assent both to The Faith, —The Faith of the whole world—as defined by the Holy and Blessed Fathers at Nicæa, and glorified and eulogized by the Holy Fathers assembled at Ephesus, and also to those Letters, written by Cyril of Blessed Memory, to John of Blessed Memory who previously to me governed this Church, in which he (Cyril) set forth the Doctrines (Orthodox) of (The True) Religion.

So also ought the same persons to assent to the Letter which the very Blessed Athanasius* wrote to the Blessed Epictetus.

We should not have (defended) advanced the progress of these Doctrines, or have laboured to convert others to them, had we not been strongly attached to them, as being (among those belonging to) Orthodox and True ones : and we always make assent to, when we preach, them.

As for those who, instead of promoting peace, prefer commotions, not only—

. . . .
. . . .
. . . .

Here the original MS. suddenly breaks off, and the blank leaf opposite represents the break—this " hiatus valde deflendus "—in it as well as the actual blank leaf in the bound Volume in the British Museum. Of the Lacunæ in the MS. this is the first one that is indicated in the Volume. The first actual break, which occurs in the early part, is not indicated by a blank vellum leaf, as we have remarked in a note at foot of the p. 27.

---

* The splendid large Volume in the British Museum, numbered Add. MS. 12,156, written against the great Chalcedon Council and attributed to the guidance, if not to the pen, of Timothy Ælurus contains in Syriac this famous Letter.

. . . .

. . . .

. . . .

in all those matters belonging to God—in order to silence intemperate tongues, but exhort those who have given credence to these calumnies, not to lend their ears to mendacious reports.

Now, as regards the Holy Church at Tyre we have had some conversation on the subject with the Honored and God-fearing Presbyters, Isaiah and Cyrus, whom, whilst we praise them as noble in their bearing and for the wisdom of their God-loving souls, we have looked upon for the time being and have regarded, as our own Clergy ; and we have admired the choice of your Piety.

We, also, requested them to repeat to your Piety all that they had witnessed, and we ask your Reverence to hold us in remembrance (in your prayers) and to gratify us with a reply in writing from all the Brotherhood that are with you.

I and those with me desire (to offer) salutation.

(Here) ends the Letter, written by Domnus the Bishop of Antioch, to the Holy Dioscorus the Bishop of Alexandria.

From this conclusion of the Letter it is evident that the preceding great hiatus, alluded to above, occurs in the Letter commencing as at the heading on page 339.

This page also is evidence of the good feelings existing between the Patriarchs, Domnus and Dioscorus up to a certain period, it may not be here inappropriate to remark.

COPY OF A LETTER WRITTEN BY THE HOLY BISHOP
DIOSCORUS TO THE GOD-FEARING BISHOP DOMNUS,
THE BISHOP OF ANTIOCH.

When any matter of grave and urgent import
presses—of a nature which would occasion a great
deal of harm to the soul, if it were neglected—then,
just then, to rest and be at ease would be the act
of a slothful mind and of one that knows not how to
awaken itself.*   May this condition of things,
however, be a great way removed to a distance from
us, so that they " who seek to find occasion " may
" obtain none occasion† ! "

For this reason I would wish to write what is
amicable at all times and to make use of a pacific
kind of writing, as well as to meet with a reciprocation ;
for, that is an indication of unanimity in the
Churches and of a consentient Catholic Faith.

But, probably, I am wanting that which is
impossible.

However, what I do say is this.   Affairs (now instant) oblige me to this by their not proceeding in a
straight path but in a tortuous one, especially in a lame
sort of way.   Even in insignificant and unimportant
matters, we should, nevertheless, not proceed insen-
sible to it, but as matters now stand, (actual) principles are jeopardized ; and how can we be exonerated
from reproach by an unjustifiable (inopportune)
silence ?

---

* Meaning, probably, " to awaken itself to energy."
† Daniel vi, 4. 2 Corinthians, ii, 12.

Knowing, then, how to exclaim with the wise Paul
and say—" Who shall separate us from the love of
" Christ ? shall tribulation, or distress, or persecution,
" or famine, or nakedness, or peril, or sword ? 'as it
" 'is written, For thy sake are we killed all the
day long,*' " I have, with this Example and
Teaching, come for the purpose of writing again
this time to urge your Piety to restrain certain
Teachers with you, leading them to what is consistent
with propriety and duty, who magnify themselves, presuming that they can speak well, and consequently
entertain very high opinion of themselves ; whilst, I
am certain, they scandalize very many people and
are naturally laughed at, "understanding neither

---

* Romans viii, 35.

The Codex Vaticanus thus gives this beautiful passage with the
quotation.

. . . . TIC
HMACXWPICEIAПOTHC
AГAПHCTOYΘYTHCE
XWIYΘΛEIΨICHCTENº
XWPIΔ HΔIWГMOCHΛEI
MOC HГYMNOCTHCH
KINΔYNOC HMAXΔIPA
" KAΘWCГEГPAПTAIOTI
" ENEKENCOYΘANATOY
" MEΘAOΛHNTHNHME
" PANEΛOГICΘHMENWC
" ПPOBATACΦAГHC·

UU

what they say nor whereof they affirm*." But it is a matter to be provided for by your Piety that you take the bridle and rein, and put restraint upon the contentions of those who war against God ; for, it is against Him that they are reported to have had the audacity to assert that the Impious and Profane Nestorius received (the punishment of) Deposition, not for having deviated from the Royal Road, nor even because he had opened a mouth of Blasphemy against CHRIST, although he mixed spurious (stuff) with The Evangelic and Apostolic Faith, but they say (it was) because he refused to put himself forward and assemble with the Holy and Œcumenical Synod which was, by the will of God, convened at Ephesus, and (they say) he was not in reality prohibited an entrance into the Blessed and Holy Synod.

It is the fact, that he did not trust himself to enter that Blessed and Holy Synod. I confess the same ; for, "what concord has belief with unbelief and "what (concord) has Christ with Satan ? "

But what really caused him to avoid intercourse with the Holy Synod, although It summoned him to (appear), was nothing else but his being kept back by a reproaching conscience. For, it is true to say :— "The wicked (man) fleeth when no one pursueth him‡."

Further, he also showed us another example¶, as far

* 1 Timothy, i, 7.
† 2 Corinthians, vi, 15.
‡ Proverbs xxviii, 1
¶ Or, perhaps, " he manifested himself to us as an example (of warning)."

as he was a Heretic and a false Scribe who in every respect resembled his Father, that is, the Devil; and he was prevented from approaching, and holding converse with, any Holy Orthodox Fathers whatever, according to a certain true old adage which declares that "it is well (and proper) for the wicked to depart "(be withdrawn) that he may not behold the "Majesty of the Lord*," · which (Majesty) then descended and blessed those assembled together, —no man can doubt it, if he use correct and holy knowledge, being also mindful of the Lord's voice promising expressly that " where two or three are "gathered together in my name, there am I in the "midst of them†." If, therefore, when only two are met together, or three for purposes of good, in the midst of them is CHRIST immediately present, causing the bystanders to fear and tremble because of (such a) Synod, how is it that some people have no hesitation in presuming to contemn the Synod of Ephesus and to separate it from the Holy Synod that took place on a previous occasion at Nicæa, whereas the task of both these‡ two Synods was one and the same: (viz.) to contend in conjunction on behalf of the Glory of Christ. The

---

* There is probably a reference in this passage to a sentence of the great Evangelical Prophet who says:—" Let favour be shown to the wicked, yet will he not learn righteousness: in the land of uprightness will he deal unjustly, and will not behold the Majesty of the Lord."

† Matthew xviii, 20.

‡ The Council of Nicæa " determined nothing new." The words of Acesius, as quoted by Canon Bright, to the Emperor Constantine,

one excommunicated Arius and the other Nestorius. The former left the whole world freed from error, whilst its successor (at Ephesus), by confirming the Decisions (of Nicæa), has woven for itself an imperishable crown—

. . . .

. . . .

. . . .

Here occurs the second of the Lacunæ in the Original MS., and the opposite blank page, with the dotted lines, represents, as the one before, the break and the vellum leaf in the MS.

Hoffman who is very competent to express a reliable opinion on the subject is of opinion that six or seven leaves are missing.

---

show that the sacred Deposit, " The Faith once and once for all delivered to the Saints," " Catholic Truth " was effectually reasserted. " The Definition of Faith agree with what I have learned by tradition from the Apostles," said he. Its dire enemy Arianism struggled on till the second General Council when the Faith's Victory was completely won. But Nestorianism, notwithstanding its Anathematisation by the Great Council of Ephesus in 431 A.D., continued afterwards and continues now to flourish in the East.

. . . .

. . . .

. . . .

—(and I hope that your Piety) will administer reproof to those who have a longing for violating—I
know not why—the peace of the Churches subsisting
with us and with you, and who have occasioned
scandal not only to many Monks in the East, but
also to Venerable Monks with us (at Alexandria) ;
for, coming over from there, they walk about in the
Monasteries of Alexandria, retailing these rumours
to persons who have withdrawn from the corrupting
influences of the world.   Consequently, these Monasteries are at present in an complete state of
commotion (excitement), and but one cry is heard ;
(viz.) "he that has disturbed us shall (some day)
"receive his punishment, whosoever he may be."

To your Piety, then, belongs the duty of reflecting
in what confusion we find ourselves ; and what will
you do to calm the multitude ?—(I will tell you)—
you should read my letter in the Assembly of the
Faithful (the Community).

If giving offence to (scandalizing) "one of the little
ones that believe in Christ " suffice to expose (us) to a
judgment (at once) complete, severe, and valid,
to what end will that scandal lead us which has
thrown so many Monks into murmuring and dis-
quietude ?

Nevertheless, we ought to reflect that our Redeemer is competent to allay all the commotion ; for, "in "Him we live and move and have our being."

(*a*) Dioscorus, Bishop of Alexandria, said :—

This Holy and Great Synod has heard what I wrote to the God-fearing Bishop Domnus when I was desirous to preserve everywhere the peace of the Churches intact and you are my witnesses that I did not permit anything beyond what propriety allows. Will your Reverences say whether I have written anything contrariant to Catholic Truth ?

(*b*) The Holy Synod, said :—

"These words agree with those of the Fathers— "These are the sentiments of the Fathers—These "are consentient with the Orthodox Faith—These "accord with the Faith of the Fathers—These are "the Doctrines of the Fathers at Nicæa—These agree "with the Two Synods—whoever keeps these secret "is not Orthodox—whoever does not proclaim these "before men is not Orthodox. He who is a calum- "niator of these is not Orthodox. He who has "written what is in opposition to these is not "Orthodox."

(*c*) Dioscorus, Bishop of Alexandria, said :—

From (these outward) expressions we discern that which characterises your Reverences and the Divine zeal settled in your hearts.

Now be induced to hear, also, what was written to me by him (Domnus).

[14] John, Presbyter and Prime Notary, read :—

To the Holy and God-loving, our Brother and Fellow-Minister, Mar Dioscorus, Domnus (sends) Greeting in our Lord :

To be intent on motives (subservient), and bent on means conducive, to peace in God,—promptly to baffle those conducive to division and strife—is righteous.

Now Your Holiness is perfectly aware of the causes of the Dispute, of that long standing Dispute, which has all but reached the ends of the world.

It was with difficulty that the efforts of the Christ-fearing and Gracious Emperors, together with the wisdom of those also who adorn our Episcopal Thrones, brought together what was dispersed. For, the Blessed John who before our Humbleness governed the East was bent on peace with all his soul. He assented to the Royal promises (propositions) ; and the Blessed Cyril, who before your Holiness used to rule Egypt, manifested a similar solicitude and desire on behalf of the same. For, when we learnt from him who is of Blessed Memory, (viz.) Paul of Emesa, that the 12 chapters were acceptable to the Easterns, he abstained making any mention of anyone of these in letters addressed to the Blessed John, but, concurring in those explanations (propositions), transmitted thence, in re-

---

The above allusion is to the Nestorian Controversy which was by no means set at rest by the Council of Ephesus A.D. 431, although the Church declared Nestorianism to be Heresy and exiled the Heresiarch, nor did it terminate with the happy results arising between the reconciliation of

lation to the INCARNATION of our Redeemer, he
indited the assenting reply, and eradicated hostility,
and restored peace to the Holy Churches of God
throughout the world; and so, by God's Grace, up to
the present time the Churches of the East and West
have had (abiding) concordant Union in God.

Now this (peace), I pray, let us preserve and not
become exciters of another Division in the Churches.
For, if the God-loving Bishops and Venerable Clerics
should learn, as well as the Faithful Communities (of
the Laity) of the East, that we make mention of
these (Articles) Chapters, your Holiness may rest
assured that they would shun communication with
me; and, if the Christ-loving ones of this Apostolic

John of Antioch and Cyril of Alexandria through the instances of the
Emperor and the Good Offices of Paul of Emesa in 433 A.D., April 23,
when the latter announced the true Doctrine as their ancestral treasure
among the delighted audience of Cyril's Church, or even after Cyril had
written his magnificent letter, beginning " Let the Heavens rejoice."

The Emperor's proferred promises, or propositions made in his last
attempt at reconciliation through the Tribune and Notary Aristolaus to
John of Antioch, refer to the acceptance by the latter, of certain
Dogmas in order to move him to peace with Cyril. Theodosius reminded him how little it became the Bishops who ought to be the
Teachers of Charity to trouble, by their misunderstanding, the peace of
the Churches and gave him distinctly to understand, that if his exhort-
ations were not sufficient to re-establish a concord with which were so
closely bound up both the welfare of religion and that of the Empire, he
would know how to resort to more cojent reasons. The " Propositions "
included the Confession that Christ was Perfect God and Perfect Man,
that there was an union of the Two Natures in the One Christ, that the
Virgin Mary was the Mother of God, &c., all which Cyril readily
accepted, notwithstanding John's showing by word of mouth his opposition
to Cyril's 12 Anathemas.

The word ܥܕܠܘܨܐ in lines 5 and 17, p. 226 means *excitatores*
from ܕܠܨ but neither Castell nor Scaaf gives the sense. Hoffman
seems to render it by a German term signifying *Pioneers*.

VV

Church now also become acquainted with that, as a fact, be assured of this, God-loving man, that they either (will) openly contemn us or allow the Churches to lie waste and desolate. To such an extent will they resist the mentioning of these (Articles) Chapters. Let us not, then, I beg, be exciters of commotion in the Churches,—commotion which (once aroused) cannot easily be allayed, but let us stand to the written (treaties or) propositions for Peace, and confirm the letter of the Blessed Cyril and that of Saint Athanasius which he addressed to Epictetus. For, one of the clauses in the Articles of Peace treats of their being mentioned ; and as regards those who are resolved on reviving commotions, and—mark my word !—on picking advantage by Divisions, let us turn away from them in disgust as the enemies of Peace : for, be well assured, God-loving man ! that we were bitterly grieved, on being informed, that when the (Eucharistic) Solemnities were celebrated, some of the Monks living with you had the audacity to shout before the congregation and to say— " whether you like it or not, *God died.*"

What is worse than this Blasphemy ? This the followers of Arius never dared to say. Your Piety, it is true, was quite scandalized by it, as we have been informed, but there was no reproof from you of those who had defiled themselves with such Impiety, as was befitting and proper, in order that the rest also might learn, through them, the heinousness of this Impiety. I, therefore, pray that they may not be allowed to enjoy any freedom of speech whatever on these subjects, and that the Anathemas should rest upon them ; for, they have, before now, agitated us with disturbance of (our) Peace.

Further, we have sufficiently convinced your Piety, on a former occasion, as regards the God-loving Bishops and Venerable Clerics of the East, that they all give assent to The Faith which was formulated (as set forth) by the Blessed and Holy Fathers at Nicæa, in Bithynia, and to which the Synod that assembled in Ephesus acknowledged its assent (and consent) also.

This (Faith) I and they most unhesitatingly preach ; and this (Faith) we teach to those who offer themselves for Most Holy Baptism. For this (Faith) we take upon our ourselves to suffer everything. We understand It just as the very Blessed Fathers did—(viz.) Damasus Bishop of Rome the Great Capital, and Ambrose of Milan, and Cyprian, the Shining Light of Lybia ; and Alexander and Theophilus and Athanasius, your Lights ; and the Very Blessed Ignatius and Eustathius who adorned the Synod of Nicæa ; and Miletius who lived (was exiled) for It a long time beyond his Province ; and Flavian who accepted the Exarchate ; and Basil and Gregory who were illustrious in the Pontic Province ; and John and Atticus who ruled the Royal City in the High Priesthood and whosoever has pronounced what is in accord with them—with these men we are in accord ; the (confessions) of these we commend : those who hold opinions opposite to these we pronounce to be strangers to Grace : these all the God-loving Bishops of the East support.

I request, therefore, of your Piety to be solicitous for and aim at peace , and not to give a single occasion for Division. As regards ourselves, being anxious for (not to disturb) this (Peace), we have not made public those letters just lately despatched (to us) by your Piety, in order to avoid kindling a great conflagration (of commotion).

That all the Brotherhood in Christ who are with thee may have Peace is the frequent prayer of myself and of those with me !

[15] (*d*) Dioscorus, Bishop of Alexandria, said :—

Who (now) seems to your Reverences to reject the twelve Chapters of our very Blessed Father Cyril ?

[3] The Holy Synod said :—

Anathema to him who rejects these !—Let him who does not receive these be Anathematised !

. . . .

. . . .

. . . .

.

The missing leaves in this hiatus, no doubt, if ever discovered will be found to report the sentences of the President of the Council and of other Bishops, as well as the commencement of Bishop Juvenal's.

. . . .
. . . .
. . . .

[*(c)* Juvenal, Bishop of Jerusalem, said :—]

* * * * * * * * * * * * * * * * *
* * * * * * * * * * * * * * * * *

what was written by the wise Solomon applies thus also to him (viz*.) " Who tears down a hedge, (fence) him will the snake bite." For, his Impiety has rendered him alien to the Honour of the Episcopate and to all the Function of the Priesthood.

(*d*) Thalassius, Bishop of Cæsarea, said :—

The letters which have just now been read to us of the Holy Archbishop Dioscorus and those that were written in reply to his Holiness by Domnus the Bishop of Antioch have not before come to our knowledge. Since, however, now that the reading of them has taken place, we have ascertained their meaning and perceive that they are at variance with the Holy Synod which was once assembled here, we for our part adjudge Domnus to be removed from (alien to) the Office of the High Priesthood.

(*e*) Stephen, Bishop of Ephesus, said :—

To how great an extent did Domnus, the late Bishop of Antioch, err, when he became infected with the Impiety of Nestorius ! For, whilst he concealed his views, he laboured to so great a degree to avoid disclosing what he really was. But since the Truth of God is superior to all intrigue, it has not allowed

---

* Eccles. x, 8.

the here (arising) injury to become serious. For, as we have ascertained from the letters just now read to your Blessedness that there is not the least excuse for any one to contend with God by taking in his own person the evil office of Calumniator, for that reason must he (Domnus) receive a punishment after the analogy of those who are charged with being Nestorians, suffering the same Deposition as they, and be removed from the Honor of the Episcopate and be considered unworthy of the Commnnion of the Pure Mysteries. For, this in concurrence with your Holy Synod is my decision.

(*f*) Eusebius, Bishop of Ancyra, said :—

Domnus, as I have learnt from the Epistolary missives which have just now been read, holds Doctrines antagonistic to those of the Blessed Cyril, and, moreover, antagonistic to the Decrees of the Holy Fathers at Nicæa and of those Fathers who assembled at Ephesus. I, for my part, adjudge him to be removed from the Honor of the Episcopate.

(*h*) Cyrus, Bishop of Aphrodisias of the Carians, said :—

It is evident from those Epistolary messages which have been just now read that Domnus of Antioch holds Doctrines antagonistic to those of the Holy Fathers at Nicæa and to those of the Holy Fathers who, on a former occasion, assembled in this place. I, therefore, assenting to the Holy Fathers before me determine that he be removed from the Honor of the Priesthood.

(*i*) Meletius, Bishop of Larissa, who also occupied the place of the Venerable Domnus, Bishop of Apameia, said :—

It has become known, through the letters that have been read, that Domnus who was Bishop of Antioch held opinions contrary to those of the Holy Fathers. Therefore, on learning this, I also along with the Holy Fathers do pronounce my decision, and I adjudge him to be removed from (alien to) all the Honor of the Episcopate and of the Priesthood.

(*j*) Diogenes, Bishop of Cyzicus, said :—

To what has been decided on by the Holy Fathers I give my assent, as well as to the transactions (directed) against Domnus of Antioch who once was Bishop (there).

(*k*) John, Bishop of Sebastia (Sebaste), said :—

For a man to make war with the teachings of the Fathers is nothing else but to inflict upon himself wounds for which there is no cure. Now Domnus, who was at one time Bishop of Antioch, in presuming (to attempt) to change those XII Chapters, formulated in conformity with the Faith and Charity by him of Blessed and Pious Memory, the Archbishop Cyril, has laboured to discompose the Peace of the Catholic Faith. He ought, for that reason, to be removed from the Grade of the Priesthood in consequence of his Blasphemy.

(*l*) Basil, Bishop of Seleucia of Isauria, said :—

Antagonism is evident between the Orthodox Doctrines of the Church and the letters, written by Domnus Bishop of Antioch, to his Perfection the Holy Archbishop Dioscorus of Alexandria, wherein he has blamed the Blessed Cyril's XII Chapters that the Synod long since received which, by the Grace of God, assembled at Ephesus. For this reason, following after you, Fathers ! I adjudge that he be removed from the Honor of the Priesthood.

(*m*) Photius, Bishop of Tyre, said :—

As regards Domnus who was Bishop of Antioch, I state for my part that I give my assent to the Holy and Blessed Synod, and I reckon he ought to be removed from the Honor of the Episcopate, because he is a follower of Nestorius.

(*n*) Theodorus, Bishop of Damascus, said :—

From the letters that have just now been read, Domnus who was the Bishop of Antioch appears to hold the opinions of Nestorius, and for that reason I also cause him to be deprived of all the Honor of the Priesthood and of Communion in the Holy Mysteries.

(*o*) Mares, Bishop of Dionysias, said :—

I, too, give my assent to the just Sentence of the Holy Fathers, which has been pronounced upon Domnus who was Bishop of Antioch, and I do deprive him of all the Honor of the Priesthood and of Communion with the Laity.

(*p*) Olympius, Bishop of Sozopolis, said :—

I give my assent to all that has been decided on in reference to Domnus, who was the Bishop of Antioch, by (this) Holy, Great and Œcumenical Synod. For that reason I likewise deprive him of the Honor of the Priesthood and of Communion in the Holy Mysteries.

Thus ends the trial of the great reticent Patriarch of the great Capital of Antioch, Domnus II ; and thus end the proceedings, under cover, not thick, of the Œcumenical Form of the ecclesiastical procedure of the Tribunal of the Catholic Church, of the celebrated Triumvirate, the over-reaching Chrysaphius, the astute but dogged Archimandrite Eutyches and the marvellously infamous Archbishop Dioscorus—proceedings which, as devoloped by the discovery of this invaluable Syriac Document purporting to be the very Acts of the latter session or sessions of the second Conncil of Ephesus, will, in the eyes of the nineteenth century, more than ever justify the appropriateness of the scarthing Epithet with which St. Leo, the Great, branded this council, when in his celebrated Letter he for ever designated it as the

LATROCINIUM EPHESINUM.

LAUS DEO.

XI.

[EDICT OF THE EMPEROR THEODOSIUS II. AVOUCHING THE AUTHORITY OF THIS COUNCIL*.]

(TRANSLATION.)

We cannot by any means allow that the Laws proclaimed for the benefit of the Community be consigned to oblivion, or, again, that the Salutary Ordinances of our (Imperial) Government be depraved by the presumption of others.   On the contrary, with that philanthropy which is constantly exercised by us, we apply ourselves to correct acts of presumption : that is, however, without (having recourse to) capital punishment, and only by a tempering of menace we reach those who are the originators (of crime) as well as prevent others from offending in the same manner. As to wit : when Nestorius attacked the Adorable Religion which the Fathers handed down (to us) and which Holy Priests assembled of old at the City of Nicæa from every quarter (of the world) for the purpose of confirming and consolidating—when (afterwards, I say,) this Nestorius publicly proclaimed positions (of Doctrine calculated to conduce) to the prejudice and injury of the simple (the Faithful), immediately our Clemency, in case the evil, creeping in by a licence of speech, should render obdurate the minds of the simple-minded, rather (if it be proper

---

* "Translation" here implies that, first, the Roman Law was written in Latin and Greek.   Then the original Greek Transcriber of that Law so written rendered into it Greek for the Church's Synod or for some of the Metropolitans, and finally the Syriac transcriber (see his note at the end) of the Greek Acts brought it into his MS. which we now possess.

to speak the truth) lest it should destroy them completely, gave orders that the Bishops should assemble, not inconsiderately and suddenly—for, it was no little or trifling subject on which there was deliberation, but one relating to our Adorable Religion, (the principles of) which uphold and consolidate our Kingdom—that, for this purpose, Expounders and Doctors of the Divine Religion, selected from the whole Empire, as is right and just to say, of the Romans, should proceed to and assemble together at Ephesus in order to search into and investigate, with a judgment prompted by Religion and Justice, certain hitherto insoluble (unsolved) questions which we brought to their remembrance, who not only consolidated and confirmed for us The Faith which was from the beginning transmitted to us, but, having proved the controversy of the aforesaid Nestorius to be groundless, deposed him from the Throne of the Episcopate and divested him of (its) Dignity.

After (the Report of) all these transactions, therefore, had been despatched and read over to our Clemency, we remitted to them their judicial sentence so pleasing to God, and, by a salutary Law which has necessarily been promulged, we enjoined that the aforementioned Nestorius and his participators in Impiety should be deprived of the company of Christians and name of (Christian).

We, further, decreed that they should be designated Simonians, because, according to the investigation of the Holy Priests, they followed the practices of that person, (Simon,) and, by a just punishment which is clearly laid down in our Injunctions, we determined that they should be so designated.

Although, then, these results had been accomplished on principles of Religion and Justice, Flavian and Eusebius resolved to resuscitate what had been set at rest by Our Clemency, and presumed to renew the depraved error of Nestorius in opposition to the Injunction of Our Clemency, and threw into the Churches the divisions and scandals of Heretics when silenced and at rest. Consequently, our Clemency, bound by necessity, commanded that Holy Bishops should go from various and distant cities and assemble at Ephesus the City afore-named in order that, on the eradication, by vigour and God-loving deliberation, of the pernicious seed from the (very) roots, The Faith alone might grow up (floursh).

Nor have we been disappointed in our expectation. For, after the whole of the investigation which they undertook had become less and less and (finally) closed, and the Holy Religion, which from the beginning had been handed down to us, become truly and powerfully strengthened, those persons, so often named above, together with their co-adjutors, (viz.) Domnus, who is said to preside over the Church of Antioch, and Theodoret and certain other persons, beguiled by the same ignorance, were deposed from the Throne of the Episcopate, because they showed themselves unworthy of so great a Dignity by corrupting the Word of Truth.

Moreover, it was resolved by a God-fearing Decree to determine that no one should by any means dare— not even partially—to deprave the Decision (Definition) of the CCCXVIII Bishops who assembled at Nicæa, nor to presume to add to, or subtract anything from, It.

.   .   .   .

.   .   .   .

.   .   .   .

The break in the MS. here which may be the loss to us of several folios interrupts the continuity of this interesting Document of the Roman Empire.

Mansi has this in Vol. VII. Interpretatio legis a Theodosio Imperatore Juniore cum seductus fuisset a Chrysaphio adversus Flavianum et socios pro Eutyche promulgata : quam religiosissimi Marciani Principis lex subsecuta destruxit.

Generalem promulgavimus legem, quae tam praedictum Nestorium quam eos qui ei similia sapiunt, damnat ; praecipientes ne Christiano saltem nomine censerentur sed ut Simoniani potius vocarentur quoniam blasphemiam Simonis dilexerunt.

. . . .

. . . .

. . . .

and considering your work as our own, seeing we honor you as a Father, we pray your Piety (Dioscorus) to draw up Circular Letters in which to insert this our God-loving Law, the Creed of our Holy Faith and the Definition of the Two Synods afore-mentioned, as well as this—that "nobody shall add to "It, even one word, or subtract from It, and that "nobody shall presume to interpret It, seeing that It "is Its own expositor and obvious to everybody."

Your Piety, having then taken copies of It, will despatch It to the Venerable Bishops of the Royal City of Constantinople and Jerusalem, and to the other Metropolitans, in order that all those Bishops, suffragan to them, may sign It also and forward It to us with those letters, notifying the same to us, and (in order that) every one of the Bishops who has a copy may read It in Church before all the people. But before anything else, your Piety, with all your Suffragan Bishops, will append your signatures, and forward the same to the Auditory of our Serene Highness. Finally, as often as your Piety receives information of Books of any author, written in antagonism to the Orthodox Faith heretofore or at the present time, or containing to the injury of mankind the polluted Doctrine of Nestorius,—seeing we know nothing of these, these could not be inserted in our Statute—your Piety will order that, on being

xx

claimed and delivered up, they must be committed to the flames by the hands of the God-fearing Bishops according to our Law which was enacted on purpose to destroy everything that is in antagonism to our Holy Faith from the (very) root.

CORRESPONDENCE BETWEEN OUR FAITHFUL AND GOD-LOVING EMPEROR THEODOSIUS AND JUVENAL THE BISHOP OF JERUSALEM*.

Seeing our Clemency has excercised great solicitude on behalf of The Holy Faith in the matter of those scandals that have sprung up concerning It and disturbed the peace of the Holy Churches of God, I now likewise command, by a God-loving Edict, all Venerable Bishops to subscribe to The Holy Faith of Nicæa and to the Definition concerning It communicated by these two Holy and Œcumenical Synods established in compliance with the will of our Clemency, and that nothing is to be added to It, not even a word, or subtracted from It, because It is final (perfect), as That Which has been accomplished by the co-operation of the HOLY GHOST.

. . . .

. . . .

. . . .

The opposite blank leaf represents another hiatus and the blank vellum leaf in the original MS.

---

* Or thus—" A letter, in reply, of our Faithful and God-loving Emperor Theodosius to Juvenal the Bishop of Jerusalem."

[XII.]

ENCYCLICAL LETTER OF THE ARCHBISHOP DIOS-
CORUS TO THE BISHOPS.—DEFICIENT AT THE
BEGINNING.

. . . . -

. . . .

(1) [The Books of Nestorius and his deposed partisans
must be destroyed,] so that we do not abandon the
country to their designs and will ; and it becomes
necessary for this to be done, when their statements,
but little Orthodox, get embellished with (are put
under the cover of) the names of other (authors),
whilst it ought at the same time to be publicly known
that the Treatises of the Blessed Fathers and of the
Orthodox Doctors who have excelled (so much) in
the Orthodox Faith or who were at the two Holy
Synods (at Ephesus), wholly possessed with the (True)
Religion, must continue (in ure) for ever ; seeing that
they possess excellence and exactitude but by no
means any human doctrines or positions injurious to
The Faith (Symbol) spoken of, to wit, to the Creed of
the CCCXVIII Bishops as well as the Definitions of
the two Holy Synods who assembled at Ephesus—
treatises that should be exhibited and, when approved,
be of force. The Books, however, (of Nestorius and
others) must be committed to the fire, seeing they
are written in antagonism with the peace of the Holy
and Immaculate Faith i.e. with the Symbol of the
CCCXVIII Bishops and with the Definition of the

two Holy Synods alluded to.   For, these, (the Symbol and the Definition) have been proved by (being received by) all the world to be unimpeachable and to be the Mothers of the Orthodox Faith.

That the Christ-loving Emperor has settled by a Law, and all of us have received that Law with gladness and thankfulness.

This point*, however, must not be omitted which the Law itself of the Community has deemed deserving of solicitude (care) : for, it says that " nobody who is a follower of Nestorius or who " holds such opinions as his shall be admitted to the " Priesthood : and further, that he who may have been " (so admitted) by surprise shall be removed from the " Grade of the Priesthood and shall not be reckoned " among the number of Priests, but that such persons " must rather be driven from every place, and not be " allowed to be received by any body into houses or " into public company, so that they may be appre- " hensive of (incurring) the punishments prescribed by " the Law, who act in violation of the Law."

This is what we would wish to urge (viz.) : it is for your Holiness to notify all this to the Metropolitans under your Authority and to require of them the observance of it, the Forms of Votes (or of

---

* Mansi vii, 497.

Sed nec habeat aliquis, aut legat, aut transcribit, proferatve Nestorii vel (decreta) terminosque, aut codices noxios, et maxime quos contra solas Porphyrius edidit Christianas literas ; neque Theodoreti scripta, sed quicunque hujusmodi codices habet, publice illos proferat, et cunctis videntibus igni tradantur.

Declarations) being transmitted to them. All, who assent to what has been decreed by the Christ-loving and Gracious Sovereign, should subscribe. All has been ordered well and shonld be observed with all vigilance. And in this way, by means of the Anaphoræ (report), it will be notified to our God-loving Emperor that legality has been observed in these (Ordinances) which Our Serene Highness has for our part determined on and arranged; whilst the execution of them has been undertaken, in a friendly manner, by his Excellency Eulogius the Prætorian Tribune and Notary, whose fidelity and ability, on many other occasions and not the least on the occasion of these present transactions at Ephesus, our Christ-loving Emperor received instances of, and we ourselves have much admired : inasmuch as we have received many proofs of his importance (intelligence)·

FORM OF SUBSCRIPTION.

I. M. Bishop of the City of N. have subscribed to what is written above in this Law, and I stand to it all, and I consent to observe everything that is written in this Letter, without adding to, or leaving out, anything inserted therein.

(HERE) ENDS THE LETTER OF THE HOLY ARCH-BISHOP OF ALEXANDRIA WHICH HE WROTE TO THE REST OF THE VENERABLE BISHOPS.

(HERE) ENDS THE SECOND SYNOD WHICH ASSEMBLED AT EPHESUS IN THE DAYS OF THE HOLY AND GOD-LOVING DIOSCORUS, BISHOP OF ALEXANDRIA AND IN THE DAYS OF THE VICTORIOUS EMPERORS, THEODOSIUS AND VALENTINIAN.

GLORY BE ASCRIBED TO THE FATHER AND TO THE SON AND TO THE HOLY GHOST—ONE PERFECT MYSTERY OF THE TRINITY—FOR EVER. AMEN.

[THE SCRIBES POSTSCRIPT.]

This book was finished* in the year MCCCXLVI, according to the reckoning ot Alexander, in the month of Jor, on the† 10th thereof, in the Holy Monastery of the Blessed Mar Eusebius of Kafra D'Bartha, in the days of the Priest-Archimandrite John, the excellent and God-loving watchful Shepherd, the Governor, full of wisdom‡, merciful to strangers, a firm adamantine wall reared for (the defence of) his Flock that none of the ravenous wolves may break through and do harm to any one of the lambs in the Monasteries which are gathered together within the peaceful fold. From that God, for whose name's sake he has laboured, and for whose Holy Monastery he has acquired this book, may he, on that great and terrible day§, when the resounding trumpet, breaking open the tombs, shall reanimate the dead and make them sing Glory—(in the day when) the Throne is set up, the judge seated and the books opened and everyone‖ receives (according to) what he has done

---

* "In MCCCXLVI according to the reckoning of Alexander," which, when 311 are substracted from it, brings it to the 535th year of our Era.

† The month *Jor* corresponding to may, the date according to the Julian Calendar would be May 16th 535 A.D.

The place *Kafra D'Bārthā* was situated in the region of Apamea (Apameia) on the river Orontes.

‡ Or "lover of guests."

§ In p. 254, l. 16, it should be ܐܽܘܣܝܐ. The word in the MS. is indistinct: ܝܳܠܕܰܬ ܐܰܠܳܗܐ is *Theotocos, Mother of God.*

‖ At p. 255, l. 22, the last word should be ܣܳܡܶܝܢ and the first word almost erased in the MS., of the next line should perhaps be ܘܣܳܡܶܝܢ,

from the Just Judge, in whose judgment is no* respect of persons—(may he) at that time hear this
sweet and pleasant voice† : "over a little thou hast
"been faithful : enter thou into the joy of thy Lord,
"and over much will I place thee ! "   And may he
with Abraham, Isaac, and Jacob and with all the
Just and Righteous, be included in the prayers of the
Blessed and God-bearing Mary.   Yea and Amen.

> Here occur eight lines in the Original MS. incapable of
> decipherment, and therefore incapable of translation or even of
> meaning except that the beginning seems to be a sort of prayer.
> A beautiful Photographic representation of this whole page
> and that of another page from the body of the MS. affording
> internal evidence as to the intended Œcumenicity of the Council
> are given in the copy of my " Ancient Syriac Document, Part
> 1 &c," drawn up to commemorate the Pan-Anglican Synod and
> presented to the late Archbishop of Canterbury and deposited
> by the present Archbishop in the Lambeth Library.

Further, this Book was written in the days of
God-loving Shining-lights of the Church, (who are)
pleasant havens, pious and holy lovers of hospitality,
influential through their manner of life, zealous for
the Catholic Faith, who are a beautiful sight to all
their beholders, from whom envy is far distant, in
whom full and perfect love is planted, and who

---

and in l. 25 the fourth word had better have had the diacritic point above,
instead of below, it.

* Or " guest-loving."

† The word ‏ܐܟܣܢܝܐ‎ is very obscured, the letter ‏ܢ‎ being indistinct
in last line of p. 254, and at p. 255, l. 2, the two words ‏ܒ‎ and ‏ܗܘ‎,
the latter being indistinct, should be ‏ܗܘܒ‎ followed by ‏ܐܝܬܘܗܝ‎

perform all good works, in whom our Lord delighteth,
—(in the days) of Mar Abraham the Governor of the
same Monastery who is from blessed Caphra.

May God,—for Whose name's sake, on behalf of
the beloved Brethren who dwelt with them, the Lord
Presbyter Abraham himself and Mar Eusebius his
disciple who is from the village of Tar and has also
charge of the Treasury of (and) the Library of the same
Monastery, weary themselves out with labour—in that
day when the good will be separated from the bad, the
goats from the lambs, the tares from the wheat,—in
that dreadful day when the trumpets speak before the
Just Judge—(may God) deem them worthy of His
Bridechamber which never passes away and of His
incorruptible Kingdom, of that which " no ear hath
heard, and no eye hath seen, and which has not
entered into human heart," as to something God has
prepared for them who love Him ; through the
prayers of the Martyrs, slain for the Gospel, (slain
for) their Lord ! Yea and Amen.

I, the sinful, miserable and imperfect John, of the
country of Antiochene, and living in the house of
Mar Eusebius of Kafra D'Birtha, have written this
Book.

But let everybody, who reads therein and learns
the power of the Orthodox Faith, pray for the poor
fellow who has written it, that the Merciful, the Long-
suffering, and very Gracious Lord will forgive him
all his imperfections, and cut in pieces his bonds, and
strike out his sins by reason of the Greatness of His

Compassion ; and that he may be deemed worthy of
the Havens of Delight in the Paradise of Light, and
in the Bridal Chamber of Promises, and (that he may)
with all those who are doers of good works, and
are instant in Prayer, and earnest in Service, and
watchful in Fasts, rejoice and leap : with the prayer
of every one who does the will of our Lord and does
it in the world that is passing away, and in the world
that does not pass away.   Yea and Amen.

And (the prayer) of all the Worshippers of Christ.
And may this prayer (be granted) to the (Tran)-
scriber and to every one who will possess it, and joy
and greeting in all.

FINIS.

EPISTOLA DOMNI AD FLAVIANUM.

Φλαβιανῷ ἐπισκόπῳ Κωνσταντινουπόλεως.

Πολλὰς μὲν ἐν τῷ παρότι καιρῷ, τὰ πάντα θεοφιλέστατε, τρικυμιῶν ἐδεξάμεθα προσβολὰς, καὶ τὸν τοῦ παντὸς ἐπικαλεσάμενοι Κυβερνήτην, ἀντισχεῖν ἠδυνήθημεν πρὸς τὸν κλύδωνα· τὰ δὲ νῦν καθ' ἡμῶν ἐπιχειρηθέντα πᾶσαν τραγικὴν ὑπερβαίνει διήγησιν. Νομίσαντες γὰρ σύμμαχον σχήσειν καὶ συνεργὸν εἰς τὰ κατὰ τῆς ἀποστολικῆς πίστεως τυρευόμενα, τὸν θεοφιλέστατον τῆς Ἀλεξανδρείας ἐπίσκοπον, τὸν κύριον Διόσκορον, ἀπεστείλαμεν ἕνα τῶν παρ' ἡμῖν εὐλαβεστάτων πρεσβυτέρων, συνέσει κοσμούμενον, μετὰ συνοδικῶν γραμμάτων, διδάξαντες αὐτοῦ τὴν θεοσέβειαν, ὡς ταῖς γεγενημέναις ἐπὶ τοῦ τῆς μακαρίας μνήμης Κυρίλλου συνθήκαις ἐμμένομεν, καὶ τήν τε παρ' αὐτοῦ γραφεῖσαν στέργομεν ἐπιστολὴν, τήν τε τοῦ μακαριωτάτου καὶ ἐν ἁγίοις Ἀθανασίου, ἣν πρὸς τὸν μακάριον Ἐπίκτητον ἔγραψεν, ἀσπασίως δεχόμεθα· καὶ πρό γε τούτων τὴν ἐν Νικαίᾳ τῆς Βιθυνίας ἐκτεθεῖσαν πίστιν ὑπὸ τῶν ἁγίων καὶ μακαρίων Πατέρων. Καὶ παρεκαλέσαμεν τοῖς τ[οι]ούτοις ἐμμένειν οὐ βουλομένους ἐμμεῖναι παρασκευάσαι. Ἀλλά τις εἰτεῦθεν δραμὼν τῶν τἀναντία φρονούντων, καὶ τοὺς [col. 1280] θορύβους τούτους ἐργαζομένων, ἐξαπατήσας τῶν αὐτόθι τινὰς, καὶ μυρίας καθ' ἡμῶν συκοφαντίας ὑφήνας, παρεσκεύασεν ἀθέσμως καὶ τῶν ἡμῶν ἐκβήσεις γενέσθαι. Ὁ δὲ θεοφιλέστατος ἐπίσκοπος Διόσκορος γέγραφεν ἡμῖν ἐπιστολὴν, ἣν οὐκ ἔδει γράψαι τὸν παρὰ τοῦ τῶν ὅλων Θεοῦ μεμαθηκότα ἀκοὴν ματαίαν οὐ παραδέχεσθαι. Πιστεύσας γὰρ τοῖς καθ' ἡμῶν εἰρημένοις, ὡς ἀκριβῶς τούτων ἕκαστον ἐξετάσας, καὶ ἐκ τῆς βασάνου μεμαθηκὼς [τ]ἀληθὲς, οὕτως ἡμῶν κατεψηφίσατο. Ἀλλ' ἡμεῖς γενναίως τὴν συκοφαντίαν ἠνέγκαμεν καὶ χρηστοῖς γράμμασιν ἠμειψάμεθα, καὶ πεπείκαμεν αὐτοῦ τὴν θεοσέβειαν, ὡς πάντα ταῦτα ψευδῆ, καὶ ὡς οὐδεὶς τῶν τῆς Ἀνατολῆς θεοφιλεστάτων ἐπισκόπων ἐναντία τοῖς ἀποστολικοῖς φρονεῖ δόγμασιν. Ἐπείσθησαν καὶ δι' αὐτῆς τῶν πραγμάτων τῆς πείρας καὶ οἱ ἀποσταλέντες παρ' αὐτοῦ εὐλαβέστατοι κληρικοί. Ὁ δὲ πᾶσιν ἐρρῶσθαι φράσας, καὶ τοῖς συκοφαντοῦσι τὰς ἀκοὰς ἐκδοὺς, πρᾶγμα πεποίηκεν οὐδαμῶς πιστευθῆναι δυνάμενον, εἰ μὴ πᾶσαν εἶχε μαρτυροῦσαν τὴν Ἐκκλησίαν. Ἠνέσχετο μὲν γὰρ τῶν ἀναθεματιζόντων ἡμᾶς ἀναστὰς δὲ καὶ προσφωνήσας ἐκείνων φωνὰς ἐπεβεβαίωσε. Πρὸς δὲ τούτοις, καὶ τινας τῶν θεοφιλεστάτων ἐπισκόπων εἰς τὴν βασιλεύουσαν ἀπέστειλεν,

1

ὡς ἔγνωμεν, πόλιν, αὐξῆσαι τοὺς καθ' ἡμᾶς θορύβους ἐλπίζων. Ἡμεῖς
δὲ πρῶτον μὲν τὸν τῶν ὅλων Ἐπόπτην πρόμαχον ἔχομεν· ὑπὲρ γὰρ τῶν
θείων αὐτοῦ δογμάτων ἀγωνιζόμεθα. Ἔπειτα δὲ καὶ τὴν σὴν ἁγιωσύνην
παρακαλοῦμεν τῆς πολεμουμένης πίστεως ὑπερμαχῆσαι, καὶ τῶν πατη-
θέντων ὑπεραγωνίσασθαι κανόνων. Ἐν ἐκείνῃ γὰρ τῇ βασιλευούσῃ πόλει
συνελθόντες οἱ μακάριοι Πατέρες, συμφώνως τοῖς ἐν Νικαίᾳ συναθροισ-
θεῖσι τὰς διοικήσεις διέκριναν, καὶ ἑκάστῃ διοικήσει τὰ ἑαυτῆς ἀπένειμαν,
ἄντικρυς ἀπαγορεύσαντες, ἐξ ἑκατέρας [ἑτέρας Neap.] τινὰ διοικήσεως
ἑτέρᾳ μὴ ἐπιέναι· ἀλλὰ τὸν Ἀλεξανδρείας ἐπίσκοπον τὰ τῆς Αἰγύπτου
μόνα διοικεῖν, καὶ ἑκάστην διοίκησιν τὰ οἰκεῖα. Ὁ δὲ τούτοις ἐμμένειν
τοῖς ὅροις οὐ βούλεται, ἀλλ' ἄνω καὶ κάτω τοῦ μακαρίου Μάρκου τὸν
θρόνον προβάλλεται· καὶ ταῦτα σαφῶς εἰδώς, ὡς τοῦ μεγάλου Πέτρου
τὸν θρόνον ἡ Ἀντιοχέων μεγαλόπολις ἔχει, ὃς καὶ τοῦ μακαρίου Μάρκου
διδάσκαλος ἦν, καὶ τοῦ χοροῦ τῶν ἀποστόλων πρῶτος καὶ κορυφαῖος.
Ἀλλ' ἡμεῖς τοῦ μὲν [μὲν addiderat Neap.] θρόνου τὸ ὕψος ἐπιστάμεθα,
ἑαυτοὺς δὲ καὶ γινώσκομεν καὶ μετροῦμεν. Τὴν γὰρ ἀποστολικὴν ταπεινο-
φροσύνην ἄνωθεν μεμαθήκαμεν. Τὴν δὲ σὴν ὁσιότητα παρακαλοῦμεν,
μήτε τοὺς ἁγίους κανόνας πατουμένους παριδεῖν, καὶ τῆς θείας πίστεως
ὑπερμαχῆσαι προθύμως. Εἰς ταύτην γὰρ ἔχομεν ἐλπίδα τῆς σωτηρίας,
καὶ διὰ ταύτην τυχεῖν προσδοκῶμεν φιλανθρωπίας.

Ἵνα δὲ μηδὲ τοῦτο ἀγνοήσῃ σου ἡ ὁσιότης, ἴσθι, δέσποτα, ὡς τὴν πρὸς
ἡμᾶς ἔσχε μικροψυχίαν, ἐξ οὗ τοῖς παρ' ὑμῖν γεγενημένοις συνοδικοῖς
ἐπὶ τοῦ τῆς μακαρίας μνήμης Πρόκλου συνεθέμεθα, τοῖς τῶν ἁγίων
Πατέρων κανόσιν ἀκολουθήσαντες· καὶ περὶ τούτου καὶ ἅπαξ ἡμῖν καὶ
δὶς ἐνεκάλεσεν, ὡς προδεδωκόσι καὶ τῆς Ἀντιοχέων, ὡς λέγει, καὶ τῆς
Ἀλε [col. 1281] ξανδρέων Ἐκκλησίας τὰ δίκαια. Τούτων μεμνημένος,
καὶ καιρὸν εὑρών, ὡς ὑπέλαβε, τὴν δυσμένειαν ἔδειξεν. Ἀλλὰ τῆς ἀληθείας οὐδὲν ἰσχυρότερον. Οἶδε γὰρ αὕτη καὶ δι' ὀλίγων νικᾶν. Παρακαλῶ δὲ σου τὴν ἁγιότητα, καὶ μνημονεύων ἡμῶν ἐν ταῖς πρὸς τὸν
Κύριον προσευχαῖς, ἵνα ἀντισχεῖν δυνηθῶμεν πρός τὰ διάφορα κύματα.

2

DUODECIM CAPITULA CYRILLI.

I.

Εἴ τις οὐχὶ ὁμολογεῖ, Θεὸν εἶναι κατὰ ἀλήθειαν τὸν Ἐμμανουὴλ, καὶ διὰ τοῦτο Θεοτόκον τὴν ἁγίαν Παρθένον· γεγέννηκε γὰρ σαρκικῶς σάρκα γεγονότα τὸν ἐκ Θεοῦ Πατρὸς Λόγον· ἀνάθεμα ἔστω.

II.

Εἴ τις οὐχ ὁμολογεῖ, σαρκὶ καθ᾽ ὑπόστασιν ἡνῶσθαι τὸν ἐκ Θεοῦ Πατρὸς Λόγον, ἕνα τε εἶναι Χριστὸν μετὰ τῆς ἰδίας σαρκὸς, τὸν αὐτὸν δηλονότι Θεόν τε ὁμοῦ, καὶ ἄνθρωπον· ἀνάθεμα ἔστω.

III.

Εἴ τις ἐπὶ τοῦ ἑνὸς Χριστοῦ διαιρεῖ τὰς ὑποστάσεις μετὰ τὴν ἕνωσιν, μόνῃ συνάπτων αὐτὰς συναφείᾳ τῇ κατὰ τὴν ἀξίαν, ἤγουν αὐθεντίαν, ἢ δυναστείαν, καὶ οὐχὶ δὴ μᾶλλον σύνοδον τὴν καθ᾽ ἕνωσιν φυσικήν· ἀνάθεμα ἔστω.

IV.

Εἴ τις προσώποις δυσὶν, ἤγουν ὑποστάσεσι, τάς τε ἐν τοῖς εὐαγγελικοῖς καὶ ἀποστολικοῖς Συγγράμματι διανέμει φωνὰς, ἢ ἐπὶ Χριστῷ παρὰ τῶν ἁγίων λεγομένας, ἢ παρ᾽ αὐτοῦ περὶ ἑαυτοῦ· καὶ τὰς μὲν ὡς ἀνθρώπῳ παρὰ τὸν ἐκ Θεοῦ Πατρὸς Λόγον ἰδικῶς νοουμένῳ προσάπτει, τὰς δὲ ὡς θεοπρεπεῖς μόνῳ τῷ ἐκ Θεοῦ Πατρὸς Λόγῳ· ἀνάθεμα ἔστω.

V.

Εἴ τις τολμᾷ λέγειν θεοφόρον ἄνθρωπον τὸν Χριστὸν, καὶ οὐχὶ δὴ μᾶλλον Θεὸν εἶναι κατὰ ἀλήθειαν, καὶ Υἱὸν ἕνα καὶ φύσει, καθὸ γέγονε σὰρξ ὁ Λόγος, καὶ κεκοινώνηκε παραπλησίως ἡμῖν αἵματος, καὶ σαρκός· ἀνάθεμα ἔστω.

VI.

Εἴ τις Θεὸν ἢ Δεσπότην εἶναι λέγει τοῦ Χριστοῦ τὸν ἐκ Θεοῦ Πατρὸς Λόγον, καὶ οὐχὶ δὴ μᾶλλον τὸν αὐτὸν ὁμολογεῖ ὁμοῦ τε θεὸν καὶ ἄνθρωπον, ὡς γεγονότος σαρκὸς τοῦ Λόγου κατὰ τὰς Γραφάς· ἀνάθεμα ἔστω.

VII.

Εἴ τίς φησιν ὡς ἄνθρωπον ἐνηργῆσθαι ὑπὸ τοῦ Θεοῦ Λόγου τὸν Ἰησοῦν, καὶ τὴν τοῦ Μονογενοῦς εὐδοξίαν περιῆφθαι ὡς ἑτέρῳ παρ᾽ αὐτὸν ὑπάρχοντι· ἀνάθεμα ἔστω.

3

VIII.

Εἴ τις τολμᾷ λέγειν, τὸν ἀναληφθέντα ἄνθρωπον συμπροσκυνεῖσθαι δεῖν τῷ Θεῷ Λόγῳ, καὶ συνδοξάζεσθαι, καὶ συγχρηματίζειν Θεὸν, ὡς ἕτερον ἑτέρῳ· τὸ γὰρ, Σὺν, ἀεὶ προστιθέμενον τοῦτο νοεῖν ἀναγκάσει καὶ οὐχὶ δὴ μᾶλλον μιᾷ προσκυνήσει τιμᾷ τὸν Ἐμμανουὴλ, καὶ μίαν αὐτῷ τὴν ὁμολογίαν συνάπτει, καθὸ γέγονε σὰρξ ὁ Λόγος· ἀνάθεμα ἔστω.

IX.

Εἴ τίς φησι, τὸν ἕνα Κύριον Ἰησοῦν Χριστὸν δοξάζεσθαι παρὰ τοῦ Πνεύματος, ὡς ἀλλοτρίᾳ δυνάμει τῇ ἰδίᾳ αὐτοῦ χρώμενον, καὶ παρ' αὐτοῦ λαβόντα τὸ ἐνεργεῖν δύνασθαι κατὰ πνευμάτων ἀκαθάρτων, καὶ τὸ πληροῦν εἰς ἀνθρώπους τὰς θεοσημίας, καὶ οὐχὶ δὴ μᾶλλον ἴδιον αὐτοῦ τὸ Πνεῦμά φησι, δι' οὗ καὶ ἐνήργησε τὰς θεοσημίας· ἀνάθεμα ἔστω.

X.

Ἀρχιερέα, καὶ ἀπόστολον τῆς ὁμολογίας ἡμῶν γεγενῆσθαι Χριστὸν, ᾖ θεία λέγει Γραφή· προσκεκομικέναι δὲ ἑαυτὸν ὑπὲρ ἡμῶν εἰς ὀσμὴν εὐωδίας τῷ Θεῷ καὶ Πατρί. Εἴ τις τοίνυν ἀρχιερέα, καὶ ἀπόστολον ἡμῶν γεγενῆσθαί φησιν οὐκ αὐτὸν τὸν ἐκ Θεοῦ Πατρὸς Λόγον, ὅτε γέγονε σὰρξ, καὶ καθ' ἡμᾶς ἄνθρωπος, ἀλλ' ὡς ἕτερος παρ' αὐτὸν, ἰδικῶς ἄνθρωπον ἐκ γυναικός· ᾖ εἴ τις λέγει ὑπὲρ ἑαυτοῦ προσενεγκεῖν αὐτὸν τὴν προσφορὰν, καὶ οὐχὶ δὴ μᾶλλον ὑπὲρ μόνων ἡμῶν· οὐ γὰρ ἂν ἐδεήθη προσφορᾶς ὁ μὴ εἰδὼς ἁμαρτίαν· ἀνάθεμα ἔστω.

XI.

Εἴ τις οὐχ ὁμολογεῖ τὴν τοῦ Κυρίου σάρκα ζωοποιὸν εἶναι, καὶ ἰδίαν αὐτοῦ τοῦ ἐκ Θεοῦ Πατρὸς Λόγου, ἀλλ' ὡς ἑτέρου τινὸς παρ' αὐτὸν συνημμένου μὲν αὐτῷ κατὰ τὴν ἀξίαν, ἤγουν ὡς μόνην ἐνοίκησιν ἐσχηκότος, καὶ οὐχὶ δὴ μᾶλλον ζωοποιὸν, ὡς ἔφημεν, ὅτι γέγονεν ἰδία τοῦ Λόγου τοῦ τὰ πάντα ζωοποιεῖν ἰσχύοντος· ἀνάθεμα ἔστω.

XII.

Εἴ τις οὐχ ὁμολογεῖ, τὸν τοῦ Θεοῦ Λόγον παθόντα σαρκὶ, καὶ ἐσταυρωμένον σαρκὶ, καὶ θανάτου γευσάμενον σαρκὶ, γεγονότα δὲ πρωτότοκον ἐκ νεκρῶν, καθὸ ζωή ἐστι, καὶ ζωοποιὸς, καὶ θεός· ἀνάθεμα ἔστω.

4

IBÆ AD MARIM PERSAM EPISTOLA.

Ἐν συντόμῳ δὲ τῇ συνέσει σου τῇ φωτεινῇ, τῇ δι' ὀλίγων τὰ πολλὰ
ἐπιγινωσκαίσῃ, οἷα πρὸ βραχέως καὶ νῦν ἐγένετο, γνωρίσαι ἐσπουδά-
σαμεν, εἰδότες, ὡς, ταῦτα τῇ σῇ θεοσεβείᾳ γράφοντες, πᾶσι διὰ τῆς
σῆς σπουδῆς τοῖς ἐκεῖσε γνώριμα γίνεται τὰ παρ' ἡμῶν, ὡς οὐδεμίαν
ἐναλλαγὴν αἱ παρὰ τοῦ Θεοῦ δοθεῖσαι γραφαὶ ἔλαβον. ποιοῦμαι δὲ
τὴν ἀρχὴν τῆς ὑποθέσεως ἐκ τῶν λόγων ὧν καὶ αὐτὸς ἐπίστασαι· ἐγένετο
φιλονεικία, ἐξ οὗπερ ἡ σὴ θεοσέβεια ἐνταῦθα ἦν, τοῖς δύο ἀνθρώποις
τούτοις, Νεστορίῳ καὶ Κυρίλλῳ· καὶ συνέγραψαν κατ' ἀλλήλων λόγους
βλαβερούς, οἵτινες σκάνδαλον ἦσαν τοῖς ἀκούουσι. Νεστόριος γὰρ
εἴρηκεν ἐν τοῖς αὐτοῦ λόγοις, καθὼς καὶ ἡ σὴ θεοσέβεια ἐπίσταται, ὅτι ἡ
μακαρία Μαρία θεοτόκος οὔκ ἐστιν· ὡς νομισθῆναι τοῖς πολλοῖς, ἐκ τῆς
αἱρέσεως Παύλου τοῦ Σαμοσατέως αὐτὸν εἶναι τοῦ φάσκοντος [MS. τὸν
φάσκοντα], ἄνθρωπον ψιλὸν εἶναι τὸν Χριστόν· Κύριλλος δέ, θέλων τοὺς
λόγους Νεστορίου ἀνατρέψαι, εὑρέθη ἐμπίπτων εἰς τὸ δόγμα Ἀπολλι-
ναρίου· συνέγραψε γὰρ καὶ αὐτὸς ὁμοίως ἐκείνῳ, ὅτι αὐτὸς ὁ Θεὸς λόγος
γέγονεν ἄνθρωπος· ὡς μὴ εἶναι διαφορὰν μεταξὺ τοῦ ναοῦ καὶ τοῦ ἐνοι-
κοῦντος ἐν αὐτῷ. συνέγραψε γὰρ τὰ δώδεκα κεφάλαια, ἅπερ νομίζω καὶ
τὴν σὴν θεοσέβειαν ἐγνωκέναι· ὅτι μία φύσις ἐστὶ τῆς τε θεότητος καὶ τῆς
ἀνθρωπότητος τοῦ κυρίου ἡμῶν Ἰησοῦ Χριστοῦ· καὶ ὡς οὐ χρή, ὡς φησί,
διαιρεῖν τὰς φωνὰς τὰς εἰρημένας, ἃς ἢ ὁ κύριος περὶ ἑαυτοῦ εἴρηκεν ἢ
οἱ εὐαγγελισταὶ περὶ αὐτοῦ· ὅσης δὲ ἀσεβείας πεπλήρωται ταῦτα, καὶ
πρὸ τοῦ ἡμᾶς εἰπεῖν καὶ ἡ σὴ ἁγιωσύνη ἐπίσταται· πῶς γὰρ δυνατόν,
ληφθῆναι τό· ἐν ἀρχῇ ἦν ὁ λόγος [Ioh. 1, 1], ἐπὶ τοῦ ναοῦ τοῦ γεννη-
θέντος ἐκ Μαρίας ; ἢ ἐκεῖνο τό· [Ps. 8, 5] ἠλάττωσας αὐτὸν βραχύ τι παρ'
ἀγγέλους, περὶ τῆς θεότητος τοῦ μονογενοῦς ῥηθῆναι ; ἡ γὰρ ἐκκλησία
οὕτως λέγει, ὡς καὶ ἡ σὴ θεοσέβεια ἐξ ἀρχῆς ἐδιδάχθη καὶ ἐστηρίχθη
τῇ θείᾳ διδασκαλίᾳ ἐκ τῶν λόγων τῶν μακαρίων πατέρων· δύο φύσεις,
μία δύναμις, ἓν πρόσωπον· ὅπερ ἐστίν, εἷς υἱὸς κύριος Ἰησοῦς Χριστός·
διὰ ταύτην τὴν φιλονεικίαν αἱ νικηταὶ καὶ φιλάνθρωποι βασιλεῖς ἐκέλευσαν τοὺς ἐξάρχους τῶν ἐπισκόπων εἰς τὴν Ἐφεσίων πόλιν συναχθῆναι,
καὶ ἐπὶ πάντων τοὺς λόγους Νεστορίου καὶ Κυρίλλου κριθῆναι. πρὸ δὲ
τοῦ πάντας τοὺς ἐπισκόπους, τοὺς κελευσθέντας συναχθῆναι, ἐλθεῖν εἰς
τὴν Ἔφεσον, προλαβὼν ὁ αὐτὸς Κύριλλος, τὰς ἀκοὰς τῷ φαρμάκῳ τῷ
τηροῦντι τοὺς ὀφθαλμοὺς τῶν σοφῶν προκατέσχεν· εὗρε δὲ αἰτίαν ἐκ
τοῦ μίσους τοῦ πρὸς Νεστόριον. καὶ πρὸ τοῦ εἰς τὴν σύνοδον παραγεν-
έσθαι τὸν ἁγιώτατον καὶ θεοφιλέστατον ἀρχιεπίσκοπον Ἰωάννην, ἐκ τῆς
ἐπισκοπῆς τὸν Νεστόριον καθεῖλον, κρίσεως καὶ ζητήσεως μὴ γενομένης.
μετὰ δὲ δύο ἡμέρας τῆς τούτου καθαιρέσεως ἤλθομεν εἰς Ἔφεσον· καὶ,
μαθόντων ἡμῶν ὅτι ἐν τῇ καθαιρέσει τῇ γενομένῃ παρ' αὐτῶν, τὰ δώδεκα

5

κεφάλαια τὰ συγγραφέντα παρὰ Κυρίλλου, ἐναντία ὄντα τῇ πίστει τῇ
ἀληθινῇ, ἀνέθηκαν καὶ ἐβεβαίωσαν, καὶ συνέθεντο αὐτοῖς ὡς τῇ ἀληθινῇ
πίστει συμφωνοῦσι· πάντες οἱ τῆς Ἀνατολῆς ἐπίσκ ποι αὐτὸν Κύριλλον
καθεῖλον, καὶ κατὰ τῶν ἄλλων ἐπισκόπων τῶν συνθεμένων τοῖς κεφα-
λαίοις ἀκοινωνησίαν ὥρισαν· καὶ μετὰ ταύτην τὴν ἀταξίαν ἕκαστος εἰς
τὴν πόλιν τὴν ἑαυτοῦ ὑπέστρεψε. Νεστόριος δέ, ἐπειδὴ ἐμισεῖτο παρὰ
τῆς πόλεως καὶ τῶν μεγάλων τῶν ὄντων ἐν αὐτῇ, ἐκεῖ ὑποστρέψαι οὐκ
ἠδυνήθη. καὶ ἔμεινεν ἡ σύνοδος ἡ ἀνατολικὴ μὴ κοινωνοῦσα τοῖς ἐπισ-
κόποις τοῖς κοινωνήσασι Κυρίλλῳ· καὶ διὰ ταῦτα λύπη πολλὴ μεταξὺ
αὐτῶν ἐγένετο, καὶ ἐν φιλονεικίᾳ ἐπίσκοποι πρὸς ἐπισκόπους ἐγένοντο καὶ
λαοὶ πρὸς λαούς· καὶ τὸ γεγραμμένον ἔργῳ ἐπληρώθη· ὅτι ἔστωσαν
ἐχθροὶ ἀνδρὸς οἱ οἰκειακοὶ αὐτοῦ, [Matth. 10, 36] καὶ ἐκ τούτου
λοιδορίαι πολλαὶ καθ᾽ ἡμῶν ἐγένοντο, Ἑλλήνων τε καὶ αἱρετικῶν. οὐ γὰρ
ἐτόλμα τις ἀπὸ πόλεως εἰς πόλιν, ἢ ἀπὸ χώρας εἰς χώραν ἀπέρχεσ-
θαι. ἀλλ᾽ ἕκαστος τὸν πλησίον ὡς ἐχθρὸν ἐδίωκε. πολλὰ δὲ, μὴ
ἔχοντες φόβον Θεοῦ πρὸ ὀφθαλμῶν, προφάσει ζήλου τοῦ ὑπὲρ τῶν
ἐκκλησιῶν, ἣν εἶχον ἔχθραν κεκρυμμένην ἐν τῇ καρδίᾳ αὐτῶν, εἰς
ἔργον ἀγαγεῖν ἐσπούδασαν· ὧν εἷς ἐξ αὐτῶν τυγχάνει ὁ τῆς ἡμετέρας
μητροπόλεως τύραννος, ὃν καὶ αὐτὸς οὐκ ἀγνοεῖς· ὅστις προφάσει τῆς
πίστεως οὐ μόνον τοὺς ζῶντας ἀμύνεται, ἀλλὰ καὶ τοὺς πάλαι πρὸς τὸν
Θεὸν ἀπεληλυθότας· ὧν εἷς ἐστιν ὁ μακάριος Θεόδωρος, ὁ κῆρυξ τῆς
ἀληθείας καὶ διδάσκαλος τῆς ἐκκλησίας· ὃς οὐ μόνον ἐν τῇ ζωῇ αὐτοῦ
τοὺς αἱρετικοὺς ἐκολάφισεν εἰς τὴν ἀληθινὴν αὐτοῦ πίστιν, ἀλλὰ καὶ
μετὰ τὸν θάνατον αὐτοῦ ὅπλον πνευματικὸν ἐν τοῖς συντάγμασιν αὐτοῦ
τοῖς τέκνοις τῆς ἐκκλησίας κατέλειψε· [. . . .] τοῦτον ἐτόλμησεν ὁ
πάντα τολμῶν ἐπ᾽ [MS. τολμῶν, ἐπ᾽] ἐκκλησίας, φανερῶς ἀναθεμα-
τίσαι, τὸν διὰ ζῆλον Θεοῦ οὐ μόνον τὴν ἰδίαν πόλιν ἐκ τῆς πλάνης εἰς
τὴν ἀλήθειαν ἐπιστρέψαντα, ἀλλὰ καὶ τὰς μακρὰν οὔσας ἐκκλησίας παι-
δεύσαντα τῇ αὐτοῦ διδασκαλίᾳ. καὶ περὶ τῶν βίβλων αὐτοῦ πολλὴ
ἔρευνα πανταχοῦ ἐγένετο, οὐ διὰ τὸ τῇ πίστει τῇ ἀληθινῇ ἐναντίας
αὐτὰς εἶναι—ἔτι γὰρ ζῶντος αὐτοῦ, συνεχῶς αὐτὸν ἐπῄνει καὶ εἰς
τὰ βιβλία αὐτοῦ ἀνεγίνωσκει—ἀλλὰ διὰ τὴν ἔχθραν τὴν κεκρυμμένην, ἣν εἶχε πρὸς αὐτόν, ἐπειδὴ ἤλεγξεν αὐτὸν φανερῶς ἐν τῇ
συνόδῳ. τούτων δὲ τῶν κακῶν μεταξὺ αὐτῶν γινομένων καὶ ἑκάστου
ὡς ἐβούλετο κατὰ τὸ γεγραμμένον ἀπιόντος, ὁ Θεὸς ἡμῶν ὁ προσκυ-
νητός, ὁ πάντοτε τῇ φιλανθρωπίᾳ αὐτοῦ φροντίζων τῶν ἁγιωτάτων
ἐκκλησιῶν, διήγειρε τοῦ πιστοτάτου βασιλέως τὸν νοῦν, πέμψαι ἄνδρα
μέγαν καὶ γνώριμον ἀπὸ τοῦ παλατίου τοῦ ἰδίου ἀναγκάζοντα τὸν
ἁγιώτατον ἀρχιεπίσκοπον τῆς Ἀνατολῆς τὸν κύριν Ἰωάννην διαλλα-
γῆναι Κυρίλλῳ· ὑπ᾽ αὐτοῦ γὰρ τῆς ἐπισκοπῆς καθῄρητο. καὶ μετὰ
τὸ δέξασθαι τὰ γράμματα τοῦ βασιλέως ἀπέστειλε τὸν τιμιώτατον καὶ
θεοφιλέστατον Παῦλον, τὸν ἐπίσκοπον Ἐμέσης, μετ᾽ ἐπιστολῶν εἰς τὴν
Ἀλεξάνδρειαν, ἀποστείλας δι᾽ αὐτοῦ τὴν ἀληθινὴν πίστιν, καὶ παραγγεί-
λας αὐτῷ, ὅτι, εἰ ταύτῃ τῇ πίστει σύνθηται Κύριλλος καὶ ἀναθεματίσῃ

6

τοὺς λέγοντας· ὅτι ἡ θεότης ἔπαθε, καὶ τοὺς λέγοντας· ὅτι μία φύσις
ἐστὶ θεότητος καὶ ἀνθρωπότητος: αὐτῷ κοινωνήσει. ἠβουλήθη δὲ ὁ Θεὸς,
ὁ πάντοτε φροντίζων τῆς ἰδίας ἐκκλησίας τῆς τῷ ἰδίῳ αἵματι αὑτοῦ λυτ-
ρωθείσης, καὶ τὴν καρδίαν τοῦ Αἰγυπτίου μαλάξαι, καὶ ἐκτὸς πόνου καὶ
σκύλσεως τὴν πίστιν δέξασθαι καὶ πάντας τοὺς ἐκτὸς ταύτης πιστεύον-
τας ἀναθεματίσαι· καὶ κοινωνησάντων ἀλλήλοις ἡ φιλονεικία ἐκ μέσου
ἤρθη καὶ εἰρήνη ἐν τῇ ἐκκλησίᾳ γέγονε· καὶ οὐκ ἔτι λοιπὸν ἐν αὐτῇ
σχίσμα, ἀλλὰ εἰρήνη ὡς τὸ πρότερόν ἐστι. τίνα δέ ἐστι τὰ ῥήματα τὰ
παρὰ τοῦ θεοφιλεστάτου ἀρχιεπισκόπου γραφέντα, καὶ ποῖα ἀντίγραφα
ἐδέξατο παρὰ Κυρίλλου, αὐτὰς τὰς ἐπιστολὰς ταύτῃ τῇ πρὸς τὴν σὴν
θεοσέβειαν συξείξας, ἀπέστειλα, ἵνα ἀναγνοὺς γνῷς καὶ πᾶσι τοῖς ἀδελ-
φοῖς ἡμῶν τοῖς ἀγαπῶσιν εἰρήνην εὐαγγελίσῃ, ὅτι ἡ φιλονεικία λοιπὸν
πέπαυται, καὶ τὸ μεσότοιχον ἤρθη τῆς ἔχθρας, καὶ οἱ ἀτάκτως κατὰ
ζώντων καὶ νεκρῶν ἐπελθόντες ἐν αἰσχύνῃ εἰσίν, ἀπολογούμενοι ὑπὲρ
τῶν ἰδίων πταισμάτων καὶ ἐναιτία τῇ πρώτῃ αὐτῶν διδαχῇ διδάσκοντες·
οὐ γὰρ τολμᾷ τις εἰπεῖν, ὅτι μία ἐστὶ φύσις θεότητος καὶ ἀνθρωπό-
τητος· ἀλλὰ ὁμολογοῦσιν εἰς τὸν ναὸν καὶ εἰς τὸν ἐν αὐτῷ ἐνοικοῦντα,
ὄντα ἕνα υἱὸν Ἰησοῦν Χριστόν. ταῦτα δὲ ἔγραψα τῇ σῇ θεοσεβείᾳ ἐκ
πολλῆς διαθέσεως, ἧς ἔχω πρὸς σέ, πεπεισμένος, ὡς ἡ σὴ ἁγιωσύνη νυκ-
τὸς καὶ ἡμέρας ἐν τῇ διδασκαλίᾳ τοῦ Θεοῦ ἑαυτὴν γυμνάζει, ἵνα πολλοὺς
ὠφελήσῃ.

APPENDICES.

A*

The following Appendices consist of the translation of extracts from various MSS in the British Museum, all of which refer, directly or indirectly, to the great Codex of Vol. i, viz., A, as well as to the great Controversy in the 5th century relative to the true Person of Jesus Christ, and some of which cite, by unmistakeable quotations, the very Volume of "the Acts" of the Second Synod of Ephesus. The value of the testimony they bear to A can hardly be over rated. In Vol. i they are all printed, line for line, like the originals except D, which would have taken too much space to have done so with it. The character of them all is given by Dr. W. Wright, formerly of the British Museum, in his three volumed Catalogue as follows, that of the magnificent Codex from which I have made no less than four extracts being fully set forth by which to judge of the rest.

That catalogue describes the Volume as consisting of "Vellum, about 12½in. by 9⅜, consisting of 137 leaves, some of which, especially near the beginning, are slightly stained and torn. The quires, 18 in number, are signed with letters. One leaf is wanting at the beginning, and four leaves after folio 8. Each page is divided into three columns, of from 43 to 51 lines. This volume is written in a fine Edessene hand of the 6th century before A. Gr., 873, A.D., 562, and contains a compilation consisting of treatises, letters, and extracts from various authors, directed chiefly against the doctrines of the Diphy-sites and the Council of Chalcedon. As the most important of these documents were composed by Timotheus (Aelurus),[*] Bishop of Alexandria,[†] under whose direction, or at whose orders the work was drawn up, it is entitled 'The Book of Timotheus against the Council of Chalcedon:' ܕܟܬܒܐ ܕܟܬܒ

ܠܥܢܝܒ ܠܡܥܕܐ ܐܕܘ܀ܐ ܐܚܣܨܐ ܘܠܐܚܣܢ܆ܢܐ ܠܐܘܡܓܕ

ܣܘܢܘܕܘܣ [ܐܡܝܕܐ] ܘܕܠܟܨܡ ܠ܀ܘ ".

Extracts B, D, I, K, in my Vol. i, were transcribed by me from that Volume. The first is the shorter of two letters on the same subject by the same writer. The very lengthy D belongs to the first Session of the Second Synod of Ephesus, the first part of which Extract gives another Version of the Imperial instrument convoking the Synod, and the latter the matter of the hitherto unknown blank page on which the President and his Coadjutors required the Bishops to inscribe their signatures. It contains also a Syriac Version of the celebrated Defence of himself, made by the Heresiarch Eutyches at the Council of Constantinople, under the Presidency of Flavian, Archbishop of that City, in 448, A.D. His "Libellus" and other intermediate Documents [are all given in Labbe, Harduin, and other Historians.

As regards the other appendices, it may be noted that C is an extract from "a volume written in a good current hand of the 6th or 7th century," but that some parts of the Extract are greatly defaced in the original.

Extracts E and F are from a Codex written in a "small elegant hand of the 6th or 7th century."

Extract G is from a volume written "in a good regular Estrangela of the 7th century, and contains the Correspondence of Sergius Grammaticus and Severus of Antioch, regarding the doctrine of the 'Two Natures of Christ.'"

H is from one "written in a small, neat hand, apparently of the 8th century."

And L is from a Manuscript written in "a small, neat hand of the 7th century, probably soon after A.D. 641."

As regard Extract C, the whole letter of Philoxenus is so important that it should be published. I hope to have it and the other mentioned by Assemanni from the Vatican Library. They are referred to at p. 37 of his Orient. Bib. Vol ii, and at p. 569 of Vol i, "Epistolae duae ad Monachos Teledenses "

B.

AN EXTACT FROM ONE OF THE ADDITIONAL MSS IN THE
BRITISH MUSEUM, NUMBERED 12,156.

FROM A LETTER OF THE BLESSED DIOSCORUS THE
ARCHBISHOP OF ALEXANDRIA, WRITTEN FROM EXILE
IN GANGRA, TO THE MONKS OF THE HENNATON :—*

I am fully aware, having been educated in the Faith,
respecting Him (Christ) that He was born of the Father,
as God, and that the Same was born of Mary, as Man.
Men saw Him as Man †walking on the Earth and they
saw Him, the Creator of the Heavenly Hosts, as God.
They saw Him ‡sleeping in the ship, as Man, and they
saw Him §walking upon the waters, as God. They saw
Him ‖hungry, as Man, and they saw Him ¶feeding (others),
as God. They saw Him **thirsty, as Man, and they
saw Him giving *drink, as God. They saw Him §§stoned
by the Jews, as Man, and they saw Him ¶¶worshipped
by the Angels, as God. They saw Him ††tempted, as
Man, and they saw Him drive away the ‡‡Devils, as God.
And similarly of many (other) things. But in order not
to make much din (trouble) in writing, I will leave the
matter for the purpose of collecting testimonies of every
one of the heads together; and I mean to collect them,
by the help of God, when a convenient opportunity bids
me to it.

---

*The Monastery was distant from Alexandria about nine miles. Hence
the designation.

† S. Mat. IV. 18.	‡ S. Mat. VIII. 24.
§ S. Mat. XIV. 25.	‖ S. Mat. IV. 2.
¶ S. Mat. XV. 36.	** S. John IV. 7.
* S, John IV. 14.	§§ S. John X. 31.
¶¶ Luke II. 14.	†† S. Mat. IV. 3.

‡‡ S. Mark v. 13.

But we leave the absurdity of those who hold opposite notions, and we confess One and the Same to be the Redeemer the Lord and God, although we see Him to have become by Œconomy Man. Hold to the Confession, therefore, of the fathers and do not listen to the soul-destroying words of Heretics, nor hold intercourse with those who divide into Two Him Who is One; for, One is our Redeemer, as I said, although out of compassion for us He became Man.

Sufficiently indeed, as I consider, to the great confusion of Heretics, the Teachings of Holy Bishops and Orthodox Archbishops have proved the fatuity of the Affirmations of Heretics and shewn at the same time that it is an Impiety to speak of Two Natures in God The Word Incarnate; for, they have excommunicated those who hold this Doctrine, and they have banished from The Hope of Christians those who do not confess God The Word to be Consubstantial with the Father, because He became Consubstantial with Man, taking Flesh, although He remained unchangeably what He was before; as they had done (excommunicated and banished) with the rest of the Heretics.

But to persuade more and more those who build their foundation upon the Immoveable Rock of the Orthodox Faith and to confute more and more the Heresies mentioned above, I adduce testimonies from the Divine New Testament written under the Spirit, along with the Expositions of the Holy Fathers, by whose aid it is possible manifestly to condemn the Heresies alluded to above and to hold to the Immoveable and Blessings-bringing Orthodox Faith Which was transmitted by the

Holy Apostles and by our Blessed and Learned Father.
Perhaps, they who have fallen from and denied the Lord
will hear and will repent, as said the Prophet, and turn
to the Lord with confession and abound in tears of Re-
pentance, in order that they may be healed; for, God
does continually take care of, and gives His hand to,[*] those
driven from him afar off, calling them to Him.

—And after testimonies from the Scriptures—

These things, then, refer to those who will not repent
and turn to The Lord, whom The Lord Jesus Christ bought
with His Own blood. For, He is Very God and the
Eternal Life of the World, as says John; for, One is
The Lord Jesus Christ, for ever and ever. Amen.

---

[*] Isaiah ix.

C.

AN EXTRACT FROM ONE OF THE ADDITIONAL MSS IN THE BRITISH MUSEUM, NUMBERED 14,663. FOL. 11, RECTO. COL. 1.

" He made for Himself a Temple in the Womb of the Virgin, and He was as one that was created."

And again ;—" he reviled the Son of God on the Cross and said—' How is He the Giver of Life who died, and how could He give Life to the dead, who was delivered into death ? He was not God—He who suffered, but Man which God took of us.' "

And again he said—" the sufferings were His, for He is passible. The Impassible is superior to sufferings. The likeness of a servant suffered."

Also, " He (Himself) truly said—*Why do ye desire to kill me ? Now, Divine Life was not killed, but only His mortal nature." And again he repeated (the statement) : —" it was not God who had suffered, but Man which God took of us."

" Therefore, in conformity with the (Gospel) Œconomy we worship, as One Son, Him who took (our Nature) and Him who was taken (of it). And we recognise different Natures, but only One Person. Just as our Lord ‡spoke of a man and his wife that " they are not twain but one flesh," so also it is befitting and proper for us to say, according to the term (implying) Union, that they are not twain but one flesh ; for, as the number does not preclude us (at all) from saying of a man and a

---

* John vii. 20.   ‡ Matthew xix. 5.

woman that they are one flesh, so the number of Natures does not preclude Unity of Person."

"When we differentiate these (two) Natures, how can we speak of the substance without (speaking of) the Person; for, the Nature of the Son of Man is perfect as is His Person, and also is Perfect the Nature of the Deity."

"When, then, we look at the Co-herence (Union), we affirm One Person, and when we differentiate the Natures, we make affirmation of the Perfect Person of the Son of Man, and the Perfect Person of His Deity."

And again, he said—"§Thomas touched Him Who rose, and worshipped Him Who raised Him." Wonder, O Heavens! at this, and be astonied, O Earth! at this, —that him who openly proclaims two Sons, this Synod receives as Orthodox, and him who utters those Blasphemies It declares to be a true Teacher, and eulogized by acclamations, as It had eulogized his fellow.

Who can now define the source of the Impiety of the Teacher of this (Heresy)? We have expounded to you only a small trickling stream from the river of his Blasphemies—how the Orthodox of that Assembly uttered those Blasphemies, and how they received with praise his sermons, contaminating the hearing; but, how was it that they did not receive openly Nestorius, since they received the praises of Nestorius and of his Teachers? Who will doubt that he (Theodoret) had in his heart the Doctrine of Paul of Samosata and of Nestorius? insomuch that The Emperor Theodosius II, worthy of remembrance, said, on hearing the Blasphemy of this man, "that if

---

§ John xx. 28.

B*

there was any doubt about the deservedness of the Deposition of Theodoret, there must be also doubt about the deservedness of that of Nestorius." Thus spake this God-loving man who well understood the subject.

But, although the man (Theodoret) was rejected by God, by men, by Kings, by true Priests, they at Chalcedon received him with applause, with the honour of the Orthodox. These accepted and welcomed him as Orthodox, but then they must accept as Orthodox other people. If, indeed, this Assembly received Jews as these, It must also receive another Jew who blasphemed more than these (people.) I allude to the Impious Ibas, who was at Edessa, who also is proved to be more impious than these by the blasphemies which he spoke, some of which—a few out of many—I am prepared to note for the purpose of arraigning (condemning) them, and for your instruction, and especially for the confusion of those who accepted as Orthodox a man excommunicated by reason of his Blasphemies, declaring and testifying that, from his words Ibas was Orthodox and deserving of being restored to the Episcopal Throne, and who gave abundant approbation to this Impious man.

True Believers, however, will perceive *what* is this impious Orthodoxy. For, thus in one place he said :— "I do not envy Christ becoming God, because I shall be what He was; for, He was of our nature.*"

And again, he said in his Homily :—"In the foreknowledge of God The Word, He knew that† Jesus would be justified by His Works."

---

* See p. 101 &c.   † See p. 101, l 24.

And again, in a Homily on the Day of the Resurection (Easter Day) he said—" ‡To-day Jesus in reality became Immortal."

And again, when he was discoursing about Gehennah he said that "that was written (only) as a threatening," dissolving by this the Word of our Lord. Again, as regards the Judgment, he denies it adding to his Blasphemies, as the Psalmist says—the wicked man says in his heart "there is no God."

And again, he said—§"It is one Person who died, and another who is in Heaven. It is one Person who had no beginning, and another who has a beginning. It is one Person who is of the Father, and another who is of the Virgin."

And again, he said—‖" If God died, who is it that vivified Him and raised Him ?" O frightful Impiety !

Again he said—* " as when the purple was insulted, the insult passed over to the King, so the suffering passed over to God.

Again, he said—" the Jews must not be elated by pride ; for, they did not crucify God," and "Mary is not the Mother of God.

Again, when writing †to the Impious Mares the Persian, he attacked the Chapters of the Blessed Cyril, saying; that " in them there was Impiety."

And again, he said—that the Deposition of Nestorius was unjust.

And again, he said that the " Blessed Theodore was a Preacher of the Truth and Doctor of the Church not only in his lifetime, but also after his death."

---

‡ See p. 104, 1 6 &c.   § See page 105, p. 21.   ‖ See p. 106, 1 2.
* See p. 106, 1 16.   † See p. 111 &c.

And again he said—"Worship is due to the Nature of God by right and only by Grace to the Nature of Him Who was from Mary—for His Union was with the Word—for, he as being composed may be divided."

And again he said, "Just as the grace replenished the Temple which (came) from Mary, so also the grace may replenish those who worship Him."

And again he said, "Just as the Sons of Jacob did contaminate the garment with blood, so also did the Lord suffer in the covering he took from Mary."

Who will not shut his ears against such Blasphemous words? How could he not suffer, and how could he not protest against them, who proclaims openly Two Natures, who affirms God to be a Creature and who denies the Virgin to be the Mother of God, who thinks our Lord to be only one of the Just who has been Justified by His works.

See, therefore, Lovers of the Faith! what Blasphemies they at Chalcedon proclaimed!

And see also how Impious is the man whom the Orthodox received with praise.

Which are the ears and minds of Believers that can uphold these Blasphemies? Notwithstanding, all those Blasphemies were assented to (by the Council of Chalcedon). True Belivers abominate hearing them, whilst these Blasphemies were sweet to the Council who proclaimed them Orthodox.

But the Holy Synod which condemned Ibas shouted— "Cease to speak these Blasphemies—*Spare our hearing "these words, fit (only) for heathens—the Devils are more

* See page 124.

"modest than Ibas—all of us excommunicate Ibas—every "body who says such things ought to be burnt."

The Fathers shouted such exclamations when they excommunicated him (Ibas), but when the true ones thus shouted—those who had departed from the Truth shouted the contrary. For they rejected him as Heathen and these received him for Orthodox. They rejected him as a Liar and these received him as a truth-speaking man; they excommunicated him as a heretic, and these honoured him as a believer.

And again, they (the Council) did more than that; for, they considered as Impious men the sons who excommunicated those Heretics: and some of them they sent into exile, and they presented a Petition to the King to the effect that the Synod (of Ephsus) should not be called a Synod.

Who, then, would not assent to the Synod which excommunicated him (Ibas) for the Impieties which he uttered? Who will assent to the Synod which received him, (Ibas), notwithstanding the Blasphemous expressions which he produced?

Who therefore would not condemn this assembly which assented to these Impieties, and to Leo, to Ibas, to Theodoret, and, with them, also to their Teachers, impious men and Doctors of evil, that calumniated The Truth?

D

EXTRACT FROM ONE OF THE ADDITIONAL MSS IN THE BRITISH MUSEUM, NUMBERED 12,156.

FROM THE SYNODICON OF THE SECOND SYNOD OF EPHESUS.

*After the (year of the) Consulate of the Illustrious Zeno and Postumianus, on the 10th of the Month Abib which, according to the Egyptians, is the 15th of Mesouri, Indiction the third, when the Synod assembled at the Metropolis of Ephesus in compliance with the commands of the God-loving and Christ-loving Emperors, Theodosius and Valentinian, and when were seated the God-loving and Holy Bishops,† in the Holy Church, which is designated Mary, John Presbyter of Alexandria, the chief Notary, said :—It has seemed good at the present time to the God-fearing and Christ-loving Emperors to command that your Great and Holy Synod should assemble here in order to make investigation into the evil that has just sprung up concerning our Orthodox and Blameless (Inerrant) Faith and to uproot it, lest it should inhere in and attract any simple minded men, and cast us into the ditch of Error and bad faith.   And it is right and just that those who love our Religion should preserve, without injury and without change, the Definitions relative to our True Religion made in the first instance by the Blessed Fathers assembled at Nicæa, and then confirmed a little while ago by those who, assembled in this City, entirely assented and agreed to them (in their fullness)

---

* See page 13.
† A list of these Bishops is given in pages 13—19.

so that no one should consider or determine anything at variance with them.

Now we bear these pure Decrees (Definitions) of the Holy Fathers, and make them known to your Holiness, in order that you may command what is your pleasure.

Dioscorus, the Bishop of Alexandria, said :—

Let the faith-full (fideles) Letters of the Christ-loving Emperors be read, which were addressed to this Holy Synod.

John, Presbyter and Prime Notary, read :—

COPY OF DIVINE (ROYAL) LETTERS.

The Imperial (Autocratic) Caesars, Theodosius and Valentinian, Victors and Illustrious by Victories, the Noble, the Worshipful, the Augusti, to Dioscorus Archbishop of Alexandria.*

It is obvious to everybody that the good order (Status) of our government and of human affairs generally is established and confirmed by an exalted Piety towards God; and so long as God is favourable to us, matters usually advance and are regulated readily, and according to our wish.

Seeing, then, that we are deemed worthy by Divine Providence to reign, we necessarily take every care of the Religion and the prosperity of those who are under our authority, whereby our True Religion and our Government may shine forth (flourish), being maintained by a true service towards God, and by Faith.

Now, seeing that all on a sudden a Controversy has just lately sprung up, touching the conservancy of the

---

* See page 8.

Catholic and Apostolic Doctrine of the Orthodox Faith,
which (controversy) so frequently leads people off into
diverse opinions and enflames and agitates the affections
and souls of men ; it has appeared to us that it would
not be well to hold back from a matter of this sort,
disgraceful though it be, lest, by disregarding it, it seem
to bring dishonour upon God Himself.   So we have ordered
that Pious and God-loving persons, of much zeal for Religion and for the Orthodox and True Faith, should assemble at one place that, an accurate investigation having
been made, the whole vain Controversy be composed, and
the Orthodox and True Faith which is so dear to God be
consolidated.   Your Piety, then, taking with you ten
Venerable Metropolitan Bishops from the Province under
you, and other ten Pious Bishops, distinguished for eloquence and integrity of life and for Orthodoxy in The
Inerrant and True Faith, and illustrious to everyone
for knowledge and learning, before the month of August,
by the first of it, must repair without delay to Ephesus,
the Metropolis of Asia—no other person besides those
mentioned above being allowed to trouble the Holy
Synod—so that, when all these Holy and God-loving
Bishops together, whom we have by our godly (divine)
Letters commanded to assemble, have reached the city
above mentioned and made an accurate investigation
and enquiry, the whole Error of deceit may be removed
from (our) midst, but the Doctrine of the Orthodox and
True Faith which loves our Redeemer Christ be confirmed
and be resplendent, as usual, so that all men may preserve It from the present to the future intact and inviolate
through the help of God.   But, if any man take upon him

to disregard this Synod which necessity demands, and which is dear to God (in accordance with God's will), and does not repair with all his might, at the time stated above, to the place selected, not a single excuse shall he be able to find (available) with God or our Piety. For, if he excuses himself from an assembly of Priests, it necessarily follows that his soul is agitated by no good conscience. But Theodoret the Bishop of the City of Cyrus, whom on a former occasion we ordered to confine himself within his own Church, we forbid to go to the Holy Synod, unless it should seem fit to the whole Holy Synod, when It has assembled, that he also should come and take part in It. But if, on his account, there should arise any division of opinion, we give order that the Holy Synod assemble without him and execute the commands (given).

(This Ordinance) was issued in the Month of Adar, on the xxxth of it, at Constantinople, after the Consulship of the Illustrious Zeno and Postumian.

The Bishop Julius, filling the place of the Holy Bishop of Rome, Leo, and interpreted by Florentius, Bishop of Lydda, said :—

According to a command similar to this (one) from the God-fearing and Christ-loving Emperors, our Holy Father of the Church of Rome, the Governor Leo, was summoned (to the Synod).

John, Presbyter and Prime Notary, said :—

Another gracious order was forwarded to our God-loving Archbishop, Dioscorus, which, too, I hold (in my hand), that your Holiness may give direction as you please (about it).

c*

Juvenal, the Bishop of Jerusalem, said :—

Let it be read and deposited among the accredited Documents.

(4) The Autocrat Cæsars, Theodosius and Valentinian, Victors and Illustrious by Victories, the Noble, the Worshipful, the Augusti, to Dioscorus.

It has come to the hearing of our Serenity that many Venerable Archimandrites of the East, with Orthodox peoples, have been troubled in one City after another of the East, by certain Bishops, said to be infected with the Impiety of Nestorius, and have had a great contest for the Catholic Faith. For this reason, then, it has seemed fit to our divinity (Serenity) that the God-loving Presbyter and Archimandrite Barsumas, who is distinguished for integrity of character and orthodoxy of faith, should proceed to the City of Ephesus, and, acting as representative of all the God-loving Archimandrites, should assemble with your Piety, and with all the Holy Fathers who are collected there ; and then you will begin your proceedings on all these matters, as it is pleasing to God. Your Piety will therefore be induced, bearing in mind our entire anxiety for the Catholic Faith, joyfully to receive the above-named Archimandrite, and to cause that he take part in your Holy Synod.

This (Ordinance) was issued in the Month of Ijar, on the second day of it.

Juvenal, the Bishop of Jerusalem, said :—

The same was addressed to me also respecting the Archimandrite Barsumas, and therefore it is with right and justice that he will assemble with the Holy Synod.

The Bishop Dioscorus, said :

If the Illustrious Count Elpidius and Eulogius, the Tribune and Notary, have any information to give us respecting this cause which we have in hand, let them speak.

THE INSTRUCTION OF COUNT ELPIDIUS.

The Count Elpidius said :—

(5) Satan, who is the originator of every evil, never ceases from making war with the Holy Churches, and the God-fearing Emperor stays not from contending, with justice, with him who so wars, rightly considering that he is fighting on his Kingdom's behalf, when he arms himself for a struggle in behalf of religion, nor does he do prejudice to himself, because from the beginning many things have been adjudged in his favour rather by reason than by arms, and for that cause he has, with you, condemned the rebellion of Nestorius, who, although he had been appointed for the service of God, became the Father and Teacher of Impious Doctrines, as if he were one who had accepted (taken) the Priestly Office on behalf of Demons, and not for the sake of Religion, but he is at present consigned to a place suited to him; being reserved for the torment that will not fail to overtake him in the world to come; seeing that he gave himself up to all this Blasphemy, and has overwhelmed many with himself, whom he has persuaded.

Now, as regards the present Controversy, the Royal (Divine) Emperor brings it before you as before Fathers and Judges, and asks of you to bring about such a solution of this controversy, as may serve for a general warning to the Community—to himself, and to all who are under his government. What those matters, then, are that the Royal (Divine) Emperor has enjoyned upon us, and has written to you, I now forthwith make known to you, adding this as being one of them who rightly, under your authority, hold to the True Religion: —To-day the Lord of all, God The Word and Saviour, submits Himself to you for judgment, and when you are judging, He is present among you, and is honoured by the authority of your sentence ; so that seeing you judge rightly matters concerning Himself, He will here honor you now, and before the Father will again own you ; and if He find some people who have estranged themselves from the True Religion by their imaginations, and who have brought into the Controversy other persons, persuaded by their eloquence, then He will bring upon both classes punishment from God and from the King. It would have been better for these not to have been born ; for, they do not confess so well as the Robber, the Publican, the Courtesan, the Canaanite woman, the pure Glory of Him Who has humbled Himself for us.

Now I will read what has been commanded to me and to you by the Faithful and God-loving Autocratic Emperor.

COPY OF THE COMMONITORY TO HIM (ELPIDIUS).

To the distinguished Count Elpidius.
(6) The Blasphemy against God of the Impious Nestorius was the cause of the Godly assembling of the Holy Synod on a former occasion at Ephesus : and he therefore received the punishment he deserved at the

hands of the Holy Fathers who assembled there. But, because another controversy also has now arisen, against The Divine Faith, we have commanded this Second Synod to take place at Ephesus; being anxious to cut away entirely the root of the evil, and that when we have driven away from all sides disturbance arising from Doctrine, we may guard in purity, by prayer, the Orthodoxy of our Belief; and that will be a protection for our government and a benefit for men. For this reason, then, we have chosen your Admirableness (Eminence) and the distinguished Eulogius, Tribune and Pretorian Notary, for the Service of The Faith, as experienced men who are both upright in other matters and hold religion purely, and able to execute our commands with efficiency relative to the transactions to be carried on at Ephesus by the Holy Synod; and you will not permit any commotion to take place on either side. But if you should perceive any man aiming at exciting commotion and disturbance to the injury of The Holy Faith, you will observe him with vigilance, and then give information of the circumstance to us, and let the proceedings of the case go on according to order, occupying yourself in taking cognisance of the cause; and you will take care that there be, speedily, a thorough examination made by the Holy Synod, of which you shall give information to us, those persons being present indeed, who sat in judgment on the Venerable Archimandrite Eutyches, but silently and not acting as judges, but expectant of the general assent of all the other Holy Fathers, since those matters that were then adjudicated upon are now again examined into.

It is not, however, permitted that any matter should be mooted, having relation to property, before those which relate to The Orthodox Faith be concluded.

In order to this end, (fortified) by the Letters addressed to the Illustrious Proconsul and with the aid from the Judges and from the Roman (soldiers) quartered there which I have assigned to you, together with your own energy—fortified by these supports, you will find yourselves competent for the accomplishment of what is commanded, which is as far superior to other advantages as the things of God are superior to those of men. And do you report to us information of all the transactions in this cause.

(This Ordinance) was proclaimed in the Month of Jar, at Alexandria.

Count Elpidius said :—
Now command that what has been written to you by the divine (Royal) Head, be received and read.

Dioscorus said :—
Let the Illustrious Letters of the Christ-loving Emperors, which have been addressed to this Great and Holy Synod, be received and read.

John, the Proto-Notary, read :—
(7) The Autocratic Cæsars, Theodosius and Valentinian, Victors and Illustrious by Victories, the Noble, the Worshipful, the Augusti, to the Holy Synod at Ephesus.

We assuredly desire that the Holy Church of God may exist without all this trouble, and that you yourselves, abiding in your Holy Churches, as usual, may exercise the function of the Priesthood in what pertains to the service of God, and that there may not arise to you so much anxiety and labour.

But, since the God-loving Bishop Flavian resolves on agitating a question touching The Holy Faith, with the Venerable Archimandrite Eutyches, and, having established a Tribunal, has begun to effect something, we have frequently sent to him (viz.,) to that God-loving Bishop, with the desire to prevent commotion arising, being fully assured that sufficient for us is The Faith, delivered by the Holy and Orthodox Fathers at Nicæa, and confirmed by the Holy Synod at Ephesus.

But seeing that we have many times requested the God-loving Bishop to desist from such an object, as there is no reason for disturbing the whole world, and that he has not assented, whilst we are of opinion that there is no objection, independently of your own Holy Synod and those first Holy Synods, to such a question concerning The Faith being mooted, we think it necessary that your Holinesses should meet in assembly when you would give instructions as to the transactions thus to take place, and as to the question to be mooted, and would cut off the whole root of calumny, and expel from the Churches those who contend for the Blasphemy of the Impious Nestorius, and work for its retention, whilst you could command the conservation of the Catholic Faith in Its true and inerrant character, because all our hopes and the consolidation of our Kingdom are dependent upon The Orthodox Faith in God and upon your Holy Prayers.

(This Ordinance) was issued in the Month of Heziran
at the City of Constantinople, during the Consulate
of Protogenes.

---

(8) The PETITON of the Archimandrite, EUTYCHES,
which was presented to the Christ-loving Emperor
Theodosius, and which moved him to convoke the Holy
Synod of Ephesus.

To the God-fearing, Faithful, Christ-loving Emperors,
Theodosius and Valentinian, the ever-August, from
the Archimandrite Eutyches :—

(Next) after the God of the Living and of the Truth
your Piety is Illumination to me. You are, too,
in no way backward in making investigation of matters
concerning The Faith and my troubles. For, as regards
the Documents that were imposed upon me by the Venerable Bishop Flavian, you read them yesterday, and
you found that the opposite of what was actually done,
was put on paper. For, what he said to me was not put
on paper, and what I did not say, they put into the
Documents. I request, therefore, of your Piety, who
are continually anxious about The Orthodox Faith, of
my Humbleness to be induced to command that the God-
loving Bishops who were then seated in the Assembly,
and the Notaries of Bishop Flavian, and the Venerable
Clerics, who were despatched by him to me, and my
Reader, who came to the Synod, and Athanasius, Deacon
of the God-fearing Bishop Basil, shall assemble in the
presence of the Venerable Bishop Thalassius, in order
to be requested to depose in writing what they are cog-

nisant of, with a view to my subscribing to it, according to usual custom, when it is done.

The Emperor, therefore, ordered that, first, the transactions at Constantinople should be investigated, and, then, he assembled the Synod at Ephesus, and sent the business to the Synod to be despatched.

(9) THE LIBEL OF EUTYCHES WHICH WAS PRESENTED TO THE HOLY SYNOD.

To the Holy and God-loving Œcumenical Synod, assembled at Ephesus the Metropolis, from the Archimandrite EUTYCHES.

I give thanks to God, Holy in all things, at the present time in which the True Religion, through your means, has received a well-established ground of trust. And I give information to your Holy Synod of what has been done against me and especially against The Orthodox Faith. My main end and object, from my childhood up to a ripe old age, has been to lead a life of quiet, apart from any business, and to continue to do so without any disturbing causes. I was not, however, permitted to continue in the enjoyment of such an object, but experienced great suffering arising from the intrigues of others, because, acceding to the Definition of your Holy Synod which took place here, I would not presume to entertain opinions contrary to The Faith set forth by the Fathers at Nicæa.

It is, however, necessary for me, before showing what had been done against me, for the satisfaction of your Holiness, again to make manifest the Confession I hold

D*

concerning Holy Dogma, calling to witness God, as well as your Holy Synod, with what power I have stood up for The Catholic Faith against Heretics.

I believe in One God Almighty, &c.

And, after he had repeated the whole Faith of the CCCXVIII, he said :— Thus, having received (the Symbol) from the beginning from my forefathers, have I believed and do I believe. For, in It, too, was I born and forthwith dedicated to God; and His own Mercy accepted me.   And in this Faith I was baptized, was signed with the cross (confirmed), and have lived up to It to this day, and in It I ask (of God) to die. This Faith, also, the first Holy and Œcumenical Synod held and, as mentioned above, confirmed, whose President was our Father, of Blessed memory, the Bishop Cyril, who drew up the Definition (of Faith) that whoever exceeded this Faith by way of addition or invented one or taught it should be subject to the punishment then prescribed, a copy of which, in writing, the afore-mentioned and Blessed Father the Bishop Cyril sent to me, which I hold in my hands.

Submitting myself to the Holy Synod I have kept this Definition till the present time, and I reckon, as well as your Piety, all those Holy Fathers Orthodox and Faithful, and I accept them as my Teachers, anathematizing Manes, Velentinus, Appollinarius, and Nestorius, and all Heretics up to Simon Magus, as well as those who affirm that the Flesh of our Lord and God Jesus Christ descended from Heaven.

But, while living according to this Faith and continuing instant in Prayer, I sustained an accusation against myself, (occasioned) by the intrigue of Eusebius, Bishop of Dorylæum, who presented Libels against me to the Venerable Bishop Flavian, and those others who, for temporary reasons, were in the Royal City; who called me a contemptible Heretic without advancing any specific Heresy in his Libel, when, suddenly having in the altercations of dispute committed those lapses of the tongue so customary in such confusion and through strong voices, I fell into mistake; then he commanded me to meet the Libel of accusation, whilst the accuser constantly continued in his company, although that accuser was not his intimate friend.

And he imagined that I, accustomed as I always was to abide in my Monastery, would not go to exhibit my presence, and therefore he could effect my Deposition, as, having not gone, I discovered when I went from my Monastery to the Royal City, being informed by Magnus the distinguished Silentiary, whom our Faithful and Christ-loving Emperor selected as one who would not suffer danger to threaten my life, when he replied to me that then my presence was superfluous, as indeed, before examination, my condemnation had taken place, which the Deposition of the Silentary, which was afterwards made, proved.

But when I went to make my Defence at the Tribunal before the Judges, and brought with me a Confession of Faith which I had subscribed, as being defined by the Holy Fathers at Nicæa, and afterwards confirmed at Ephesus by the Holy Synod there—*that* he would neither accept nor permit to be recited. The agitation and tumult (confusion) took place in the Tribunal, many

persons being agitated and pressing forward with cries
from every quarter, as asserting the different Depositions (statements) which afterwards were taken down
in writing by the Judges relating to that disturbance.
Subsequently, I was ordered to proclaim myself my Confession of Faith, and I said, I believe according to the
Definitions of the Holy Fathers of Nicæa, which Definitions were confirmed by the Holy Synod of Ephesus.
Then he told me that I had before confessed something
different from the Symbol of Nicæa and Ephesus.

But, through fear of exceeding (transgressing) the
Definition set up by the Holy Synod which formerly by
the will of God assembled here, and those things touching The Faith that were settled by the Holy Fathers who
assembled at Nicæa, I requested to make known *this* to
your Holy Synod, because I am prepared to stand by
what will be investigated and settled by your Highness.
But whilst I was saying that, all on a sudden my Condemnation, long ago drawn up against me, as it had
pleased him (Flavian), was read out, as being the con-
tinuation (sequence) of words uttered by them and by
me and of other Depositions. Then I Confessed that I
believed, as has been defined by the Holy Fathers
assembled at Nicæa and by those assembled at Ephesus,
before the Documents asserting the contrary were drawn
up, as it has been proved by the writings drawn up afterwards at my request and at the request of the Faithful
and Christ-loving Emperor, but the Pious Bishop Flavian
did not make any mention at all of the appeal I had
made to your Piety, nor had he any regard for my grey
hairs, with which I have grown old in wars against

Heretics and in the Confession of the Orthodox Faith, but, being in possession of power to do every-thing alone touching The Faith and reserving no authority whatever for your Piety on the (subject of the) equity of such a sentence, he pronounced condemnation upon me and cut me off from the Church, as he thought, and deprived me of the Priesthood, as he supposed, and inhibited me from Communion in the Divine Mysteries, and unjustly expelled me from the Government of the Monastery, and handed me over to the multitude who were prepared to drag me through the Episcopal and (other) public places, as a Heretic, a Blasphemer, and a Manichæan, if Divine Providence had not liberated me and this day delivered me to the guardianship of your Holiness.

He, moreover, at various Feasts of the Saints, after that tumult and my taking exception to his judgment, ordered this sentence against me to be proclaimed, and he ex-communicated me, and those who visit me and converse with me he estranged (inhibited) from the Holy Communion, without waiting for the judgment of your Holy Synod, and he obliged the Monks to subscribe to the Condemnation made against me, although such a practice had never been done, as your Charity well knows, even against Heretics. He, also, sent papers to the East and to different parts in order that other God-fearing Bishops and Monks, although they took no part in adjudicating, might subscribe to them, and although it would appear far preferable and proper for the High Priests to have subscribed before everybody, to whom I made appeal.

At this present time, then, whilst I am scarcely liberated

I have made known these transactions by Libel to your Piety. And I ask the God-fearing and Faithful Emperor that you, who are Pious and God-loving and despise all Calumny and Detraction, should become Judges of what was adjudicated upon, and I ask now of your Holiness to consider the Calumny and Injury that have been heaped upon me, and the commotion that, from this cause, has been occasioned to the Holy Churches everywhere, and the scandal that has thence arisen to many, and, by the Christ-loving wisdom which you possess, to subject to ecclesiastical rules those who have occasioned these evils, and so cut off the whole root of Blasphemy and Impiety. For, from the beginning, I appealed to the Tribunal of your Blessedness, and I bear witness before Jesus Christ, Who before Pontius Pilate witnessed a good Confession, that thus I believe, I understand, I think, as The Faith which was delivered to us by the Holy Fathers who assembled at Nicæa, and which also the Holy Fathers at the First Synod of Ephesus confirmed. And, if any man thinks contrary to this Faith, I anathematize him according to their Definition.

The Subscription of Eutyches, Archimandrite.

Thus I believe, as is written above, having subscribed the Document by my own hands and presented this Libel.

(9) After the Reading of the Royal Letters before the Holy Synod at Ephesus, DIOSCORUS, the Archbishop of Alexandria, said :—

It is evident to us that the Faithful Letters of our

God-loving Emperor, when the matter was mooted at Constantinople for a Synod to take place, commanded that the claims of those Synods should first be made known, because it is not proper for us to depart from those ascertained Definitions and Canons which the Synods have decreed. Our Christ-loving, Faithful Emperor, seeing that a certain controversy has arisen, commanded that this Holy Synod should assemble, not to formulate our Faith, which already our Fathers have done, but to examine what has arisen, and to see if it be in accordance with what has been determined on by the Holy Fathers. It is right and just, then, that what has arisen be first examined and scrutinized by us to see if things are in accordance with the Definition of the Holy Fathers; and if it is so, you will again proclaim The Symbol of the Holy Fathers.

The Holy Synod Said :—

"Whoever rejects It let him be anathematized—who-"ever perverts It let him be anathematized—The Faith "of the Fathers preserve."

Dioscorus, the Archbishop of Alexandria, said :—

For the sake of peace to everybody and of the confirmation of The Faith and for the annihilation of what has arisen, I examined The Faith of the Fathers at Nicæa and at Ephesus.

The Holy Synod said :—

"That saves the world—that maintains The Faith."

Dioscorus, the Bishop, said :—

Although two Synods are mentioned, yet only One Faith has been delivered.

The Holy Synod said :—

"With perfection did the Fathers determine every-
"thing—he who goes beyond them is excommunicate—
"no man must add to or subtract from."

Dioscorus, the Bishop, said :—

Seeing that God accepts your voices and that you
yourselves accept what is true and pleasing to God,
whoever, as an enquirer, or investigator, or teacher, exceeds what was done and what was decreed by the Holy
Fathers who assembled at Nicæa, and who gathered
together in this place, must be excommunicate.

The Holy Synod said :—

"To the great preserver of The Faith, to Dioscorus
"the Archbishop, many years."

Dioscorus, the Archbishop of Alexandria, said :—

Another thing, too, I would mention—one of fear and
trembling—(viz.), that, if one man sin against another,
let him pray for him to the Lord ; but if he sin against
the Lord, who will pray for him ? If, then, the Holy
Ghost is present with the assembly of the Fathers, as
He assuredly is, and decrees what is decreed, he who
rejects them ignores the Grace of the Blessed Spirit.

The Holy Synod said :—

"We all say the same—let him who rejects them be
"excommunicate."

Dioscorus, the Archbishop of Alexandria, said :—

Nobody now defines what has been defined.

The Holy Synod said :—

"That is the voice of the Holy Spirit—Preserver of
"the Canons! in thee the Fathers live! Preserver of
"The Faith is Dioscorus, the Archbishop."

Dioscorus, the Archbishop of Alexandria, said :—

The order, as well as that which is right and proper, is—that, first, the transactions in this cause should be read, and, then, the Letters of the God-loving Archbishop of Rome ; and therefore, as it is agreeable to the Holy Synod, let the transactions be read.

John, Presbyter and Prime Notary, said :—

Your Great and Holy Synod has ordered that the transactions, in the Royal City of Constantinople, respecting this cause which is now mooted, should be read. Since, then, the God-loving Bishop of the City of Constantinople, Flavian, has presented these Documents and the Venerable Presbyter and Archimandrite, Eutyches, has also given a copy, I now read them according to your orders.

And, when the Documents had been presented, the Praxis was read—both the second and the third—in which were reported some conversations of Flavian's party against The Faith, from which are extracted the following,

Basil, Bishop of Seleucia, said :—

When the discourses (compositions) of the Blessed Cyril have been read, who will arraign the sentences of our Blessed Father Cyril who, by his wisdom, has checked the Impiety of Nestorius, which (Impiety) was rending the world and dividing into two Persons and into two Natures our ONE LORD and GOD and Redeemer CHRIST? For, he showed that, in ONE Person, in ONE Son, and in ONE LORD of Creation we acknowledge a PERFECT DIVINITY and a PERFECT HUMANITY. We receive, then, all that was written and sent forth by him (Cyril), as being

E*

The Truth and full of Piety; and we worship ONE
LORD JESUS CHRIST, Whom we acknowledge to be
of Two Natures.   For, He was indeed before the worlds,
as One Who is the Splendor of the Glory of the Father,
but He, as One born of His Mother for our sakes, took
Corporeity from her, and was called PERFECT GOD
and The SON of God, as well as PERFECT MAN and
SON of Man, by which he seeks to make us all Life.
But we affirm of those who stand up against (oppose)
such Doctrines that they are the enemies of the Church.

Julius, the Bishop of Cos, said :—

Nobody of a sound way of thinking can stand up
against The Faith established by the Holy Bishops at
Nicæa, and again by the Holy Synod of Ephesus.   We
confess, therefore, TWO NATURES in ONE PERSON,
and, because of that, we confess the ONE SON and
ONE JESUS CHRIST our LORD.   And, whoever
adopts the insanity of Satan and brings his own ideas
to be like His, having opinions contrariant to what we
have received from the Holy Fathers, let him be anathematized.

Audoxius, Bishop of Bosphorus, said :—

When our Father Cyril, worthy of Blessedness, sustained the Holy Synod of Nicæa, he made known clearly
to us the origin of our Lord and Redeemer that He was
GOD, Who, The SON of the FATHER, before the Worlds,
was born as man at the end of the ages in order to tear
in pieces the engagements (hand writing) which existed
against us (men), and took Perfect Manhood for our
Redemption.

The Notary, who was the Reader at Ephesus, said :—

By what has been read we are certain that another Faith, other than that which the Fathers formulated, is that of those who have thus spoken.

Olympius, the Bishop of Evasa, said :—

If dissolvers of The Faith appear by the Documents which they present, let them (the Dissolvers) be anathamatized.

Then Seleucus, the Bishop of Amasia, said in his Deposition :—

We believe in our Lord Jesus Christ, in The Word from God, in the Light of Light, in the Two Natures after the INCARNATION and the Assumption of Flesh which was received of the Holy Mary. And we proclaim him who thinks differently from this to be estranged from the Church (as excommunicate).

And when these things were read, the Holy Synod at Ephesus said :—

"No body proclaims our Lord to be Two after The IN-"CARNATION—nobody Divides that which is Indivisible "—Nestorius did this. Thus Nestorius thought—but not "the Bishop of Amasia—not the Bishop of Amasia of "Sinope."

Dioscorus, the Bishop of Alexandria, said :—

Wait a little to hear other Blasphemies—you indeed charge only Nestorius. Lo! there are now many Nestorians.

And in another place the Notary of Flavian made Deposition against Eutyches, saying :—

Of the Two (Natures) before the Union he said not Two, but worhips One Nature of GOD Who took body.

And, in another place, he said concerning Him :—

I confess that He is Perfect GOD and Perfect MAN Who was born, but He had not Flesh Con-substantial with us.

Again, he made another Deposition concerning Him, saying :—

He said—spare me speaking of Two Natures in our LORD or investigating into the Nature of my GOD.

And, when the same Eutyches was asked by Flavian to affirm that His Flesh was Consubstantial with us, he spoke thus :—

Because I confess the body of God, I do not confess that the body of God is the body of man. But it is a human body, and I affirm that our Lord took body of the Virgin. But if it is befitting and proper to speak of the Virgin as Consubstantial with us, *this* also, my Lord, I confess. Nevertheless, of the Only Begotten Son of GOD, I confess that He is LORD and KING with the FATHER, with Whom He is also seated and glorified. For, I am not speaking of the same Nature when I deny that He is The SON of God.

Florantius said to him :—

Do you affirm of our Lord that He is Consubstantial with us and of Two Natures after INCARNATION by the Virgin, or not?

Eutyches said :—

I confess that our LORD was of Two Natures before the Union, but after the Union I confess Him to be of One Nature.

Dioscorus and the Holy Synod at Ephesus with Him, said :—

"We all assent to this,—yes, all of us."

Again, there was read the conversation of Basil, Bishop of Seleucia, with Eutyches at Flavian's Synod.

And if you do not speak of Two Natures after the Union, you speak of mixture and of a con-fusing.

And when this sentence was read at Ephesus, immediately Basil stood up and denied that sentence to be his, saying, that "this sentence which they affirm I said, I did not say in those words, and I am certain that I did not speak them."

Juvenal, of Jerusalem, said :—

This sentence, therefore, was altered.

Basil said :—

I do not remember and I do not know if I did say so.

Again, from the Documents of Flavian, Eusebius, Bishop of Dorylæum, after the reading of Cyril's Letter, said :—

Does Eutyches assent to what has now been read of the Blessed Cyril and Confess that there is a Union of the Two Natures in ONE Person and ONE Substance, or not ?

Florantius said :—

Do you hear, Archimandrite! what your accuser says ?

Eutyches said :—

Yes, I affirm our Lord to be of Two Natures.

Eusebius, of Dorylæum, said :—

Do you confess Two Natures, my Lord Archimandrite, after the Incarnation ? and do you affirm of Christ in the Flesh that He is Consubstantial with us ?

And when this was read the Holy Synod at Ephesus said :—

"Take and burn Eusebius—this man ought to be burnt
"alive—this man ought to be divided into two, as he
"divided."

Dioscorus, Bishop of Alexandria, said :—

Is it pleasing to you to affirm, after the Incarnation,
Two Natures ?

The Holy Synod said :—

"Anathema be to him who affirms so."

Dioscorus of Alexandria, said :—

I want both your voices and your hands. Let him
who cannot shout put up his hand.

The Holy Synod said :—

"Whoever affirms Two Natures let him be Anathema-
"tized."

Whilst these and other things were shouted, after a
little, Basil, the Bishop of Seleucia, said :—

I assent to The Faith of the Holy Fathers at Nicæa,
and of those at Ephesus who confirmed It. And them
who think at all oppositely, whether to those at Nicæa
or at Ephesus, I abhor; and I anathematize those who
separate the Two Natures after the Union or the Substance or the Person of The ONE JESUS CHRIST our
LORD, whilst I blame and arraign my own statement
which I made concerning the Two Natures in the Documentary Transactions at the Royal City of Constantinople; and I worship One Nature of the Divinity of
The Only Begotten (Son) Who became Incarnate and
assumed corporeity (took body).

Seleucus, Bishop, said :—

I assent and consent to what was formulated at Nicæa,
and confirmed at Ephesus, and I blame the expression

which I made in the splendid (City of) Constantinople, in which (expression) I (affirm) it is right to confess our Lord to be of Two Natures after the Union, and I anathematize those who divide our Lord Jesus Christ into Two Natures or Two Persons or Two Substances after the Union, and I look upon them as alien from Ecclesiastical Communion; and so also said others.

Moreover, he (the Notary) read that, after the charges against Eutyches, preferred by the Notary of Eusebius, and after the sentence of Basil against him, the Synod in conjunction with Flavian and Basil stood and excommunicated him. And then Flavian made some observations thus.

(10) THE DEPOSITION OF EUTYCHES.

The Bishop Flavian said—when Eutyches was by those things convicted, who formerly had been Presbyter and Archimandrite—that, in consequence of what had already been done, and from his own present Deposition (shewing that) he was infected with the false doctrines of Valentinus and Apollinarius and (yet) unalteringly entertained their Blasphemies, who also revered not our admonition and teaching and refused to assent to Orthodox Doctrine, we, whilst weeping and lamenting for his entire ruin, determine, by our Lord Jesus Christ Whom he has Blasphemed, that he be alien from the whole Order of the Priesthood and from Communion with us and from the government of a Monastery, whilst all those who, after this, converse with him and meet him (in company), are quite aware that they subject themselves to the pain of Excommunication, in consequence of not having ceased to hold intercourse with him.

Then (follow) the Subscriptions.

When these transactions before Flavian had been read before the Holy Synod at Ephesus, Dioscorus, the Archbishop of Alexandria, said :—

Now that what has been read is known to all, let everyone .of the Bishops here present say in what he knows the Archimandrite to be true to The Faith, and (say) what he determines respecting him.

Juvenal, of Jerusalem, said :—

Inasmuch as he (Eutyches) has frequently made the declaration that he is Orthodox, I withdraw what I said about him. And I, also, decree and vote that he be restored to his Monastery and to his Grade.

The Holy Synod said :—

"That is a correct judgment."

Domnus, the Bishop of Antioch, said :—

Because of what was once forwarded to me by the Holy Synod that assembled at the Royal City, relative to the Archimandrite Eutyches, I subscribed to his Deposition. But by the Libel which he has now presented he confesses to assent to The Faith of the CCCXVIII Holy Fathers and of the CL at Ephesus, and so I agree with your Piety that the Dignity of the Presbyterate ought to be restored to him as well as the Government of the Brethren under his authority.

Stephen, the Bishop of Hieropolis, said :—

What appears good and right to the Holy Fathers to be done respecting the God-fearing Presbyter and Archimandrite Eutyches, I likewise give my assent to, because from what has been read I agree that he is Orthodox; and, therefore, I adjudge him worthy of exercising the office of the Priesthood and of the Government of the Monastery.

John, the Bishop of (Massana,) Messena, said :—

As one who has transgressed in nothing with reference to what was formulated as a matter of The Faith by the Holy Fathers at Nicæa as well as by the Holy Fathers at Ephesus, he ought to be in the enjoyment of the Dignity of the Priesthood, and, according to his former custom, likewise, he ought to be reinstated in the government of the Venerable Monastery of Brothers.

And Basil of Seleucia and all the Holy Bishops up to the Archimandrite Barsumas delivered their addresses in the same way.

Dioscorus, the Bishop, said :—

Agreeing with the opinions of all this Holy and Œcumenical Synod, which have been expressed relative to the Venerable Archimandrite Eutyches, I also unite my mind with yours (viz.) that he be replaced in the Order of Presbyter and be allowed to govern his Monastery as heretofore.

Now when all had delivered their addresses and absolved Eutyches and when the whole Synod had justly contemned Flavian and Eusebius, such (condemnation) did not take place in consequence of any acts committed by them, but because they did not repent and confess the offences they committed and ask pardon, as the rest did with whom they had condemned Eutyches. For that reason their Deposition ran thus :—

F*

11. THE DEPOSITION OF FLAVIAN AND EUSEBIUS.

When the whole Synod had condemned Flavian, the Archbishop Dioscorus said :—

Because that great and Holy Synod which, by the will of God, assembled of old at Nicæa formulated for us that Orthodox and Inerrant Faith which the Holy Synod, assembled a little while since here, confirmed, I determine that this only shall be adhered to and proclaimed in Churches, decreeing likewise this (viz.), that nobody shall formulate a Faith other than this, or bring forward or introduce any thing new, or at all moot any matter connected with our pure Religion. But those who, contrary to this, are resolved to think or desire or set up something of the kind, or venture at all to change what has been decreed, I shall put under certain punishments, so that if they be Bishops they shall be removed from the Episcopate, but if Clerics from the clerical roll, if laymen they shall be deprived of Communion.

We learn from the Documents that have just now been read that these things are proved, as this Holy Synod perceives, (viz.) that Flavian, who was Bishop of the Church of Constantinople, and Eusebius of Dorylæum unsettled and altered everything, in many respects, and became a cause of scandal and of commotion to the Holy Churches and to the Communities of the Orthodox, some of whom have subjected themselves to punishments which then were determined on, at the Synod, by the Holy Fathers. And therefore also we, confirming these things, adjudge them whom we have called to remembrance, (viz.) Flavian and Eusebius, alien from

all the Honor of the Priesthood and of the Episcopate
But let everyone of the God-loving Bishops here present
speak his own mind and openly authorise it to be put in
the Documents. But all that has been done and written
to-day must be made known to the God-fearing and
Christ-loving Emperors.

Flavian said :—

I repudiate you. I protest.

Hilarius, Deacon of Rome, said :—

To *that* will be made a reply.

Juvenal, the Bishop of Jerusalem, said :—

Flavian and Eusebius have shown themselves alien
from the Priesthood and the Dignity of the Episcopate,
because they have dared to add to, or substract from,
The Catholic Faith.

And after many observations (he continued) :—

And therefore I decree the very same as the Holy and
Pious Archbishop Dioscorus, removing them from the
Dignity of the Episcopate.

Erasistratus, the Bishop of Corinth in Hellas, said :—

Being present and knowing from what was written,
that Flavian and Eusebius are not consentient with The
Orthodox Faith, and do not assent to the Holy Synod
of Nicæa and to that which a little while since assembled
at Ephesus, I am, too, consentient with the Holy
Bishops assembled, and I regard them as alien from the
Dignity of the Episcopate—I allude to Flavian and
Eusebius.

Stephen, the Bishop of Hieropolis, said :—

I for my part, also, assent to the punishment assigned
by your Piety to Flavian and Eusebius, who formerly

were Bishops, and who lately were present here, as having transgressed the Holy Canons of Nicæa. And, considering that they thus have been and are aliens from the Episcopate, I assent to what has been decreed by you.

And in a similar manner to this, Basil also, and all the other Bishops and Archimandrites decreed.

WHEN ALL THIS HAD BEEN DONE, THE WHOLE SYNOD UNITED IN ADDRESSING THE EMPEROR THEODOSIUS thus :—

(12) If any person should designate your Illustrious and Christ-loving Kingdom a source of (the true) Religion, and of a good Confession, and of Faith, he would not be surpassing the bounds of the truth. But it is possible for him to remain under the mark in using words which are not adequate for enlarging upon the greatness of the Godly love which attaches to you, O Glorious and Victorious Emperors! For, every day there flows from you, O Venerable (Sires)! a (refreshing) drink of the true knowledge of God upon those who are under your authority, and in continuous descent it comes, as a spiritual and life-giving power, copious upon all the earth, so that the powerful authority of the Kingdom will perpetually abide, not so much by (the force of) arms as by prevailing through service toward God. By *that* you will prevail over your enemies, and prevail abidingly, since the King of Kings, on account of your watchfulness over The Catholic Faith, raises up invisible hosts against them (enemies), whilst that preserves the Sceptre of your Kingdom from destruction and renders it terrible to

those who set themselves up in opposition to you.

On you lies the responsibility (care) not only of guarding the human race from the army of the barbarians but of its continuing completely unmolested and preserved from novelties of language used by those who, with adverse notions, spread mischief (impiety), like some deadly poison upon an arrow, and shoot destructively against the souls of the simple a shot which, it is true, causes no wound to the body, but lasting death to the soul. Further, it is now known that both formerly this Faithful and Christ-loving desire moved and at present moves your Venerableness to be zealous for the Lord and has very rightly been diligent (exercised) in serving, in accordance with the expression of the Prophet, spiritual weapons and a shield, and in standing up in defence of your Orthodox and Spotless Faith which people have been caught— and they are not far off—bent on unsettling. They have too, unmasked themselves by their works (deeds), (shewing) that they discuss other things than the disciples of Christ discuss, and preach to them error strange to themselves. For this reason you commanded us by Royal and Illustrious letters to assemble at the City of Ephesus and to repair to John the Theologian, with whose (help) the Fathers had already (before this) cut off, with the Sword of the Spirit, the tongue of Nestorius who had armed himself against the Glory of Christ, whilst in this noble contest they had the Blessed Cyril as their Leader, who was our Father and Bishop.

As soon as the Letters of your Serenity, like a loud-voiced and devout Trumpet summoned us to fight for The Faith, we hastened hither, everyone from a different side, this from afar, that from near, another out of the midst, and all from all quarters to the City of John and Timothy, where all of us assembled and reached (repaired to) the Temple of the Holy Church, named Maria (Mary) and—so that the place itself will become a monument and a witness of our True and Divine Belief—we thereupon directed our thoughts to the investigation of the matter.

Now there passed (before us) and stood in our midst the Venerable Archimandrite Eutyches, who presented to us his complaint (plea) in which—invoking CHRIST as a witness of his thoughts and speech—he said at the end that he had learnt from his youth the Holy Confession of Faith of the Fathers of Nicæa and that he had kept that (Faith) intact up to the present time and had never varied at all from the principles which they had decided on.

Subsequently, in a similar way, he had adhered to the principles decided on a former occasion at the City of Ephesus by the Holy Synod assembled there, and to the Laws then promulged to protect The Orthodox Faith.

After the Presbyter had communicated this, and as they were present who had adjudged him in the Royal City, we caused, as a matter of obligation, an investigation to be made into the matter; for, *that* the Revered Words of your Christ-loving Authority commanded us to do.

When the (documentary) Acts were then presented, we ordered them to be read aloud, without leaving out anything whatever therein laid down, so that, by that means, the Truth should be elicited and traced out.

We forbear to relate that some of our official Brethren

who were at Constantinople charged some of the
(determinations) depositions that were put in the Acts
as their own personal ones, with being falsely returned,
(distinctly) affirming of them—"they are frauds"—and'
that others, on their part, blamed what was affirmed of
them (the latter) as not well-done.

We leave off speaking, abbreviating the prolixity of
the subject with the view of not being tiresome.

As we found, however, that the Archimandrite Eutyches
confessed as well by his own voice after coming, on the
third citation, before the Holy Synod, as by means of the
Libel which he now presents to us, that he held fast to
the confession of The Orthodox Faith and that he has
not undertaken to introduce any novelty whatever or
anything alien from what was defined by the Holy
Fathers who assembled at Nicæa and Ephesus—for that
reason have we, on the one hand, expressed to him our
approbation, in the matter of his faith which is Orthodox
and which does not deviate (from the true one) on any
side, and accordingly have decided that he shall exercise
the Office of the Priesthood, as he has done hitherto;
and on the other hand, we have shed tears not so much
over him who was unjustly condemned, as over those
who condemned him, that is, the astute accuser and the
wonderful (!) judge. Not in this only have they acted
with unwisdom—for, how often is a sinner to be found
who can easily be healed—but they presumed to throw a
false Doctrine in the ways of God and to cause innocent
people to overstep the bounds of True Religion and—as
if from the first—for the second time to introduce again
into our midst the Impure and Blasphemous Doctrines

of Nestorius which (doctrines) the enactment of your faithful Laws have ejected from our midst as well as the Synod which, on a former occasion, assembled at Ephesus—it was not without the entrance and enlightenment of the Holy Spirit—when you decreed the following among other matters (viz.)—No one shall have the authority to formulate a Faith other than that proposed at Nicæa, still less to seek one out, or to renew one, or to alter unalterable things. But they who do so, if Bishops, shall be removed from their Bishoprics, if Clerics, from the (number of the) Clerus, if Laymen, from Communion in the Holy Mysteries. For, It (the Synod) was aware and was convinced—seeing that It was, of a truth, speaking by the Spirit and was filled with men (richly) endowed with the Word of faultless Doctrine—that to wrangle with useless words would chiefly contribute to confuse the hearers, as also the wise Paul says, continuing thus—" But abstain from vain and strange words, for they will still (more) increase in Impiety, and their speech will spread around like a canker." To these belong Flavian and Eusebius, who, after having erred from the Truth, were ejected from the Dignity of the Priesthood, and deprived of all the Honour of the Episcopate, inasmuch as they were pronounced guilty by us all unanimously, and with one voice and tongue have been condemned by the assembly, because they went beyond what was formerly established in Ephesus, and because they stood forth as inventors and teachers of idle subtleties.

Further, inasmuch as they brought a violent storm on the Churches, and have thrown disquiet and alarm into the minds of the Faithful, and as they do not well nor skilfully understand how to pasture their flock; it should consequently be said to them:—Go hence in your own light, and in the flame which you have made to blaze on high. Now, may these eat the fruit of their own ways, and be satisfied with their own devices, as it is *written; but, with respect to our Catholic and Holy Faith, we have decided only to hold fast that which the Fathers resolved upon, who were earlier assembled in Nicæa, and lately in Ephesus, seeing that we have learnt, out of the Divine Scripture,†—this: "Displace not the ancient boundaries " which thy fathers have placed"; for, it is not allowed us to add anything to them nor to take anything away from them.

Now, we beg your Invincible Power that you would have compassion on the bodies of us, who are become old, and, through being weary with the journey upon our long way, are sick and cast down, especially in consequence of the bad atmosphere in Ephesus; and that you will command, that we depart from this place somewhat quickly, particularly on account of the long delay, so that every one may get back to his own Church and Town, and may offer up prayers for the pure and Christ-loving Dignity of the Sovereign.

AND THIS ALL SUBSCRIBED. ‡

---

* Proverbs, chapter i, v. 31.   † See Proverbs chapter xxii, v. 28.

‡ It should be remembered that these are the. words of Timothy Ælurus, stating that all the Fathers of the Council subscribed to the Document (12), and it was, at the end of its first Session, that they gave their signatures to it. Now Historians relate (Mansi, Héfélé, &c.,) that at the council of Chalcedon mention was made of Bishops at the Ephesine Synod being forced to subscribe to a blank paper. The Greek Acts of the latter, of which A is a translation, make no allusion to any letter written upon it. But Timothy, in his great work directed against the former Council, gives the whole letter, of which the above is a translation into English.

*G

E.

AN EXTRACT FROM ONE OF THE ADDITIONAL MSS IN THE
BRITISH MUSEUM, NUMBERED 14,602.   FOLS 95. AND 96.

CANON THE 70TH OF THE HOLY APOSTLES.

If a Bishop be accused of any Crime, by persons who
are believers and worthy of credit, he must be cited by
Bishops ; and, if he appear and confess it, let him be
admonished, and some punishment inflicted upon him.
But if, when cited, he should not obey, let him be cited
a second time.   But if, in this case, he should not pay
attention, let him be cited a third time by sending two
Bishops again to him.   If, however, he should even
then show contempt, and refuse to appear, let the Synod
of Bishops pronounce against him what seems befitting
to them, in order that he may not seem to be advantaged
by flying (from the trials).

[Here] ends Chapter the Second.

CHAPTER THE THIRD.

Ibas and Theodoret were excommunicated by Dioscorus and his Synod, although they were not cited (to
appear at it).   So, also, was Domnus, Patriarch of
Antioch, although Libels (bills of indictment) against
him were presented by persons of credit, as is evident
from their Synodicals.

REPLY TO, AND SOLUTION OF, THIS (DIFFICULTY).

"Who will make my head a fount of waters and my eyes a source of weeping, that I may lament with bitterness?" For, behold! again is Jesus "numbered with the wicked" by those of his own people. Behold! again is the Blessed Paul (of Antioch) likened to the arrogant Egyptian and Imposter. Look, (Regard) Lord! and be not silent. Awaken, Lord!—why sleepest thou? Arise and be not far removed from us, and turn not thy face away from us." Have mercy upon Thy little flock, seeing that now, O Lord! we are despised by all the Gentiles and brought low in all the Earth, by reason of our transgressions and sins, lest we should mercilessly injure and devour one another, and exterminate each other, and beco.ne a terror (derision) to the Gentiles. Why, then, do we love schism and speak up for division? Why do we fuse together what is infusible?

Let us see if the affair of our Blessed Patriarch, whatever it may be, has some likeness to the causes of Ibas and Theodoret and Domnus.

And, first, let us examine the circumstances of Ibas. Now, who does not know the cause of Ibas, although he may be as insignificant as I am, after having perused the ecclesiastical annals? In those annals it is seen that the people of Edessa, being tired of his Blasphemies against Christ (God) and of his crimes without end, presented a Petition to the Memorable Theodosius the Emperor, complaining of and deploring his excessive Profanity. The God-fearing Emperor, compassionating them, commanded Photius, Bishop of Tyre, and Eustathius, of

Berytus, and Uranius, of Himeria, to investigate the charges made against Ibas, so that, whatever they are, anyone who wished to know might easily learn from those Acts that were drawn up at Berytus.*

When, however, delay arose about the judgment pronounced upon him (from a reason which we are prepared to give information about from the voice of the judges) and when his accusers became pressingly urgent upon the Emperor, he commanded the Second Synod of Ephesus to investigate the circumstances of the case as well as the judgment they (the Bishops) had given against him at the City of Berytus.

When, then, the Bishops Photius and Eustathius were asked by the Synod what judgment they pronounced upon Ibas, they replied in the following words :—

* As regards Ibas, indeed, great action was first taken against him in writing, touching The Faith, and seeing that many witnesses would be necessary and long journey to bring them, we determined that the Clerics of the City Edessa should affirm on oath before (upon) the Evangelists, whatever they were cognizant of in reference to the accusation advanced against him (Ibas) touching the matter of The Faith.   For, much was committed to Documents at the same (city of) Edessa, which were brought also to the cognizance of the Faithful and Gracious Emperor.   Because, then, the Victory-Clad Emperor assented to them, and received the affidavit of all the persons who gave testimony in the Praxis, as your Holiness has just now heard, we make request that these Documents be read before you.*

---

* See pages 10—13, 41—43.

—And after other things.—

" But this we apprise your Highness of (viz.), that, after the hearing of these men (at the Tribunal), we were not inclined to hold communication with Ibas referred to." *

I, myself, am of opinion that from this Deposition alone of these Commissioners, as well as from their refusal to hold communion with him, it is tolerably patent and manifest that they pronounced a definite (adequate) judgment in consequence of his false Faith.

† But how many are the accusations heaped upon him, and written in the Documentary Acts drawn up at Edessa—for, these judges decreed that the testimonies received against him there should have a full value—it is possible to see by those Documents drawn up at Edessa. For, from all the Civil Dignities and classes of men in that City, and from its neighbourhood, and even from Women, formal accusations were advanced against him (Ibas) before Cheræas, the (Hegemon) Governor of that City, charging Ibas before him who put down the charges in minutes, with all the evil Doctrine of Nestorius and with committing Sacrilege in holy things, and (especially) with the silver Vessels of the Altar, some of which he even melted down for the purpose of making utensils for his own table, while others he sold, and pilfered the purchase money, along with a good deal of property belonging to the Poor and the Captives. They charged him, also, with exercising the art of Incantation, naming certain persons who were his companions in such things; and they called him by

* See p. 43.   † See p. 44—73.

the nickname of *jockey*, because he used to take pleasure in certain foul practices of inebriety and such like.

For the certification of all these counts (of indictment) they drew up Documents which were brought to the cognizance of the Serene-minded Emperor Theodosius, who received and examined them, and approved of them, and despatched them to the Holy "Second Synod of Ephesus," which, on their being read to It, together with the Impious letter Ibas wrote to Mares the Persian, the Bishops Photius and Eustathius being present, as well as those accusers of his, then and there, after the scrutiny, prononounced upon him a judgment in accordance with Law.*

This we have narrated with brevity about the affair of Ibas: and (we have seen) how much care was used in all the investigation which was instituted concerning him everywhere and how, after all that investigation, and after the assent of the Emperor himself, the Holy Synod † did not hesitate (contemn) to investigate it again, as it was right to do, notwithstanding the personal detestation in which Ibas was held.

Now, were these new investigations necessary after all that careful examination?

And now, (let me ask) has something of the same kind been done relative to the holy Patriarch of Antioch, Mar Paul?

I pray and adjure every hearer of me to judge and to

---

* See p p. 134—145.

† Or, "even the Holy Synod did not neglect the necessary examination although an (absolutely) necessary examination was not required in the person of Ibas." The original seems patient of this rendering.

decide for himself, as before Christ-God, the Searcher of all.

And as to Theodoret, how can anybody with any simplicity relate his history? Who is ignorant of that history? Who is ignorant of his efforts on behalf of Nestorius? With what power he contended in written and unwritten ways for Theodore and Diodore, Heretics? Who is ignorant of his writings and his ardent attacks upon St. Cyril, the Doctor of the Church? For the moment I forbear to speak of all the other things he has done. I should like to recite, in its entirety, his letter to John of Antioch, after the death of the Blessed Cyril, in which he despises, derides, and ridicules the death of the Saint, and his God-pleasing Faith; and in that way I could show to what a pitch it was possible for Satan to excite this man (Theodoret). But not to prolong that history I will only cite a part, and that, the beginning of that Letter which is truly the bitter product of his impure heart, and of his diabolical tongue.

F

AN EXTRACT FROM ONE OF THE ADDITIONAL MSS IN THE
BRITISH MUSEUM, NUMBERED 14,602. FOL. 97.

FROM A LETTER WHICH HE (THEODORET) WROTE, AFTER
RETURNING FROM EPHESUS, TO THE MONKS OF THE EAST.

---

* Now, the cause of this are those who want to deprave
the Apostolic Faith, and desire to introduce, what is
changeable, into the Evangelical Doctrine; and they
accepted the Impious Chapters of Cyril, which they also
despatched to the Royal City, confirming them, as they
thought, by their subscriptions. These evidently germi-
nate from the bitter root of Apollinarius, and are par-
ticipaters of the Blasphemy of Arius and of Eunomius.
If, however, anybody will, with minute accuracy investigate them, they will be found to be not free from the
Impiety of Valentinus, and of Manes, and of Marcion,
and such like who were the offspring of the Egyptian,†
truly an evil offspring of a more evil sire.

---

* See p. 220, l. 4—18   † See p. 221, l. 9, and p. 222, l. 23.

G

AN EXTRACT FROM ONE OF THE ADDITIONAL MSS IN THE BRITISH MUSEUM, NUMBERED 17,154. FOLS. 31 & 32.

Because, as I heard, people declared of the letters I (Dioscorus) wrote once to you, that they are not very agreeable to the words of the Holy Cyril, from a want of learning or from bold treatment, they set themselves up to make it known that they were adverse to those holy contests against the Synod which took place at Chalcedon.

For, Dioscorus, a witness for Christ, who alone did not himself bend the knee to Baal in the assembly of Schism, thus wrote to Domnus, who at that time sat on the Throne (Episcopal) at Antioch, concerning those who dared to compose evil (calumnious) statements against some writings of the wise Cyril.

DIOSCORUS.

"*Moreover, they composed treatises exceedingly reprehensible and not in accordance with, but in contradiction to the Holy Scriptures and to those of our Blessed and universally praised Brother, the Bishop Cyril. For, this proves assuredly that they are reprehensible and not in accordance with the Holy Words (of God). For, our wise and distinguished Father became an Universal Teacher. Now he wrote, if any other man did, in a manner Catholic and unblameable, and, being not

---

* See page 333.

H*

only a skiful elaborator of words—for, he was glorious in this last (mentioned thing), as he shone in this from his early youth—but, being richly endowed with gifts from above, he gave an exact Exposition, as It admitted of it, of the Mystery of the INCARNATION of the Only-Begotten Son of God. And nothing proceeded from him, in which he did not excel to all admiration. For, indeed, whether a Treatise be mentioned, or a Letter, or an Exposition, or an extempore Commentary, or a Homily for the Community, or a Chapter, or Anathematisms—all was exact and accurate, and neat and appropriately wrought, and in consonance with the Divine Words, so that it would be not inappropriate to say of his writings —'Who is wise? and yet he may not know them; and who is intelligent? and does not understand them—that the ways of the Lord are right, and that the Righteous walk therein, but transgressors shall fall thereby.' " *

How, then, can modesty condemn them?

(Here) ends the Second Letter of the Patriarch Severus to Sergius the Grammarian.

---

* See page 333.

Ħ

The CHAPTERS, on account of which Theodoret was ex-communicated by "the Second Synod of Ephesus;" without having required of him a retractation of which, the Synod of Chalcedon received him.

From the Synodicon of "the Second Synod of Ephesus," respecting the Deposition of Theodoret.

Pelagius, the Presbyter of Antioch, said :—

I possess a Volume, also written by Theodoret against the first Holy Œcumenical Synod which assembled here, and against what was written from time to time by the Blessed Cyril; and, with it, a treatise drawn up afresh against him* after his communion with the Blessed Cyril.

THEODORET.

From a Volume which was read before the Synod.

A little after the beginning,—speaking against Cyril and against the Synod which received his Chapters, and ex-communicated Nestorius,—they aimed (he says†) at depraving the Apostolic Faith, and were antagonistic to the Doctrine of the Evangelical teaching, to which they dared to add the impious Chapters of Cyril, which they received along with the Anathema-

---

* See page 218, line 7.   † See page 220, line 4, to page 221, line 7.

tisms and despatched to the Royal City and confirmed, as they thought, by their (own) subscriptions, which manifestly sprung from the bitter root of Apollinarius. Further, they are participative of the Blasphemies of Arius and Œunomius. But, if any one wishes minutely (accurately) to inspect them, they will be found to be not free from the Impiety of Valentinus and Manes and Marcion. For, in the first Chapter, he (Cyril) proceeds to dilate upon what took place on our behalf, teaching that God did not (really) take human Nature, but was changed into flesh, teaching that the INCARNATION of Our Redeemer took place in appearance and in phantasy, and not in reality. This, however, is the offspring of the Impiety of Marcion, and of Manes, and of Valentinus.

But, in the second and third Chapters, as if he had forgotten what he had put at the beginning, he introduces an Hypostatic (Personal) Union and a concursus constituting a Physical Union, teaching (thereby) a Commixture and Con-fusion.

And, again, after a little :—

*We confess Our Lord Jesus Christ to be Perfect GOD and Perfect MAN, of a reasonable soul and body, Who, as to His Divinity, was born of the Father before the worlds, but, in the last times, for us and for our salvation the Same was born, as to His Humanity, of the Virgin Mary—consubstantial (co-essential) with the Father as to The Divinity, and consubstantial with us as to The Humanity.

---

*See page 223, line 13.

The Union consists of The Two Natures. On this account we confess One Christ, One Son, One Lord: for, we do not dissolve the Union.

—And after other things :—

"He was crucified through weakness, but He liveth by the power of God."* By the term "weakness" we should learn that not He Who is Almighty, Inexhaustable, Unchangeable, Immutable, was crucified by nails, but That Nature, Which became by the Power of God among the Living, according to the teaching of His Apostle, died and was buried — two circumstances appertaining to the likeness of a Servant.

After the reading of Theodoret's Volume,

John, Presbyter and Prime Notary, said :—

The Book, presented by Pelagius, bears upon it the following Title :—*Bishop Theodoret: an Apology for Diodorus, Warrior of (The True) Religion.*

The Holy Synod said :—

That alone suffices for his Depositon.

SOME OF THE BLASPHEMIES FROM THE BOOK PRESENTED.

† "And what shall I say about the Athenians, (such) par-"ticular worshippers of the unknown God. The Divine "Peter himself, when discoursing to the Jews, did not "designate our Lord Christ (as) God, but he even ex-"tended his address about Him, as Man."

And, again, when arraigning Cyril's Treatises against Diodorus, he said :—

---

* see page 223, line 9.   † See page 241, line 15.

* " For, the whole Deed (writing) of Arraignment
" is full of such (expressions) as these—He (Christ) did
" not take (upon Himself) Man : He did not actually
" become Man : He was not a Son of Man, but acted in
" the manner of men : He, the Only Begotten, suffered :
" He tasted of Death."

And, again, against Cyril he amplifies in this Treatise.

† " And show, then, what there is against Diodorus,
" but you have nothing to show."

And, again, from the same Treatise.

‡ " How do you, then, fail to perceive this, that, when
" you arraign Diodorus for having affirmed that the
" Nature, which was assumed, was the Son of Grace,
" you implicate yourself (in the charge)? because you
" have blamed him for not having affirmed Him to be
" the Very Son of the Father, Who is of the Seed of
" David; for, how is that Nature, which was derived
" from David, the Very Son of the God of All ? for, He,
" Who was begotten of the Father before the worlds,
" owns this Name."

And, again, from the same Treatise, when he is
speaking about Cyril :—

§ " But again forgetting these words, and, having also
" abandoned the other Teaching, he turned to the evil
" peculiarly his, and covertly advanced the Blasphemy of
" Apollinarius, and exclaimed that we speak of One (Only)
" Son, just as the Fathers did, and of One (Only) Nature
" of THE WORD INCARNATE. Look at the bitter-

---

* See page 242, line 2. † See page 242, line 9 ‡ See page 243, line 2.
§ See page 248, line 19.

"ness of Orthodox Teaching. For, having postulated what
"is evidently confessed by the Just—One SON—he intro-
"duces after it "ONE NATURE," a thing which grew
"out of the Blasphemies of Apollinarius. But he added this
"—INCARNATE—being apprehensive of a disclosure
"of his Blasphemies. He must tell us, however, what
"Fathers brought up this expression. For, the very con-
"tradictory to this we can discover among the Holy Fathers,
"since, in their Sermons, they have perfected The Two
"Natures. Dost thou name Apollinarius, and Eunomius,
"and Asterius, and Ætius? For, it was they who gave
"birth to this Blasphemy."

Hence this is an ascertained fact—that, what was recovered by Cyril, Theodoret put into this writing
(Treatise) which has received condemnation by Dioscorus
and by his Synod from the testimony brought to it by
Cyril, who says—We affirm One Son, &c. For, Cyril
put this in the first letter to the Synod in which Cyril
firmly avows that he wrote it after he had received the
Easterns (into Communion).

Again—what specially belongs to Theodoret—from an
Exposition he delivered in the Church of Antioch, when
Domnus, too, the Patriarch of Antioch, stood up and
delivered an Exposition :—

* "Thomas touched Him Who rose, and worshipped
"Him Who raised Him."

And, again, when he was expounding in the Church of
Antioch, he said :—

---

* See page 294, lines 20, and 26.

"God took Man, although it was not apparent (agreeable) to men."

[After the above Extract from the thick and closely indited Volume (12, 155) there follows a passage from "the Acts of the Synod of Chalcedon" (451 A.D.) referring to Bishop Theodoret. Then, after six more lines follows an extract from an address of the Bishop of Antioch, Maximus. After eleven more lines, a sentence from Theodoret thus :]

THEODORET. From the refutation of the first Anathematism of Cyril.

There is, assuredly, ONE PERSON, and ONE SON and CHRIST. To confess *these* is Catholic. But to make affirmation of Two BEINGS, and of Two NATURES is not only hateful, but it is, likewise, to *add to* (The Catholic Faith).

The Syrac is—

ܡܢ ܬܘܪܥܐ ܕܚܪܡܐ ܩܕܡܝܐ ܕܩܘܪܝܠܠܘܣ .

ܚܕ ܡܢ ܦܪܨܘܦܐ ܘܚܕ ܒܪܐ ܘܚܕ ܡܫܝܚܐ . ܗܘ

ܗܟܘܬ ܠܡܘܕܝܘ ܬܪܝܨܐ . ܬܪܬܝܢ ܕܝܢ ܩܢܘܡܐ ܐܘ

ܬܪܬܝܢ ܟܝܢܐ ܠܡܐܡܪ ܠܐ ܣܢܝܐ . ܐܠܐ ܘܬܘܣܦܐ .

One Person indeed, and One Son, and One Christ, &c.

I.

AN EXTRACT FROM ONE OF THE ADDITIONAL MSS IN
THE BRITISH MUSEUM, NUMBERED 12,156.

FORMULARY OF THE HOLY SYNOD OF THE CL AT CONSTANTINOPLE.

I BELIEVE IN ONE GOD, THE FATHER, ALMIGHTY
—THE MAKER OF HEAVEN AND OF EARTH (AND) OF
ALL THINGS VISIBLE AND INVISIBLE:

AND (I BELIEVE) IN ONE LORD JESUS CHRIST—
THE ONLY SON OF GOD, WHO WAS BEGOTTEN OF
THE FATHER BEFORE ALL WORLDS—LIGHT OF
(FROM) LIGHT—VERY GOD OF (FROM) VERY GOD—
WHO WAS BEGOTTEN AND WAS NOT MADE—CO-ESSEN-
TIAL WITH THE FATHER—BY WHOM ALL THINGS
WERE MADE—WHO, FOR THE SAKE OF US SONS OF MEN
AND FOR OUR SALVATION, CAME DOWN FROM HEAVEN
AND BECAME INCARNATE BY THE HOLY GHOST
AND BY THE VIRGIN MARY AND WAS MADE MAN;
AND WAS CRUCIFIED FOR US IN THE DAYS OF PONTIUS
PILATE AND SUFFERED AND WAS BURIED AND
ROSE AGAIN ON THE THIRD DAY, ACCORDING TO THE
SCRIPTURES, AND ASCENDED INTO HEAVEN AND
SAT DOWN ON THE RIGHT HAND OF HIS FATHER
AND WILL COME AGAIN IN GLORY TO JUDGE THE
QUICK AND THE DEAD—WHOSE KINGDOM HATH NO
END:

I *

AND (I BELIEVE) IN THE HOLY GHOST, THE LORD AND THE LIFE-GIVER, WHO PROCEEDETH FROM THE FATHER, WHO, WITH THE FATHER AND THE SON, IS WORSHIPPED AND GLORIFIED, WHO SPAKE BY THE PROPHETS; AND (I BELIEVE) IN ONE, HOLY, APOSTOLIC, AND CATHOLIC, CHURCH. I CONFESS ONE BAPTISM FOR THE REMISSION OF SINS; AND I ACKNOWLEDGE THE RESURRECTION OF THE DEAD AND THE LIFE OF THE WORLD TO COME. AMEN.*

---

* This Symbol was not received, as a Creed of the Church, until the Council of Chalcedon A.D. 451, which Council, even afterwards, speak of the Creed of the 318, as the *one* summary of Teaching.

It was not known to S. Cyril of Alexandria in 429 or 430, chiefly through the circumstances of the times.

One Nestorius quoted the Nicene Creed with C P addition; and S. Cyril the actual creed, and then speaks of the addition as " an innovation of this man." This he could not have done, had he known that the words were added in Council of CP.

This Creed was never purposely interpolated, and the Filioque probably came into Latin Copy of the Nicene Creed from the Uniform Western Use. (DR. PUSEY).

K.

AN EXTRACT FROM ONE OF THE ADDITIONAL MSS IN
THE BRITISH MUSEUM, NUMBERED 12,156.

But, in reference to those who affirm that there was a
time when He (Christ) was not, or who affirm that He is
of another Being or Essence, or is Changeable, or is a
Mutable Son of God, the Catholic and Apostolic Church
which is One and Only, anathematizes them.

She Formulates against Arius.*

---

* The sum and substance of the Arian Heresy is that it holds that the
Son of God is " a Creature;" and this is more than implied in the above
which was, originally, part of the Nicene Creed. It began at Antioch.
Lucian broached similar ideas, but Paul of Samosata, and Theodore of
Mopsuestia, were the great Fautors of it. Socrates the Historian, relates
how the Heresy broke out, how Bishop Alexander in discoursing declared
" in the Unity there was a Trinity," and how Arius accused him of Sabel-
lianism and asserted " that, if the Father begat the Son, there was a time
when the Son was not, He who was begotten had a beginning to His existence; whence it is manifest that there was a time when the Son was
not, as a consequence that He had His Person out of non-existence. In
short, he asserted that our Lord was a creature."

The Arians grounded their arguments on such passages of Scripture
as these,—" The firstborn of every creature," which means that He was
begotten before all creatures,—" The Lord created me in the beginning
of his way," which some misinterpretated, taking 'Εκτήσατο for ἔκτισε.
—" But of that day knoweth . . . . . neither the Son . . . . . . ," which
shows, in assuming human nature, he assumed human ignorance,
as one of the accidents of humanity—" Jesus increased in wisdom and
stature . . . ," which He did, not as The Word, but as He was man.
Then there could be no phantasm (δοκήσιν) instead of a real manifestation of God. So all things, by which human nature is characterized, are
related of him in Scripture, the propensity to sin excluded. (BISHOP
FORBES.)

L.

AN EXTRACT FROM ONE OF THE ADDITIONAL MSS IN
THE BRITISH MUSEUM, NUMBERED 14,526.

SYNOPSIS OF MATTERS BELONGING TO THE SYNODS.

The Synod which assembled at Nicæa in the days of
Constantine the Great :—
The Heads were Alexander the Archbishop of Alex-
andria and, in the place of the Pope of Rome, were
Vantonius and Vancentius, Priests of Rome.

The Synod which assembled at Constantinople in the
days of Theodosius the Great :—
The Heads were Nectarius Bishop of the same Constantinople, and Timothy the Great, Bishop of Alexandria.

The Synod which assembled at Ephesus in the days of
Theodosius the Less :—
The Heads were Calistinus, Bishop of Rome, and
Cyril, Bishop of Alexandria, and Memnon, Bishop of
Ephesus.

The Synod which assembled at Chalcedon, in the days
of the Emperor Marcian :—
The Heads were Anatolius, Bishop of Constantinople,

and Leo of Rome, represented by his letter and by those who filled his place.

———

Again: the Synod that assembled at Nicæa has reference to the Impious Arians, who predicated of the Son that the Son (proceeded) from the Nature of the Father, but against His being Begotten of the Father. They called Him "one made," and "a creature," but not "Consubstantial with the Father."

———

Again: the Great Synod which assembled at Constantinople dealt with the Impieties of the Macedonians who Blasphemed against The HOLY GHOST and refused to designate Him GOD, and (to declare Him) to be of the same Essence and the same Nature as The Father and The Son, but only a certain Spirit sent forth.

———

Again: The Synod which assembled at Ephesus regarded Nestorius and his fellow thinkers as Impious, that is, John of Antioch in Syria, and Theodoret of Cyrus, and Ibas the Bishop of Edessa, with some others.

———

Again: the Synod at Chalcedon assembled nominally, indeed, about the tenet of the Impious Eutyches who avowed that the Divine Nature was changed into a certain thick and corporeal nature, like that of our Humanity. We, however, affirm that It assembled really—from the sense of Its Confession and from Its Symbol determined and set forth—to confirm and to strengthen the Doctrine of the Impious Nestorius; and this is perfectly evident, because It accepted the Letter of Leo of Rome, which Letter affirmed of the following expressions that they do not relate to the same Nature, when Christ said:—"I and my Father are One," and "My Father is greater than I."

FINIS.

Lightning Source UK Ltd.
Milton Keynes UK
176376UK00007B/28/P